Humanism in Crisis

STUDIES IN MEDIEVAL AND EARLY MODERN CIVILIZATION
Marvin B. Becker, General Editor

Charity and Children in Renaissance Florence:
The Ospedale degli Innocenti, 1410–1536
  Philip Gavitt

Humanism in Crisis: The Decline of the French Renaissance
  Philippe Desan, editor

Humanism in Crisis

The Decline of the French Renaissance

Philippe Desan, Editor

Ann Arbor

THE UNIVERSITY OF MICHIGAN PRESS

Copyright © by the University of Michigan 1991
All rights reserved
Published in the United States of America by
The University of Michigan Press

1994 1993 1992 1991   4 3 2 1

Distributed in the United Kingdom and Europe by
Manchester University Press, Oxford Road,
Manchester M13 9PL, UK

Library of Congress Cataloging-in-Publication Data

Humanism in crisis : the decline of the French Renaissance / Philippe Desan, editor.
    p. cm. — (Studies in medieval and early modern civilization)
    Proceedings of a conference held at the Institut collégial europeén in Loches, France in 1988.
    Includes bibliographical references and index.
    ISBN 0-472-10239-7 (alk. paper)
    1. French literature—16th century—History and criticism—Congresses. 2. Classical literature—Appreciation—France—Congresses. 3. France—Civilization—Classical influences—Congresses. 4. French literature—Classical influences—Congresses. 5. France—Intellectual life—16th century—Congresses. 6. Education, Humanistic—France—History—Congresses. 7. Renaissance—France—Congresses. 8. Humanists—France—Congresses. 9. Humanism—France—Congresses. I. Desan, Philippe. II. Series.
PQ239.H8 1991
001.1'0944'09031—dc20   91-9832
                                                                                     CIP

British Library Cataloguing in Publication Data
Humanism in crisis : the decline of the French Renaissance.
— (Studies in medieval and early modern civilization).
1. France. Humanism, history
I. Desan, Philippe
144.0944
ISBN 0-472-10239-7

Paperback ISBN: 978-0-472-75102-0

Acknowledgments

This book is the fruitful result of a conference on the decline of the French Renaissance held at the Institut Collégial Européen in Loches (France) in 1988. I would like to thank the Humanities Division of the University of Chicago, which assisted financially in the sponsoring of this conference. Moreover, I am grateful to Constance Spreen, who painstakingly and meticulously helped me in editing this book. She spent much time double-checking references in the library and also translated into English numerous passages available only in French. I must say that she has mastered the *Chicago Manual of Style* and successfully harmonized all the essays presented in this volume. Without her assistance this book would have been an inferior product.

Contents

Introduction
  Philippe Desan 1

The Worm in the Apple: The Crisis of Humanism
  Philippe Desan 11

The Failure of Humanist Education: David de
Fleurance-Rivault, Anthoine Mathé de Laval, and
Nicolas Faret
  James J. Supple 35

Ruined Schools: The End of the Renaissance System of
Education in France
  George Huppert 55

Humanism and the Problem of Relativism
  Zachary S. Schiffman 69

Unreadable Signs: Montaigne, Virtue, and the
Interpretation of History
  Timothy Hampton 85

Writing the Crisis Differently: Ronsard's *Discours* and
Montaigne's *Essais*
  François Rigolot 107

The Idea of Meaning and Practice of Method in
Peter Ramus, Henri Estienne, and Others
  Timothy J. Reiss 125

The Crisis of Cosmography at the End of the Renaissance
  Frank Lestringant 153

The Crisis of the Science of Monsters
Jean Céard.. 181

The Erosion of the Eschatological Myth (1597–1610)
Claude-Gilbert Dubois 207

Fin de Siècle Living: Writing the Daily at the End of the Renaissance
Marc E. Blanchard................................ 223

De Arte Rhetorica: The Gestation of French Classicism in Renaissance Rhetoric
Bernard Crampé................................... 259

Marie de Gournay and the Crisis of Humanism
Cathleen M. Bauschatz 279

Descartes and Humanism: The Critique of *Bricolage*
Fernand Hallyn.................................... 295

Contributors....................................... 315

Index of Names 319

Introduction
Philippe Desan

Some years ago, in an introductory course on French Renaissance literature, while I was giving a broad review of the most important concepts usually associated with the Renaissance in view of a forthcoming exam, a first-year science major asked: "When can one cease speaking of humanism?" I asked him to clarify his question. He wanted to know what crucial changes in values separate the times we live in from the Renaissance. At the time, I had no ready, straightforward answer. There I was, in front of twenty-five eager students poised to take notes, and I could not find any "scientific" tangible fact that would have saved the day. When and why can one stop speaking of the Renaissance? This was (and still is) a very good question.

It is with this question in mind that I conceived of a colloquium that would precisely address some of the issues associated with the decline of the French Renaissance. I contacted the best specialists of the French Renaissance and offered them the opportunity to meet and exchange views on what this question meant in their various fields of expertise. We met September 1–3, 1988, at the Institut Collégial Européen in Loches (France). After a few presentations, it appeared that the notion of a "crisis of humanism" was shared among scholars and that the decline of the French Renaissance was somewhat the result of a series of crises. After three days of intense intellectual dialogue, everyone went home with a better idea of what the others meant by "decline" and "crisis." What were then only works in progress addressing a very vague topic slowly became the essays that make up this book. I had requested that conference participants take into consideration ideas contributed by other scholars during this colloquium and that essays refer as much as possible to points raised during the various roundtable discussions. I believe that this book reflects the rich intellectual debate that took place in Loches.

I have always entertained doubts about humanism—this set of universal values accepted by all during the early Renaissance. The more I read in graduate school, the more I became aware of a movement that was more form than content. It seemed to me that, from very early on, the ideals presented in the texts of the ancients and replicated by humanist education simply did not convey or reflect the historical preoccupations of the intellectuals who read those texts. Nonetheless, my assumption was that these people were certainly not stupid and that they must have understood that what they were reading in classical works did not relate much to their daily experience. I suspected either that they must have enjoyed living in a dream world or that some kind of dissidence also existed. Of course, the idea of a counter-Renaissance is not new; it was remarkably argued by Hiram Haydn more than forty years ago. Instead of searching for a French counter-Renaissance (which methodologically accepts the historical period called the Renaissance and starts from there), the contributors to this book chose to study some of the most fundamental tenets of humanism and to see how those tenets ultimately corrupted from within the very notion of humanism and consequently precipitated the decline of the French Renaissance.

I developed the idea that if the Renaissance is to be associated with a golden apple (a beautiful form), there was certainly a worm inside from the beginning. The further the Renaissance progressed, the more dissension was heard from the inside, though it remained somewhat contained. A series of crises took bites at the apple: education, cosmology, cosmography, science, politics, ethics, religion, and language are only a few important areas where reality did not fit the neatly packaged vision of man and the world the ancients had given us. The worm fed on the apple, leaving its outside shape intact but slowly emptying its core. Soon there was no content left, just an empty form that did not even offer aesthetic pleasure to the eyes of intellectuals, who by now had more real and practical problems on their hands. The world had grown more complex than it had seemed to the ancients. New theories, accompanied by novel forms of expression, had to reflect this unprecedented complexity. Mannerist and baroque styles, for example, could be said to have been attempts to express this newly discovered complexity. Knowledge (of man and the world), which had been so stable for so long, suddenly generated more questions that it could answer. The worm (crisis) continued to feed on the apple (humanism) and finally consumed it. In a sense, the essays collected in this book, each dealing with a particular aspect of the crisis of humanism, are the stories of one series of bites at the apple.

Intellectual movements and cultural attitudes do not materialize from thin air; rather, they are often the result of a system of education. The decline of the Renaissance, and consequently of the values it stood for, is visible in the institutions that served to educate the elite of the time. James Supple analyzes the nobiliary ideal as it was reproduced and diffused in the education of the aristocracy. The humanist's educational system, which emphasized letters almost exclusively and ignored arms in the curriculum, was a favorite target of the *noblesse d'épée,* who reacted against what they saw as a vain and useless education based on the reading of ancients who offered very little when it came to concrete and practical situations in life—especially on the battlefield. Numerous treatises written by the members of the aristocracy recommended a more practical education that would emphasize mathematics (ballistic), geography, and history. This utilitarian approach to learning had for its function to give primacy to action over theory. The "useless subjects" taught in the humanist colleges had to make way for a more realistic vision of man and the world. As one of these reformers from the *noblesse d'épée* put it, "a man would profit more by gaining practical experience in the world than in studying Aristotle." This sentiment was also shared by a great number of intellectuals who had become disenchanted by the humanist values still taught at the end of the Renaissance. In the long run society's practical needs were to produce a more rigorous education that would in the seventeenth century fall under the control of religious orders. Instead of teaching universal values without regard to class origin and with little concern for a practical use, colleges specialized in order to meet particular demands. Families now sent their children to institutions where determinate programs with which they closely identified were provided. The universal system of education so dear to the humanists had finally splintered into exclusive and more suitable programs designed to please specific classes.

Colleges played an important role in diffusing the humanist ideology from the 1520s until the late 1570s. George Huppert examines what took place between the decade of the 1530s, a period that saw an unprecedented founding of new colleges, and the last decade of the century, which saw these same colleges literally in ruins. As Huppert shows, in the 1530s every small city wanted to have a college modeled after the best Parisian institutions and where Greek, Latin, and classical literature were taught as part of the curriculum. Not only was it profitable for a city to create a college, but it also added considerably to the city's prestige. Everybody wanted to be part of the humanist movement, and one of the best ways to achieve this was to create a college. Such a rapid and ambitious foundation was soon followed, however, by an unprecedented crisis in education. In fact, before fifty years had passed, most of these small colleges were bankrupt. Set up too rapidly, they had failed to establish any kind of endowment and were too dependent on city budgets. Priorities do change over time, and Huppert notes that what had changed was "the will to sacrifice in favor of education." Religious congregations soon took over the role that cities had played in the 1530s. Instead of the independent scholars who had been nourished on humanist values, priests were now teaching to young pupils a more orthodox approach to life. Too rigid in its program, the humanist educational system had failed to create a system that could adapt to the changing aspirations of society.

As every student of the Renaissance knows, philology proved to be the cornerstone upon which humanism was built. However, in France philological investigations were undertaken in a particular fashion: most tended to assert the "precellence" of French (Gallic) civilization and to help develop a nationalistic sentiment by showing the relativist relationship between history and its institutions. Zachary Schiffman demonstrates how the very notion of normative standards taken from antiquity was challenged in France. Historians used relativism as a weapon against the cultural domination of Latin (and therefore Italian) culture. But if relativism became a valuable weapon in favor of the superiority of French culture, the demonstration could easily be turned around. Therein lies the theoretical problem of relativism during the Renaissance: it is a never-ending process and therefore cannot be invoked to create a cultural order among civilizations. Montaigne was perhaps the first modern thinker to go all the way in developing a true relativist vision of history. As Schiffman suggests, Montaigne was "the first to reject all these traditional solutions, leaving him with no alternative but to turn the mind away from the now impossible task of knowing the world and toward the more feasible one of knowing itself." This inward turn implied a new definition of the thinking subject and reaffirmed the uniqueness of the individual in relation to its historical and social environment.

Relativism is a recurrent theme throughout the essays of this book. The question asked by Pasquier, La Popelinière, Montaigne, Charron, and Descartes is after all basically the same: Is knowledge accessible in a definitive state? The answer to this question, as probably best expressed by Descartes, is that the subject forges his own truth by means of what is historically given to him (the provisionary *morale*, for example) in order to think his own relationship to the world. Whereas reality refers to a concrete knowledge visible in nature and discoverable through a series of investigations, truth, on the contrary, refers to a reality that exists only in the mind. The world is an intrinsic part of the thinking process, and the subject can construct the world and demonstrate its truth by exercising his own reason and judgment.

There are very few periods in French history in which politics and culture become as closely intertwined as they do during the Renaissance. It is this relationship between political practice and cultural heritage that Timothy Hampton addresses in his essay. Post-Machiavellian politics have redistributed the cards of classical ethics, and virtue and cruelty are among the concepts most debated at the time. Hampton shows how historical exemplary figures suddenly become problematic and produce a crisis of representation visible in the texts written in the late Renaissance. As a result, an irreconcilable tension develops between exemplarity and narrative. Classical models of public life do not concur with this new era of creative politics and changing morals. As Hampton points out, "this divorce between act and virtue has a destructive effect upon the social body." Virtue and public action become the subject of one of Montaigne's most intense reflections. The author of the *Essais* suggests two distinct strategies to cope with this irreconcilable dichotomy, a public one and a private one. The public body has lost its identity and is now functioning with its own political logic, which tends to blur conventional ethics. It has become difficult to enter public life without abandoning some of the values one has received through a humanist education. The past is no longer a guide for public action, even if it provides valuable examples for one's personal life. This crisis between public and private life leads to a new definition of virtue, or rather to a dual meaning that applies to both spheres of human action.

Ronsard and Montaigne express their views of the political crisis in different literary forms: the *discours* and the *essai*. François Rigolot compares these two forms in terms of the political views they convey and sets for himself the task of evaluating "to what extent the 'poetic' colors the 'political.' " He contends that Ronsard sees rhetorically and aesthetically what Montaigne sees semiotically. If Montaigne attempts to reconcile the contradictions of his time within his own text, in a semiotic fashion, Ronsard seems more determined to salvage what is left of a divided France. Poetry serves to legitimate the political model still in place. Once more, it is the problematic relation between the individual and the social body that has to be reassessed. Rigolot embarks on a demonstration of how the "literary" can sometimes influence one's vision of politics. He reaches the conclusion that "the *essai* distinguishes itself from the *discours* to the extent that the first form accommodates the general deliberations of a private subject, the 'individual,' whereas the second can only allow individual expression of public subjectivity." In the end the poetics of Ronsard and Montaigne, by addressing ideology via literary forms, show new ways to perceive political situations.

The idea of method is central to any scientific or philosophical investigation. But too often we take what is said about method for the method itself. For this reason Timothy Reiss shows the necessity of putting in context the development of the idea of method in the sixteenth century. The practice of method is in fact far more complicated than its theoretical implications. One can say that "the method had not itself been the aim, but was more or less a side effect of the endeavor to set the relation between idea, word, and thing on some firm philosophic and linguistic ground." The elaboration of a method serves to simplify the issues that are debated, but it is never conceived as an end in itself. Ramus and Henri Estienne set out to develop a method that would help them to teach or present philosophical and philological theories. Central to the reordering of knowledge, method offers a way to reorganize a world that has become fragmented and needs to be represented in a new, more orderly fashion. New scientific or philosophical paradigms require an accompanying discourse dependent upon a method that always claims its novelty from tradition. The idea of method is closely linked to the crises that rocked the social and scientific order at the end of the Renaissance. A study of the development of method (more specifically the way it was practiced in particular situations) helps us to understand how the world can be theoretically rebuilt and how modern epistemologies are born.

The crisis of cosmography was principally a crisis of experience and description. At the end of the Renaissance it was often asked why one should pay any attention to the cosmographers, who had not even traveled to the places they wrote about. Montaigne expressed this sentiment better than anybody else, personally preferring the testimony of sailors and merchants, those who had the "experience" of the places they described. Frank Lestringant presents the crisis of cosmography in the following terms: "How could one reconcile the practical cartography of deep-sea navigators with the erudite geography of the humanists? And how could one proclaim the primacy of autopsy—or personal observation—while at the same time claiming to modernize and revise a scientific tradition that was over fifteen hundred years old?" Theory and practice of the physical world clashed when scholarly cartography was confronted with the more precise portolan charts drawn by travelers. Cosmography declined among the humanists as it became clear that the ancients offered unreliable sources for a practical knowledge of the world. Collections of travelers' particular accounts accompanied by maps slowly replaced the cosmographies popular at the height of humanism. Individual experience, even if very subjective, had finally prevailed over the authority of a Ptolemy or a Strabo.

Teratology and demonology anticipated modern scientific discourse in the way they attempted to establish a scientific explanation of natural causes. Jean Céard sees the crisis of the science of monsters as having led to a crisis in the idea of nature. It was held that monsters, although closely associated with divination, remind us of God's power over nature's activity. However, this important notion became challenged at the end of the Renaissance, and when it came time to explain marvelous occurrences, the articulation that had thus far been accepted between a physics and a theology of monsters gave way to a belief in the autonomy of nature. As Céard remarks, "the idea of a natural order endowed with a certain autonomy is gaining ground." The same trend toward an autonomy of nature can also be seen in the field of demonology. Nature, as it was "read" by science in the early seventeenth century, was gaining its scientific independence. The crisis of the science of monsters offers in this sense a symptom of a much larger crisis in the representation of nature and its subordination to the Creator.

Claude-Gilbert Dubois studies a related subject, treating the erosion of the eschatological myth at the end of the Renaissance. Dubois shows how, from being a purely imaginary figure in the Middle Ages, suddenly the Antichrist acquired a historical perspective with the Reformation: the pope became the Antichrist. As one might expect, civil peace precipitated the decline of this eschatological myth. But there is more in this legend than a simple rise and decline of anti-pope literature. Dubois takes the image of the Antichrist as a model for what he calls "the phantasmagorical representation of the Other" in Christian civilization. When one segment of society does not tolerate another part, it creates an imaginary Other, which then becomes the enemy. An entire literature may thus develop around this demonic threat to the well-being of society, and political interests are often served by the resurgence and the exploitation of the cultural *imaginaire*. The decline of the Antichrist legend follows a political and social pattern and for this reason needs to be analyzed within a specific historical context.

Marc Blanchard asks why people wrote their personal experiences during the Renaissance. This new kind of writing had nothing to do with a classical tradition and did not attempt to build upon a newly acquired knowledge of man; instead it was made of a daily recording of small events that nonetheless marked one's personal life. The idea of history was reduced to that of the Self who attempts to give a trace of his own existence amid a series of carefully reported incidents. The central position occupied by the subject had much to do with this new form of self-expression. At the end of the Renaissance, more than ever, man sensed himself as having been a body flung into turmoil, searching desperately for points of reference in his own life, either in the present or at least within the limits of his own life's history. Proximity became an essential way of understanding the world: "the overall narrative perspective, to which a humanist subject would have been used, shrinks more and more to the dimensions of a descriptive discourse whose references are more and more proximate to the writer." Blanchard speaks of a certain obsession with recording daily events. The desire to leave a trace of what might not otherwise exist anymore tomorrow can also be explained by a new perception of human time. Knowledge was no longer fixed but represented an ever-moving set of personal experiences that slowly supplanted the transmitted knowledge of the ancients. Personal experience replaced the texts of the ancients as the case of Montaigne proves to us. Practice counted more than ever, relegating theory to the second place. Truth itself was reduced to a series of repeated experiences determined by the subject. The writing of everyday experience not only reaffirmed the subject's sense of his own importance in the world, but also placed him on an equal footing with any other source of authority.

The best ideological control one could have over society is the control of language. Bernard Crampé traces the origin of classicism in Soarez's

De arte rhetorica and shows how rhetorical teaching was central to the destruction of vernacular literary practices developed in the sixteenth century. In fact, Soarez's work served as a model for numerous rhetorical manuals used in schools in the first decades of the seventeenth century. These manuals (in Latin or in French) are the best examples we have of the decay of the *arts poétiques* so popular in the mid-sixteenth century. A unified classical doctrine was soon to emerge of these rhetorical treatises that helped language to stabilize. This linguistic consolidation in turn permitted an ideological and cultural unification around a single vernacular language now clearly shared by all.

In the seventeenth century the language of Malherbe and Guez de Balzac replaced the language of Ronsard and Montaigne. It was precisely this phenomenon of linguistic banalization that inspired Marie de Gournay to write. The covenant daughter of Montaigne defended the outmoded language of the Renaissance. But oral usage of language was replacing the written language as the conversations taking place in Salons soon supplanted the reading of the ancients. As we know, the ideal of the *honnête homme* was strongly colored by an ingenious and versatile use of language. The "art de la conversation" was nowhere more visible than in the practice of the "précieuses" so well ridiculed by Molière and so avidly criticized by Marie de Gournay. Cathleen Bauschatz claims, as Marie de Gournay herself repeatedly asserted, that women could be blamed for doing away with the humanist definition (and use) of language. In fact, Bauschatz suggests that the decline of humanism, and therefore of its language (Latin), might have been prompted by women through the language they spoke. Whereas during the height of humanism language was directly associated with ideas, in the seventeenth century it often became an end in itself. The crisis of language was related to the fact that the vernacular had overtaken Latin as the means of education and intellectual discussion. From Montaigne to Descartes, we witness challenges to the notion that Latin was a better language with which to explore the Self (or even to embark on philosophical investigations). The decline of the Renaissance produced a new approach to language: to understand the subtleties of the Self one must address it in its own vernacular.

Descartes can be considered the best example of the desire to break with humanism. It seems therefore appropriate to end this collection of essays on the decline of humanism with what Fernand Hallyn calls the "critique of *bricolage*" in Descartes's work. One must understand *brico-*

lage to be the practice of accommodation and re-accommodation that sums up human activity before Descartes. For Hallyn, "the discursive break that Descartes seeks to bring to light ... can be read as the opposition between the work of a *bricoleur* and that of an *ingénieur*." A new mode of thinking, identified with the work of the *ingénieur*, had definitely replaced the intellectual patchwork of humanist thinkers. The world was now ready for the *tabula rasa* that so loudly announced the modern era.

History has continually taught us that following periods of crisis we must think the world anew and build a "better" science that will help us explain the relationship between nature and man. The Renaissance soon became an idea whose time had passed. From a succession of crises, a new paradigm of human knowledge had emerged, and it was now the task of seventeenth-century thinkers to prove to their contemporaries that their revised understanding of man and the world was in fact more true than the "old" and "desuet" Renaissance gloss over ancient literature, which too often sounded like a "clatter of so many philosophical brains," to use Montaigne's expression. The seventeenth century's desire for a quantification of science and its need for social pragmatism and realpolitik implied a rejection of the humanist culture—a culture that perhaps had been only an idealist dream, but a dream that nonetheless had shaped reality and served as the cornerstone of modernity. What is at stake in this book is precisely the very notion of modernity, which is still very much with us today in spite of all the arguments claiming we are in a new era of postmodernism.

The Worm in the Apple: The Crisis of Humanism

Philippe Desan

> Decline anticipates death's hour and intrudes even into the course of our progress.
>
> —Montaigne

"On December 31, 1494, at three o'clock in the afternoon, Charles VIII's army entered Rome, the military procession lasting well into the night, by torchlight. Not without terror, the Italians pondered this new French presence, seeing in these barbarians an art, a new martial organization that they had never thought possible."[1] Thus begins Jules Michelet's *Renaissance et réforme,* the ninth volume of his *Histoire de France.* Entering Italy under a cloud of gunpowder and the boom of cannons, French troops discovered a "new" world. The French historian continues: "These barbarians heedlessly clash one morning with this highly civilized culture; it is the shock of two worlds and more, the shock of two ages seemingly so removed from each other. It is the shock and the spark; and from the spark, the colossal burst of flames that would be called the Renaissance."[2]

With these words Michelet describes the "birth" of what was to become the French Renaissance (a veritable birth in the sense that, for Michelet, it is a precise, datable event—December 31, 1494, at 3:00 P.M.). Born late in comparison to the Italian Renaissance, which had been fathered by Petrarch two centuries earlier, the French Renaissance would experience an agitated childhood. Textbooks inform us that there was indeed a French Renaissance and that it was accompanied by the humanist movement. We also know that the seventeenth century had little to do with this famous humanism and that the "Grand siècle," preoccupied with its own notion of "classicism," was not a part of the Renaissance.

Something, therefore, happened during the sixteenth century to undermine the foundation of humanism and divide these periods into two distinct historical categories. Since we cannot furnish a death certificate for the French Renaissance in the same way that Michelet provides a birth certificate, we must speak instead of a "decline" or an "autumn."[3] Both historians and literary critics have preferred these terms in characterizing what happened in France between 1580 and 1630—i.e., between Montaigne and Descartes. As everyone will accept the "fact" that Montaigne belongs to the French Renaissance while Descartes opens a new era, something that happened during those fifty years must have been the basis for our historical perception. Yet the causes of the decline of the French Renaissance are as obscure as a precise date for its "death." The investigation of these causes is what interests us here. I myself would like to have the historical certainty of a Michelet and be able to propose a date and time that marks the end of the Renaissance; this would greatly facilitate the teaching of students who eagerly seek to assimilate causes, effects, and dates.

One thing is certain: declines do not happen by themselves. In the case of the French Renaissance, several "crises" within the humanist movement that began at the end of the fifteenth century led to the decline. The idea of crisis applied to the French Renaissance is not new. V. L. Saulnier saw a "crisis of humanism" in the fact that toward the end of the sixteenth century almost no new translations of ancient texts were being undertaken; he saw this period as a "loosening, where writers started to ignore Latin and Greek."[4] Likewise, in his insightful study *Society in Crisis: France in the Sixteenth Century*,[5] J. H. Salmon had already used the term *crisis* to describe French society during that politically and socially troubled time. Because the term remains vague and because it is quite impossible to pinpoint a definitive cause for the decline of the French Renaissance, I propose instead to investigate a series of what I shall call "axes of crisis." This essay will focus on these axes, not so much to offer a global explanation for the decline of the French Renaissance as to examine several paths that may have led to the crisis of humanist canons, which included universalism of scholarship (gloss of the ancients), Latin as the privileged tongue for the acquisition and diffusion of knowledge, the unchallenged papal authority, a shared

Ptolemean cosmology, and the prevailing Aristotelian vision of the world.

I shall begin with the problem of the organization and presentation of knowledge, i.e., the discussion surrounding the idea of method during the French Renaissance.[6] During the second half of the sixteenth century, individuals put themselves to the task of mentally reconstructing a world that was crumbling theoretically. The erosion of the scientific humanist canon unveiled new methodological questions, and it became apparent that a new order was needed. This discussion surrounding the idea of method attempted to address problems directly tied to such diverse factors as the decline of the Latin language and the explosion of the vernacular, the crumbling of the authority of the Sorbonne, the parceling out of scientific thought, the demise of Ciceronian morality and Aristotelian metaphysics, and, of course, the Protestant schism. The accumulation of these problems, all directly or indirectly responsible for the decline of the Renaissance, culminated in a veritable crisis of the humanist ideals that were inherent to the notion of a universal knowledge and morality, a notion that in the past had stood unchallenged, regardless of physical or mental boundaries.

Let us play the devil's advocate for a moment. Were there ever really a French Renaissance and a French humanism comparable, for example, to their Italian counterparts? Probably not. It is my argument here that France never developed a humanist tradition as well defined as the one that existed in Italy, for example. In fact, from its inception the French Renaissance carried within it a deep contradiction that undermined the values it was supposed to embrace.[7] In a sense, the "discovery" of Italy as it is ornately described by Michelet happened too late: I would like to suggest that when France picked the golden apple—in a certain way the troops of Charles VIII could be compared to Jason and his Argonauts embarking on the quest for the golden apples of the Hesperides' garden—the worm was already inside the apple, eating it away from within. I believe this image of a golden apple—with a glittering peel (form) but a problematic content—is a pertinent one for understanding the French Renaissance. Visual representations are often more powerful than words. We will have the opportunity to return to this image later.

The period that we conveniently designate as the Renaissance does not in reality constitute a temporally stable and coherent entity. Beginning in the first few decades of the sixteenth century, humanist principles were attacked by those who advocated a traditional culture based on a distancing from other cultures. The emergence of national sentiment during the sixteenth century, for example, played a crucial role in the reclamation and establishment of a unique French culture.[8] The golden form of humanism soon barely covered its increasingly problematic content. It is this crisis in the content of humanist values (politics, ethics, religion, cosmology) that brought into question the very form (rhetoric, topoi, syllogism, method) of humanist discourse. Because of this crisis of content, intellectuals began to conceptualize a new form, a new discourse, before becoming truly interested in its ends. This explains the interest in questions of method during the second half of the century. It was only when the intellectuals understood that the content of their values was threatened that they began to conceive of this problem as a crisis. The decline, like a worm devouring the core of the apple, happened slowly, although, in a way, it enriched the future of French intellectual thought.

When studying the French Renaissance, one feels that the packaging of ideas often assumed greater importance than the ideas themselves. For example, Ramus's dialectical method, as opposed to the Aristotelian syllogism, was viewed as a way to approach knowledge from a new angle, with a new method. People had not yet begun to realize that it was not the form of knowledge but its content that was truly undermined. Not until the beginning of the seventeenth century was the notion of "truth" applied to the content of arguments (redefined principally by Descartes) and finally seen as part of the method itself. As we know, such an understanding required the development of a *tabula rasa* and the abandonment of traditional rhetoric as the principal means of discovering knowledge. Experience and experimentation in the end prevailed. Instead of forming long linear arguments, knowledge assumed a more fragmented form accompanied by a more fragmentary discourse. The new form of discourse that emerged in the early seventeenth century strikes all students of literature: Seneca had definitively replaced Cicero, and the short form prevailed—the maxims of a La Rochefoucault, the characters of a La Bruyère, the *pensées* of a Pascal, and even the fables of a La Fontaine.

From the mid-sixteenth century onward, the humanist ideal of universality came under attack from all sides. On a linguistic level, the explosion of the vernacular undermined universal education based on Latin. The *Deffence et illustration de la langue françoise* (1549) by Du Bellay offered a true manifesto for the French language. It is clear that France was starting to discover its origins and was struggling to free itself from Latin influence, particularly from the image of Rome. While the Petrarchian sonnet was seen as a form to copy, poets nonetheless intended to give it a French content. French heroes, too, started to emerge in the Renaissance. This was the period of "our ancestors the Gauls,"[9] the Gallic Hercules,[10] the Trojan legend,[11] and the myth surrounding the creation of the city of Paris.[12] The principal function of all these legends was to create a new mental space distinct from Roman culture, which was increasingly perceived as "Italian."

As they became less inclined to identify with Greek and Roman traditions, French intellectuals had fewer difficulties rejecting the authorities that had for so long rooted themselves on the other side of the Alps. Indeed, Petrarch, Valla, and other great humanists were identified as Italian very early on. The very foundation of the humanist movement—the universalization of thought and the designation of a source for a common tradition of knowledge—came under attack by intellectuals who were beginning to feel more French and who expressed this nationalism by writing in the vernacular. These writers rapidly began to see that teaching based on Greek and particularly Latin models could not correspond to their everyday life experiences. While the rhetorical tradition became more closely associated with the Italian tradition, many intellectuals were seeking a mode of thought that would correspond more fully to their national and cultural specificity.

Rabelais, the poets of the Pléiade, and Montaigne all write in French and provide significant literary evidence of the tensions that arise when a personal consciousness of regional heritage clashes with the ideals of a classical universal education. Rabelais and Montaigne, and later Descartes, tell us that they have rejected Latin and the rhetorical science that accompanies it. Sebillet, Du Bellay, Peletier, and Ronsard choose to write *arts poétiques,* by freeing poetry of its designation as an Art of Second Rhetoric, which it retained until 1548. Ramus's prejudice against Italian orators and his resentment of a method organized around rhetoric are symptomatic of this desire to reestablish a harmonious relationship among eloquence, logic, and mathematics. In all these instances, this burgeoning poetic and scientific spirit is often tied to a latent patriotism: as Ramus declares, for example, in his preface to *Dialecticae partitiones,* mathematics were transmitted from Greece to Italy in order to wind up in France; Du Bellay says exactly the same thing of the French language.

On a moral level, Machiavelli's work is a veritable time bomb. The theorization of the *raison d'état,* largely appreciated in France, at least until the Saint Bartholomew's Day massacre in 1572, brings into question Ciceronian ethics. The topos of the lion and the fox, for example, illustrates this dramatic change in the humanist ideal throughout the sixteenth century (Cicero, Machiavelli, Montaigne). The question is whether the prince can combine both aspects, as Machiavelli recommended. At stake in such a choice is the issue of keeping a promise. Should the governor of a besieged place go out in order to parley with the enemy? This is the question Montaigne asks. Lies are becoming common practice and the *chevaleresque* moral of one's kept promise is degenerating. It is in fact difficult to write a political treatise in the wake of the Saint Bartholomew's Day massacre, difficult to proclaim a harmonious order when this order is based on a cosmological and ethical system that is dissolving day by day.

One must admit that the spirit of humanism underwent a serious crisis during the last quarter of the sixteenth century. Ciceronian ethics were systematically replaced by what was now called the "politique." Machiavellian pragmatism had left an indelible mark on the development of political thought, even if the Florentine author had currently fallen out of favor. Let us recall Jean Bodin's eulogistic statement from his 1566 *Methodus,* in which he declared Machiavelli to be "the first...to have written on the subject of the government of the state after twelve hundred years of universal barbarism."[13] Ten years later, in his *Six livres de la république,* Bodin apparently changed his mind, since he now declared, with a vehemence of tone that leaves no doubt as to his position, that Machiavelli was responsible for all the woes of France. The rumor circulated that the queen mother, Catherine de Medici, had taken *Il principe* as her Bible and that the idea of a Saint Bartholomew's Day massacre had come to her while she was reading these "sacred" pages. In spite of this newfound hostility toward it in France, Machiavellianism is nevertheless central to the redefinition of the French idea of politics.

Montaigne, perhaps the best witness of this humanist crisis in the realm of ethics, echoes the moral vacuum that reigns in France. The interest that he takes in the topos of the "useful" and the "honest" is evident throughout his *Essais* and in a sense sums up the problematic of his time. Yet "Of the Useful and the Honorable," the first chapter of the third book of the *Essais,* addresses a deeper question concerning the ideology of the whole period, an ideology that clearly surfaced after

1580 and that reflects a deep-seated historical hesitation as to whether one should, on the one hand, defend the ideals of chivalry, Ciceronian ethics, and the values of the nobility or, on the other, emphasize the practical, pragmatic, and commercial bourgeois conception of society.[14] David Schaefer, for example, argues that at the end of the sixteenth century the traditional morality based upon the idea of beauty was slowly being replaced by a utilitarian ethical system, which is the basis for modern bourgeois morality.[15] The useful is replacing the honest in the most mundane aspects of everyday life as well as in the political, social, and economic spheres. Montaigne attempts to counterbalance the invasion of the "useful" in society by defending the "honorable."

The first essay of the third book of the *Essais* perhaps illustrates better than any other what I have elsewhere called the "heterology" of the *Essais*,[16] that is, the realization of the impossibility of reconciling the useful—be it in the public, private, or economic spheres (and this before the theorization of utility and mercantilism by such seventeenth-century economists as Sully, Montchrestien, Laffemas, and even Colbert)—with the conception of honesty as it was understood at the end of the Renaissance. "Honesty" at this time presaged the seventeenth-century *honnête homme*, the dilettante, idle champion of noble values and ideals that are nonetheless eroding away. Montaigne's language oscillates between these two discursive poles. The useful/honest distinction creates conflict within the *Essais*. Marcel Tetel has rightly noted that "it is the search for the resolution of an inner conflict between honesty and utility, such as Montaigne defines them in the context of a *vita activa*, that animates his work."[17] The idea of conflict is indeed evident in the lexical oppositions throughout the third book of the *Essais* and is symptomatic of a larger problem of two ideologies competing for dominance in French society.

The end of the sixteenth century redefined the rules of politics by virtue of an ethical reorientation. All political power had to seek to explain its existence in the context of a cosmogonic order: it was morally incumbent upon the thinkers of this period to find a geometry or arithmetic to justify the forms of government. Justice operated according to this same model. Thus, politics, justice, and the cosmos had to form a coherent whole, and it was precisely this veiled coherent system that interested intellectuals at the end of the French Renaissance. Political order also underwent a crisis at the same time, resulting in a profound disequilibrium. Jean Bodin's *Methodus ad facilem historiarum cogni-*

tionem responds to the need to create a new equilibrium among the monarchy, the church, the nobility, and the people.[18] As a jurisconsult, Bodin conceives this new order in legal terms and bases his conception on a numerology reminiscent of that of Plato. His goal is to achieve harmony, both cosmogonic and political, by finding new, stable order in this period of instability.

The theoretical conception of the cosmos is also unstable at this time. The author of the *Essais* perceives the project upon which he embarks as being structurally unsound: "the vain construction of human knowledge."[19] Certainly Plato and the Pythagoreans provide a total vision of the cosmos and of the world, one that would serve as the ground for the stabilization of the "branloire perenne" to which Montaigne alludes. Yet the belief in an essential relationship between macrocosm and microcosm persists. In this context, 1543 is an important date in the erosion of Aristotelian science and philosophy; this is the year in which Copernicus published his *De revolutionibus* and Ramus submitted his *Dialecticae institutiones* and his *Aristotelicae animadversiones,* in which he criticizes Aristotle and the authority of the Sorbonne. These two authors, who represent space in a similar fashion, provide a radically different formulation of the universal from that of their predecessors. For this reason they can be considered the key figures of an increasing tendency toward formulating a logical representation of man's world by interposing spatiotemporal variables. Copernicus criticizes the Ptolemean system and rejects all qualitative aspects of Ptolemean cosmology; for Copernicus, the universe is above all an ensemble of geometric relationships that can be approached and understood through mathematics. Ramus, in his conception, quantifies method by placing equal value on numeric relationships among differing cognitive propositions. He intends to expose his philosophical demonstrations through a geometric and arithmetic use of a methodological space.[20] In so doing, he believes he has found in Plato a mathematical panacea absent in Aristotle.

It is crucial to understand the importance of the "discovery" of Plato after 1550 in France as well as the profound influence that his thought and especially his method exercise on ideology at the end of the Renaissance. At a time when Aristotle could no longer convincingly present an ordered world, the *Timeus* offered a complete system that takes the cosmos as a point of departure in order to arrive at man. Plato's text offered its reader a teleological explanation in which the world and man are intimately bound together. Plato starts with the universal (the cosmos) and arrives at the particular (man), thus offering a new cosmogony that temporarily patches up gaping holes in the Aristotelian system. We know, for example, that the historical method as it is developed during the end of the French Renaissance was strongly influenced by Plato, to Aristotle's detriment. No doubt the numerous translations of Plato during the second half of the sixteenth century contributed largely to the development of a new vision of the world. We can see the influence of a text such as the *Timeus* on the work of Le Roy, for example. Here I am thinking of Le Roy's treatise *De la vicissitude ou variété des choses en l'univers...*, which attempts to provide a cosmological understanding amid the apparent chaos of all human and natural phenomena.

Aristotle, then, became the object of constant criticism, as did many other ancient Greek writers. In 1550, the humanist movement began to attack the founder of the Peripatetician school with an intensity and vigor heretofore unknown. To be sure, Ramus had already launched the anti-Aristotelian movement in France with his declaration before the Sorbonne in 1536: "Quaecumque ab Aristotele dicta essent, commentitia esse" ("everything Aristotle has said is but falsehood"). But it was during the second half of the sixteenth century that the perception of Greek philosophy in France changed definitely: humanists turned away from Aristotle and looked toward Plato. It is not mere coincidence that most of Plato's works were translated into French between 1550 and 1560.[21] Poetry, especially the Pléiade, was strongly influenced by this Neoplatonist movement.[22] Although intellectuals still invoked Aristotle in matters pertaining to philosophy, he was no longer considered an infallible authority. As Aristotelian method became subject to scrutiny, Renaissance humanists ascertained that numerous laws in the *corpus aristotelium* simply no longer corresponded to their experience. Aristotelian order did survive in spite of it all, for better or for worse; until Descartes established a new cosmogonic and ontological paradigm, however, a philosophy of accommodation prevailed.

The question remains: Why did Plato experience a popularity in France unequalled in other countries in the mid-sixteenth century? If we take as an indication the number of Plato's texts published in major European cities, we see that the largest number was indeed printed in Paris. It was only in the following generation, during the 1570s and the 1580s, that Platonism became recognized as subject matter worthy of being taught in Pisa and in Farrare.[23] And even then, the Neoplatonic

Renaissance in Florence, under the influence of the Medici family, could not compare with the scientific monopoly of Paduan Aristotelianism. The reason for Plato's popularity in France may be found in the structural difference between the French humanist movement and the humanist movements in Italy, Germany, and Spain. Let us not forget that the French Renaissance, contrary to the Italian Renaissance, for example, extends over a relatively short period of time, one that corresponds roughly to the sixteenth century.

Plato unconsciously proposes solutions to many problems that arise in Artistotle's texts, yet, in spite of the attacks, Aristotle remains the foremost philosopher at the end of the Renaissance. According to Montaigne he is still "the god of scholastic knowledge"[24] and "the monarch of modern learning."[25] As Alexandre Koyré points out, "they could not take Aristotle away from the professors without giving them something in his stead. Until the time of Descartes, there was nothing, absolutely nothing, to give them."[26] A simple glance is all that is needed to confirm that the Aristotelian world is crumbling, but just as a paradigm will not disappear unless it can be replaced by another,[27] Aristotelianism survives and remains more or less intact. As I have already stated, this is a philosophy of accommodation and of "patching-up" to which Montaigne refuses to adhere. He understands perfectly the desperate situation in which the Aristotelian religion finds itself, and the questions he asks himself lead him to doubt:

> The god of scholastic knowledge is Aristotle; it is a religious matter to discuss any of his ordinances, as with those of Lycurgus at Sparta. His doctrine serves us as magisterial law, when it is peradventure as false as another. I do not know why I would not as readily accept either the Ideas of Plato, or the Atoms of Epicurus, or the Fullness and Void of Leucippus and Democritus, or the Water of Thales, or the Infinity of Nature of Anaximander, or the Air of Diogenes, or the Numbers and Symmetry of Pythagoras, or the Infinite of Parmenides, or the One of Musaeus, or the Water and Fire of Apollodorus, or the Similar Parts of Anaxagoras, or the Discord and Friendship of Empedocles, or the Fire of Heraclitus, or any other opinion out of that infinite confusion of theories and views which this fine human reason produces by its certainty and clear-sightedness in everything it meddles with.[28]

Montaigne sees man at the end of the sixteenth century as "patched with a thousand false and fantastic bits."[29] The works of Nicholas of Cusa, Copernicus, Thomas Digges, and Giordano Bruno lay the groundwork for the breaking up of Aristotelian spheres, the ensuing notion of a heliocentric cosmos, the idea of an open-ended world, and finally the acceptance of a universe in constant motion. These successive stages inevitably lead to what has judiciously been called the "dissolution of the universe." At the time Montaigne is writing his *Essais,* this dissolution is not yet complete, but the process has already been put into motion. Our essayist easily detects the first tremors of Aristotelianism's ultimate collapse. Montaigne declares science unstable, useless, sterile, and full of pitfalls; he sees nothing in it but "dreams and fanatical follies,"[30] fantasies, "twaddle and lies."[31]

The ideas proposed by Copernicus in his *De revolutionibus orbium caelestium* (1543) spread slowly, yet we can affirm that by 1570 the notion of a heliocentric world was well enough known that Montaigne, who had no scientific pretensions and shared only the common knowledge of his day, made reference to these ideas in his *Essais:*

> The sky and the stars have been moving for three thousand years; everybody had so believed, until it occurred to Cleanthes of Samos, or (according to Theophrastus) to Nicetas of Syracuse, to maintain that it was the earth that moved, through the oblique circle of the Zodiac, turning about its axis; and in our day Copernicus has grounded this doctrine so well that he uses it very systematically for all astronomical deductions.[32]

Imagine Ptolemy and Aristotle, pillars of Western civilization for fifteen centuries, suddenly beginning to quiver. The entire humanist structure is on the verge of collapse. Once again, Montaigne is the witness of his day: "Ptolemy, who was a great man, had established the limits of our world; all the ancient philosophers thought they had its measure."[33] Suddenly everything gives way. Who should be believed? What should be held for truth? These two questions function as a leitmotif at the end of the French Renaissance.

Copernicus's theories also raise questions of religious order. How, for example, can God and man coexist in an infinite universe? If man is no longer the center of the universe, what becomes of the relationship between the microcosm and the macrocosm? If the earth is simply one planet among many, how can one continue to consider it a privileged place? Is there life on other planets? If so, are these creatures equally the sons of Adam and Eve? How could they have inherited original sin? If the universe is infinite, where is God's throne situated? So many embarrassing questions prevent the ecclesiastical authorities from taking an official position before 1616. These questions surface again in 1633 when the authorities forbid the teaching of the doctrine that the sun is the center of the universe and Earth a mere planet. Although the ecclesiastical authorities were able to integrate Aristotle and Ptolemy into Catholic dogma during the twelfth and thirteenth centuries, the questions raised by Copernicus and his disciples prove unacceptable at the beginning of the seventeenth century. They meet with even stronger opposition in Protestant circles.

Having destroyed Aristotelian physics, metaphysics, and ethics, the Renaissance finds itself in a veritable vacuum. Indeed, humanism can no longer accept the Aristotelian notion of a "natural place," of a finite universe where everything has its place and there is a place for everything. Ernst Cassirer observes that from this time on, "there is no absolute 'above' or 'below,' and, therefore, there can no longer be just one direction of influence. The idea of the world organism is here expanded in such a way that every element in the world may with equal right be considered the central point of the universe."[34] Objects wander aimlessly within the infinite cosmos, everything is in constant motion, and man himself is surprised by his newfound ontological nudity. Everything must be rethought; everything must be redone.

Koyré points out that it is not until the seventeenth century that a new ontology of man can be elaborated. This period of transition between two ontologies explains the deep interest that French society takes in alchemy, magic, and astrology at the end of the Renaissance.[35] Even the most distinguished scientists and intellectuals of the day become caught up in the occult and lend credence to the most unlikely theories. Ambroise Paré firmly believes in demonic intervention; Bodin refers to witches; Postel orients himself toward the Cabala. This is the time when the most unbelievable superstitions enjoy widespread popularity, when magic and sorcery are a part of daily life. Should we not see in all of this a desperate attempt to latch onto a "replacement science" that would allow practitioners to span the chasm that characterizes the end of the sixteenth century? The question remains open to debate, but it seems that many marvelous explanations surface during such periods of crisis when the existing scientific paradigms are under attack from all sides. At the end of the Renaissance, man can only be described as "credulous": the world collapses under his feet and he is suddenly predisposed to believe any explanation. This is the period when all things seem possible. Man stands in awe before the idea of a New World, and wild rumors circulate about its nature. To borrow Koyré's expression, man in the Renaissance is taken prisoner of a "magical ontology"; he gets lost exploring a thousand paths that all lead nowhere. Yet this apparent disorder allows for the expression of innumerable ideas, some of which become highly developed. These ideas lay the groundwork upon which seventeenth-century science and philosophy will be able to build.

One can find evidence of other attempts to create a new order in the numerous utopias that are conceived of in the late sixteenth and early seventeenth centuries, of which the *Civitas solis* (1602) by Tommaso Campanella and *The New Atlantis* (1629) by Francis Bacon are only the most famous. This period of utopias and of occultism inevitably culminates in Descartes, the first thinker to propose a cosmos in which things, once again, find their place. With Descartes the abyss is finally bridged by a safe, strong, and solid structure, and the unstable footbridges that utopias and the occult had offered will once again disappear for a time.

A deep sense of confusion as well as chaos marks French thought at the end of the sixteenth century. Etienne Pasquier chooses precisely the term *chaos* to define the situation in which the France of 1589 finds itself. In a letter to the Count of Sanzay, Pasquier speaks of the "chaos of our troubles"; he picks up on the term again in book 6 of his *Recherches de la France:* "a pell-mell chaos in all things."[36] Yet perhaps this chaos of which he speaks attests more to a proliferation of new orders than it does to a veritable disorder. When several possible authorities are in competition to prove "their" truth, truth can no longer be considered an absolute category. A historicist and relativist vision of the world reigns at the end of the Renaissance, a vision that blatantly contradicts the humanist canon and the humanist order itself. Montaigne once again sums up the new definition of truth: "Our truth of nowadays is not what is, but what others can be convinced of."[37]

Montaigne is not immune to the doubt that now characterizes truth; he is surprised by the philosophical vacuum that reigns in his era. Doubt, for Montaigne, is not a deliberate philosophical choice (in this way he is neither skeptic nor Pyrrhonian) but a simple ineluctability. Doubt is the logical conclusion for a period that becomes conscious of its historicity and sets itself apart from the ancient precepts that no longer reflect a verifiable empirical reality. The practical supersedes the theoretical, or, as Montaigne himself says, "it is a fine thing to learn the theory from those who well know the practice."[38] The practical aspects of ethics and politics as well as of science have changed; the theory, therefore, must be rewritten. This, then, in summary fashion, is the philosophical position of many intellectuals at the end of the Renaissance.

Montaigne, for example, advocates a return to the naked man, to man's natural condition. The inhabitants of the New World offer a new paradigm that generates yet another crisis: that of the human essence. Only after stripping man of reason and rhetoric, both scientific and philosophical, can true philosophy emerge: "men who have tried everything and sounded everything, having found in that pile of knowledge and store of so many various things nothing solid and firm, and nothing but vanity, have renounced their presumption and recognized their natural condition."[39] We now understand what interests Montaigne so deeply about these newly discovered societies in the New World. The author of the *Essais* feigns surprise that the Greek philosophers were unable to foresee the existence of these societies that irremediably contradict the very basis of Aristotelianism, as much by their customs and ethical codes as by their "philosophy" of life: "This story of Aristotle does not fit our new land."[40] In this regard, cannibals play a fundamental role in the essays pertaining to Aristotelian philosophy precisely because the cannibal serves as a living response to the doctrines proposed by the author of the *Organon:* "This answer would be good among the cannibals, who enjoy the happiness of a long, tranquil, and peaceable life without the precepts of Aristotle and without acquaintance with the name of physics."[41] The cannibal symbolizes the last man to be corrupted by the texts of the ancients. Montaigne expounds at great length upon the consequences of such a reality and finally decides that cannibals, in their ignorance, are no worse off than their European contemporaries.

The cannibal of the New World, however, is not the only example of man still in his vulgar and naive state; Montaigne also finds a more contemporary model in the French peasant. At a time when idols are burned, the peasantry forms a last bastion of true philosophy; they are seen to hold real truth: "The least contemptible class of people seems to me to be those who, through their simplicity, occupy the lowest rank; and they seem to show greater regularity in their relations. The morals and the talk of peasants I find commonly more obedient to the prescriptions of true philosophy than are those of our philosophers."[42] What Montaigne appreciates about the peasant is his simplicity of speech (a tendency that we find in the new style favored in the form of the novella throughout the sixteenth century). The difference between a philosopher and a peasant can almost be reduced to the problem of the brain: "the peasant and the shoemaker go their way simply and naturally talking about what they know; while these men, though waiting to exalt themselves and swagger around with this learning that is floating on the surface of their brain, are perpetually getting confused and tangled up in their own feet."[43] We find here the opposite poles of humanity, what Montaigne calls "the two extremes, philosophers and rustics."[44] Rural people, like the cannibals, provide a response to the abuses of Aristotelianism and allow Montaigne to offer a critique of philosophy in general.

Another crisis arising in the Renaissance, more social and economical in nature, involves the *noblesse d'épée,* whose power is slowly eroding in favor of a new rising class, the bourgeoisie. As the bourgeoisie imposes more and more of its own values on society, the tensions produced by the two conflicting systems of values (conflicts not only on the political level but also on economic and legal levels) generate two discursive paradigms that even while coexisting are inevitably in competition. The old nobiliary model, previously dominant in the literature and still present in the early Renaissance, claims to be representative of sublime and universal values such as glory, virtue, and other nobiliary ideals. This somewhat idealistic paradigm is suddenly confronted by a more realistic and materialistic discourse in which literary images center on individual experience and the particular. The resulting discursive tensions can be seen in Montaigne's *Essais.* In fact, in the *Essais* we witness Montaigne's conscious desire to reproduce and extend the language and values of the *noblesse* while he recognizes, at the same time, the impossibility of escaping the intrusion of a new commercial discourse and economic discursive structures. The confrontation of these two models implies a deconstruction of authority and the assertion of the individual.

This discursive change has tremendous ideological implications that exceed the individual author. Montaigne is not an isolated case; his discursive practice, as revealed in his diction, indicates a qualitative change in the linguistic and ideological tendencies of an entire era. Already in Du Bellay's *Deffence et illustration de la langue françoise* we can find an emerging economic mode of reference: he speaks of a language that can be enriched, that has a price, etc. It is perhaps in discourse itself that this crisis becomes most visible. We may consider the *Essais* an essential text for the analysis of social discourse at the end of the Renaissance, because it is to be understood in an interpersonal context as a series of verbal exchanges with others.

The discursive heterology present in the *Essais* (the opposition between the mercantile discourse and the nobiliary discourse) coincides with the social and political crisis that characterizes the end of the sixteenth century. A profound linguistic transformation accompanies the economic success and the social mobility of the merchant bourgeoisie at this time. The communal nature of the language is being redefined in order to accommodate a new world vision and to adapt to the mercantile discourse. It would seem that the way in which society apprehends and describes social interaction—indeed, all human activity, including artistic and literary activity—overlaps with the mode of economic organization beginning in the sixteenth century.

From this point on, one may view the literary text as a commercial object: conceived and organized as such, the text characterizes itself as merchandise and as a commodity. It is therefore hardly surprising that not only the content of the literary work—the text—but also its structure—the physical book—is closely tied to the economic sphere. The end of the Renaissance marks a decisive moment on both a linguistic and an ideological level. A battle for control of the language is being fought between two ideological systems with opposing sets of values. Economic discourse, as it expands beyond the marketplace, will eventually emerge victorious, and the literature of the seventeenth century, in particular the theater of Molière,[45] will provide the stage for the representation of this new discourse. During the final stages of the Renaissance, social relationships begin to correlate mimetically with economic relationships. Infrastructure and superstructure become superimposed; social discourse merges with economic discourse and soon becomes indistinguishable from it.

These are, very briefly, several of the axes of crisis to which I alluded at the beginning of this essay. I would now like to elaborate further the "worm in the apple" metaphor I used earlier. I have already characterized French humanism as a movement born with the seeds of its own destruction. The apple is indeed the famous golden apple of the garden of the Hesperides, an image frequently invoked in the Renaissance. Ronsard, for example, refers to it in his *Hymnes:*

> The Ancients also admiring your virtue
> Have the sheep from Helles with fine gold covered,
> They have in your favor the apples honored
> By Venus and Atlas all made golden[46]

And again:

> Alcide acquired praise in no small degree
> For having won the rich golden apples:
> Having acquired the beautiful MARGUERITE,
> You alone have the world's treasure.[47]

To summarize the legend briefly: Hercules' eleventh task is to pick the golden apples from the garden of the Hesperides despite the dragon that guards the place (a serpent in Apollonius of Rhodes's *Argaunotic,* a dragon in Sophocles' *Trachiniae* and Euripides' *Heracles*), but Prometheus warns Hercules not to go himself to take the golden apples. He suggests to send Atlas for them, and, in the meantime, to support the heavens in his place. It is therefore Atlas who obtains three apples from the three Hesperides—Hesperia, Aegle, and Erythie, who inhabit the garden in the Far East that Mother Earth had given to Hera. The Hesperides are also called maidens of the night because they sing with sweet and melodious voices. Once he has taken the apples, Atlas wants to bring them himself to Eurystheus. Hercules feigns agreement with Atlas but asks him to hold the heavens again while he makes a pad to put on his head. Atlas is easily tricked and Hercules finally leaves with the golden apples. In *The Greek Myths,* Robert Graves tells us that "the names of the Hesperides... refer to the sunset. Then the sky is green, yellow, and red, as if it were an apple-tree in full bearing; and the Sun, cut by the horizon like a crimson half-apple, meets his death dramatically in the western waves."[48] This sun of the Renaissance that finally sets once the golden apples have been picked suggests not only the result of a quest (that of the Argonauts) but also a newly engendered irony. For, as in the garden of Eden, once picked, the apple brings problems or begins to rot. It is for this reason that I suggest that the apple transmitted from Italy is already badly damaged when it arrives in France and that much of its splendor is already tarnished.

Yet the idea of an ongoing cycle of decline and renewal may be symbolized by the figure of the worm itself: the worm turns into a butterfly, who lays new eggs that in turn become worms, and so on. Ronsard himself provides the metaphor:

> After having vomited all his silk
> (That a good laborer in many thin threads
> Must join to the gold for the garments of a King),
> This fatigued worm, as though tired of himself,
> Suddenly changes, and flies away through the meadows
> Made butterfly with colorful wings
> Of red, green, azure and vermillion.
> Then tired of being so much a butterfly
> Becomes caterpillar and lays eggs, in order
> That by his death he can live again.[49]

The sense of decline is therefore systematically reintegrated into a positive model of cyclical renewal. Just as the caterpillar becomes a butterfly with all of its marvelous colors, so the crisis of humanism and the decline of the Renaissance engender the "Grand siècle."

It is not coincidental that history becomes one of the privileged fields for intellectual reflection at the end of the Renaissance, for it raises precisely the issues of continuity, degenerescence, decline, and progress. As we have seen, if the breaking down of humanist values marks the crisis, the questioning of this degeneration also suggests the idea of progress. After all, the rotten apple nourishes the caterpillar who will eventually become a colorful butterfly, as Ronsard describes it. Intellectuals of the end of the French Renaissance ask themselves how this decline occurs. As Michelet had stated, and as writers of the sixteenth century also saw it, military conquests always give birth to new eras. Such conquests will invariably lead to a renaissance in the arts. But this view is problematic, because, as so many writers from Machiavelli to Bodin and Le Roy have agreed, it is only when the arts attain their peak in a given society that the society's military begins to decline. Loys Le Roy best expresses this conflicted attitude vis-à-vis decline and progress in his 1575 text *De la vicissitude ou varieté des choses en l'univers*. This paradox, in fact, lies at the root of Le Roy's philosophy of history: the literary and artistic fame a civilization achieves would therefore be regarded as the first sign of its decline. Since this final stage of progress encourages idleness, Le Roy thinks, it would inevitably lead to a civilization's military decline and its eventual subjugation by another race or people. Le Roy detects this implacable mechanism in the rise and fall of all the great civilizations; the tendency attains the status of a historical law. Let us not forget that Du Bellay has exactly the same attitude vis-à-vis language.

Moreover, Le Roy finds proof of the accuracy of this law during his lifetime. Although there were many technological discoveries during the sixteenth century, Le Roy is appalled by the degree of barbarity and social chaos that characterizes his era and, more particularly, France:

> Thus this century was admirable in strength and wisdom and in all the arts: it was also full of maliciousness and extraordinary changes. As if it were necessary that the same age produce horrible monsters and illustrious marvels. For one commonly sees that where people's knowledge is the greatest, virtuous and vicious men come together, authors of great things both good and evil. As if virtue and vice, which are things so contrary and mutually repugnant, had their summits nearby.[50]

All great periods of history have demonstrated such contradictions; the paradox is inherent in the very notion of civilization.

The fundamental question that Le Roy asks himself is: Are things ever comprehensible? More explicitly, was there ever a golden age when things existed in harmony with people? The answer to both questions is no. Le Roy does not believe in the existence of a golden age, and he breaks with those who call for a return to the past. But neither does he believe that things go from bad to worse; like Ronsard, Le Roy is an optimist who professes unlimited confidence in slow and cumulative progress. He distrusts abrupt revolutions. Claude-Gilbert Dubois has noted that "the optimism of the author does not base itself solely on the triumph of life over death: there is for him a metaphysics of progress."[51] Le Roy's optimism derives from an almost metaphysical faith in progress and in the technological developments that accompany it. He believes that the developmental stage of a civilization may be viewed as a function of its technical advances and its military prowess.

For Le Roy and many other historians of the end of the French Renaissance, the separate notions of cyclical history and linearly progressive history are brought together, allowing us to figure historical thought as a series of cycles placed on an ascending linear axis. Mircea Eliade has commented that by the beginning of the seventeenth century the idea of progress had come to dominate the Western vision of the world and that, for many authors of this period, a cyclical view of history survived side by side with a new, progressive view of history. Eliade cites Tycho Brahe, Kepler, Cardan, Bruno, and Campanella to illustrate this new vision of the world: "By the seventeenth century, the linearism and the progressive notion of history continue to assert themselves, establishing the belief in an infinite progress."[52] We have in Le Roy probably the best example of this new mental attitude vis-à-vis history. Already present in the *Deffence et illustration de la langue françoise* (1549) by Du Bellay, but theorized and developed more fully by Le Roy in *De la vicissitude*, this progressive mentality linked to a double vision of history allows for the development of a synthesis of the cyclical tradition of humanism and Christian "linearity." It is perhaps the fusion of these two ideas of history, combined with the cosmological, political, social, and moral crises in humanist values, that mark what we could call in a larger way the crisis of humanism, a generalized crisis that led to the decline of the French Renaissance. The golden apple had become a perfect form but with an empty core; the butterfly had flown away toward a new life, a new century, and new problems.

NOTES

Epigraph from Montaigne, *The Complete Essays of Montaigne,* trans. Donald M. Frame (Stanford: Stanford University Press, 1958), III, 13, 846 B: "La mort se mesle et confond par tout à nostre vie: le declin praeoccupe son heure et s'ingere au cours de nostre avancement mesme." In this and subsequent references to Montaigne, a letter (A, B, or C) following the page number indicates one of the three major textual strata: 1580, 1588, or 1595.

 1. Jules Michelet, "La Renaissance," in *Renaissance et réforme,* vol. 9 of *L'Histoire de France* (Paris: Robert Laffont, 1982), 83. My translation.

 2. Michelet, 175.

 3. See, for example, *L'Automne de la Renaissance, 1580–1630,* ed. Jean Lafond and André Stegmann (Paris: J. Vrin, 1981).

 4. V. L. Saulnier, *La Littérature française du siècle classique* (Paris: Presses Universitaires de France, 1967), 18.

 5. J. H. Salmon, *Society in Crisis: France in the Sixteenth Century* (New York: St. Martin's Press, 1975).

6. I have traced this discussion around method in my book, *Naissance de la méthode: Machiavel, La Ramée, Bodin, Montaigne, Descartes* (Paris: Nizet, 1987).

7. Hiram Haydn (*The Counter-Renaissance* [New York: Harcourt, Brace and World, 1950]) has proposed a somewhat similar theory with regard to England and has shown how this counter-Renaissance "originated as a protest against the basic principles of the classical renaissance, as well as against those of medieval Scholasticism" (xi).

8. See Philippe Desan, "Nationalism and History in France during the Renaissance," *Rinascimento* 24 (1984): 261–88.

9. On the Gallic craze in France during the last twenty-five years of the sixteenth century, it suffices to see Ronsard, *Les Quatre premiers livres de la Franciade* (1572); François Hotman, *Francogallia* (1573); Guy Le Fèvre de la Boderie, *La Galliade, ou De la revolution des arts et sciences* (1578); Claude Fauchet, *Recueil des antiquitez gauloises et françoises* (1579); Etienne Forcadel, *De Gallorum imperio*... (1579); Nicolas Vignier, *Traicté de l'estat et origine des anciens françois* (1582); Noël Taillepied, *Histoire de l'estat et republique des Druides* (1585); and Claude Fauchet, *Les Antiquitez gauloises et françoises* (1599). For a discussion of these books, see Claude-Gilbert Dubois, *Celtes et Gaulois au XVIe siècle, le développement littéraire d'un mythe nationaliste* (Paris: J. Vrin, 1972).

10. See Marc-René Jung, *Hercule dans la littérature française du XVIe siècle* (Geneva: Droz, 1966).

11. See Edmond Faral, *La Légende arthurienne* (Paris: H. Champion, 1929); and Sándor Eckhardt, *De Sicambria à Sans-Souci: histoires et légendes franco-hongroises* (Paris: Presses Universitaires de France, 1943).

12. See Du Breul, *Theâtre des antiquitez de Paris,* text reproduced by Antoine Le Roux de Lincy and L. M. Tisserand, *Paris et ses historiens aux XIVe et XVe siècles* (Paris: Imprimerie Impériale, 1867), 247–55.

13. Jean Bodin, *Methodus ad facilem historiarum cognitionem,* in *Oeuvres philosophiques de Jean Bodin,* ed. Pierre Mesnard (Paris: Presses Universitaires de France, 1951), 167: "multa quoque Maciavellus, primus quidem, ut opinor, post annos mille circiter ac ducentos quàm barbaries omnia cumularat."

14. See Philippe Desan, "De l'utile, de l'honnête et de l'expérience: le cadre idéologique du troisième livre des *Essais,*" in *The Order of Montaigne's Essays,* ed. Daniel Martin (Amherst, Mass.: Hestia Press, 1989), 200–220.

15. David Schaefer, "The Good, the Beautiful, and the Useful: Montaigne's Transvaluation of Values," *American Political Science Review* 73, no. 1 (1979): 139–54.

16. See Philippe Desan, "Quand le discours social passe par le discours économique: les *Essais* de Montaigne," *Sociocriticism* 4, no. 1 (1988): 59–86.

17. Marcel Tetel, "De l'*honneste*' chez Montaigne: réversibilité et subver-

sion," in *La Catégorie de l'"honneste' dans la culture du XVIe siècle* (Saint-Estienne: Institut d'Etudes de la Renaissance et de l'Age Classique, 1985), 233.

18. See Philippe Desan, "La justice mathématique de Jean Bodin," *Corpus: revue de philosophie* 4 (1987): 19–29.

19. Montaigne, II, 12, 415 A: "le vain bastiment de l'humaine science."

20. See Nelly Bruyère, *Méthode et dialectique dans l'oeuvre de La Ramée: Renaissance et âge classique* (Paris: J. Vrin, 1984); and Walter Ong, *Ramus, Method, and the Decay of Dialogue: From the Art of Discourse to the Art of Reason* (Cambridge, Mass.: Harvard University Press, 1958).

21. On Plato's translations into French during the Renaissance, see Albert-Marie Schmidt, "Traducteurs français de Platon (1536–1550)," in *Etudes sur le XVIe siècle* (Paris: Albin Michel, 1967), 17–44; and Frédéric Hennebert, *Histoire des traductions françaises d'auteurs grecs et latins pendant le XVIe et XVIIe siècles* (1881) (Amsterdam: B. R. Grüner, 1968).

22. See Robert V. Merrill and Robert J. Clements, *Platonism in French Renaissance Poetry* (New York: New York University Press, 1957).

23. See Charles B. Schmitt, "L'introduction de la philosophie platonicienne dans l'enseignement des universités à la Renaissance," in *Platon et Aristote à la Renaissance* (Paris: J. Vrin, 1976), 93–104.

24. Montaigne, II, 12, 403 A: "le dieu de la science scholastique."

25. Montaigne, I, 26, 107 C: "le monarque de la doctrine."

26. Alexandre Koyré, *Etudes d'histoire de la pensée scientifique* (Paris: Gallimard, 1971), 19.

27. Thomas Kuhn has shown that to reject a paradigm is at the same time to accept a different one that proposes a different and more rigid definition of a field (*The Structure of Scientific Revolutions* [Chicago: University of Chicago Press, 1970]).

28. Montaigne, II, 12, 403 A: "Sa doctrine nous sert de loy magistrale, qui est à l'avanture autant fauce qu'une autre. Je ne sçay pas pourquoy je n'acceptasse autant volontiers ou les idées de Platon, ou les atomes d'Epicurus, ou le plain et le vuide de Leucippus et Democritus, ou l'eau de Thales, ou l'infinité de nature d'Anaximander, ou l'air de Diogenes, ou les nombres et symmetrie de Pythagoras, ou l'infiny de Parmenides, ou l'un de Musaeus, ou l'eau et le feu d'Apollodorus, ou les parties similaires d'Anaxagoras, ou la discordet amitié d'Empedocles, ou le feu de Heraclitus, ou toute autre opinion de cette confusion infinie d'advis et de sentences."

29. Montaigne, II, 12, 401 A: "rapiecé de mille lopins faux et fantastique."

30. Montaigne, II, 12, 400 A: "songes et fanatique folies."

31. Montaigne, II, 12, 403 A: "fadesse et mensonge."

32. Montaigne, II, 12, 429 A, C: "Le ciel et les estoilles ont branlé trois mille ans; tout le monde l'avoit ainsi creu, jusques à ce que Cleanthes le Samien ou, selon Theophraste, Nicetas Siracusien s'avisa de maintenir que c'estoit la terre

qui se mouvoit par le cercle oblique du Zodiaque tournant à l'entour de son aixieu; et, de nostre temps, Copernicus a si bien fondé cette doctrine qu'il s'en sert tres-regléement à toutes les consequences Astronomiques."

33. Montaigne, II, 12, 430 A: "Ptolemeus, qui a esté un grand personnage, avoit establi les bornes de nostre monde; tous les philosophes anciens ont pensé en tenir la mesure."

34. Ernst Cassirer, *The Individual and the Cosmos in Renaissance Philosophy* (Philadelphia: University of Pennsylvania Press, 1979), 110.

35. On the importance of magic, sorcery, and occult sciences in general during the Renaissance, see Wayne Shumaker, *The Occult Sciences in the Renaissance: A Study in Intellectual Patterns* (Berkeley: University of California Press, 1972).

36. Etienne Pasquier, *Ecrits politiques* (Paris: Droz, 1966), 306.

37. Montaigne, II, 18, 505 A: "Nostre verité de maintenant, ce n'est pas ce qui est, mais ce qui se persuade à autruy."

38. Montaigne, II, 10, 302 A: "il faict beau apprendre la theorique de ceux qui sçavent bien la practique."

39. Montaigne, II, 12, 370 A: "les hommes ayant tout essayé et tout sondé, n'ayant trouvé en cet amas de science et provision de tant de choses diverses rien de massif et ferme, et rien que vanité, ils ont renoncé à leur presomption et reconneu leur condition naturelle."

40. Montaigne, I, 31, 151 A: "Cette narration d'Aristote n'a non plus d'accord avec nos terres neufves."

41. Montaigne, II, 12, 404 A: "Cette response seroit bonne parmy les Cannibales, qui jouissent l'heur d'une longue vie, tranquille et paisible sans les preceptes d'Aristote, et sans la connoissance du nom de la physique."

42. Montaigne, II, 17, 501 C: "La moins desdeignable condition des gents me semble estre celle qui par simplesse tient le dernier rang, et nous offrir un commerce plus reglé. Les meurs et les propos des paysans, je les trouve communément plus ordonnez selon la prescription de la vraie philosophie, que ne sont ceux de nos philosophes."

43. Montaigne, I, 25, 102 A: "le paisant et le cordonnier, vous leur voiez aller simplement et naïfvement leur train, parlant de ce qu'ils sçavent; ceux cy [les philosophes], pour se vouloir eslever et gendarmer de ce sçavoir qui nage en la superficie de leur cervelle, vont s'ambarrassant et enpestrant sans cesse."

44. Montaigne, III, 10, 780 B: "les deux extremes, des hommes philosophes et des hommes ruraus."

45. On this subject see Jean-Marie Apostolidès, "Molière and the Sociology of Exchange," *Critical Inquiry* 14, no. 3 (1988): 477–92; and Ralph Albanèse, "Argent et réification dans *L'Avare*," *L'Esprit Créateur* 21, no. 3 (1981): 35–50.

46. Ronsard, *Les Hymnes*, in *Oeuvres complètes*, 18 vols., ed. Paul Laumonier, 8:191, ll. 261–64: "Aussi les Anciens admirantz ta vertu / Ont le mouton

d'Helles de fin or revestu, / Ilz ont en ta faveur les pommes honorées / De Venus & d'Atlas faictes toutes dorées."

47. Ronsard, "Inscriptions en faveur de grands seigneurs," in *Oeuvres complètes,* 9:197, ll. 41–44: "Alcide acquit louange non petite / D'avoir gaigné les riches pommes d'or: / Ayant acquis la belle MARGUERITE, / Tu has tout seul du monde le thresor."

48. Robert Graves, *The Greek Myths,* 2 vols. (Baltimore, Md.: Penguin Books, 1955), 1:129–30.

49. Ronsard, "Discours à Maistre Juliain Chauveau," in *Oeuvres complètes,* 15:156, ll. 69–78: "Apres avoir vomy toute sa soye / (Qu'un bon ouvrier en meinte estroite voye / Doibt joindre à l'or pour les habitz d'un Roy), / Ce ver fasché, comme ennuyé de soy, / Soudain se change, & vole par les prées / Fait papillon aux aesles diaprées / De rouge, verd, azur & vermillon. / Puis se faschant d'estre tant papillon / Devient chenille & pond des oeufs, pour faire / Que par sa mort il se puisse refaire."

50. Loys Le Roy, *De la vicissitude ou varieté des choses en l'univers, et concurrence des armes et des lettres par les premieres et plus illustres nations du monde, depuis le temps où a commencé la civilité, et memoire humaine jusques à present,* ed. Philippe Desan, Corpus des oeuvres de philosophie en langue française (Paris: Fayard, 1988): "Mais ainsy que ce siecle fut admirable en puissance et sapience et en tous ars: aussi fut il plein de toute meschanceté et de changemens extraordinaires. Comme s'il falloit que mesme aage produist monstres horribles et merveilles illustres. Car l'on void communément où les entendemens des personnes sont plus grands, se rencontrer ensemble hommes tresvertueux et vicieux, autheurs de grandes choses bonnes et mauvaises. Comme si la vertu et le vice qui sont choses si contraires et repugnantes avoient leurs sommitez prochaines" (222).

51. Claude-Gilbert Dubois, *La Conception de l'histoire en France au XVIe siècle (1560–1610)* (Paris: Nizet, 1977), 93. See also Herbert Weisinger, "Louis Le Roy on Science and Progress (1575)," *Osiris* 11 (1954): 199–210.

52. Mircea Eliade, *The Myth of the Eternal Return,* trans. Willard Trask (London: Routledge and Kegan Paul, 1955), 168.

The Failure of Humanist Education: David de Fleurance-Rivault, Anthoine Mathé de Laval, and Nicolas Faret

James J. Supple

Before speaking of the "failure of humanist education," it is essential to decide what one means by "humanism." It is generally agreed that humanism did not involve acceptance of any particular philosophical position. It simply involved study of the *lettres humaines:* grammar, rhetoric, poetry, history, moral philosophy, and, of course, Latin and Greek.[1] According to Philip Hallie, on the other hand, one would be wrong to neglect the moral significance of the humanist program, which endeavoured to teach us not only how to speak and write well but also how to live well.[2] I have myself adopted a similar position in an earlier study in which I tried to demonstrate that there is a kind of humanist ideology according to which man cannot be fully human unless he cultivates the two gifts that separate him from the animals—speech and reason. As Guillaume Budé, one of the acknowledged leaders of the French humanist movement, put it,

> man differs most of all from the beasts because learning and speech enable him to express all the ideas formed in the human mind; indeed, the seeds of intelligence in human minds cannot reach maturity except in the school of philosophy, when they come together to form Reason, which is nothing other than Nature brought to its full development.[3]

Humanism was not, of course, a monolithic movement; but this ideology was a central element, as is shown by the humanists' own name and by the name they gave their studies: "they are called the humanities because they perfect and adorn mankind"; "for this reason, you are pre-eminently called Human Letters since you summoned Man to fulfil his true human potential."[4]

I attempted in the study to which I have already referred to analyze Montaigne's often ambiguous and sometimes hostile reactions to the humanist ideal. My intention in this essay is to examine the reactions of a social class that was one of the humanists' favorite targets: the *noblesse d'épée*. There had always been exceptions, but, traditionally, the military aristocracy had contented itself with a rudimentary education, preferring to cultivate the military arts rather than letters, which were accused of making them effeminate.[5] The humanists' own self-interest (they needed patrons and protectors at court), the interests of the state (which needed an educated governing elite), and their concept of man encouraged humanists as different as Jean Bouchet, Guillaume Budé, Lancelot de Carle, Symphorien Champier, Jacques Colin, Antoine Du Saix, and Claude de Seyssel to attack this prejudice against letters.[6] It would seem, therefore, that study of some of the educational programs recommended for the *noblesse d'épée* will provide us with an ideal opportunity to study the successes and the failures of the humanist cause.

First of all the successes. As P. D. Bourchenin, François de Dainville, George Huppert, Paul Porteau, and others have shown,[7] the humanists' educational program became solidly implanted in the network of colleges in which, as Roger Chartier has indicated, *nobles d'épée* often sat side by side with *robins* and magistrates. Even if they preferred to be educated at home by a tutor, they were usually exposed to the same cultural model.[8] Complaints about the ignorance of the military aristocracy continued throughout the sixteenth and the seventeenth centuries; but it is significant that many of the most vocal critics—François de La Noue and Brantôme, for example—were themselves *nobles d'épée*.[9]

As Paul Porteau has suggested, on the other hand, the military aristocracy were not always satisfied by an educational program that, from their point of view, seemed to be too exclusively directed toward the cultivation of eloquence.[10] It was perfectly natural, therefore, that the *nobles d'épée* should look elsewhere for their educational ideal—to Antoine de Pluvinel's riding academy, for instance, where they could perfect the military arts and pick up a rudimentary knowledge of studies with an obvious military relevance, such as geography and fortification.[11] This example tells us a great deal about the educational ideals of the *noblesse d'épée*, which seemed to prefer practical to purely "literary" training. For our purpose, however, we will need to look at educational programs where the emphasis on letters is sufficient for us to measure the strength of the author's reaction to the humanist ideal.[12] In order to avoid the trap that awaits the historian who finds only what he sets out to look for, I have chosen two different kinds of examples: first of all, an educational program that shares and even develops a certain number of humanist presuppositions; and, second, two programs that react, directly or indirectly, against the humanist program. The fact that all three were published toward the beginning of the seventeenth century should help us to study the transition between the Renaissance and the classical period, a study that is one of the main aims of the present volume.

I will begin with David de Fleurance-Rivault (1571?–1616), who is the most enthusiastic of our three authors. The breadth and universality of his studies take him, indeed, well beyond the traditional humanist program. His knowledge of Latin and Greek, together with his translation of Archimedes,[13] puts him firmly in the humanist tradition; but his interest in mathematics, geometry, physics, and physiology shows him to have been influenced by scientific and encyclopedic tendencies that go beyond the disciplines normally associated with his humanist forbears.[14] Until 1608, he was also a practicing soldier and had taken part in two expeditions abroad, one to Hungary, and one to the Mediterranean to fight against the Turks. As he also composed a lengthy political treatise and wrote some verse, a work on honor, and a short account of his campaign in Hungary, Rivault can clearly claim to be something of an *uomo universale*.[15]

These military, literary, and scientific gifts were not, moreover, cultivated in isolation. Far from seeing any conflict between them, Rivault earnestly attempted to make them serve one another, as in *Les Elemens de l'artillerie* (Paris, 1605), in which he applies his knowledge of physics to artillery and ballistics. The treatise is dedicated to Maximilien de Béthune, who, as *capitaine de cent hommes d'armes des ordonnances de sa Majesté*, would have a natural interest in the subject. Both in the preliminary epistle (fol. a iiij-r) and in the preface (not paginated), Rivault is concerned to demonstrate that artillery is a part of the contemplative arts. The kind of machinery that Archimedes produced was, as Rivault reminds Béthune, sufficient to withstand the might of the Romans. The warrior should remember, therefore, that physics and "philosophie" (the word Rivault uses) can be of the greatest use to him.

This kind of exhortation is a recurring theme in Rivault's works. We find it again in the preface ("Nobilibus gallis pro mathematicis") to his translation of Archimedes (fols. e iij-r–i iij-v) and in a rather traditional arms and letters treatise, *Minerva Armata: De conjugendis literis et armis* (Rome, 1610). It is not at all surprising, therefore, that, when he was made tutor to Louis XIII in 1612,[16] he used his influence to try to create a court academy on the lines specified in a short treatise entitled *Le Dessein d'une académie et de l'introduction d'icelle en la Cour* and in what seems to have been the Academy's first and only lecture, *La Leçon faicte en la première ouverture de l'Académie Royale*.[17] In some ways, Rivault's plans were wider than this,[18] but his main aim was to create an academy in which "Arms and Letters will be united equally" ("les lettres et les armes se joindront de pareille recommandation," *Leçon*, 4–5). The nobles, who were to meet two or three times a week, were to cultivate the same "learned courage" ("sçavante générosité") as the ancient Greeks and Romans. The two "Lecteurs" were to be military men and would teach "in the manner of the ancients, with their sword at their side" ("à l'antique, l'espée au costé"). Aided by *maréchaux* and other captains, one of them was to teach nothing but military subjects: the art of war, the qualities needed in a commander, the conditions governing a declaration of war, military discipline, battle formations, etc. The other was to range more widely, covering moral philosophy, "la police," "l'oeconomie," virtue, the various kinds of state and similar political considerations (*Dessein d'une Académie*, fols. 10r, 2r–v, 15r–16v). Apart from this, there were also to be wide-ranging talks on "toute autre chose," including philosophy, the humanities, literary or historical exegesis ("l'éclaircissement d'un Auteur vieil ou récent"), the art of war again, "in brief, everything that a gentle soul could desire and seek to know" ("et bref tout ce qu'une ame gentille peut concevoir et rechercher"). Poetry readings, songs, and madrigals were also to figure among the academicians' activities, as well as lectures on one's duty to the king and exhortations to virtue (*Dessein d'une académie*, fols. 11r–13r).

Such a marriage of arms and letters would have fulfilled the most cherished dreams of many a humanist. But Rivault knew full well that he had to face the opposition of those nobles who still felt that study is debilitating, "as if Letters made man stupid, cowardly and worthless."[19] He stresses, therefore, the importance of studies with a practical military value, such as astronomy, geometry, and especially mathematics, which is particularly useful in areas like fortification and logistics (*Estats*, 117–18, 220–21; "Nobilibus gallis," fols. i ij-v, i iiij-r). In arguing in this way, he is broadening the humanist educational program, in which such studies did not normally have a central role. When he insists, on the other hand, that one year's study of the theory of war would help a soldier more than would ten years' experience (*Dessein d'une académie,* fol. 5r–v), he is echoing an idea dear to Erasmus, who (in a very different domain, admittedly) had also insisted on the superiority of theory over practice.[20] Even more significantly, he takes up one of the humanists' essential themes when he argues that courage is in no way reduced by knowledge; that it is, indeed, increased by a knowledge of good and evil ("la connoissance du bien et du mal," *Leçon,* 25). Like the best of the humanists,[21] he is prepared to admit that a learned man can be evil ("Nobilibus gallis," fol. e vj-r–v); but, unlike Montaigne, he is not prepared to separate learning and virtue.[22] On the contrary, he insists that it is impossible to act honorably without a deep knowledge of moral philosophy: "Even though the Will desires only the Good, seeking evil only when it bears the outward signs of its opposite, it still needs skill in recognising the true signs of the Good... so as not to choose badly."[23] The will, therefore, must be given the criteria according to which it can make a choice. These criteria, Rivault tells us with all the enthusiasm of the early humanists, will be provided by knowledge: "But what is the eye of the Will if not the Intellect? What refines it more than knowledge? What makes it more prudent than a great knowledge of all things?"[24] It is easy for him to conclude, therefore, like Antoine Du Saix some eighty years before,[25] that study will solve our moral problems: "Letters, therefore, teach us what we should will."[26] Such is his confidence, in fact, that he echoes Budé's most chimerical dreams. Where the latter had dreamed of a moral revolution that would heal a Europe torn by dynastic wars,[27] his emulator believes that, if he can persuade the French nobility to frequent his academy, the ills created by the still-recent religious wars will be cured: "saeculi reparabitur infelicitas" ("Nobilibus gallis," fol. e vj-r–v).

In some ways, however, Rivault modifies the humanist program. Assuming that the nobles have already been to college (*Dessein d'une académie,* fols. 3v–4r), he puts very little weight on the study of Latin or Greek, and gives only passing attention to the necessity for the nobleman to cultivate eloquence.[28] For him, the unifying principle of the encyclopedia is not philology, as it had been for Budé, but mathematics. Knowledge, he claims, is a matter of distinguishing one thing from another, and this is the same as counting. Disciplines such as philosophy, physics, metaphysics, logic, and even theology are often presented in mathematical form, while virtue and justice are equally dependent on distinguishing good from bad, what is equal from what is unequal (*Archimedis opera*, 446; "Nobilibus gallis," fols. e vj-r, i-r). Such an argument may seem flimsy to us, but it confirmed Rivault in his belief that the art of war, which has many links with mathematics (ballistics, for example), will have a natural place in his academy: "Plato quite rightly legislated that boys should study all the parts of mathematics if they were ever to win any honour or praise. Honour, indeed, is not won just by contemplation, but also by action, especially in war."[29] If he emphasizes the practical advantages of mathematics, geometry, and astronomy, therefore, it is not (as Frances Yates has suggested) merely because he "anticipates adverse criticism":[30] it is above all because he genuinely believes that action and contemplation cannot be separated: "Man does not have different ends. There is but one honour that is proposed for him, and it is to be won by action and contemplation alike" ("Non est hominum multiplex finis: unus est ipsis honos propositus, qui contemplatione simul et actione comparatur"). He is convinced, therefore, that the *noblesse d'épée* will provide a natural audience for his theories: "Nobles, believe me: you have been born both to act and to learn."[31]

We have here, therefore, an original and interesting development of the humanist educational program, well adapted—in theory—to the needs of the *noblesse d'épée*. One notes, however, that Rivault's enthusiasm is literally encyclopedic: "What is there in the world which is not found in our Academy? What are you looking for that you don't find here? What is there from the First Mobile to the centre of the Earth which we cannot discover?"[32] As a result, the range of studies that he intends to cover increases in an unrealistically encyclopedic way ("toutes les sciences et toutes les cognoissances tant divines qu'humaines," *Leçon*, 12–13). Rivault tried to get around this problem by admitting members of the *noblesse de robe longue* as well as the *nobles d'épée*[33] but his project seems to have collapsed after only one meeting. This failure suggests that, though elements in the humanist ideal survived—sometimes in exaggerated form—into the seventeenth century,[34] the ideal itself was still far from winning acceptance by large numbers of the military aristocracy.

Like Rivault, Anthoine Mathé de Laval (1550–1630) seems to have been in a position where he could attempt to influence the educational practices of the *noblesse d'épée*. Henri IV asked that Laval's *Desseins de professions nobles et publiques*,³⁵ which, following the death of his eldest surviving son, the author was tempted to destroy, should be published; Ludovic de Gonzague asked for his advice on the kind of mathematical education needed by his heir; and the *grands* of the court consulted him on such matters as writing letters and speaking well (*Desseins de professions*, fols. a ij-v, 6v–19r, 201r). Laval does not appear to have the same depth of erudition as Rivault; but he became *géographe du roi* at some time before 1583, was well known to members of Pibrac's academy, and was something of a poet and translator as well as a prolific author of treatises.³⁶ In order to underline the wide-ranging nature of his accomplishments, the frontispiece to the *Desseins de professions* shows him holding a helmet resting on a book and bears the punning motto "Idem undique valla."

With such a background, Laval was no more likely to approve of the philistinism to which substantial sections of the aristocracy were still prone than was Rivault. He does not hesitate, indeed, to criticize "the common error of our age and even of our ancestors" ("l'erreur commune de nôtre âge et de nos ancéstres mesmes") that resulted in their traditional disdain of letters: "Why should a soldier need to study letters so much, say the ignorant. As long as he can keep his weapons polished..., as long as he has a good sword and courage, he has all he needs to be an *honnête homme*." Like Budé, Laval argues that to regard the nobility as a mere fighting machine is to deny its members the possibility of being great captains.³⁷ At the same time, he uses the diminishing military monopoly of the nobility to imply that an ignorant noble who knows no more than how to fight is no better than a Swiss or German mercenary. Like Rivault (*Estats*, 117–18), he argues that the great captains of antiquity achieved as much with their heads as with their hands. Among the disciplines he recommends are geography, history, and (to Rivault's approval, no doubt) mathematics. He also advocates a knowledge of languages and of disciplines that will help the captain "to learn to speak well and to form his judgment."³⁸

The military sphere, however, is not Laval's main concern. If he is especially anxious about the nobles' ignorance, it is because he feels that it is disadvantaging them politically. The meanest "soliciteur de Palais" who can put two words together is able to shame great lords, "to whom, because of their ignorance, you would not dare entrust the smallest office in the world."³⁹ The *nobles d'épée* feel aggrieved at this change in their status; but, ultimately, they have no one to blame but themselves:

"We want to be in the first rank everywhere and cannot bear to be helped by a man whose grandfather served ours even though we cannot get out of our difficulties without him."[40]

The idea that the ignorance of the nobility was prejudicial to their own interests goes back at least as far as Deschamps.[41] It had been echoed at the beginning of the sixteenth century by Claude de Seyssel and a little later by Antoine Du Saix,[42] but seems to have become particularly common in the latter part of the century, when the nobles themselves began to complain that offices were being withheld from them.[43] The view that nonmilitary (and especially judicial) office was somehow *dérogeant* persisted, of course;[44] but it is precisely to combat this prejudice that Laval has written the *Desseins de professions nobles et publiques*. He recommends acceptance of posts in the royal administration (as secretary to the king or as finance secretary), but is above all concerned with the legal profession, which the *noblesse de robe longue* has used as its stepping-stone to power: "which today rules the world and which alone in this state is in a position of perpetual dictatorship." It is *la chicane* "which holds tyrannical power over the honour, the life, goods and fate of the best families in this kingdom." The *nobles d'épée* naturally resent this; but their resentment is pointless since they refuse to remedy the situation by educating themselves, preferring more "gentlemanly" exercises like hunting, as Laval so bitterly puts it: "becoming dumb by continually chasing after dumb animals."[45] Laval does not demand a specialist knowledge of law except for those who are going to make it their main profession, but the knowledge he demands of the others is, even so, considerable: the *Instituts du Droit,* the *Digeste,* the *Code,* and the *Authentiques,* as well as all royal ordonnances and local customs. Thus equipped, the noble will be able not only to help others, but also to defend his own interests more capably and prepare himself "for office" ("à quelque charge," *Desseins de professions,* fols. 101v–103r).[46]

Laval's earnest exhortations seem to put him in the same tradition as humanists like Guillaume Budé and Antoine Du Saix, who had also insisted on the political value of study.[47] There is, however, a difference, since Laval is much more rigidly utilitarian. Where Rivault—who also sought to prepare the noble to serve the king[48]—attempts to create a harmonious balance between action and contemplation, Laval insists on the primacy of action: "man is born to act, and to act usefully" ("l'homme est nay pour agir, et pour agir utiliment"). Where a theologian is concerned, this would imply outstanding erudition; but, for a noble who is not destined to a church career, things are different. No one can envisage "une carrière honnorable" without having studied letters first; but there is no room for any kind of encyclopedic project. In common with other authors of pedagogical treatises, Laval argues, therefore, that the *nobles d'épée* should know "just as much as they need to" ("justement autant qu'ils en ont besoin," *Desseins de professions,* fols. 2v, 4v–5v, 20v, 348v).[49]

This restriction is, in part, the result of a reaction against the humanist colleges I mentioned earlier. The regents, Laval affirms, impose excessive discipline and devote too much time to useless subjects, especially unnecessary and trifling wordplay ("la Logomachie ou questions de mots si peu necessaires"). In this way, they actually encourage the nobility in its prejudices against letters and leave it "rough," "uncultivated," and totally incapable of proper action: "for in the end, one sees that the most learned are far from being the most wise, unless they have used their learning in the world, which is the school where one really becomes educated."[50]

More important, Laval—who had himself abandoned his interest in poetry for fear of inspiring his son with a passion for "céte vraye Lote des compagnons d'Ulisses" (fols. 350v–351r)—fears the influence of humanist disciplines because they might distract a young gentleman from the more useful studies he prefers. He condemns, for example, a learned nobleman who knew a lot about languages, philosophy, and especially poetry, but who, being ignorant of law, was unable to help one of his peasants, who committed suicide in despair. Thus, where the humanists insist on the moral and spiritual benefits of letters, Laval gives them only a subordinate role:

> and it is not enough to have a knowledge of Polite Letters, which for the most part serve only as an ornament, for, if one has to know something, and devote time to it, one would be better off spending one's time on some useful subject, which will be of benefit to oneself and to the state.[51]

If Laval is willing to sacrifice "polite letters" so readily, it is not just because of his utilitarian preferences, however. It is also because he has underlying doubts about the value of the humanist program. As a staunch Catholic, he rejects, in terms that recall those of the earliest critics of the humanist movement,[52] both rhetoric and philology:

> It is pride which has destroyed so many souls, pride caused by some knowledge of the humanities which made people believe that they were more capable of interpreting Holy Writ than the ancient Fathers, who, in their saintliness, were always more concerned with truth and with good sense than with beautiful language.[53]

His assertion that, from an early age, he has always studied at night when he has not found time during the day to give himself "quelque consolation parmy les bonnes létres" ("some consolation in good letters," *Desseins de professions*, fol. 350r) shows that he can still appreciate the almost religious appeal that study had for the humanists, for whose ideals he has much more than just a residual admiration. Hence his defence of moral philosophy against the sneers of his fellow *nobles d'épée:* "Here you could tell me, like most of the ignorant people in our kingdom, that there is not much point in talking about Aristotle to a man with a sword at his side." However good we are naturally, he replies, study of Aristotle's *Ethics* will strengthen our virtues, which will become more familiar and better understood "when we know their names, their effects, and the limits within which they should be maintained."[54] This argument is undoubtedly sincere. But, as a Christian, Laval is very conscious of the fact that Aristotle was a pagan who regarded as virtues emotions and motives (anger, ambition, the pursuit of honour and advancement, luxury, magnificence, and revenge) that he and his readers must regard as sins (*Desseins de professions*, fol. 37v). It is not surprising, therefore, that, where Josse Clichtove urged his readers to study moral philosophy night and day,[55] Laval denies that one should devote one's best years to a "meandering argument which entangles rather than untangles the thread of an argument."[56] The ancients contradict each other, in any case, and can thus provide only the most uncertain of moral guides. It is for this reason that the true Christian will ultimately turn to the Bible and to the writings of the Church Fathers, which will teach him "more than all the syllogisms and subtleties in the *Ethics* of Aristotle, Plato or anybody else."[57]

The Jesuits adopted a much less severe stance toward the ancients when they drew up their *Ratio studiorum*.[58] It would be wrong, therefore, to regard Laval's reactions completely typical of the Counter-Reformation. One notes, however, that, once its claim to provide a sure path to moral improvement is undermined, the humanist ideal begins to look vulnerable. This can be seen even more clearly in our third and final example, *L'Honnête homme ou l'art de plaire à cour,* published by Nicolas Faret in 1630.[59]

The son of a cobbler, Faret (1596?–1646) was not even an *anobli*. Under the patronage of the comte de Harcourt and Richelieu, however, he occupied a high place among the *beaux esprits* in Paris and was something of an authority on cultural matters.[60] He was also the author of a treatise on the prince (*Des vertus necessaires à un Prince* [Paris, 1623]), and perhaps found the step between this and a treatise on the courtier a natural one. Like Rivault and Laval, he cannot tolerate "the ill-formed souls who, as a result of their beast-like stupidity, cannot conceive that a nobleman can be both learned and a soldier." He affirms, for his part, that "learning is becoming and most useful for those who are highly born." Like Montaigne, he feels that learning's true role is not to be found in universities, lawcourts, or doctors' operating "theatres": "it seems that its true function is to rule peoples, to lead armies, to win over foreign princes, and all those other glittering actions which make states prosper."[61]

Faret's attitude toward letters is, however, less positive than it might seem. Like Montaigne, who insists that only the *âme bien née* can derive proper benefit from study,[62] Faret argues that learning, which can raise some minds to "a condition approaching the divine" ("une condition approchante de la divine"), is often accompanied by stupidity and extravagance. Again like Montaigne—and like Laval (*Desseins de professions,* fol. 22v)—he has nothing but contempt for those whose knowledge of Greek and Latin has just made them more impertinent and stubborn.

This is to be expected in a writer who is developing the ideal of *honnêteté*, according to which pedantry is to be eschewed quite as much as the inane behavior of the braggart soldier (*L'Honnête homme,* 14–15, 79). More worrying, on the other hand, is his apparently deliberate failure to determine the exact nature of the relationship between the military and the literary ideals. He rejects, as we have seen, the prejudices of the more philistine members of the military aristocracy, and is quite prepared, as we will see shortly, to recommend disciplines that will be of use to the soldier; but, this apart, he seems not to give the subject a thought. This is particularly striking because of its importance in his main model, Castiglione's *Il cortegiano*. The conclusion apparently arrived at in the latter work (that arms must be regarded as the noble's main profession) is as firmly military as Faret's own assertion (which, because of its exclusiveness, would have vexed Laval) "that there is no more becoming or more essential profession for a nobleman than Arms."[63] Castiglione's work is, however, a dialogue, in which more than one voice can be heard. Thus, Bembo is permitted to challenge Count Lodovico's assertions: "I don't know why, Count, you want this courtier, who is learned and endowed with so many other virtuous qualities, to regard everything as serving to adorn the military profession, and not Arms and the rest as embellishing his knowledge of Letters)." Bembo seems to lose the argument in that it is Lodovico who has the last word; but one notes that the count is unable to answer Bembo's main argument, which bears on the superiority of things spiritual over things corporal: "Letters, all on their own, are as much superior in dignity to Arms as the soul is to the body." Indeed, he could not reply since, while condemning the French nobility's disdain for letters, he has himself argued that the latter are not only "Utili e necessarie" but also God's *supreme* gift to mankind: "which God has given to man as a supreme gift."[64]

It is this kind of belief in the value of letters that justifies G. Toffanin's description of the arms-versus-letters discussion in *Il cortegiano* as based upon "the complete humanist ideal."[65] The topic's failure to appeal to Faret would seem, on the other hand, to derive from his relative lack of enthusiasm for the humanist ideal. His initial assertion about the moral value of letters, which he describes in typically humanist vein as a source of virtue,[66] is soon qualified in a very pragmatic way: though letters are useful and pleasurable, he does not value them to the point of believing that "their teachings can make us happy or unhappy" ("leurs enseignements puissent nous rendre heureux ou malheureux"). The encyclopedic knowledge aspired to by Rivault and so many others is rejected as the daydream of "certain minds whose curiosity has made them ill" ("certains esprits malades de trop de curiosité"). In accordance with the growing tendency to believe that the moderns are as good as if not better than the ancients,[67] Faret also refuses to agree that our happiness might depend on the vagaries of "people whose dreams were not always more rational than ours today."[68]

This naturally affects the kind of education that he proposes for his *honnête homme*. Philosophy, which (like Laval) he regards as inferior to divine wisdom anyway (*L'Honnête homme*, 33), suffers particularly severely. Unlike Laval, who seems to be somewhat hesitant on this point,[69] Faret bluntly affirms that a man would profit more by gaining practical experience in the world than by studying Aristotle. When he argues that the nobleman should not get involved in the limitless quarrels of the philosophers, he sounds more like Laval; but he is really going much further, reducing the sublime aspirations of the humanists to a mere social adjunct of value only in the important but relatively limited world of *la conversation mondaine:* "it is enough that he should have a middling knowledge of the more agreeable questions which are sometimes raised in good company" ("c'est assez [que le gentihomme] ait une médiocre teinture des plus agréables questions qui s'agitent quelquefois dans les bonnes compagnies"). The difference between Faret and the humanists is, once again, made apparent by a comparison with Castiglione. Where the latter demands that the courtier should be "more than just a little learned" ("più che mediocremente erudito," *Il cortegiano*, 109), Faret reduces those "agreeable questions" that he does recommend to a mere topic of conversation, that is of value only because the courtier who can talk of only one thing (usually war) is obliged to be silent too often (*L'Honnête homme*, 26).

This limitation on the studies proposed extends even to the more practical ones. Castiglione recommends both Latin and Greek for his courtier (*Il cortegiano*, 109); and even Brantôme argues that the future ambassador should study Latin as well as Spanish and Italian.[70] Faret, on the other hand, settles for the last two languages on the grounds that Latin and Greek may be too difficult (*L'Honnête homme*, 31). As concerns the mathematical disciplines that are at the heart of Rivault's encyclopedia, he admits only those that are absolutely essential: "As long as he knows enough mathematics for a captain, for correct fortification or drawing up plans, it's not at all important for him to have delved deeply into the secrets of geometry or the subtleties of algebra."[71]

Politics, moral philosophy, and especially history, "which has always been called the proper subject for kings, and which is hardly less necessary for those who serve them" ("qui de tout temps a esté nommée l'estude des Roys [et qui] n'est guères moins nécessaire à ceux qui les suivent"), are received with more enthusiasm. Yet even here there are restrictions. To begin with, Faret does not appear to recommend either of the first two studies as separate disciplines. They are not mentioned except briefly and are presumably to be studied as part of history, which he describes as "the purest source of civil wisdom" ("la plus pure source de la sagesse civile," *L'Honnête homme*, 27). As far as the latter subject is concerned, we know that Faret was something of a historian,[72] and that he praises history as a valuable storehouse of experience in his treatises on the prince (48). In *L'Honnête homme*, however, he concludes his discussion of the best historians with a remark that a knowledge of the past is not a sure guide to wisdom: "It serves only as a guide for those who seek it: wisdom is found in the understanding, not in the memory."[73] This does not mean, of course, that Faret's belief in the value of history is not serious. He is merely making a point that most people (and Montaigne certainly) would be inclined to accept; but comparison with the enthusiastic utterances of earlier (perhaps unduly enthusiastic) admirers of history aptly indicates the change in attitude.[74] This is visible, too, in his attitude to poetry. As a minor poet himself, he claims to be ashamed of the disrespect in which this "admirable language" is held; but he is above all concerned with the fact that the ability to write well will help improve one's chances of obtaining social advancement, by turning successful "compliments d'amour," for instance (*L'Honnête homme*, 30–31).

Faret's treatise is, indeed, an admirable indicator of the change in intellectual climate. There were, of course, many different treatises in which authors continued to claim, like Rivault, that study is the source of virtue. There were, as we have seen, a number of academies in which the nobility could obtain a rudimentary education, and colleges like La Flèche, which, with its much more extensive educational program, was attracting more and more noblemen.[75] As Laval argues, it was increasingly accepted that any noble who wished to obtain advancement would have to be reasonably well educated. One notes, however, in the case of Laval and Faret—and elsewhere—that this is achieved at a price. The humanists' more sublime—but essentially unrealistic—claims concerning the direct relationship between learning and virtue are toned down or jettisoned, and educational programs become ever more closely tied to the practical needs of the *noblesse d'épée*. This view is best exemplified in what is probably the least inspiring but certainly the most successful of our three treatises: Faret's *L'Honnête homme ou l'art de plaire à la cour*.[76]

NOTES

1. Paul O. Kristeller, *Renaissance Thought* (New York: Harper, 1961), 9–10, 110.

2. Philip Hallie, *The Scar of Montaigne* (Middletown, Conn.: Wesleyan University Press, 1966), 10.

3. Quoted in James J. Supple, *Arms versus Letters: The Military and Literary Ideals in the "Essais" of Montaigne* (Oxford: Clarendon Press, 1984): "il n'y a rien parquoy l'homme diffère tant des bestes brutes que par parler fondé en science, par lequel un homme peult donner à entendre... toutes les conceptions formées en l'entendement humain"; "in humanis autem mentibus intelligentiae inchoatae perfici nequeunt nisi in officina philosophiae; atque ex his notionibus ratio coagmentatur, quae nihil est aliud quam in se perfecta et ad summum perducta natura."

4. L. Bruni, quoted in Giocchino Paparelli, *Feritas, Humanitas, Divinitas* (Messina and Florence, 1960), 33; Etienne Pasquier, *Le Pourparler du Prince* (Paris, 1560), fol. 61r: "Humanitatis studia nuncupantur, quod hominem perificiant atque exornent." "Pour ceste cause [vous] fustes par singulière prééminence nommées lettres humaines, en recognoissance de ce que [vous] appelastes les hommes à une deuë humanité."

5. See Supple, *Arms versus Letters,* 67–68.

6. See James J. Supple, "'Nobilium culpa iacent literae': Guillaume Budé and the Education of the French Noblesse d'Epée," in *Acta conventus neo-latini Sanctandreani,* ed. Ian D. McFarlane (Binghamton, N.Y.: Medieval and Renaissance Texts and Studies, 1986), 207–22.

7. P.-D. Bourchenin, *Etudes sur les académies protestantes en France au XVIe et au XVIIe siècle* (Paris: Grassart, 1882); François de Dainville, *La Géographie des humanistes* (Paris: Beauchesne, 1940); George Huppert, *Public Schools in Renaissance France* (Chicago: University of Chicago Press, 1984); Paul Porteau, *Montaigne et la vie pédagogique de son temps* (Paris: Droz, 1935).

8. Roger Chartier et al., *L'Education en France du XVIe au XVIIIe siècle* (Paris: Société d'Édition d'Enseignement Supérieur, 1976), 177, 179.

9. Jack H. Hexter, "The Education of the Aristocracy in Renaissance France," in *Reappraisals in History* (London: Longmans, 1961), 45–70.

10. Porteau, 17.

11. Ellery Schalk, *From Valor to Pedigree: Ideas of Nobility in France in the Sixteenth and Seventeenth Centuries* (Princeton, N.J.: Princeton University Press, 1986), 181ff.

12. Note, however, that Pluvinel himself hoped for the creation of royal

academies in which letters would have a reasonably important place (*L'Instruction du Roy* [Paris, 1625], 150ff).

13. David de Fleurance-Rivault, *Archimedis opera quae extant* (Paris, 1615).

14. See, however, A. H. T. Levi, "Ethics and the Encyclopaedia," in Peter Sharratt, ed. *French Renaissance Studies* (Edinburgh: Edinburgh University Press, 1976), 170–84.

15. For a general study, see A.-F. Anis, *David Rivault de Fleurance* (Paris-Laval, 1893).

16. Prior to this date, he was mathematics tutor only (Anis, 58, 96).

17. For a discussion of Rivault's plans in the context of the Renaissance academic tradition, see Frances A. Yates, *The French Academies* (London: Warburg Institute, University of London, 1946), 276–82. For their apparent failure, see Paul Pellisson-Fontanier and l'Abbé d'Olivet, *Histoire de l'Académie Française*, 2 vols., ed. C. Livet (Paris: Didier, 1858), 1:476.

18. Rivault hoped to improve the courtiers' social graces, to give them practice in ambassadorial skills, and to make them generally better able to serve the king (*Dessein d'une académie* [Paris: Robert Estienne, 1612], fols. 1r–v, 4r, 13v–14r).

19. Rivault, *Les Estats* (Lyon: Benoist Rigaud, 1595), 355–56: "comme si les lettres rendent l'homme stupide, sans courage ny valeur."

20. Erasmus, *Declamatio de pueris statim ac liberaliter instituendis*, ed. Jean-Claude Margolin (Geneva: Droz, 1966), 401–3.

21. Erasmus, 415.

22. Supple, *Arms versus Letters*, 272ff.

23. Rivault, "Avant-Propos," in *Elemens* (Paris: Adrian Beys, 1605): "Or iaçoit que la volonté n'aime que le Bien et ne soit portée au mal que quand il paroist revestu du manteau et des couleurs de son contraire, elle a toutesjois besoin d'adresse en la recognoissance des légitimes marques du Bien ... pour ne prendre party mal à propos."

24. Rivault, "Avant-Propos": "Mais qui est l'oeil de la volonté que l'intellect? qui la subtilise que le sçavoir? qui la rend plus advisée qu'une grande cognoissance de toutes choses?"

25. Antoine du Saix, *L'Espéron de discipline* (Paris, 1532), fol. d iij-v.

26. Rivault, "Avant-Propos": "Les Lettres donc enseignent ce qu'il faut vouloir."

27. Budé, *De philologia* (Paris: Jodocus Badius, 1532), fol. lxvi-v.

28. See, however, Rivault, *Leçon* (Paris: Pierre Lecourt, 1612), 15–16, 23–24.

29. Rivault, "Nobilibus gallis," in *Archimedis opera*, fol. iij-r: "Quinimo meritissimo iure Plato legem tulit, qua iubebantur pueri partes omnes Matheseos addiscere, si qui unquam honoris et laudis essent adepturi: Honos vero non contemplando solum, sed agendo quoque inter arma potissimum, comparatur."

See *Republic,* bk. 8, where Plato insists on the need for both the soldier and the Guardian to study mathematics.

30. Yates, 278.

31. Rivault, *Minerva Armata: De conjugendis literis et armis* (Rome: Stephanus Paulinus, 1610), 8: "Viri nobiles, mihi credete, ad hoc nati estis, ut discatis, et agatis."

32. Rivault, *Leçon,* 25: "qu'y-a-il au monde qui ne se trouve dans nostre Academie? de quoy estes-vous en peine, dont on ne vous informe parmy nous. Qu'y-a-il depuis le premier moblile jusques au centre de la terre dont nous ne descouvrirons l'essence?."

33. See Rivault, *Leçon,* 23.

34. See Nicolas Pasquier, *Le Gentilhomme* (Paris, 1611), 13; Thomas Pelletier, *La Nourriture de la noblesse* (Paris, 1604), fol. 20r–v; Antoine de Nervèze, *Les Oeuvres morales* (Paris, 1605), fol. 30r–v.

35. Antoine Mathé de Laval, *Desseins de professions nobles et publiques* (Paris: Abel l'Angelier, 1605). I have used the second, slightly augmented edition (Paris: Abel l'Angelier, 1613).

36. Henri Faure, *Antoine de Laval* (Moulins: Place, 1870), 291–93; Claude Longeon, *Les Ecrivains foréziens du XVIe siècle* (Saint-Etienne: Centre d'Etudes Foréziennes, 1970), 391–93, 399–402.

37. See Supple, "'Nobilium culpa iacent literae,'" 402.

38. Laval, fols. 34r–37r: "Qu'est-il besoin de tant de létres à un soldat (disent les ignorans); pourveu qu'il sçache tenir ses armes bien fourbies . . . , qu'il ait une bonne épée et du courage: le voilà en équipage pour paroître honnête homme"; "former la parole et solider le judgement."

39. Laval, fol. 36v: "ausquels, à raison de leur ignorance, vous n'oseriez avoir fié la moindre charge au monde."

40. Laval, fol. 35r: "nous voulons tenir les premiers rangs partout: et souffrons malaysément qu'un homme de qui l'ayeul servoit le nôtre soit veu nous redresser en un mauvais pas, bien que nous n'en sçachions sortir sans son ayde."

41. La Curne de Sainte-Palaye, *Mémoires sur l'ancienne chevalerie,* 2 vols., ed. Charles Nodier (Paris: Girard, 1826), 1:407–8.

42. See Supple, *Arms versus Letters,* 46–47.

43. Davis Bitton, *The French Nobility in Crisis* (Stanford: Stanford University Press, 1969), chap. 3.

44. See Pelletier, fol. 23v–24r. Laval himself feels that none of the professions he recommends should be exercised for financial reward (*Desseins de professions,* fols. 36v–37r).

45. Laval, fol. 91v: "la Profession qui régente aujourd'huy le monde, et qui se void seule parmy cét Etat en Dictature perpétuelle"; fol. 93r: "qui tyranise l'honneur, la vie, les biens et la fortune des meilleures familles de ce Royaume"; fol. 35r: "à devenir béte, courans sans interruption aprés la béte."

46. F. C. Marois (*Le Gentil-Homme parfaict* [Paris: Cardin Besogne, 1621], 542) also recommends a restricted knowledge of law for the noble. François de l'Alouëte (*Traité des nobles* [Paris: Guillaume de la Nouë, 1577], fol. 16r–v) suggests that special digests should be made.

47. See Supple, "'Nobilium culpa iacent literae,'" 401; *Arms versus Letters*, 47.

48. As a councillor, ambassador, or delegate (Rivault, *Dessein d'une académie*, fols. 4v–5r).

49. La Noue comes to a similar conclusion (James J. Supple, "François de La Noue and the Education of the French *Noblesse d'épée*," *French Studies*, no. 36 [1982]: 270–81).

50. Laval, fols. 10r, 348v, 22v, 48v: "car à la longue on reconnoit combien il s'en faut que les plus sçavans ne soient les plus sages, s'ils n'ont pratiqué leur sçavoir en l'exercice du monde, qui est la vraye Ecole où l'on se dresse."

51. Laval, fols. 102r–104r: "et ne suffit pas de sçavoir des létres polies, qui ne servent pour la pluspart que d'ornement, car s'il faut sçavoir quelque chose et y employer du tans, il est mieus dépendu à l'étude de quelque science utile, servant et au public et au particulier."

52. See Noël Béda, *Annotationum in Iacobum Fabrum Stapulensen libri duo* (Paris: Badius, 1526), fol. Aai-v.

53. Laval, fol. 1v: "Ce qui a perdu tant d'Ames a été l'outrecuidance: pour quelque cognoissance de létres humaines ... s'estre creu plus capable de l'interprétation des Livres sacrés que ces bons Pères anciens: la sainteté desquels ... fut tousiours plus soucieuse du bon sens et du vray, que du beau langage."

54. Laval, fol. 37v: "Icy me pourras-tu dire (comme font la pluspart des ignorans de nôtre France, qui font gloire de dire qu'ils ... ne veulent rien sçavoir) qu'il n'y a pas grande apparance de parler d'Aristote à un homme qui a l'espée au costé"; "quand nous en sçavons les noms, les effects, et les termes dans lesquels elles doivent demeurer."

55. Josse Clichtove, *Dogma moralium philosophorum* (Strasbourg: Mathias Schurerianus, 1512), fols. 1v–2v.

56. Laval, fols. 37v–38r: "qui emmêle plus le fil d'un discours plus qu'il ne le dévelope."

57. Laval, fol. 22v: "[plus] que tous les syllogismes et subtilités de l'Ethique d'Aristote, de Platon, ny d'autre quel qu'il soit."

58. See Dainville.

59. Nicolas Faret, *L'Honnête homme ou l'art de plaire à la cour*, ed. M. Magendie (Paris: Presses Universitaires de France, 1925).

60. See Magendie's introduction to Faret, xi–xii.

61. Faret, 24: "les esprits malfaits, qui par un sentiment de stupidité brutale, ne peuvent se figurer qu'un Gentilhomme puisse estre sçavant et soldat"; "la doctrine ... est de bonne grace et très utile à ceux qui sont nays à de grandes

fortunes"; and "il semble que son propre usage soit d'estre employée à gouverner des peuples, à conduire des armées, à pratiquer l'amitié d'un Prince . . . et à toutes ces autres actions éclatantes qui . . . font fleurir les Estats."

62. See Supple, *Arms versus Letters*, 285–86.

63. Faret, 12: "qu'il n'y a point [de profession] plus honneste ny de plus essentielle à un Gentilhomme que celle des armes."

64. Castiglione, *Il libro del cortegiano,* ed. Vittorio Cian (Florence: Sansoni, 1947), 112: "Io non so, Conte, come voi vogliate che questo Cortegiano, essendo litterato, e con tante altre virtuose qualità, tenga ogni cosa per ornamento dell'arme, e non l'arme e'l resto per ornamento delle lettere"; 102–3: "le [lettere], senza altra comagnia, tanto sono di dignità all'arme superiori, quanto l'animo al corpo"; and 106: "le quali veramente da Dio sono state agli omini concedute per un supremo dono." The Arms versus Letters topic also figures prominently in one of Faret's other main sources, Stefano Guazzo's *La civil conversazione* (Brescia, 1574), fols. 100r–103v.

65. Giuseppe Toffanin, *Il "Cortegiano" nella trattatistica del Rinascimento* (Naples: Libreria Scientifica Editrice, 1951), 104.

66. Toffanin, 24. Letters are mentioned, however, along with more traditional noble values: the desire for glory and the example of one's predecessors.

67. Hubert Gillot, *La Querelle des anciens et des modernes* (Paris: H. Champion, 1914), esp. 278–305.

68. Faret, 25: "des personnes qui ne resvoient pas tousjours plus raisonnablement que l'on faict aujourd'huy."

69. Laval argues that the world is the real school of life (fols. 22v, 48v), but reacts angrily against philistine nobles who argue that a knowledge of *le monde* is sufficient education, arguing that their view of virtue is superficial (fol. 37v).

70. Pierre de Bourdeille, seigneur de Brantôme, *Oeuvres complètes*, 11 vols., ed. Ludovic Lalanne (Paris: Renouard, 1864–82), 7:73–76.

71. Faret, 26: "Pourveu qu'il ait des Mathémathiques ce qui sert à un Capitaine, comme de fortifier régulièrement et de tirer des plans . . . , il est fort peu important qu'il ait pénétré dans les secrets de la Géométrie et dans les subtilitez de l'Algèbre."

72. See Faret's *Histoire chronologique des Ottomans,* printed at the end of J. Lavardin's edition of the *Histoire de Georges Castriot* (Paris, 1621).

73. Faret, *L'Honnête homme,* 27–29: "[Elle ne sert] que de guide à ceux qui la cherchent: son siège est dans l'entendement, et non dans la mémoire."

74. See Jacques Colin's preface to Claude de Seyssel's *Histoire de Thucydide,* fol. a iiii-r.

75. Chartier et al., 179–80.

76. It was reprinted thirteen times between 1630 and 1681.

Ruined Schools: The End of the Renaissance System of Education in France

George Huppert

In a recent statement quoted in *Le Monde,* the mayor of the city of Roanne, M. Jean Auroux, gave his views on the demand for higher education in provincial centers: "The cities I represent," said M. Auroux, who is an official of the association of medium-sized cities in France, "these cities, 150 of them, demand their share in the intellectual investments to be made in this country. Put it another way: they want institutions of higher learning, within their walls, just as the rural communes demanded primary schools a century ago."[1]

Actually a more accurate parallel would result from a comparison with educational trends much earlier in French history. It was in the sixteenth century that these middle-sized provincial cities—the same ones represented by M. Auroux and his colleagues today—it was then, in the 1530s especially, that each of these provincial centers began to clamor, for the first time, demanding higher education on the spot, *intra muros.* Each wanted high-level municipal classical grammar schools in which Greek and Latin languages and literature would be taught "in the manner of Paris."

The motives of Renaissance mayors and city councils were just about the same as those of their modern continuators. They wanted to revive the commercial and cultural life of provincial cities, so that their best forces should not be drained and swallowed up by the Parisian metropolis. It was important, too, to have the local youth studying locally instead of going off, at great expense, to distant university centers in Paris or Toulouse. The argument was well put by the sixteenth-century principal of one of these cities, Amiens: "Having a college in town is of great profit to any city, because the money and the supplies, which would otherwise leave town, stay right here," wrote Master Descaurres.[2]

As for the need to have the highest possible level of learning available to the local youth, there is little doubt in Master Descaurres's mind on that question as he lobbies the city council of Amiens for financial support: "The first matter for concern in any community, the first and the most useful and necessary, is a college. It is in everyone's interest that young people should be well educated, whatever career they may eventually choose to follow."[3] This college should be "magnificently built so that even the sons of great lords will take pleasure in being there and so that all those with good minds shall find delight in studying in such surroundings, stimulated as they will be by the magnificence of the sumptuous buildings and by the serenity of the site."[4] The most telling and audacious claim made by Master Descaurres, it seems to me, is that such a college—i.e., a classical high school—"serves as the nursery and foundation of Republics, that it is the repository of all learning and the workshop in which young minds are molded: such an establishment is of greater profit to the community, without comparison, than are all the hospitals in the world."[5] This triumphant praise of the utility of the public college, its superiority even to hospitals for the community, is not an exceptional claim. It was already, in 1584, when Descaurres's book was published, something of a commonplace. For example, in 1565, a similar claim was made in the small provincial city of Condom, in Gascony, where the establishing of a public college is said to constitute a "far greater work of charity than is the construction of hospitals, because it is a matter of nourishing both minds and bodies, rather than bodies alone."[6]

These were not empty words. Without getting any financial help from Paris, each of these middle-sized towns found the means necessary for the leasing or even for the building of a new college in the center of town. They found the money to pay teachers competitive salaries as well, and these expenses were carried on the municipal budget, so that the sons of residents were generally able to attend the municipal college free of charge. The instructors were expected to be "scholarly persons of good character, capable and proven, experienced in the teaching of rhetoric, dialectic, philosophy, Greek and Latin languages, poetry and oratory." Finally, these paragons of academic virtues were expected to teach "in the manner and form used in the most famous colleges, as in the colleges of Paris."[7]

In the manner of Paris: in other words, according to the new humanist formula. It was no longer sufficient, in the 1520s and 1530s, to acquire enough Latin to say a mass or write a contract. Now the need was for "good letters," a knowledge of the Roman poets and even a smattering of Greek literature. In order to achieve these new and difficult objectives, a standardized system came into existence, almost at once, almost everywhere. A boy started out in the lowest class, the Sixth, at age seven or thereabouts. Here he would learn "the alphabet, Greek and Latin"; here he was to learn to write, to read, to pronounce, and to decline "both Greek and Latin nouns." In the Fifth class one read Cicero and Terence and "from time to time the boys would be taught to turn French sentences into Latin." In the Fourth class, Virgil, Ovid, and Valla were added to the curriculum and the work tended to become more rigorous and demanding: twice each day a brief theme or argument in French would be handed out to be translated into Latin. In the Third class, one read, inter alia, Cicero (*De amicitia, De senectute*), Virgil (*Georgics*), and Ovid (*Metamorphoses, Epistles*), but one also studied Greek grammar. The Second class read Cicero's *De officiis,* the *Aeneid,* Horace's *Odes* and *Satires*—"as well as other poets, both Greek and Latin." In the final year, for the small number of pupils who had kept up with this severe regime, Sallust, Livy, Juvenal, Persius, Aristotle, Xenophon, and other authors were added to those already familiar. This was the program of the municipal school in the small town of Auch, in Gascony, when the school was in the charge of the principal Massé, in 1565.[8]

What is striking, in those years of the sixteenth century, is the scale on which schools were founded—the scale, the enthusiasm associated with it, the mobilization of financial resources, and the ambition exhibited in the building programs, in the curriculum, in the demands placed on both teaching staff and student body. Money was not easy to find. Neither the State nor the Church was prepared to contribute. "Never mind," was the attitude of local elected officials: "We must go on with this, no matter what the cost," in the words of Master Le Saige of the little town of Condom, near Auch. Why should local citizens impose such heavy financial burdens on themselves? Because "learning magnifies the glory of God and proclaims it to the world." Learning also "honors the King" and it "preserves, augments and maintains the Republic" (i.e., the commonwealth, the city).[9] Similar views are expressed in other small towns in the kingdom. In Sens, in the Ile de France, Master Hodoard, a local dignitary, goes on record to say that "there is nothing in the world that is more suitable and necessary for the preservation and augmentation of the commonwealth than the securing of teachers, masters and instructors for her young—this is proven both by the opinion of the wise ancient philosophers and by experience."[10]

City councils and leading citizens everywhere went to work to establish the best possible classical high schools in their own towns. They sent delegations of headhunters to Paris to recruit the most renowned humanist professors. Someone of the stature of Mathurin Cordier, for instance, was signed up in 1529 to take over the nascent school at Nevers, installed, three years earlier, in a truly princely mansion in the center of town.[11] In Toulouse, a much larger and wealthier city, the new municipal high school was housed in a splendid building erected expressly for the purpose. The construction project cost over five thousand livres and took five years to complete. No efforts were spared in hiring the most renowned professors, either. Jean Bodin applied for the principal's post in Toulouse, but the city council rejected his application and tried to interest the best-known hellenist in France, Adrian Turnèbe, in the position. Turnèbe declined and Toulouse eventually settled for a highly competent jurist, Dr. Bertrand de Lapointe. Once entrusted with the principalship, Lapointe was sent to Paris to recruit four other staff members; upon his return, the city went ahead with a flourish, appropriating a further sum for its school to pay for the writing and performance of plays both in Latin and in French, with the goal of "keeping up the ardor of the students."[12] It is clear that the ardor of city councillors, of philanthropists, of the entire bourgeois *élite* for the teaching of the humanities, knew no bounds in the first half of the sixteenth century. But it is equally clear that this enthusiasm for the new learning and its widest possible dissemination does not last. In most cities, a period of ambitious school foundations is followed by exhaustion. Eventually the entire *élite* stops investing in education. The qualifications of the teaching staff tend to diminish in time. The students, too, appear to lose their motivation. Expressions of concern about this decline are heard everywhere. Sooner or later, the cities simply get used to lower expectations.

"The school is in ruins. The building keeps sliding downhill. When it rains a lot, water comes right through and the floor boards fall apart," complains the principal at Angoulême. Furthermore, he insists, his teachers are "naked," because they do not receive their wages. The situation here is said to be "pitiful." "The children are left without masters."[13]

The case of the prosperous little city of Vienne, south of Lyon, in the

Rhône valley, is instructive in this respect. As late as 1563, under the principalship of Dr. Lecourt, a jurist like his colleague at Toulouse, things seem to be working fine in the local municipal school. Lecourt has a staff of four teachers, all said to be "learned, erudite, of good character and conversation." The city's budget for its school is five hundred to six hundred livres, which is quite generous. The principal is expected to reside at the school "together with his wife and family," a standard provision of the contracts that remain the chief source for our knowledge of the schools of this period.

Even so, a note of alarm has already sounded in this idyllic setting. Perhaps it is not to be taken too seriously, since it comes from an envious teacher who, no doubt, is maneuvering to take over the principal's post. The complaint, addressed to the city council, asserts that "the students speak only French," instead of Latin, and that they waste their time "playing cards with Lecourt and his wife." Ten years later, in 1573, there is a shortage of funds made available for the school. Another four years go by and the school is stopped dead in its tracks: in 1577 classes cease for lack of money. The school at Vienne is moving toward its eventual ruin, just as are most of the schools that had been established thirty or forty years earlier in an atmosphere of jubilant enthusiasm.

The process is a gradual one. As early as 1566, the principal at Vienne is released from his obligation to maintain a staff of four teachers. In the years that follow, the school holds on, just barely. At times it stops operating. Then it revives, amid complaints that the school "is in bad shape and that a really capable and learned man must be found to run it." But such men are hard to find now. In 1581 the school at Vienne has only two teachers. The following year, a candidate for a teaching post presents himself. Hopes are raised. But the school board, having examined the candidate, finds that he is incompetent and sends him on his way. It is not just teachers that are missing; it is also that there is no money. In 1588, the principal complains that he is out of grain and wine; lacking these basic supplies, the school will be forced to close down. Two years later the school is literally in ruins, following the street fighting between royalists and the supporters of the ultra-Catholic party. When the fighting ends, the city hires a teacher at the modest salary of forty livres per year. He is asked to take up residence in the battered school building with his wife and family and to run the school as best he can.

What sort of teaching could one expect under those circumstances, in 1590? The ambitious curriculum set up a generation ago is only a nostalgic memory now. The time is past when even a small provincial town could afford to have five classes, to teach the humanities at the highest level, and to offer instruction in classical Greek as well as Latin. Now the single teacher is asked only to teach "piety and the Catholic religion." An effort will be made to find an assistant teacher to help with the younger children, a man "of mediocre learning for the time being, while waiting that it may please God to let this town recover a little and so, in time, to increase the number of teachers and to improve the instruction available to the children."[14]

The case of Vienne is in no way exceptional; the pattern is a general one. In every city there is a first stage during which one observes an all-out mobilization of resources in favor of an expensive, ambitious program of school building. The key to success in this early effort is the ability to attract first-rate teachers. These men often appear overqualified. They tend to have advanced degrees, and they are often genuine intellectuals who publish books.

This first stage is followed, sooner or later, by a catastrophic collapse. Here again, the heart of the problem is the quality of the teaching staff. All at once, city after city fails to attract the talented men who had served so well, year after year, in the past. The reason the schools could be brought to ruin so suddenly is clear: they were vulnerable because they were never set up as permanent operations. Few had any kind of endowment; all were dependent upon the vagaries of the annual municipal budget. They had always operated in this way. As for the teachers, here again, there had never been any premium placed on permanence; on the contrary, all contracts were for one year only. There was no tenure: every teacher's job was up for grabs each year, since new candidates could compete with those teachers who had been in place the previous year. It was an entirely competitive situation in which teachers moved from town to town looking for the best offer. This system worked marvels as long as there was a plentiful supply of qualified teachers. But when candidates stopped presenting themselves, the schools could collapse overnight.

The question, then, is: Why did competent teachers compete less frequently for these posts in the 1560s and 1570s? Why did they all but vanish from the scene in the 1580s and 1590s? A quick and easy reply would be: because of financial difficulties. Certainly, the cities did run into difficulty. The documentary evidence points unanimously to lack of funds as the source of the school crisis. But these documents—minutes of city council meetings, which are the chief sources for the history of the municipal schools—would naturally deal almost exclusively with budgetary matters.

However, the financial squeeze is by no means universal, even in the worst years. Some cities can afford to hire at the old level, but they still can't find first-rate teachers. Even those cities that are in trouble seem to make no real effort to solve the problem. Private benefactors, who were legion in the 1520s and 1530s, now appear to have become extinct as a species. What has changed is the will to sacrifice in favor of education. It is by no means clear that in every case there was more money available a generation before the crisis. It would be more accurate to say that spending on education always involved a hard choice. In the earlier period, the choice was made in favor of humanist learning, which was seen by the local *élite* as a panacea for all ills and as a benefit, an investment safer and more profitable than others. For example, on the question of which was more important, the teaching of the humanities or charity for the poor, the answer always used to be a resounding vote for Latin grammar and Greek philosophy. As the end of the century approaches, local officials are no longer so sure. In Vienne, around 1600, we hear for the first time a statement that would have been unthinkable a generation earlier: "The school is not really needed."

What has happened, in the meantime, in Vienne and many other towns, is that the iron grip of the local *élite*, a self-perpetuating oligarchy of wealthy bourgeois families, has loosened enough so that the voice of the middle and lower bourgeoisie can be heard. This voice is radical in tone and full of accumulated grievances against the *familles* who have directed the cities' fortunes all along. These lesser citizens now dare to say, openly, that the expensive municipal Latin school is the pet project of a minority of twenty or thirty families, "which have usurped all power in the conduct of the city's affairs." The old *élite* admits that the school is really their project, although funded with tax money. "The building of the new school was approved only by the consuls, supported only by a handful of the most notable and zealous citizens, while all the rest of the population was dead set against it."[15]

This division along class lines will harden in time. In Provins, the issue will be spelled out with great clarity in the seventeenth century. Here, too, there has been a *belle époque* in the history of the municipal school. Here, too, this is over, and the school is moribund. Should it be revived? In the debate over this issue, the case against the local *élite,* who supported further expenditures for education, is made in the following terms: "We are told that the education of our children is a very important matter. One could well reply to this that it would be wrong to deprive the poor and the community as a whole so as to assist the children of a few persons who have the means, anyway, of having their children educated."[16] In sum, classical learning, which had once been praised to the skies, is now criticized as a class privilege of no consequence to any but the richest citizens.

So far, in trying to explain the crisis of the late sixteenth century, we have spoken of budget difficulties, of choices made according to class lines, of an administrative system with no permanence. We have also heard complaints about the scarcity of competent teachers. Now why should teachers vanish overnight? Were they simply reacting to tighter budgets and looking for opportunities elsewhere? And in the absence of qualified teachers, what could school boards do, short of closing down the schools?

It seems reasonably clear that there was no shortage of qualified teachers until after 1560 or so. For some years after that, it was still possible to staff the schools even in remote towns hidden away in the mountains, a case in point being the city of Mende, in the Cévennes. Year after year, these marginal schools were able to function to everyone's satisfaction. Each fall, enterprising young teachers with university degrees would present themselves, compete for the available positions by giving a sample lecture, and, if chosen, stay on for a year's contract. The turning point came rather late in Mende. It was not until 1629 that the city council finally could not staff the school. In desperation, they turned to a religious order to replace the free-wheeling secular professionals of the past. This strategy often worked in other places. It worked in Vienne, for instance, which was a substantial enough city to be attractive to the Jesuits, whose reputation was considerably better than that of other religious orders. A small town like Mende did not have the resources to attract the Jesuits, who insisted on an endowment with three thousand livres. Mende turned to the Carmelites, but this did not work out. The Reverend Fathers, it seems, failed at this job, "so that most of the schoolboys have quit, there being seven or eight left for each master."[17] Hard-pressed to hire someone, such cities often wound up with men of questionable character, as in the case of the town of Condom, which had to fire a teacher because, it was alleged, he was in the habit of "going out at night to make love."[18] Actually, this was not a new problem, although complaints about debauchery appear with greater frequency in the crisis years. One could go back as early as 1540, in the heyday of the school-foundation movement, and easily find teachers who had acquired reputations as wild and disreputable men. This was the case with Hubert Sussanneau, for instance, a brilliant young humanist, a friend of Rabelais, who was principal at the municipal school in Grenoble, until the city council got upset: "He gives a bad example," the council complained. "He blasphemes and he is drunk most of the time, showing a bad example to his pupils, carrying a sword, fighting with anyone who comes his way."[19]

Whatever Sussanneau's moral failings may have been, he was definitely an inspired and learned man. Half a century after he was fired, the problem was no longer moral turpitude. It was not a question of the local bourgeoisie's indignation directed at some bohemian, provincial James Joyce. The problem became altogether different: drunk or sober, qualified humanists were now hard to find.

And why was that? Well, in the first place, young men with the requisite learning tended to be attracted to alternative careers and to give a wide berth to the teaching profession, which had become stifling, stultifying, and, with the advent of the Counter-Reformation, downright dangerous. Humanist learning now automatically invited suspicion. Some sort of formal adherence to Catholic orthodoxy became a requirement. One could say that this was not a new development either. Suspect teachers had been fair game as early as 1530. In Loches, for example, three schoolteachers were arrested on suspicion of heresy in 1530, among them Master Jean Moreau. Forty years later, it was still a Moreau who represented classical learning in Loches. This Pierre Moreau, perhaps the son of Jean, was a married man, a hellenist of some repute. He had taught in the school at Loches all his working life. But when the Counter-Reformation triumphed there in 1575, Moreau would be eased out and replaced by less suspect—but also less learned—teachers.[20] From this point onward, the independent, secular classics teacher, a family man and a man of the world, peripatetic by nature or necessity, may be said to belong to an endangered species.

If the municipal schools were to continue to function at all—as indeed most of them did—they would have to lower their sights. Instead of pining for famous hellenists from Paris, or even for experienced academics with doctorates in law or medicine, most towns would henceforth have to settle for men of mediocre learning or hand the school over to a religious order. This choice was not as humiliating as we might think, because much had changed in these cities since the early years of the sixteenth century. The schools had once been almost the private fiefs of the local *élite*, who had used them to propel their sons into important careers, so they had to have been intellectually demanding. Their highly motivated clientele was composed of young bourgeois who aspired to careers in the law courts and in the royal administration. This is how things used to be, we are told, in Autun. By 1610, the school at Autun was clearly serving a new kind of student: not the sons of the best families, groomed for the *parlement*, but "a great number of clerics, priests and monks, most of them, not having the means to acquire an education because of the poverty of their parents, have remained ignorant until now."[21]

By 1610 the Counter-Reformation dominated French life, as much as the Reformation had a century earlier. And the Counter-Reformation had a specific social foundation: it expressed the point of view of a "second bourgeoisie," in Henri Drouot's formulation, a class full of grievances, excluded from offices and benefices by the powerful "first bourgeoisie" which had created the humanist schools and which had made skillful use of humanist culture in the pursuit of power and prestige. Now on the attack, the lesser bourgeoisie found ready allies in the Catholic Church establishment. Espousing the cause of ultra-orthodoxy and conformity, joining the Church in its battle against heresy—and the semblance of heresy—this lower-middle class worked hard at unseating the old families ensconced in municipal office. In this battle one of the most effective strategies was to accuse the older *élite* of being far too open to new ideas, of favoring the hiring of suspect laymen on the municipal teaching staff.

Where new men won power, they tended to demand an end to what we might call the Renaissance system in education. In practice, this meant the replacement of independent scholars with priests or religious congregations. In this way, while educational standards were not guaranteed to rise, at least orthodoxy was assured.

It seems reasonable to ask whether the departure of the Renaissance classics teacher, a familiar figure in the French landscape for a century, can be seen as a clear instance of the decline of Renaissance culture in France. There are a number of reasons why I should hesitate to pronounce on this matter, as yet. First of all, the new tenants of the public schools, Jesuits, Oratorians, and Doctrinaires, continued the work of their secular predecessors. They continued to teach the same corpus of Latin authors, in any case, although certainly they did so in a different spirit. They might have wished to cut off or diminish certain components of the curriculum established by the Renaissance tradition, especially where the teaching of Greek was concerned. They certainly made every effort to redirect the purpose of the schools to serve as proto-seminaries, as training schools for future priests. But there was a limit to how many changes they could introduce. The watchful city councils remained the theoretical trustees of these schools, and they could resist such changes.

As for the secular teachers, they did not necessarily vanish. They continued to function, and to pass on their profession from father to son, in one way or another. Plenty of towns had not turned over their schools to religious orders. In those towns, which usually were not large centers with unusual resources, a place remained for the independent teacher, who could continue his work, unhindered by the political passions that blazed in more strategically placed cities. And when he was not employed as a teacher, the itinerant scholar could always count on making a living as a dependent of the old families who may have been forced to curtail their political activities, but who still possessed money and influence.

Rather than speaking of the end of Renaissance culture, I would say that academics who had once provoked the ire of the clerical establishment in a hundred provincial cities now tended to keep a low profile. Even Jesuits could not help transmitting subversive ideas, in spite of their best efforts, since these ideas were inherent in the Greek and Roman models of civilization that were still habitually turned to as guides for proper behavior. Hence, it is not surprising that men such as Descartes, Voltaire, or Robespierre were to acquire the tools of their trade, as critics of contemporary culture, in educational establishments directed by mentors whose entire purpose was to ward off such criticism.

NOTES

1. Jean Auroux, *Le Monde,* June 16, 1988.
2. Jean Descaurres, *Oeuvres* (Paris, 1584): "Il y a un grand revenu pour la ville où il y a un collège, car l'argent et vivres qui seroient transportez ailleurs demeurent."
3. Descaurres: "La chose et la premiere qu'on doit avoir en soin et la plus utile

et necessaire qui soit en toutes sortes de Republiques. Tout le monde a interest que les jeunes gens soient bien instruits, quelque vocation qu'ils prennent."

4. Descaurres: "Magnifiquement basti, que les enfans des grand seigneurs mesmes y prennent plaisir d'y demeurer et que tous bons esprits se delectent a y estudier estans conviés et excitez par la magnificence des beaux bastimens et par la serenité des lieux."

5. Descaurres: "Le fondement et pepiniere des Republiques, commune boutique de tout scavoir et comme l'ouvroir des esprits pueriles. De plus grand profit que ne sont sans comparaison aucune tous les hopitaux du monde—icy les esprits sont nourris, là seulement les corps corruptibles."

6. Cited by Joseph Gardère, "Les écoles de Condom," *Revue de Gascogne* 26 (1885): 483: "Oeuvre charitable beaucoup plus grande" because it means "nourrir les esprits avec le corps" rather than "le corps seulement."

7. This formulation in the three-year contract was signed in the city of La Rochelle, in 1560, by Master Guillemelle, "principal regent et super intendent des escholles publiques de ceste ville." Cited in *Ephemerides de La Rochelle* (1859), 24. The formula is just about universal. For Rennes, for instance, the phrase is "endoctrinez, regiz et gouvernez en tout honneur bonne litterature à l'exsemple des colleges de Paris."

8. See Paul Bénétrix, *Les Origines du college d'Auch* (Paris: H. Champion, 1908).

9. See Gardère, 483.

10. Sens, Archives communales, G.G. 2. See also Gustave Julliot, "Fondation du college du Sens," *Bulletin de la société archéologique de Sens* 11 (1877): 132ff.

11. Nathanaël Weiss, "Le Collège de Nevers," *Revue Pédagogique* 18 (1891): 400–416.

12. Abbé Corraze, "L'Esquille, collège des capitouls," *Mémoires de l'Académie de Toulouse* 15 (1937): 155–228.

13. The grievances of the principals are recorded in the minutes of city council deliberations, Angoulême, Archives communales, B.B. 2, fol. 23, cited in Prosper Boissonade and Jean Bernard, *Histoire du collège d'Angoulême* (Angoulême: L. Coquemard, 1895).

14. See Claude Faure, *Recherches sur le collège de Vienne* (Paris: A. Picard, 1933).

15. Faure, 113, 129.

16. Rivot, "Histoire ecclesiastique de Provins," MS. 99, Bibliothèque municipale, Provins.

17. Mende, Archives communales, B.B. 4, fol. 97r.

18. Gardère, 273.

19. A. Prudhomme, "L'enseignement secondaire à Grenoble," *Bulletin de l'Académie Delphinale* 14 (1900): 93–139.

20. On Pierre Moreau's retirement in 1575, see Jean-Claude Margolin, "A. Ysore et la fondation du collège de Loches," *Loches au 16e siècle* (Marseille, 1979).

21. Anatole de Charmasse, *Les Jésuites au collège d'Autun* (Autun: H. Champion, 1884), 24: "toujours le college d'Autun estoit bon et qu'il y avoit infinité d'étrangers et de la ville qui depuis se sont trouvez en parlement et autres justices." This is in 1580. In 1613, we hear the prospective clientele for the school is to be composed of "gens de l'église, prestres et religieux, la plupart desquels, pour n'avoir moyen de s'instruire aux bonnes lettres, par la pauvreté de leurs parents, sont demeurés ignorants."

Humanism and the Problem of Relativism

Zachary S. Schiffman

Montaigne arranged the first edition of the *Essais* to highlight the problem of relativism. The first essay of book 1, "By Diverse Means We Arrive at the Same End," introduces this problem in its conclusion: "Truly man is a marvelously vain, diverse, and undulating object. It is hard to found any constant and uniform judgment on him."[1] The first essay of book 2, "Of the Inconsistency of Our Actions," amplifies it: "There is as much difference between us and ourselves as between us and others."[2] And the last essay of book 2 reiterates it in the concluding lines of the first edition: "There never were in the world two opinions alike, any more than two hairs or two grains. Their most universal quality is diversity."[3]

Relativism was intensely problematic for Montaigne because he had been trained to think as a humanist. Underlying the humanists' fascination with Latin eloquence was the belief that the study of letters could provide practical wisdom for daily life, as opposed to the useless philosophical abstractions of the scholastics. This contention was based on two assumptions: that universal norms underlay the apparent diversity of examples found in humane letters, and that they could be illuminated by the skeptical mode of reasoning *in utramque partem,* on both sides of a question. These assumptions were compatible only so long as the humanists had access to a small number of classical texts. But with the spread of printing in the sixteenth century, virtually the whole corpus of classical literature—Greek as well as Roman—became available, along with medieval and modern works. Throughout the *Essais* Montaigne showed that when the mode of reasoning from both sides was applied to diverse examples, it undermined the ability to demonstrate universal norms.[4]

The *Essais* provide the most eloquent expression of a problem that was first experienced acutely in sixteenth-century France. Of course an awareness of relativism was intrinsic to the humanist movement from its very beginning. Bruni, for example, had criticized as unhistorical the notion of perennial Rome, which obscured the political and cultural achievements of the Florentine republic. But Florentine humanists nonetheless debated whether their city had been founded by Caesar's or Sulla's veterans; in other words, they could not entirely free themselves from the pull of the classical norm, despite their sense of their own historical and cultural specificity. Not until the sixteenth century, when humanism spread northward to France, was the primacy of ancient culture effectively challenged. The classical revival made Frenchmen more aware of the distinctiveness of their own culture, with its feudal rather than classical roots. By the mid-sixteenth century, they had begun to assert the equality or superiority of French culture to that of antiquity. This challenge to classical hegemony derived special impetus from the rise of humanist philology in France, and its impact on the study of Roman law. Philology demonstrated the relativity of laws and institutions, undermining the notion of normative standards derived from antiquity. The popularity of legal education grew apace with the royal bureaucracy, increasing the general awareness of the problem of relativism and the need for a solution.[5]

The period from the mid-sixteenth to the mid-seventeenth century witnessed no fewer than five different types of response to the problem, mostly by thinkers who had received both humanistic and legal training. Their responses covered a wide range of human inquiry, indicating the extent and severity of the problem. Legal theorists like Bodin, Baudouin, and Hotman proposed a "neo-Bartolist" solution, in which they attempted to distill the principles of universal equity from the laws of the most noteworthy states. Historians like La Popelinière, Vignier, and Pasquier put forth an essentially taxonomic solution, in which they attempted to classify the diversity of historical entities. Moral philosophers like Du Vair and Charron sought a neo-Stoical solution, in which they attempted to transcend diversity with a revised and revitalized form of universal reason; whereas Montaigne accepted diversity and proposed using his self as his point of orientation amid it. And finally, in reaction to Montaigne and Charron, natural philosophers like Descartes attempted to redefine human knowledge, and consequently human wisdom, so as to exclude the problem of relativism altogether. The variety and ingenuity of these solutions highlight the fundamental intractability of relativism as a problem for the early modern mind, which simply did not have the conceptual techniques to deal with it in a satisfactory manner. The thinkers of this period were thus trapped in an intellectual cul-de-sac, from which there could be no exit until the advent of an idea of historical development released the humanities from the problem of relativism.

François Hotman's *Antitribonian* exemplifies the ambivalence of the neo-Bartolist response to relativism. The work is a critique of a French system of legal education based on the study of the *Corpus juris civilis*, the only extant body of Roman law, compiled by Tribonian at the behest of the emperor Justinian. In the fourteenth and fifteenth centuries, the followers of the Italian jurist Bartolus of Sassoferrato had regarded the *Corpus juris* as the embodiment of universal law, which had only to be interpreted properly for contemporary use. But in the sixteenth century this *mos docendi italicus*, or Italian method of teaching law, was challenged in France by the followers of the *mos gallicus*, who wanted to cleanse the *Corpus juris* of accumulated scribal errors before interpreting it for contemporary use. The application of humanist philological techniques to the *Corpus juris*, however, revealed that Roman law was not universal law but rather that of a past society, promulgated in response to that society's own particular needs. This insight led Hotman to question the relevance of the *Corpus juris* for French legal education.

He began the *Antitribonian* by boldly declaring that Roman public law was relative to the historical circumstances of that state and thus inapplicable to France. In the bulk of the treatise, he extended this relativistic argument to Roman private law as well. But no sooner had he dethroned the *Corpus juris* than he gave it pride of place in the proposal for legal reform that concludes the *Antitribonian*. Although Roman law was no longer *the* standard of jurisprudence, it still embodied legal principles, as did the laws of other noteworthy states, from which a new body of universal law could be distilled. In the context of this undertaking, Hotman likened the *Corpus juris* to a "priceless treasury" providing not only the best examples of "natural equity" but also the model for the organization of the new legal code.[6]

The paradoxical, pro-Tribonian conclusion of the *Antitribonian* underscores Hotman's ambivalence toward the legal and historical relativism that he had begun by boldly asserting. One might explain this paradox in terms of the widely recognized need for a codification of French private law: although public law necessarily reflected historical circumstances, private law could be analyzed according to the universal principles evident in the *Corpus juris*. The only problem with this explanation is that Hotman ended up including public law in his proposal. The very acuteness of his sense of relativity compelled him to assert that public law, too, had normative characteristics, lest he undermine the possibility that universal principles existed for the codification of private law.[7]

Hotman's ambivalence toward relativism is also apparent in his *Francogallia,* an examination of French public law that complements his treatment of private law in the *Antitribonian*. The *Francogallia* was really a polemic for a return to the ancient constitution of France, which supposedly originated with the union of the Frankish and Gallic peoples. The ancient constitution Hotman described was ultimately based on the classical ideal of mixed government, combining monarchic, aristocratic, and democratic elements. Hotman extolled this mixed constitution as the most perfect form of government, citing the authority of Plato, Aristotle, Polybius, and especially Cicero; and he established its universality as a political norm by referring to examples of noteworthy states both ancient and modern. He thus subsumed the historical uniqueness of French public law under the universality of a classical norm, the appropriateness of which his relativism had already made questionable.[8]

Whereas ambivalence toward relativism led legal theorists like Hotman to impose an extrinsic order upon diversity, it led historians like La Popelinière, Vignier, and Pasquier to seek an intrinsic one. Lancelot Voisin de La Popelinière's theory of "perfect history," which was put into practice by Nicolas Vignier, reveals the fundamentally classificatory nature of this response to the problem of relativism. And Estienne Pasquier's notion of *recherches* reveals the taxonomic underpinnings of historical classification. The intrinsic order sought by these historians was ultimately based on the principles of Aristotelian essentialism.[9]

La Popelinière's awareness of relativism no doubt stemmed from his humanistic and legal education, which ultimately bore fruit in 1599, when he published a volume of works proclaiming the need to reform the writing of history. These works—the *Histoire des histoires,* the *Idée de l'histoire accomplie,* and the *Dessein de l'histoire nouvelle des françois*—constitute sequential parts of a sustained argument. First, La Popelinière criticized the inadequacies of all previous historiography; then in response to this criticism, he formulated his theory of "perfect history"; and finally, he sketched out the practical application of this theory to the history of France. The idea of perfect history was an attempt to accommodate the writing of history to the expanded historical horizons revealed by legal scholarship.

La Popelinière maintained that the state was the true subject of history—rather than kings and battles—and that previous historians had failed to describe it in sufficient detail. Because each state was characterized by its own unique laws and institutions, one could not understand it unless he gave a perfect—that is, complete—account of its history, beginning with its origins and moving forward, step by step, to encompass each of its subsequent periods. La Popelinière ignored the role played by historical actors in this account, emphasizing instead the distinctive structure of the state in each of its phases. Perfect history was thus characterized by the sequential overlay of discrete historical strata, each defined by its own particular institutional composition. Given the absence of historical actors, La Popelinière located the temporal dynamic not in the state's development in relationship to its ever-changing circumstances, but rather in the unfolding of the potential inherent in its primal matter, which was represented by the customs, laws, and institutions that had given the state its first form.

In the final analysis, perfect history was a form of classification. To insure completeness La Popelinière recommended that history be organized topically, according to the general kinds of institutions all states possessed, and chronologically, according to the mutations of these institutions. He likened this plan to a blueprint for a building that would rise stage by stage, each divided into topics—such as religion, administration, justice, military discipline, finances, and business—that would be subdivided into the units appropriate for the state and period under consideration. Perfect history would be a topical repository for all knowledge pertinent to the state. La Popelinière thus overcame the problem of relativism by ordering, in a vast storehouse, the multitude of historical entities revealed by legal scholarship.

According to La Popelinière, the man who came closest to realizing the goal of perfect history was Vignier, a physician turned historian, whose monumental *Bibliothèque historiale* was published in 1587. The

Bibliothèque was a comprehensive summary of history, encompassing all the known peoples of Europe, Asia, and Africa, and extending from the time of Adam to the accession of Francis I. This massive work of three folio volumes was ordered chronologically, year by year, with the world events of any given year being correlated with as many as two dozen dating systems. The variety of chronological systems was thus subordinated to a universal one, enabling Vignier to order the profusion of historical events and entities. In essence, this epitome of perfect history relegated all known historical information to its appropriate place on a huge time line.

Pasquier, a humanist scholar and practicing lawyer, offered an alternative means of ordering historical material that enabled him to circumvent the encyclopedic impulse of perfect history. In his monumental *Recherches de la France*, Pasquier contrasted his program of historical inquiry with that of perfect history: "Any man of understanding, without seeing a perfect history, can almost imagine the overall temper of a people when he studies its ancient statutes and ordinances; and by the same token can make a sound conjecture about what its laws must have been, by looking at its manner of life."[10] In other words, one could understand a people by studying its original customs, laws, and institutions, which embodied its characteristic essence.

The notion of *recherches* reveals how the fascination with origins, which characterized the historical thought of this period, was fundamentally taxonomic. Although Pasquier was very conscious of historical change, he tended to attribute the distinctive features of modern French culture directly to the "genetic" material of ancient Gaul. In book 1 of the *Recherches*, he ascribed the success of the ancient Gauls—who had once sacked Rome and conquered the bulk of Europe—to the power of their Druidical assemblies, which unified the Gallic tribes under a combined civil and religious administration. In books 2 and 3, he traced the origins of Parliament and the Gallican church back to these assemblies. Modern French civil and religious institutions were thus differentia of the genetic material of ancient Gaul, to which Pasquier also attributed the distinctive features of French literature and language in books 6 and 7. The intervening two books of the *Recherches* concern obscure customs and neglected historical figures, the former being whenever possible traced back to Gallic precedents. The bulk of the work, therefore, attributes the uniqueness of French culture to the Gallic essence from which it unfolded.

Cultural taxonomy proved to be as unwieldy a solution to the problem of relativism as perfect history. The final edition of the *Recherches*, for example, comprises over three hundred chapters on various aspects of French history and culture.[11] Like perfect history, Pasquier's historical "researches" tended to reduce France to a collection of disparate bits of information that obscured the unity of the culture. In short, both types of classificatory solution were conceptually sterile; they provided a means of describing the complexity of historical reality, without affording an understanding of it.

Like that of his contemporaries, Montaigne's relativism originated from a humanistic and (presumably) legal education. Unlike his contemporaries, though, Montaigne's solution to the problem of relativism transcended both the normative and the classificatory modes of thought. These two tendencies were reflected in the Renaissance genre of commonplace literature, which gathered similar examples around a central theme or moral. When Montaigne began writing the *Essais* in 1572, he attempted to imitate this genre, but the diversity of examples consistently prevented him from illustrating commonplace norms. In frustration he then began to assert the validity of the ideal of the sage in his so-called Stoical essays, but the diversity of examples soon began to undermine even this once-hallowed norm. By the time he composed the Pyrrhonistic core of the "Apology for Raymond Sebond," around 1576, he had given up any hope of finding what he sarcastically termed "the bean in the cake" (II, 12, 383 C).

In a world devoid of apparent norms, the only alternative to complete skepticism was to base knowledge on what was actually accessible to the mind, namely itself as mirrored by its manifold operations in a complex world. Montaigne found his new intellectual orientation in the process of essaying his mind, of testing, weighing, and measuring his judgment against the diversity and variety of the world. The nature of human existence dictated the inconstancy of these measurements, for the mind that perceived itself through its own operations fluctuated with the movements of body and soul. All these movements, however, were equally revealing of the thinker; and Montaigne affected to record them "naturally," as they occurred. By the time he published the first edition of the *Essais* in 1580, he conceived of the work as a dynamic record of the moment-to-moment fluctuations of his mind, as it engaged with the complexity of a world that was itself in constant motion.

The word *essai*, with which Montaigne denoted his new intellectual process, is now so mundane that it tends to obscure for us its significance as a means of understanding the world. The process of essaying himself provided Montaigne with a new cognitive standpoint in a complex reality that defied normative analysis. Amid the natural motion of the world, he acquired such knowledge as befitted his condition as a mere man, knowledge not of unchanging essences but of instances of flux. The mind served no longer to transcend the flux of reality but to engage with it. In place of the normative view of the world, which could not accommodate itself to the mobility of existence, Montaigne substituted a form of cognition in which the self-conscious mind interacted spontaneously with reality, registering its own specific movements within the general flux of the world.

Although the record of each movement of his mind immobilized only a transitory aspect of himself, it was he who moved, he who essayed himself: "So, all in all, I may indeed contradict myself now and then; but truth, as Demades said, I do not contradict" (III, 2, 611 B). Truth resided not only in the honesty of the portrait but in the reality of the self as a mental object. The multiple perspectives he took upon himself revealed his *forme maistresse,* the shape of his personality (III, 2, 615 B). This pattern underlying the many instances of self gave unity and substance to a being that could apprehend itself only fleetingly.

Montaigne's new cognitive standpoint enabled him to mediate between the extremes of binding rationalism and skeptical relativism. The rationalist believes that reason has access to normative truths that transcend diversity, whereas the relativist believes that such diversity invalidates any so-called truth. The activity of essaying himself complemented Montaigne's sense of relativity without engendering a skeptical denial of truth; it accorded with his awareness of the limitations of his perception while, at the same time, serving as a link to the reality he sought to understand. On the one hand, it presented all knowledge as relative to the observer; on the other, it presented the observer as an entity that could be known "objectively." That entity, existing in and of the world, represented the portion of reality accessible to human understanding. Individuality thus served as the point of orientation amid relativity.

This ingenious solution to the problem of relativism made those of Montaigne's contemporaries who understood it very nervous. They were bothered by his delight in a diversity that appeared to them chaotic. They were disturbed by his denial that one could transcend or classify this diversity. And they were distressed by his reliance on the self as the only anchor in a sea of relativity. Indeed, Montaigne had such a rare degree of existential stability that his solution to the problem of relativism was destined to remain idiosyncratic.

One of the contemporaries who best understood Montaigne and who attempted to circumscribe his relativism was Pierre Charron, a priest with both humanistic and legal training. Having experienced the last and most violent phase of the Wars of Religion, Charron attempted to formulate a systematic distinction between religion and morality. This distinction served both to express and to resolve his own profound sense of relativism. Civil war had catalyzed his need to find a new standpoint in a complex reality where religious truths no longer provided satisfactory answers to political and ethical questions. The catalyst of civil war reacted with the compound of his humanistic and legal education, which revealed fundamental differences between the classical, pagan world and the modern, Christian one. In his widely read treatise, *De la sagesse,* Charron articulated a new moral science appropriate for life in this more complex world. His work represents one of the most thorough attempts at a neo-Stoical solution to the problem of relativism.[12]

Book 1 of *De la sagesse,* on self-knowledge as the prelude to wisdom, is based largely on the *Essais.* Here Montaigne's rambling critique of the vanity, inconstancy, and weakness of man received powerful, systematic expression. This indictment of man served to sweep the reader forward into a comparison between man and the animals—borrowed largely from the "Apology for Raymond Sebond"—that dethroned man utterly, casting him into the flux of the world along with all of God's other creatures. Having been reduced to his proper place in the universe, man was then subjected to a detailed analysis that explained the physiological causes of the human condition. For Montaigne self-knowledge led to self-acceptance, whereas for Charron it served as the prelude for the project of moral reformation in book 2 that would provide certainty amid flux.[13]

Skepticism was the basis for moral reformation, because it prepared the mind to receive truth. Charron's skepticism in book 2 is clearly indebted to Montaigne's in the "Apology," but he did not so much borrow the latter's skepticism whole as modify it to suit his own purposes. Charron's motto, *Je ne sais,* was in conscious contrast to Montaigne's *Que sais-je?* By substituting an unequivocal statement for Montaigne's equivocal one, Charron underscored his belief that there was a universal standard of judgment accessible to all those who used skepticism to cleanse their minds of dogmatism.

Charron found this standard in the natural law of reason, "the first and universal law and light inspired by God."[14] Living by this standard entailed not only *preud'hommie*, or moral integrity, but also piety. Charron distinguished between piety born of universal reason, and religion born of habit and custom, asserting that piety preceded religion. He then went on to declare that if piety preceded religion, so too did *preud'hommie*, which flowed from the same fountainhead as piety. By definition *preud'hommie* was the source of all virtue, and religion was relegated to the status of "a special and particular virtue" ("une vertu speciale et particuliere," 2:151–52). Indeed, it was subsumed to one of the four cardinal virtues, justice, which teaches us to render to each thing whatever is appropriate to it. Religion was nothing other than the particular human virtue of rendering obeisance to God, and it varied according to habit and custom.

Like Montaigne, Charron used relativism as a weapon to combat all forms of dogmatism, which he decried as an *esprit municipal,* a narrow-mindedness that elevated local usage to the level of absolute truth (1:334). Montaigne, however, was a sincere enough relativist to recognize that this weapon was double-edged, and wisely chose not to wield it systematically, for fear of wounding himself in the process. Charron had no such fear, because he believed that relativism revealed the essential nature of reality. He could boldly declare that religion and morality were autonomous realms, because in the final analysis they were ruled by the same sovereign, whose universal law anchored him in the sea of relativity. The weapon he wielded, though, ended up undercutting religion, and his contemporaries were quick to label *De la sagesse* the "Breviary of the Libertines."

Even Charron's biographers have characterized him as *l'herbier de Montaigne,* who desiccated the fruits of the *Essais* by attempting to systematize them. But Charron was no slavish admirer, content to tidy up after his master. He had assimilated enough of Montaigne's relativistic insights to know that he could neither ignore nor fully accept them; instead, he used them in the cultivation of a new moral science that would provide stability without denying complexity. It is ironic that the fruits of Montaigne's mind, far from being desiccated by Charron's systematizing, became instead hypertrophied, further disseminating the problem he had tried to uproot.

To some extent Descartes inherited the problem of relativism from Montaigne and Charron. Although he was notoriously reticent about his sources, the *Discours de la méthode* in particular bears the traces of many ideas popularized by his two skeptical predecessors.[15] But the seeds of this problem first germinated during a humanistic education at the Jesuit Collège de La Flèche that had failed to fulfill its promise: "From my childhood I have been nourished upon letters, and because I was persuaded that by their means one could acquire a clear and certain knowledge of all that is useful in life, I was extremely eager to learn them."[16] The promise was not of scientific but of moral clarity and certainty, the moral utility of humanist education being a long-established commonplace. Skepticism about the ability of his education to provide him with moral norms amid the diversity of opinions led him to abandon the study of letters after receiving his degree in law from the University of Poitier.

Having failed to find moral certainty through erudition, Descartes sought it through travel as a gentleman in military service. But the book of the world offered him no greater certainty than the world of books, because the diversity of customs was just as bewildering as that of learned opinions. At this point of confusion in his life, Descartes found a mentor in the Dutch savant Isaac Beeckman, who reawakened his interest in mathematics. Under Beeckman's influence, Descartes enjoyed a year of intense creativity that culminated with his famous meditations in the *poêle* on November 10, 1618, when he had the vision of a "wonderful science" that would bring unity to previously distinct areas of human inquiry (10:216). A powerful urge to find the intrinsic order of human knowledge underlay his intellectual vision.

In the *Discours* he would subsequently amplify this notion of order in the four deceptively simple rules of his new logic: to accept as true only what he apprehended so clearly and distinctly that there was no room for doubt; to divide each problem into as many parts as possible; to think in an orderly manner, from simple to complex; and to make the enumerations so complete as to omit nothing. These "long chains of reasonings" expressed relations between entities that were characterized by proportions—such as greater, lesser, and equal—rather than by a shared substance or essence (6:19). Descartes assumed that his new logic mirrored the structure of a reality in which the sciences were linked like a "series of numbers," reflecting the sequential nature of human knowledge (10:215). He elaborated a plan of study that began with the new logic, proceeded to metaphysics and physics, and culminated with medicine, mechanics, and morals. This new intellectual orientation supplanted the normative one of his humanistic education, which had focused on the essential nature of entities rather than the measurable relations between them.

The famous *cogito* provided the logical foundation upon which Descartes erected his new intellectual edifice. "I think, therefore I am"—a proposition that expressed the necessary relationship between thinking and existing—was doubly suited as the basis for knowledge in a complex world.[17] First, it transformed what we would today term the "subjective" act of thinking into a mental object that could serve as the basis for certainty. Second, it expressed not a normative truth but a propositional one that was relative to its two elements, "thinking" and "existing." Although this truth was at first alive only in Descartes's own mind, it could also come alive for anyone who considered the proposition attentively. In other words this proposition, though both "subjective" and relative, was nonetheless universal. It thus offered an ingenious solution to the problem of relativism.

Descartes's solution reflects some of the same intellectual constraints as Montaigne's. Both men had been searching for *sagesse*. Both eventually came to realize that in a complex world the only real knowledge accessible to the mind was that of its own operations. Both, then, focused their attention on the mind's self-conscious experience of the cognitive moment. But Montaigne's awareness of the uniqueness of each moment compelled him simply to record it, whereas Descartes went on to analyze it, stripping it bare of all contextual detail in order to reveal its quintessential nature as a propositional relation. Descartes thus distilled a logical unit, empty of content, from the very existential moment of cognition that lay at the heart of Montaigne's relativism. In place of the mind's rich experience of itself in the world, he had substituted the mind's bare experience of itself in isolation.

By draining the cognitive moment of content, Descartes ultimately reified the problem of relativism. His new method demonstrated how the mind that produced mathematics could, in the same manner, also produce a unified science of nature. Difficulties arose, however, when he tried to extend his method to metaphysics in the *Meditationes*, and to morals in *Les Passions de l'âme*. In the former, he had trouble explaining how one could move from the inner certainty of the *cogito* to knowledge of extra-mental reality; and in the latter, he had trouble explaining how the thinking substance of the soul, revealed by the *cogito*, interacted with the material substance of the body. These difficulties, which ultimately stemmed from his having transformed the cognitive moment into a logical unit, undermined his whole intellectual edifice. Ironically, the collapse of this edifice would further substantiate the problem of relativism by separating the natural sciences, unified under mathematics, from the human ones.

Relativism remained an intractable problem for the early modern mind, because it lacked an idea of historical development. In lieu of this idea, which would have explained diversity as part of an ongoing process, most thinkers resorted to traditional solutions that were necessarily of limited utility. Neo-Bartolists supplanted the normative view of the world with a meta-normative one, which was nonetheless still exposed to the corrosive effects of relativism. Historians sought a classificatory solution based ultimately on the principles of Aristotelian taxonomy, despite the fact that skeptical relativism had called these essentialist principles into question. And neo-Stoics attempted to reassert the universal norm of reason in the face of diversity.

Montaigne was the first to reject all these traditional solutions, leaving him with no alternative but to turn the mind away from the now impossible task of knowing the world and toward the more feasible one of knowing itself. Oddly enough this inward turn represents a potential advance toward historical knowing by emphasizing the uniqueness of the individual, which then might have been explained in terms of its development in relationship to its circumstances. Montaigne, however, viewed his individuality not as produced by his unique circumstances but simply as reflected in them; in other words, that he was a Catholic, Frenchman, and Gascon served to describe who he was but not to explain why he was that way. In the final analysis, the historical potential inherent in his individualizing view of the world was never realized, because hardly anyone had so strong a sense of self as to use it comfortably as a point of orientation amid complexity.

In response to the persistence of the problem, Descartes had no choice but to travel further down the route indicated by Montaigne, delving into the existential moment to isolate the existential act of thinking. On this basis he attempted to rebuild first the natural and then the moral sciences, purifying them of the errors born of custom and opinion, and molding them into the unified structure of human knowledge that was the true image of wisdom. The difficulties he encountered in this undertaking virtually precluded any further systematic attempts to resolve the problem of relativism, until the advent of an idea of historical development in the eighteenth century laid the foundation for the human sciences.

NOTES

1. Montaigne, *The Complete Essays of Montaigne,* trans. Donald M. Frame (Stanford: Stanford University Press, 1958), I, 1, 5 A: "Certes, c'est un sujet merveilleusement vain, divers, et ondoyant, que l'homme. Il est malaisé d'y fonder jugement constant et uniforme." In this and subsequent references to Montaigne, a letter (A, B, or C) following the page number indicates one of the three major textual strata: 1580, 1588, or 1595.

2. Montaigne, II, 1, 244 A: "Et se trouve autant de difference de nous à nous mesmes, que de nous à autruy."

3. Montaigne, II, 37, 598 A: "Et ne fut jamais au monde deux opinions pareilles, non plus que deux poils ou deux grains. Leur plus universelle qualité, c'est la diversité."

4. In general see Zachary S. Schiffman, "Montaigne and the Rise of Skepticism in Early Modern Europe: A Reappraisal," *Journal of the History of Ideas* 45 (1984): 499–516. For humanist education in general, see also Anthony Grafton and Lisa Jardine, *From Humanism to the Humanities: Education and the Liberal Arts in Fifteenth- and Sixteenth-Century Europe* (Cambridge, Mass.: Harvard University Press, 1986); and, for the mode of arguing *in utramque partem,* Victoria Kahn, *Rhetoric, Prudence, and Skepticism in the Renaissance* (Ithaca, N.Y.: Cornell University Press, 1985).

5. On French humanism in general, and legal humanism in particular, see J. G. A. Pocock, *The Ancient Constitution and the Feudal Law* (Cambridge: Cambridge University Press, 1957), chap. 1; Donald R. Kelley, *Foundations of Modern Historical Scholarship* (New York: Columbia University Press, 1970); Julian H. Franklin, *Jean Bodin and the Sixteenth-Century Revolution in the Methodology of Law and History* (New York: Columbia University Press, 1963); and George Huppert, *The Idea of Perfect History* (Urbana: University of Illinois Press, 1970).

6. François Hotman, *Antitribonian* (Paris, 1603; facsimile edition, Publications de l'Université de Saint-Etienne, 1980), 153–55.

7. On the paradox of the *Antitribonian*, see Ralph E. Giesey, "When and Why Hotman Wrote the *Francogallia*," *Bibliothèque d'humanisme et renaissance* 29 (1967): 596–604.

8. In general see the editors' introduction to François Hotman, *Francogallia*, ed. Ralph E. Giesey and J. H. M. Salmon (Cambridge: Cambridge University Press, 1972).

9. For a more detailed analysis of these authors, and bibliography of their work, see the following articles by Zachary S. Schiffman: "An Anatomy of the Historical Revolution in Renaissance France," *Renaissance Quarterly* 42 (1989): 507–33; and "Estienne Pasquier and the Problem of Historical Relativism," *Sixteenth Century Journal* 18 (1987): 505–17.

10. Estienne Pasquier, *Les Recherches de la France* (Paris: Laurent Sonnius, 1611), 421: "Tout homme de bon entendement, sans voir une histoire accomplie, peut presque imaginer de quelle humeur fut un peuple, lors qu'il lit ses anciens Statuts & Ordonnances, & d'un mesme jugement peut tirer en conjecture quelles furent ses loix, voyant sa maniere de vivre." My analysis of the work is based on the 1611 edition, comprising seven books, which was the last edition published during Pasquier's lifetime.

11. See *Les Oeuvres d'Estienne Pasquier*, 2 vols. (Amsterdam: Compagnie des Libraires Associez, 1723).

12. See Günter Abel, *Stoizismus und Frühe Neuzeit* (Berlin: Walter de Gruyter, 1978), which also provides a recent bibliography on Charron.

13. My analysis is based on the first edition of *De la sagesse*, published in 1601 and revised in 1604; see the three-volume variorum edition edited by Amaury Duval (Paris, 1824; reprint, Geneva: Slatkine Reprints, 1968); all references in the text are to the volume and page number of this edition.

14. Charron, 1:xliii: "la premiere et universelle loi et lumiere inspirée de Dieu."

15. See the extensive commentary in René Descartes, *Discours de la méthode*, ed. Etienne Gilson (Paris: J. Vrin, 1925).

16. Descartes, *Oeuvres de Descartes*, 12 vols., ed. C. Adam and P. Tannery (Paris: J. Vrin / C.N.R.S., 1964–76), 6:4: "J'ay esté nourri aux lettres dés mon enfance, et pource qu'on me persuadoit que, par leur moyen, on pouvoit acquerir une connaissance claire et assurée de tout ce qui est utile à la vie, j'avois un extreme desir de les apprendre."

17. I am here following the "existential" interpretation of the *cogito* put forth in John Cottingham, *Descartes* (Oxford: Blackwell, 1986), 35–42; for other interpretations, see Willis Doney, ed., *Descartes: A Collection of Critical Essays* (Garden City, N.Y.: Doubleday, 1967).

Unreadable Signs: Montaigne, Virtue, and the Interpretation of History

Timothy Hampton

The collapse of French humanism in the late sixteenth century is a phenomenon that raises important questions about the relationship of politics and culture. For the social and political disarray marking the last years of the sixteenth century led not only to the bankruptcy of the humanist idealism that had flourished at the court of Francis I. It also brought about essential redefinitions of the relationship between rhetoric and poetry, between intellectuals and political power, between learning and public action, and between the self, history, and society. These intellectual realignments and revisions of central tenets of humanist thought developed as responses to political chaos precisely because humanism was, in its very foundations, an intellectual movement concerned with the relationship between politics and culture. From the development of civic humanism in the Italian city-states of the fifteenth century, humanist culture had served a specifically political function. With the first generation of *quattrocento* humanists, humanist culture had attempted to break with what Hans Baron has called "the half-monastic *vita solitaria* ideals of the Trecento humanists."[1] By promoting the study of history and rhetoric, humanists such as Bruni and Salutati envisaged the creation of an educated *élite* prepared specifically for public service, for meeting the needs of a newly developing urban economy and society—an *élite* that would much later become the bureaucracy of the centralized absolutist state. As humanism was transferred to northern Europe in the early sixteenth century, the close relationship between the study of letters and public action remained one of its distinguishing characteristics. Erasmus, for example, attempted to link humanist political rhetoric and Christian piety, to bring the activities of secular rulers under the sway of moral strictures. In France, humanism allied itself with the nationalist projects of the Valois court. Guillaume Budé's *Institution du prince*, written in 1517 for Francis I, linked humanist ideals of public action to the promotion of a glorious and unified French state. And Rabelais's *Pantagruel* is itself on one level nothing but a fictionalized *speculum principis* that recounts the education of an aristocratic hero for public service.[2]

The principal humanist pedagogical vehicle for defining and promoting ideals of public action was the study of history. For humanist historiography—as, indeed, for all secular historiography up to Hegel—history is seen as a reservoir of models for present action. "History is philosophy teaching by example," ran the commonplace taken from Dionysius of Halicarnassus. The privileged element in this exemplar theory of history is the heroic or virtuous model from antiquity who offers the Renaissance reader an ideal image of the self. By studying the words and deeds of the illustrious ancients the Renaissance reader learns the lessons of the past and is formed upon tested images of excellence. Indeed, Montaigne himself reaffirms this central topos of humanist culture in his essay on the education of children (I, 26)—a text normally seen to be profoundly antihumanist in its pedagogical message. Montaigne recommends that the self can best be formed through the study of men. But he adds that the men who make the most profitable study are the illustrious men of the past: "In this association with men I mean to include, and foremost, those who live only in the memory of books. He will associate, by means of histories, with those great souls of the best ages."[3]

The image of the exemplary figure or "great soul" stands as the textual locus at which culture and politics, the moralistic interpretation of history and ideals of public action, overlap. As such, it offers a privileged topic for understanding the specific ramifications of the crisis of humanism. In the face of the political chaos of the civil wars, humanist culture, which had earlier sought confidently to influence political action, suddenly discovered the limits of its effectiveness. This bankruptcy of humanist idealism is registered in the changing representations of exemplary figures in late sixteenth-century texts. The text of Montaigne's *Essais* offers the richest meditation upon the relationship between public action and the difficulties of forming the self according to historical models. Yet, paradoxically, it is through his attempt to confront the difficulty of imitating models of comportment from antiquity that Montaigne opens up new articulations of the relationship between self and society and points, ultimately, to the new models of selfhood that define the seventeenth century.

The humanist promotion of heroic exemplars is essentially a problem in the interpretation of history. Most precisely it is a problem in the interpretation of a particular form of historical discourse—the exemplary biography. The heroic ancients come to the Renaissance as a series of narratives, as the *Lives* of Plutarch, Xenophon's *Cyropaedia,* and Petrarch's *De viris illustribus.* This structuring of the heroic life as a narrative is a central component in the promotion of the exemplary figure as a model of excellence. Thus, for example, the Spanish humanist Antonio de Guevara, whose vastly influential *Dial of Princes* was the favorite book of Michel de Montaigne's father, recommends that his reader place his own life in parallel with the story of Marcus Aurelius by taking the Roman as a guide in all activity: "as teacher in youth, as father in government, as leader in war, as guide on expeditions, as friend in labor, as example in virtue, as master in learning, as target in ambition and as rival in deeds."[4] The deeds of Marcus offer an entire course in moral philosophy that helps to mark the reader of history, to define him and place him in history and society.[5] The excellence of Marcus Aurelius, his status as a model of selfhood for the reader of Guevara's advice book, is contingent upon the coherence of his life as a unified representation of a personality through time. As Roland Barthes has observed, the "self" or "personality" of a character in literature is in fact merely a collection of features (what Barthes calls *semes*) that, when read chronologically, make up the character's biography. In Renaissance texts the moral homogeneity of these characteristics defines the exemplary value of the heroic figure. And this coherence is represented narratively, through a series of acts signifying virtue. If the ancient model's narrative fails to present a unified vision of consistently moral activity, his value for the reader of history is undermined.[6]

This tension between exemplarity and narrative, between a unified image of virtue and a life's story, marks the major advice tract of French humanism, Budé's *Institution du prince.* Budé focuses attention in the early portions of his text on the figure of Alexander the Great, whom he promotes as the model for his patron Francis I. Budé praises both Alexander and Francis in similar terms, urging the French king to imitate the great deeds of the Macedonian. Yet whereas Guevara's Marcus Aurelius offers a narrative of consistently virtuous actions, Alexander's story is fragmented by the moral heterogeneity of his acts: "Alexander was famous for many things, for after he had great fortune and conquered the kingdom of the Persians, he became intoxicated, so to speak, with the great delights of the Orient, and let himself go into other reprehensible novelties and barbarian insolences, leaving behind the customs of Greece and bringing about the degeneration of the house of Macedonia." The moral ambiguity of certain moments of Alexander's life, his weakness for what Budé euphemistically calls "the delights of the Orient," places the unity of his narrative and the integrity of his exemplary self in question.[7] Exemplary narrative is splintered into a group of discreet, morally heterogeneous moments; Alexander's inconsistent behavior renders problematic any attempt to promote him as a perfect model of kingship.

Budé's response to this breakdown in the coherence of the exemplary life is simply to change directions in the middle of his treatise and replace Alexander with Pompey as the ideal model for Francis I. This easy replacement of one model by another tells us much about the relationship between the interpretation of history and public life in the heyday of French humanism. Interpretation, as Jürgen Habermas has noted, must be grounded in a general agreement between members of a given interpretive community as to what constitutes meaning.[8] Thus, though Renaissance humanists may differ drastically in whether they believe Alexander's acts offer an adequate model of political virtue, they generally agree as to what constitutes an act and as to what they mean by virtuous action. It is this general agreement which makes possible socially productive hermeneutic activity. For Budé, Alexander and Pompey are virtually interchangeable, since both are read as examples of the same type of civic-oriented virtue. By the late sixteenth century, however, ideological struggle has rendered problematic the easy substitution of one model for another. Pompey's republicanism and Alexander's imperial conquests take on radically opposed political significance in the world of the civil wars.

This relationship between the interpretation of virtue and public action is confronted most directly by Montaigne in the essay entitled "Of Glory," which begins thus: "There is the name and thing. The name is a sound which designates and signifies the thing; the name is not a part of the thing or of the substance, it is an extraneous piece attached to the thing, and outside of it." This *res/verba* distinction recasts exemplarity as a problem of semiology.[9] The "name" is the exemplar's renown, and the "thing" is his virtuous soul, whose excellence must be signified by signs in the form of acts. The precise nature of the virtuous soul can only be known through the hero's actions, or what Montaigne elsewhere calls "effects." Acts are signifiers that represent the virtue of the great soul. And Montaigne's attack on heroic action stems from the fact that the relationship between act and virtue, between signifier and signified, is unstable.

This instability is caused by the fact that the relationship between act and virtue, between signifier and signified, may be mediated by a variety of factors that have nothing to do with heroism. Chief among these is the passion for glory, which can drive people to momentary achievements of excellence that misrepresent the true states of their souls. As Montaigne says in "Of Virtue," the deeds of the heroic ancients are frequently signs not of excellence but of a momentary passion that drives the self "out of itself."[10] Montaigne's disdain of public action not only flies in the face of humanist ideals; it effectively drives a wedge between virtue and act and undermines any attempt to read history as a series of moral examples. For once it becomes conceivable that virtuous acts may be committed merely to win glory, rather than from some foundation in the virtuous soul, the acts of all exemplars become open to suspicion. The force of public adulation and the desire for glory are so powerful that the most illustrious of exemplars may have only been acting with an eye to the crowd. This being the case, the reader of history can never know the true virtue of an exemplar from studying his illustrious deeds.

This divorce between act and virtue has a destructive effect upon the social body. For if virtue is only desirable for the glory that accompanies it, men would act virtuously only when in public, regulating "the movements of the soul" (II, 16, 470 A) only when in the presence of others. Given the fact that this danger results from the split between the public sphere and the private sphere, it is not surprising that Montaigne gives two distinct strategies, a public one and a private one, for dealing with the difficulty of interpreting exemplary acts. First he suggests that if princes see that the people praise the memory of Trajan and abominate the memory of Nero, the desire for glory may actually serve to keep men in line. The thought is expanded a few lines later to include not merely the powerful but all members of society: "Since men, because of their inadequacy, cannot be sufficiently paid with good money, let false be employed too" (477 A). The images of virtuous acts are cast as bad coins, which circulate to assure that people will fufill their proper function in society.

The notion that public virtue may be illusory is offset by the claim made three pages earlier that, if virtue cannot be unambiguously represented through public action, its presence may be seen elsewhere, in a zone free of the dynamics of exchange. In response to the ambiguity of public action Montaigne favors a turn to the private. The self's virtue becomes clear only in its relationship to itself, which takes preeminence over the relationship to others, who see only "events and external appearances" (474 A). In place of the false money that circulates to pacify the crowds, Montaigne seeks a true richness achieved through self-contemplation: "I do not care so much what I am to others as I care what I am to myself. I want to be rich by myself, not by borrowing" (474 A).

The skepticism toward public action seen in "Of Glory" reappears in "Of Cruelty" as a prolonged meditation on the problems of reading and the representation of exemplarity. In the opening passages of "Of Cruelty" Montaigne contrasts two types of virtue. He observes that, though there is clearly a difference between true virtue and mere goodness ("the inclinations toward goodness that are born in us," II, 11, 306 A), merely good acts frequently wear "the same face" as virtuous ones. Yet, he says, there is something more active about virtue that sets it apart from goodness: "Virtue means something greater and more active than letting oneself, by a happy disposition, be led gently and peacefully in the footsteps of reason."[11] The near-tautology of Montaigne's formulation (virtue injects something "active" into action) suggests from the outset the problems of reading acts as signs of virtue. He goes on to locate the expression of true virtue in struggle; one knows virtue is present in an act if the act evinces a struggle against vice, since "virtue...cannot be exercised without opposition."[12] Yet this struggle, which is the sign of virtue's presence, cannot be read in every virtuous act. For the perfectly virtuous soul—the soul of the exemplar—is perfect precisely because it suffers no stain of vice and thus reveals no sign of struggle. How then, Montaigne wonders, is one to know that the actions of perfectly virtuous characters like Socrates, "the most perfect that has come to my knowledge" (II, 11, 308 A), are truly virtuous? This recognition of the difficulty of reading exemplary acts leads to a conflict in Montaigne's text between what he "knows" about Socrates' excellence and what he can "read" within the limits of the interpretive model he is presenting.

Like a good humanist, Montaigne "knows" about Socrates' excellence ("I know this reason to be so powerful and so much the master in him"), yet he cannot imagine how that excellence might be represented in a specific action so that it might be read by another ("I can put nothing up against a virtue as lofty as his").[13] If virtue can only be represented by struggle with vice, Socrates' action would be marked by a legible trace of defeated vice. But no such trace can be seen. Socrates' deeds are, in this formulation, unreadable signs, gestures whose blankness prevents them from being interpreted as signifiers of the virtue that Montaigne, trained in the conventions of humanist moral philosophy as he was, "knows" to lie behind them.

As if in response to this dilemma, Montaigne immediately suggests another criterion for interpreting action. The truly perfect soul not only conquers vice as soon as it enters his soul; he actually enjoys his trials. Thus it is not struggle but pleasure that becomes the sign of absolute virtue: "If I assign (virtue) unpleasantness and difficulty as its necessary condition; then what will become of the virtue which has climbed so high that it not only despises pain but rejoices in it and feels tickled by the pangs of a bad colic . . . ?"[14] The sign of true virtue is no longer pain, but pleasure. The perfectly virtuous soul rises to a point at which the barbs of adversity are mere tickles.

But if the introduction of joy draws a line between the virtue of Socrates and that of lesser beings, it still offers no solid criterion for interpreting action. It merely adds another level of mediation, a new set of signs that point to other signs. For though absolute virtue produces joy, it does not follow that every manifestation of joy signifies the presence of absolute virtue. Montaigne is clearly aware of this problem, and he immediately tests his model for interpreting virtue on one of the *loci classici* of humanist moral philosophy—the suicide of Cato. He evokes the scene as a kind of visual tableau, and includes himself among its viewers. He begins with the affirmation that Cato actually enjoyed his pain: "Witness the younger Cato. When I see him dying and tearing out his entrails, I cannot be content to believe simply that he then had his soul totally free from disturbance and fright. . . . I believe without any doubt that he felt pleasure and bliss in so noble an action, and that he enjoyed himself more in it than in any other action of his life."[15] Yet through his "reading" of the scene, one can trace Montaigne's own uncertainty about pleasure as the sign of the presence of virtue:

[A] I seem to read in that action I know not what rejoicing of his soul, and an emotion of extraordinary pleasure and manly exultation, when it considered the nobility and sublimity of its enterprise: [B] *Prouder for having chosen death*. [A] This enterprise was not spurred by some hope of glory, as the plebeian and effeminate judgments of some men have judged (for that consideration is too base to touch a heart so noble, so lofty, and so unbending), but was undertaken for the beauty of the very thing in itself, which he, who handled the springs of it, saw much more clearly in its perfection than we can see it.[16]

Montaigne's doubts about Cato's motives are suggested by the very movement of his language. One slides almost imperceptibly from morality to aesthetics, from nobility to a beauty that is preeminently theatrical rather than ethical. By the end of the passage Cato's excellence seems to stem from a peculiar kind of Pygmalionism, in which the artist falls in love with his creation *before* he creates it. In place of the typical Stoic death, unreadable in its blankness, we are now given a portrait of a dying soul rapt in a beatific vision of its own creation. Cato's greatest act is to have created a death admirable "for the beauty of the very thing in itself."

At the center of this depiction of Cato as an admirer of beauty, as a kind of stage manager who manipulates the drama of his suicide, Montaigne emphasizes the difficulty of interpretation through the contrast between Cato's "manly exultations" and the "plebeian and effeminate judgments" of those who see Cato's joy as the sign of a show-off in search of glory. In contrast to these skeptic interpreters whom he himself has introduced, he affirms his confidence in the hero's excellence:

if his goodness, which made him embrace the public advantage more than his own, did not hold me in check, I should easily fall into this opinion, that he was grateful to fortune for having put his virtue to so beautiful a test and for having favored that brigand [Caesar] in treading underfoot the ancient liberty of his country.[17]

Montaigne's suspicion toward the reading of history leads him to wonder if Cato might not have been pleased at the opportunity that Caesar's destruction of the Roman republic offered for a noble death. The crisis of public life experienced by Montaigne's age returns obliquely here, through Cato's desire to express private nobility, a desire that edges toward the negligence of public duty. Yet what prevents Montaigne from siding with the cynics who condemn the hero is Cato's "goodness, which made him embrace the public advantage more than his own." The appearance of the term *goodness* is striking, for it recalls the essay's first sentence, where virtue and goodness were set in opposition. Virtue was seen as active, whereas goodness simply implied a complexion that steered one away from vice. Montaigne's initial inquietude about this opposition stemmed from the fact that virtue and goodness show the same face to the world. Here, however, when the virtue of the most excellent exemplar's death is in question, goodness reemerges as the criterion upon which to base an interpretation of his death. If Montaigne earlier rejected a model of exemplary action based upon struggle, suggesting that struggle always tainted virtue with an element of vice, he here seems to suggest that perfect virtue—a virtue beyond the reach of vicious contamination—can only be decisively read from the perspective of goodness. The difficulty of interpreting heroic action has led him to collapse two opposing categories that he "knows" to be different.

What is more important than the philosophical paradox here, however, is that the shift to goodness takes us both from private action back to public action and from the isolated moment of the suicide back to the heroic life as narrative. To be certain of Cato's commitment to individual conscience one must be aware of his *habitual* preference for the public good over his private interests. One must insert the moment of death into a sequence of signs or acts signifying an entire identity. The crisis of public life and the disintegration of selfhood are both resolved in the fantasy of Cato's suicide. The fragmentation of the heroic life, suggested both by Budé's anxiety over the figure of Alexander and Montaigne's own assertion in "De la vertu" that heroism is the product of isolated moments during which we are "out of ourselves," is forestalled here, as Montaigne reintegrates the heroic death and the heroic life by insisting that they must be understood together. As Montaigne says a moment later, "when we judge a particular action we must consider many circumstances and the whole man who performed it, before we baptize it" (311 A).

Obviously, this integration of life and death is not as easy to achieve as Montaigne might wish it to be. His very formulation suggests the focus of the problem. Normally, it is not acts that one "baptizes," but "the whole man." Indeed, one might object that the reader of Cato is faced with a vicious hermeneutic circle, since the privileged moment of death can only be interpreted when seen against the "tendency" of a life—itself composed of a sequence of individual acts, each of which must be interpreted in the same fashion as the death. These difficulties, to be sure, are skirted by the death of Cato—a relatively simple example, since the outward appearence of his death seems consistent with his general comportment. A more difficult case would be a heroic death that seemed out of step with the rest of the life. This problem is in fact suggested by the line from Horace inserted for the 1588 edition into the depiction of the scene: *"Prouder for having chosen death"* (*"Deliberata morte ferocior"*). The allusion is to Cleopatra, who, in 1.37 of the *Odes,* attempts to redeem her reprehensible life with a noble death. Cleopatra seems to illustrate Montaigne's claim that heroism takes us "out of ourselves," since Horace's ode asserts that this most feminine of ancient figures actually took leave of her femininity at the moment of death: "Yet she, seeking to die a nobler death, showed for the dagger's point no woman's fear."[18] Thus if Montaigne seems to base an interpretation of Cato's death upon the strength of his "goodness"—i.e., upon the general tendency of his life—the line from Horace introduced in the B level of the text complicates that model. Using the life to interpret the death may not be as easy as first supposed.

In the absence of any firm phenomenological ground for interpreting heroic action, Montaigne slips, immediately following the depiction of Cato's suicide, into an aesthetic register. An addition made for the final version of the text seems to fix interpretation once and for all by asserting that a principle of coherence, a kind of moral equivalent of the Aristotelian theory of plot, can ground judgment: "Philosophy has given me the pleasure of judging that so beautiful an action would have been indecently located in any other life than Cato's, and that it belonged to his alone to end thus" (309 C). Montaigne's philosophy answers the "extraordinary pleasure" experienced by Cato at death with the "pleasure" of a doctrine that asserts the essential unity of the beautiful life and the beautiful death. The exemplary life must form a "decent" unified whole with a beginning, a middle, and an end: "I always interpret the death by the life. And if they tell me of a death strong in appearance, attached to a feeble life, I maintain that it is produced by a feeble cause corresponding with the life." In this formulation the self must be coherent ("Every death *must* be the same as the life"). The strong death turns out to be only "strong in appearance." By an interpretation that insists upon the coherence between life and death, an overarching unity is imposed upon the signs constituting the life. A virtuous "self" is either affirmed or denied, regardless of evidence to the contrary adduced by particular acts. By imposing this totality through a call to "decency" (Montaigne's own term) or decorum, instead of through reference to a specific illustration of a consistently moral life lived in history (as Budé tried to do with his use of Alexander), Montaigne both saves and loses exemplarity. He disregards the semantic slipperiness of the act, in order to preserve the coherence of the life and hence the myth of the virtuous man.

This reintegration of the exemplary life as narrative is, however, temporary. Montaigne changes registers a moment later, as he turns from Cato back to the figure of Socrates. He describes the philosopher's last days in terms that are familiar by now, claiming that Socrates' response to his trials went beyond mere constancy to joy. But the moment in Socrates' life that Montaigne picks to illustrate this joy contrasts with the pathetic scene of Cato's self-immolation. He pictures Socrates scratching his leg at the moment his chains are removed:

[C] By that quiver of pleasure that he feels in scratching his leg after the irons were off, does he not betray a like sweetness and joy in his soul at being unfettered by past discomforts and prepared to enter into the knowledge of things to come? [A] Cato will pardon me, if he please; his death is more tragic and tense, but this one is still, I know not how, more beautiful.[19]

It is curious that, while we see Cato tearing out his entrails, we see Socrates in quite a different situation. Montaigne has carefully placed this moment of pleasure between two famous tableaux in the life of Socrates—the trial and the drinking of the hemlock. Indeed, unlike the protracted death of Cato, with its rapture and fascination, this scratch is over as soon as it begins. It seems to satisfy Montaigne's need for an exemplary moment removed from the public eye. For certainly one would be hard put to misinterpret Socrates' reflex as a publicity stunt aimed at the promotion of glory. In fact, one would be hard put to interpret it at all.

Yet Montaigne does just that. First, he draws a parallel between body and soul in which it is unclear whether corporeal pleasure signifies spiritual pleasure or spiritual pleasure actually originates in corporeal pleasure. Thus far he follows Plato's presentation of the same anecdote in the *Phaedo*. Yet he departs from Plato in the second half of the sentence added for the C version. Montaigne shifts to an allegory that reinscribes the isolated and seemingly insignificant gesture of Socrates into a narrative movement. At the moment of exemplary action, the recourse to Platonic allegory takes us out of the realm of history altogether. The body's release from its irons prefigures the soul's imminent release from the body and from life as it enters into the knowledge of things to come.

This interpretation of Socrates' scratch offers a rare glimpse of a Platonism that Montaigne usually avoids, averse as he is to all forms of mysticism. Allegorical discourse is generally absent from the text of the *Essais*, and might even be said to run counter to its habitual strategies of signification. Yet Montaigne enlists allegory here as a rhetorical solution to the interpretive problem explored throughout the opening pages of "Of Cruelty." We see here the integration of the great life and the great death, framed by Montaigne in aesthetic terms a moment ago. If the narrative of the heroic life is a journey of the soul, then the life has a direction, and even the most offhand gesture becomes a sign of greater purpose. Platonic allegory offers a momentary rhetorical resolution to the problem of working out a model for interpreting the deeds of the ancients.

The fragility of the resolution is suggested by the fact that Montaigne immediately turns from exemplarity to an analysis of ethical action, which, he asserts, can be furthered more easily through the elimination of vice than the promotion of virtue. Vice, he suggests, is a "simpler" subject than virtue, since the virtuous man acts with all of his virtues in consort, whereas the vicious man is motivated by one vice at a time. The question of vice permits Montaigne to come at last to the theme announced in his title. The greatest vice, he says, is cruelty ("Among other vices, I cruelly hate cruelty," II, 11, 313 A). And the most striking and needless illustration of cruelty is that stylized training exercise for the rigors of true battle, the hunt. As we pass from a discussion of virtue to a discussion of vice we move from the murder of the self as a heroic act to the murder of animals, from a crime against God and nature to nature's actual destruction as the test of heroic spirit. Yet all conventional descriptions of the hunt as the domestic ritual through which martial virtue is demonstrated are undercut by Montaigne. The hunt is figured here as the ceremony of a type of lust. If the passion for glory can lead men to feign virtue, the excitement of the hunt can lead the hunter to lose control of his faculties. The traditional aristocratic pastimes—love and war—are compared as we learn that the lust for blood can possess the hunter more powerfully than sexual desire. Moreover, in the heat of the chase men are driven to commit the worst of offenses—cruelty toward the innocent. If Montaigne took "pleasure" in the contemplation of Cato's suicide, he expresses his "displeasure" at the spectacle of the murder of innocent beasts.

There is more to this condemnation than mere eccentric resistance to fashion. Montaigne's interjection of a line from Virgil describing Ascanius's murder of the stag to set off the war over Italy raises the stakes of the discussion, suggesting that the harmless beasts whose part he takes may themselves be figures for the victims of the civil wars, which he points to as the source of "incredible examples" of cruelty. This condemnation of murder is extended a few lines later, as cynegetic cruelty becomes the sign of a generally bloodthirsty character and cruelty turns out to be a component of the human soul: "Nature herself, I fear, attaches to man some instinct for inhumanity" (316 B).

The corrective to this naturally vicious instinct is a recognition of the ethical social contract linking beast and man. Montaigne develops this solution on the essay's last page, arguing that men are attached to animals through a certain respect and a general human duty. Justice is owed to men, and kindness to others, since a mutual obligation connects man and animal. Men's natural "instinct to inhumanity" can only be overcome by a "general duty of humanity" that acknowledges the mutual obligations of man and beast within the larger scheme of nature. A recognition of the other's right to exist will put a stop to the exercise of cruelty—against both men and beasts.

The close of "Of Cruelty" certainly stands as one of the most intensely ethical moments in the *Essais*. Its importance for our concerns lies in the fact that the model of transformation and correction it presents dispenses with both exemplarity and the notion of virtue explored in the essay's first passages. Man and beast are now seen as linked through their common relationship to nature. The essay's unfolding development from an analysis of the representation of *virtue* to a recognition of the power of *nature* may be seen as an attempt to save ethical action in the face of the crisis in reading history, a crisis illustrated by the opening pages. The humanist understanding of exemplarity, in which model and imitator share a common historical tradition, has been exploded by the fragmentation of French political and social life. Through the working out of

"Of Cruelty," an extraordinary conceptual shift occurs. Nature emerges to supplant virtue as that which defines the morality of humanity action.[20]

The stakes of this rejection of traditional humanist virtue and of narrative can best be seen in "Of Experience," the last chapter of the *Essais*. For it is here that Montaigne addresses the questions of his own life as narrative and of his own exemplarity. Near the center of "Of Experience" Montaigne points out that as he grows older he turns increasingly from history and the world around him to focus on himself. True education, he says, takes place not through "foreign examples" but through study of the self's example to itself. This affirmation of self-reliance has both political and philosophical implications. It appears at the end of a long discussion of the difficulty of personal independence amid the dangers of the civil wars, suggesting the importance of placing and defining a self now largely cast loose from the moorings provided by common tradition and political consensus. Skeptical of the value of ancient precedent and horrified by the chaos of his age, Montaigne attempts to work out a model of self-education in which the present self is to learn from its own past mistakes. If the self contemplates its past attentively, that past will be seen to contain a reservoir of negative images to be avoided: "He who calls back to mind the excess of his past anger, and how far this fever carried him away, sees the ugliness of this passion better than in Aristotle, and conceives a more justified hatred of it."[21] The humanist privileging of historical example over philosophical precept reappears here, but in a totally private context. When neither history nor society can educate, life in perilous times demands that the self teach itself. The act as sign returns, disposed upon a temporal axis defining the self's relationship to its own history.

But the very temporal structure, the narrative movement, of this model proves a problem. Not only does it lead to an ever-more-constricted vision of the self's capacity for self-transformation, but, more important, it relies upon memory, Montaigne's weakest faculty. For the man with a bad memory, personal history is no easier to judge than ancient history:

> The slips that my memory has made so often, even when it reassures me most about itself, are not vainly lost on me; there is no use in her swearing to me now and assuring me, I shake my ears. The first opposition offered to her testimony puts me in suspense, and I would

not dare trust her in any weighty matter, or guarantee her in another person's affairs.[22]

Even at the moment Montaigne's memory tries to convince him of its authority he knows that it is wrong, since he recalls all of the times that it has deceived him. Moreover, this very act of recalling is itself paradoxical, since it may be yet another mistake of memory. Unable to trust his memory, Montaigne is at the mercy of the opinions of others, whom he makes it his practice to mistrust. He is left with no solid ground upon which to rest in "weighty" matters.

Yet the failure of this temporal model of self-exemplarity opens up the possibility for affirming a model that stands beyond the dynamics of history. For though Montaigne's memory is bad, he points out that its very weakness is a strength saving him from reliance upon the judgment of others, since what he does from a bad memory they do through ill will ("what I do for lack of memory, others do still more often for lack of good faith" [822 B]). Montaigne escapes the deleterious effects of his bad memory and the influence of others through the strength of his "faith." Unlike those around him, who act from bad faith, he merely acts from bad memory, and hence from good faith (recalling the "good faith" of his book's first sentence). This places him once again on firm ground.

The precise nature of this "faith" becomes clear a moment later, as Montaigne turns to praise his own judgment, which, he says, holds "a magisterial seat" and remains uncorrupted by the vicious forces around it. Self-correction cedes to the reaffirmation of autonomy, as Montaigne replaces anxiety toward others with friendship toward himself. The emphasis upon judgment removes Montaigne from the model, defined a moment ago, of selfhood as narrative. For judgment is that faculty that is both constantly tested against the world (and the self) and inherent in Montaigne's aristocratic nature. Exemplarity as narrative is diffused into an image of an ahistorical "self" standing free of the sum of its actions: "Not only do I find it hard to link our actions with one another, but each one separately I find hard to designate properly by some principal characteristic, so two-sided and motley do they seem in different lights."[23]

Through a constant dialectic between public and private Montaigne responds to the crisis of humanist culture with an image of the self that stands beyond the narrative tradition of exemplary biography and the myth of the great man. Yet the very precariousness of Montaigne's model of the self, with its famous instability and contradictions, is itself the product of his attempt to define the relationship between private virtue and public action through a meditation upon the humanist topos of history as guide for action. Moreover, it is precisely the tension between public and private, between past and present, which Montaigne so productively explores in the complex rhetoric of "Of Cruelty" and "Of Experience," that those who follow in his footsteps will attempt to reduce. Thus, for example, his disciple Pierre Charron claims that his master's project of studying the self—set forth in the passage just cited from "Of Experience"—is the guiding principle of his own *De la sagesse*. Near the outset of his book he describes his enterprise by quoting (without attribution of course) both Montaigne's attempt to work out a model in which the self could be its own example and his claim that by remembering past errors one can correct the self.[24] Yet this very model, which was rejected by Montaigne on the grounds that it made him vulnerable to the vicious motives of those around him, is taken as a path to self-knowledge by Charron. *De la sagesse* presents a world in which questions of moral philosophy are asked in solitude, with little attention to the relationship between virtue and the public sphere. Where Montaigne attempts to define the self in history by appropriating humanist ideals of public virtue, Charron rejects the public sphere altogether.

Yet whereas Charron seeks to remove exemplarity from the realm of politics and the sphere of public action by promoting an image of the isolated individual who is his own exemplar, Corneille will move, three decades later in *Le Cid*, in the opposite direction by redefining exemplarity in terms which place it at the service of political absolutism. The quarrel between Don Gomès and Rodrigue's father, Don Diègue, which sets Corneille's drama in motion, is a courtier's dispute over the king's choice of who is to be the tutor to his son. Though the king has chosen Don Diègue, Don Gomès asserts that the post should have been his. Their argument appropriates the humanist discourse of exemplarity, as each man claims to be the hero whose deeds the young prince would most benefit from emulating. Don Gomès ironically taunts the aging Don Diègue, urging him to show the young prince how to act:

> Show him how to harden himself against pain, how to render himself unequalled in the profession of Mars, how to pass entire days and nights on horseback, how to rest at arms, how to capture a fortress

and make himself the sole reason for a victory. Teach him by example and make him perfect, explaining your lessons to him by your acts.[25]

Don Diègue's response to this challenge is simply to point out that the young prince can read history: "To learn from example, to spite envy, he will simply read the story of my life."[26] Don Gomès replies that living examples are more potent than written ones, and that he is still young enough to teach the prince by taking him into the field.

The conflict between past history and present history, between a written model and a living one, reaches its apogee when Don Gomès challenges Don Diègue to a duel. Don Diègue's awareness of his weakness provokes his famous soliloquy on the misery of old age: "O rage! o despair! o old age my enemy! Have I thus lived this long in order to suffer infamy? And did I age in martial labors in order to see my laurel crown branded with shame?"[27] What is remarkable in this speech is the way in which Corneille blends the humanist concern for the consistency of the exemplary figure with the ideology of honor taken from his Spanish source material. The heroic figure of humanism, whose deeds must be consistently virtuous if his self is to be exemplary, has been metamorphosed here into the Spanish Don, whose single moment of disgrace is enough to undermine his hard-won honor. A moment of weakness late in life undercuts the exemplary power and coherence of "the story of my life."

Don Diègue's solution to his problem is to turn to his son Rodrigue, who, as the valiant son of a valiant father, is guided by the blood of a warrior and dedicated to serving the king. The scandal of old age is redeemed by generational succession, which in turn assures national security. The family of Don Diègue thus offers the reader of the play two types of exemplarity: that of the father, set down in written history as "the story of my life," and that of the son, demonstrated in action. Don Gomès is eventually killed by Rodrigue, not merely because Rodrigue is the better swordsman, but because he, Don Gomès, has questioned the king's choice of Don Diègue as the tutor for his son. Thus Corneille's play reveals the ideological importance of exemplary figures and the importance of narrative in defining excellence. Yet Corneille offsets the fragmentation of exemplary narrative seen in Montaigne through an appeal to family continuity and the excellence of the warrior caste. By copying his father's valor and avenging his disgrace Don Rodrigue effectively extends his narrative, transforming it into an unbroken story of exemplary excellence. Corneille recuperates exemplarity and rewrites virtue as submission to royal authority.

Corneille's redemption of exemplarity stands in direct contrast with Montaigne's complex meditation on the difficulty of reading the words and deeds of heroic figures as models for virtuous action. Montaigne's rumination on the question of appropriating models of comportment from antiquity unfolds within the general problematic of the crisis of public life in late sixteenth-century France. The interpretive problem produced by the difficulty of reading public action as virtuous action is registered in Montaigne's anxiety over the narrative structure of the exemplary life. Yet this very collapse of narrative as a model of selfhood is itself the occasion for an articulation of a newly independent self, free of the contingencies of history and narrative. This liberation of the self from narrative is, however, only temporary. The history of the seventeenth century is the history of the birth of a new model of selfhood, that of the bourgeois self, which possesses its own autonomy and defines its authority not through ideals of public action and through reference to figures such as Cato and Socrates, but through its relationship to itself. This new model of the self will in turn find its narrative not in the epic or the heroic biography, but in the novel. Montaigne's *Essais* constitute a pivotal moment in the genesis of this new model of selfhood. Working from within a humanist vocabulary, the *Essais* redistribute the terms of humanist discourse and mark the passage from aristocratic humanist faith in history to bourgeois notions of autonomy, turning the tomb of humanism into the cradle of modernity.[28]

NOTES

1. Hans Baron, *The Crisis of the Early Italian Renaissance* (Princeton, N.J.: Princeton University Press, 1966), 112. Baron's study remains the classic description of the break between the humanism of figures such as Petrarch and Boccaccio and the civic humanism of the fifteenth century.

2. On the traditions of humanist pedagogy, see Eugenio Garin, *L'educazione in Europa, 1400–1600* (Bari: Laterza, 1957); as well as, more recently, Anthony Grafton and Lisa Jardine, *From Humanism to the Humanities: Education and the Liberal Arts in Fifteenth- and Sixteenth-Century Europe* (Cambridge, Mass.: Harvard University Press, 1986). On Erasmus's advice literature and its political importance, see James Tracy, *The Politics of Erasmus* (Toronto: University of

Toronto Press, 1978), chap. 1; and J. H. Hexter, *The Vision of Politics on the Eve of the Reformation* (New York: Basic Books, 1973). I have dealt with the implications of Budé's advice to Francis I in "Guillaume Budé Dedicates His *Institution of the Prince* to Francis I," in *A New History of French Literature*, ed. Denis Hollier (Cambridge, Mass.: Harvard University Press, 1989). For a full-scale study of the problems addressed in this essay, see Timothy Hampton, *Writing from History: The Rhetoric of Exemplarity in Renaissance Literature* (Ithaca, N.Y.: Cornell University Press, 1990).

3. Montaigne, *The Complete Essays of Montaigne*, trans. Donald M. Frame (Stanford: Stanford University Press, 1958), I, 26, 115 A: "En cette practique des hommes, j'entends y comprendre, et principalement, ceux qui ne vivent qu'en la memoire des livres. Il practiquera, par le moyen des histoires, ces grandes ames des meilleurs siecles." In this and subsequent references to Montaigne, a letter (A, B, or C) following the page number indicates one of the three major textual strata: 1580, 1588, or 1595. For background on the exemplar theory of history, see George H. Nadel, "Philosophy of History before Historicism," *History and Theory* 3, no. 3 (1964): 291–315, as well as Reinhart Koselleck, "*Historia Magistra Vitae:* Über die Auflösung des Topos im Horizont neuzeitlich bewegter Geschichte," in *Natur und Geschichte: Karl Löwith zum 70. Geburtstag* (Stuttgart: W. Kohlhammer Verlag, 1976), 196–219; and Myron P. Gilmore, "The Renaissance Conception of the Lessons of History," *Facets of the Renaissance*, ed. W. H. Werkmeister (New York: Harper and Row, 1959), 71–101.

4. I translate from the edition of the *Reloj de príncipes* prepared by Angel Rosenblat (Madrid: Signo, 1936), 21. Montaigne notes his father's fondness for this text in "Of Drunkenness."

5. My use of the masculine pronoun to refer to the reader of history and philosophy throughout this essay is not intended to suggest that the reading subject is male. Rather, it is designed to reflect a historical reality in which the vast majority of students were men. Indeed, since the promotion of exemplary figures is an ideological operation for "marking" or defining the subject, the question of which models are presented to which readers is a crucially important one. My aim here is simply to offer steps to an understanding of how exemplary figures function, or don't function, in late Renaissance texts.

6. On the semiotic construction of character see Roland Barthes, *S/Z*, trans. Richard Miller (New York: Hill and Wang, 1974), 67ff., as well as Kenneth Burke's essay "What are Signs of What? A Theory of Entitlement," in his *Language as Symbolic Action* (Berkeley: University of California Press, 1966), 359–79.

7. I translate from Claude Bontems's edition of the *Institution du prince*, in his *Le Prince dans la France des XVIe et XVIIe siècles* (Paris: Presses Universitaires de France, 1965), 129. For a discussion of Budé's humanism, see

David O. McNeil's *Guillaume Budé and Humanism in the Reign of Francis I* (Geneva: Droz, 1975). On the importance of the coherence of the heroic life for exemplarity, see Aristotle, *Nichomachean Ethics*, 1.7.

8. See Jürgen Habermas, *Knowledge and Human Interests*, trans. Jeremy J. Shapiro (Boston: Beacon Press, 1971), 71ff., as well as Habermas's reply to Hans-Georg Gadamer in "Der Universalitätsanspruch der Hermeneutik," in *Hermeneutik und Ideologiekritik,* ed. Habermas et al. (Frankfurt: Suhrkamp, 1975), 120–59.

9. Montaigne, II, 16, 468 A: "Il y a le nom et la chose: le nom, c'est une voix qui remerque et signifie la chose; le nom, ce n'est pas une partie de la chose ny de la substance, c'est une piece estrangere joincte à la chose, et hors d'elle." For a detailed analysis of "Of Glory" with reference to philosophical debates over nominalism, see Antoine Compagnon, *Nous, Michel de Montaigne* (Paris: Editions du Seuil, 1980), 120ff. On military glory generally in Montaigne's work, see James J. Supple, *Arms versus Letters: The Military and Literary Ideals in the "Essais" of Montaigne* (Oxford: Clarendon Press, 1984). Other important discussions of the essay can be found in François Rigolot's *Poétique et Onomastique* (Geneva: Droz, 1977), 235–37, and in Hugo Friedrich's *Montaigne*, trans. R. Rovini (Paris: Gallimard, 1968), 173ff. On the problem of Montaigne's relationship to public life, see Timothy J. Reiss, "Montaigne and the Subject of Polity," *Literary Theory / Renaissance Texts,* ed. Patricia Parker and David Quint (Baltimore, Md.: Johns Hopkins University Press, 1986), 115–49.

10. See Montaigne, II, 29, 533 A: "Et ès vies de ces heros du temps passé, il y a quelque fois des traits miraculeux et qui semblent de bien loing surpasser nos forces naturelles.... Il nous eschoit à nous mesmes... d'eslancer par fois nostre ame, esveillée par les discours ou exemples d'autruy, bien loing au delà de son ordinaire; mais c'est une espece de passion qui la pousse et agite, et qui la ravit aucunement hors de soy."

11. Montaigne, II, 11, 306 A: "Mais la vertu sonne je ne sçay quoy de plus grand et de plus actif que de se laisser, par une heureuse complexion, doucement et paisiblement conduire à la suite de la raison."

12. Montaigne, II, 11, 307 A: "il semble que le nom de la vertu presuppose de la difficulté et du contraste, et qu'elle ne peut s'exercer sans partie."

13. See Montaigne, II, 11, 308 A: "Socrates, qui est la plus parfaicte qui soit venuë à ma conoissance, seroit, à mon compte, une ame de peu de recommandation; car je ne puis concevoir en ce personnage là aucun effort de vitieuse concupiscence. Au train de sa vertu, je n'y puis imaginer aucune difficulté et aucune contrainte; je connoy sa raison si puissante et si maistresse chez luy qu'elle n'eust jamais donné moyen à un appetit vitieux seulement de naistre. A une vertu si eslevée que la sienne, je ne puis rien mettre en teste."

14. Montaigne, II, 11, 308 A: "si je luy donne pour son object necessaire l'aspreté et la difficulté: que deviendra la vertu qui sera montée à tel point que

de non seulement mespriser la douleur, mais de s'en esjoüyr et de se faire chatouiller aux pointes d'une forte colique."

15. Montaigne, II, 11, 308–9 A: "Temoing le jeune Caton. Quand je le voy mourir et se deschirer les entrailles, je ne me puis contenter de croire simplement qu'il eust lors son ame exempte totalement de trouble et d'effroy.... Je croy sans doubte qu'il sentit du plaisir et de la volupté en une si noble action, et qu'il s'y agrea plus qu'en autre de celles de sa vie."

16. Montaigne, II, 11, 309: "Il me semble lire en cette action je ne sçay quelle esjouissance de son ame, et une émotion de plaisir extraordinaire et d'une volupté virile, lorsqu'elle consideroit la noblesse et hauteur de son entreprise: [B] *Deliberata morte ferocior,* [A] non pas esquisée par quelque esperance de gloire, comme les jugemens populaires et effeminez d'aucuns hommes ont jugé, car cette consideration est trop basse pour toucher un coeur si genereux, si hautain et si roide; mais pour la beauté de la chose mesme en soy: laquelle il voyoit bien plus à clair et en sa perfection, lui qui en manioit les ressorts, que nous ne pouvons faire."

17. Montaigne, II, 11, 309 A: "Et si la bonté qui luy faisoit embrasser les commoditez publiques plus que les siennes ne me tenoit en bride, je tomberois aiséement en cette opinion, qu'il sçavoit bon gré à la fortune d'avoir mis sa vertu à une si belle espreuve, et d'avoir favorisée ce brigand [César] à fouler aux pieds l'ancienne liberté de sa patrie."

18. I cite, for both text and translation, C. E. Bennett's edition of Horace's works in the Loeb Classical Library (London: Heinemann, 1978): "quae generosius / perire quarens nec muliebriter / expavit ensem."

19. Montaigne, II, 11, 310: "[C] A ce tresaillir, du plaisir qu'il sent à gratter sa jambe après que les fers en furent hors, accuse il pas une pareille douceur et joye en son ame, pour estre desenforgée des incommodités passées, et à mesme d'entrer en cognoissance des choses à venir? [A] Caton me pardonnera, s'il luy plaist; sa mort est plus tragique et plus tendue, mais cette-cy est encore, je ne sçay comment, plus belle." On the central function of bodily actions as signs of the soul in Stoicism, see Victoria Kahn, *Rhetoric, Prudence, and Skepticism in the Renaissance* (Ithaca, N.Y.: Cornell University Press, 1985), 118ff.

20. On the ethical implications of this essay, see Phillip P. Hallie, "The Ethics of Montaigne's 'De la cruauté,'" in *O un amy: Essays on Montaigne in Honor of Donald M. Frame,* ed. Raymond C. La Charité (Lexington, Ky.: French Forum, 1977), 156–71. On the interrelationship between human death and animal death, see Claude Blum, "La mort des hommes et la mort des bestes dans les *Essais* de Montaigne: sur les fonctions paradigmatiques des deux exemples," *French Forum* 5 (1980): 3–13.

21. Montaigne, II, 12, 822 B: "Qui remet en sa memoire l'excez de sa cholere passée, et jusques où cette fièvre l'emporta, voit la laideur de cette passion mieux que dans Aristote, et en conçoit une haine plus juste."

22. Montaigne, II, 12, 822 B: "Les faux pas que ma memoire m'a fait si

souvant, lors mesme qu'elle s'asseure le plus de soy, ne se sont pas inutilement perduz; elle a beau me jurer à cette heure et m'asseurer, je secoüe les oreilles; la premiere opposition qu'on faict à son tesmoignage me met en suspens, et n'oserois me fier d'elle en chose de poix, ni la garentir sur le faict d'autruy."

23. Montaigne, III, 13, 824–25 B: "Non seulement je trouve mal-aisé d'attacher nos actions les unes aux autres, mais chacune à part soy je trouve mal-aysé de la designer proprement par quelque qualité principalle, tant elles sont doubles et bigarrées à divers lustres." On Montaigne's understanding of judgment see Raymond C. La Charité, *The Concept of Judgment in Montaigne* (The Hague: Martin Nijhoff, 1968). On Montaigne's self-exemplarity see Marcel Gutwirth, *Michel de Montaigne ou le pari d'exemplarité* (Montreal: Presses Universitaires de Montréal, 1977).

24. Charron, *De la sagesse* (Paris, 1621), 27: "Pour devenir sage et mener une vie plus reglé et plus douce, il ne faut point d'instruction d'ailleurs, que de nous. ... Qui remet en sa memoire et remarque bien l'excez de sa cholere passee, jusques ou ceste figure l'a emporté, verra mieux beaucoup la laideur de ceste passion, et en aura horreur et hayne plus juste, que de tout ce qu'en disent Aristote et Platon, et ainsi de toutes les autres passions, et de tous les branles et mouvements de son ame." It is interesting that Charron groups Plato and Aristotle together as moral philosophers to be rejected, and that he recasts Montaigne's "fever" of anger as the "figure" of anger.

25. Corneille, *Le Cid,* in *Oeuvres complètes,* ed. André Stegmann (Paris: Editions du Seuil, 1963), ll. 178–84: "Montrez-lui comme il faut s'endurcir à la peine, / Dans le métier de Mars se rendre sans égal, / Passer les jours entiers et les nuits à cheval, / Reposer tout armé, forcer une muraille / Et ne devoir qu'à soi le gain d'une bataille. / Instruisez-le d'exemple, et rendez-le parfait, / Expliquant à ses yeux vos leçons par l'effet." The translation is mine.

26. Corneille, ll. 185–86: "Pour s'instruire d'exemple, en dépit de l'envie, / Il lira seulement l'histoire de ma vie."

27. Corneille, ll. 237–40: "O rage! ô désespoir! ô vieillesse ennemie! / N'ai-je donc tant vécu que pour cette infamie / Et ne suis-je blanchi dans les travaux guerriers / Que pour voir en un jour flétrir tant de lauriers?"

28. For analyses of the seventeenth-century transformations of humanist traditions, see Kahn's *Rhetoric, Prudence, and Skepticism;* and Timothy J. Reiss's *The Discourse of Modernism* (Ithaca, N.Y.: Cornell University Press, 1982), chaps. 4–8; as well as, in a specifically English context, John G. A. Pocock's *The Ancient Constitution and the Feudal Law* (New York: Norton, 1967).

Writing the Crisis Differently: Ronsard's *Discours* and Montaigne's *Essais*

François Rigolot

It is not always easy to define the attitude of Renaissance writers toward the bloody civil wars between Catholics and Protestants, which began in France around 1560. Confronted by the political and religious turmoil ("troubles") of their time, Pierre de Ronsard and Michel de Montaigne were obligated, in varying degrees, to declare themselves openly, reaffirming their loyalty to the prince and condemning the social disorders resulting from the innovations of the Reformers. For them, the political order was inextricably linked to ancestral values and to monarchy; it was unthinkable that it be otherwise—unless one wished to see French society in anarchy and its cultural heritage destroyed.[1]

To be sure, both Ronsard and Montaigne regretted what they saw as a profound crisis in contemporary society. Signs of internal disintegration were only too obvious to these writers, imbued with humanism, who felt compelled to warn their readers of the growing threat to the very fabric of French society.[2] Though these writers both recognized the evils around them, they expressed their political unease in very different ways. And their views were shaped, at least in part, by the literary in which they expressed those views. For this reason, it would be impossible to reconstitute each writer's unique perspective without considering the characteristics of the literary genre in which it was articulated. As Jean Plattard said long ago of Rabelais, one must determine how the literary form has modified the author's thinking, or, as Marshall McLuhan later phrased it, to what extent the medium has become the message.[3]

In these pages, we will compare the two literary forms that our authors chose to adopt: *discours* (Ronsard) and *essai* (Montaigne). A comparative analysis may allow us to uncover, in particular, the "poetic indices" that redefine the political meaning of each work. Henceforth, one can no longer speak of Ronsard's "engagement" or of Montaigne's "tolerance" without judging them in relation to the intentionality of the literary genre—*discours* or *essai*—within which these ideas appear. In other words, one must determine to what extent the "poetic" colors the "political": how, for example, the choice of a rhetorical mode or a poetic form influences the expression of the specific political crisis of the 1560s or of the 1580s.

We may suggest at once that Ronsard tends to see rhetorically and aesthetically what Montaigne sees semiotically. Whether in the *Discours des miseres de ce temps* (May, 1562), the *Continuation du discours des miseres de ce temps* (August, 1562), the *Remonstrance au peuple de France* (December, 1562) or the *Responce de P. de Ronsard aux injures et calomnies, de je ne sçay quels predicans, et ministres de Geneve* (1563), Ronsard's primary objective is to borrow from classical antiquity the means of expression that will bring him literary success and renown. In trying his hand at biting satire, he must look to classical latinity for exemplary models and then choose between Horace and Juvenal. He must mimic the ancients' expression of indignation; the expression need not be sincere, provided it is couched in verse so perfect that it will remain forever in French memory. The "troubles" thus provide opportunity to make heard the great Voice of Reprobation and to put into service the traditional procedures of classical rhetoric: to admonish, attack, warn, blame, threaten, ridicule, propose, supplicate. The aims of conventional eloquence must be reproduced according to the well-known tripartite schema: *docere, movere, delectare*.

Etienne Pasquier was not off the mark when in praising "la memoire du grand Ronsard" he saw in the militant poetry of the *Discours* above all "a means of diversifying his style." He concluded:

> Surely he [Ronsard] was interested in this project, because the words that were written against him stimulated his anger and his mind in this way... so that there is *nothing more beautiful* in all his works than the responses that he made to them, whether it be in fending off their insults or in divinely praising the honor of God and his Church.[4]

In his *Oraison funèbre* for Ronsard (1586), Jacques Davy du Perron insists on "the elegance and sweetness of humane letters" ("toute l'elegance et toute la douceur des lettres") produced by Ronsard in his "poésie engagée." It is less the militant nature of the *Discours* that interests the future cardinal (perhaps because he was himself a former Huguenot) than their rhetorical resources—this "science profane" that Ronsard knew how to deploy for "the defense and greater glory of the Church."[5]

Even Agrippa d'Aubigné, who was a champion of the Reformers and therefore an opponent of Ronsard's position, had for this predecessor what Claude-Gilbert Dubois calls a "hyperbolic deference" ("déférence hyperbolisée").[6] One finds d'Aubigné imploring his readers to read and reread this poet above all others:

> It is he who cut the string that France had under her tongue, perhaps in a style less delicate than that of today, but with advantages to which I see all writers of our time conforming.[7]

There is, indeed, a certain *distance* between Ronsard and his reader that only highlights the aesthetic preoccupations of the poet. Unlike d'Aubigné, who leads his reader to conversion by the strength of his words, Ronsard is satisfied with presenting a picture and leaving the final judgment to the reader's preferences. If one contrasts (as Ullrich Langer has) a passage from the *Princes* with another from the *Eloge à Des Masures,* one can see two very distinct ways of relating to the reader.[8] D'Aubigné declares:

> You who gave this subject to my pen,
> You also who brought to my anvil
> This red-hot lightning, raging with furor,
> Do read it: you will be horrified at your own horror.[9]

Ronsard, by contrast, committed though he may be, borrows the image of a banquet, treating his readers as guests whose opinions he will respect. Nothing could be further from his mind than to pressure his opponent to convert:

> I never force anybody to enjoy my poetic verse,
> Let him who wishes read it or buy it.[10]

Strangely enough, one could almost say that the grim realities of the civil wars find a place in Ronsard's poetry only insofar as they serve the aesthetic intentions of the poet (cf. Pasquier's earlier statement: "nothing more beautiful"). These "misfortunes," totally subservient to the work of art into which they are inscribed, have no true existence on their own: they must "serve"—in other words, be subservient to Ronsard's poetic project, which has less to do with the spirit of combat than with the great models of antiquity.

The "savage tone" of certain works such as the *Chant triomphal pour jouer sur la lyre* or the *Hydre deffaict* thus comes less from the political convictions of Pierre de Ronsard—whatever they may be—than from the all-powerful fury of the poet.[11] There has been much quibbling about why Ronsard engaged in the polemic: loyalty of the *poëte royal*? religious convictions? opportunism and self-interest? "Necessity, linking together many reasons, made him speak," concludes Marcel Raymond, who notes "the tragic serenity of the voice which falls from above and in no way resembles that of the partisan blinded by passion and fear."[12]

This "serenity of voice" is substantiated by Ronsard's conception of his poetic role. Even in the passages of the *Discours* that seem the most politically committed, Ronsard never seems to forget that his first duty is to poetry. Daniel Ménager emphasizes the conscious distance between the poet's muse and the religious upheavals of his time.[13] This distance is certainly evident in the *Responce* (1563), where Ronsard constantly reminds us of the exemplary status associated with his name and fame. One is struck by the assured tone with which he proclaims: "I am the master singer of the French Muse."[14]

Another famous declaration, toward the end of the *Responce*, reaffirms the fecundity of this poet of poets, the French Homer to whom all other poets are necessarily secondary:

> For you are all filled
> With my own plenitude: I alone am your object of study;
> You all spring forth from my own greatness;
> You are my subjects and I am your law giver.
> Your are my tributaries and I am your fountain,
> And the more you exhaust me, the more fertile is my vein:
> Pushing the sand aside, it provides an *eternal*
> *Font* of spring water to *you, small streams.*[15]

In his study *Origin and Originality in Renaissance Literature*, David Quint compares these lines to the *Ode à Michel de l'Hôpital*, noting a drastic change in meaning. Whereas in the *Ode* the source of inspired poetry ("le vif surgeon perennel," l. 130) is found in the oceanic depths of Jupiter's palace, in the *Responce* Ronsard finds in himself the "surgeon eternel" that nurtures the new French poetry. The "divine plenitude" of the original source is displaced between 1550 and 1563 until it ultimately coincides with the generative power of the one and only poet of modern times: Ronsard.[16]

Having created this image of himself, Ronsard is obliged to enter the arena of religious polemics. Was it not he—as he claims in the *Responce*—who single-handedly raised French language and poetry to the level of Greek and Latin?

> Thus, wishing to perfect my mother tongue,
> I labored for it, regardless of the work.
> I created new words, unearthed old ones
> To raise the fame of French up to the heavens.
> Like the Ancients, but in different ways,
> I made compound words and poetic phrases;
> And I established such rules for poetry
> That French was raised to the level of Greek and Latin.[17]

After Joachim Du Bellay died in 1560, Ronsard appropriated his role of *Deffenseur* and *Illustrateur* of the French language. He felt compelled to speak in the name of France and to link her destiny with his own. Politics had become the condition sine qua non of poetics.

Clearly, Ronsard could not be further from Montaigne, a man always hastening to denigrate his own work and to underscore its shortcomings. The derogatory terms Montaigne uses to describe his *Essais* are well-known: "bundle" (II, 37, 574 A), "patchwork" (III, 9, 736 C), "fricassee" (III, 13, 826 B), etc. In the chapter "Du Dementir" ("Of giving the lie") he expresses his desire for a personal and unpretentious work:

> I am not building here a statue to erect at the town crossroads, or in a church or public square.... This is for a nook in a library, and to amuse a neighbor, a relative, a friend, who may take pleasure in associating and conversing with me again in this image.[18]

For this reason one may speak of a "marginal" poetics in the *Essais*, in contrast to the more self-centered message of Ronsard's works.[19] Montaigne refrains from confronting head-on the problems that concern him; he prefers to approach them *de biais, obliquement,* sneaking up on them, testing them, as he says, "sounding the ford from a good distance" ("sondant le gué de bien loing," I, 50, 219 A). Such is his attitude toward the "troubles" of his time.[20]

Montaigne's observations on the civil wars do not constitute a separate, independent commentary; they are scattered throughout the *Essais,* without a unified platform. Life was not simple for Montaigne. When he took sides in the hot debates over contemporary ideology and declared himself in favor of the legitimacy of the monarchy and the succession to the throne, he also criticized several extreme "Ligueurs" and praised the virtues he perceived in some of the Reformers: "In the present broils of this state, my own interest has not made me blind either to the laudable qualities in our adversaries or those that are reproachable in the men I have followed."[21]

As a person of the law—one who respects the law and asks others to do the same—Montaigne has a duty to uphold the fundamental principles of political order and social conduct. By definition, lawyers and administrators are conservative: they exist to maintain the smooth functioning of the city. Montaigne the administrator, however, cannot completely eclipse Michel, the private man, painter of the "passage" and lover of the "distinguo," although Montaigne hastens to distinguish between his official political position (he was defending the legitimacy of the monarchy) and his strictly personal feelings: "I adhere firmly to the healthiest of the parties, but I do not seek to be noted as especially hostile to the others and beyond the bounds of the general reason."[22]

Montaigne refuses the generalizing statements wherein the public figure speaks for the private conscience. He wants to remain in tune with experience in a period of confusion, when often one must accept a life of uncertainty and contradiction or suffer even greater moral disintegration. He admits, "I do not know how to involve myself so deeply and so entirely" ("Je ne sçay pas m'engager si profondement et si entier," III, 10, 774 B).

Hence the necessity of a "plural consciousness," which requires a complementary worldview in constant response to that which denies it. And one finds, in the area of political ruminations, the interplay of antagonistic forces that oppose the *jurisconsulte* to the *honneste homme,* the admirer of Henri de Guise to the friend of Henri de Navarre, the engaged politician to the advocate of tolerance:

I condemn extraordinarily this bad form of arguing: "He is of the League, for he admires the grace of Monsieur de Guise." "The activity of the King of Navarre amazes him: he is a Huguenot." "He finds this to criticize in the King's morals: he is seditious in his heart."[23]

To be sure, a polemical writer would not so adamantly eschew generalizations and simplistic reasoning. According to the Ronsard of the *Discours,* the satiric mode does not lend itself well to subtle distinctions because "clear separations" are essential. (Interestingly, Montaigne uses the same phrase himself when distinguishing between his private self and his other self as the mayor of Bordeaux [III, 10, 989 B].) The essay, on the other hand, given its open-ended form, naturally accommodates the complexities of thought that may also be subtly expressive of an uneasy conscience. In the essayist's act of expression, there are always secondary issues (reservations, questions, objections) that graft themselves onto the main logic of the discourse. In this way, Montaigne follows his exemplar, Socrates, who "is always asking questions and stirring up discussion, never concluding, never satisfying; and says he has no other knowledge than that of opposing."[24]

If Ronsard opposes himself to the "preachers and ministers of Geneva," he does so in the hope of exalting himself in triumphant, mocking conquest. The poetry he embodies requires this. His role as *poëte royal* demands it. His mission is to end the "troubles" because the role of the poet, like that of the prince, is to calm the rebels, to reassure those in fear, and to convince countrymen that they are marching toward a golden age of justice and truth guaranteed by France's mythical history and nature's profound serenity.[25]

Nothing could be further from the outlook of Montaigne, who repeatedly refuses to take solace in the sweet consolations of Utopia—even those of the "bel art Poëtique." In his *Responce* Ronsard takes malicious pleasure in defending the preeminence of his art, a realm of complete pleasure, over the grim reality of the civil wars:

Neither your verses nor mine are oracles:
For me the Muses are but a subject of amusement.
With laughter I compose, with laughter I intend to read;
And this is the only reward I seek from writing.
Those who do otherwise fail to elect

The verses intended only for pleasure.
And this is why great kings marry music
(Except in private Councils) with beauties of Poetry.[26]

To admit such pleasure in the face of the civil wars might seem to proclaim a shocking insensitivity on Ronsard's part, a concern solely with personal glory. And yet his chosen genre of "discourse" demands this. In other words, Ronsard must deny the deep reasons for the guilty conscience of the sixteenth century.

Conversely, for the author of the *Essais,* the "troubles" emanating from the political and religious unrest are the symptoms of a much more profound crisis that shakes the very foundation of the society of his time. This crisis can be called *semiotic* to the extent that it has to do with the system of representation on which the dominant ideology relies. The humanist way of thinking, which had been crucial to the development of a Renaissance self-identity, finds itself jeopardized by the very process of history. Ronsard confidently heralds national unity; with equal gusto he proclaims that all conflicts will be resolved by the inspired rituals ("ébas," l. 922) of the "bel art Poëtique" (l. 928); yet he is never able to silence the voice of the Protestant opposition, whose very existence posed far greater problems than those of arrogance and temporary misconduct.

To be sure, Montaigne shares with Ronsard, at least in appearance, a disdain for the useless agitation of the common herd. He is quick to declare that the Protestant innovations often result from vanity, pride, and presumption. The real danger he sees is in the proliferation of various sects, each believing itself closer to the truth than the other. Erasmus has already written: "ex una secta complures in dies nascuntur."[27] Montaigne takes this one step further in the beginning of his chapter "De l'experience": "I have observed in Germany that Luther has left as many divisions and altercations over the uncertainty of his opinions, and more, as he raised about the Holy Scriptures."[28]

Yet Montaigne's goal is not, in effect, to go the way of Lutheranism—nor is it to call back the stray sheep to the fold. The context of this passage invites us to ponder a completely different idea: "Our disputes are purely verbal. I ask what is 'nature,' 'pleasure,' 'circle,' 'substitution.' The question is one of words, and is answered in the same way."[29] Montaigne is concerned here with a problem of hermeneutics. He has just spoken of the human being's insatiable desire to impose meaning on things. He rejects any illusion that would have us believe we can attain truth through the practice of interpretative commentary: "glosses increase doubts and ignorance" ("les gloses augmentent les doubtes et l'ignorance," III, 13, 817 B). One recalls as well this famous passage: "There is more of a job to interpret the interpretations than to interpret the things, and there are more books about books than about any other subject: we do nothing but write glosses about each other."[30]

For Montaigne, everything happens as if the growing multitude of heresies was symptomatic of a much more universal problem, that of the "quest of knowledge"—a veritable "sickness" of the human mind ("Men do not know the natural infirmity of their mind" ["Les hommes mescognoissent la maladie naturelle de leur esprit," III, 13, 817 B]), since such a quest results in the contamination of all practical search for truth: *Mus in pice,* a mouse stuck in a pitch barrel.

But Montaigne does not count himself among those who can condemn such an inclination to seek for truth—even if, as with silkworms or Aesop's dogs, he risks suffocation. His *Essais* are precisely an interminable search, detouring and meandering, for meaning. This "sickness" of Luther's is indeed quite curious: it encumbers the human mind while at the same time creating dignity. Montaigne comes back to this point to reformulate the question in a more positive light:

> It is a sign of contraction of the mind when it is content, or of weariness. A spirited mind never stops within itself; it is always aspiring and going beyond its strength; it has impulses beyond its powers of achievement. If it does not advance and press forward and stand at bay and clash, *it is only half alive.*[31]

To live life only half alive is not the plan of such a "spirited mind" as that of the author of the *Essais*. It is necessary, therefore, to view Montaigne's "political" commentaries, scattered throughout his chapters, not only in their immediate context but also in the larger poetic perspective of the entire work. One cannot speak of a "Montaigne engagé" without considering the cogency of the whole text. Dealing with partial utterances is perhaps a necessity of criticism; but this necessity must be complemented by serious precautions when concerned with a genre as "variable and elusive" ("divers et ondoyant") as the subject (the human being) under consideration: "it is hard to found any constant and uniform judgment on him" ("il est malaisé d'y fonder jugement constant et uniforme," I, 1, 5 A). Thus, for Montaigne, the *semiotic crisis* of which the civil "troubles" are a symptom affects above all the relation between words (*verba*) and things (*res*). Signs have become opaque; they can mislead at any moment; deception rules. No other chapter from the *Essais* expresses this better than "Of Glory": "There is the name and the thing. The name is a sound which designates and signifies the thing; the name is not a part of the thing or of the substance, it is an extraneous piece attached to the thing, and outside of it."[32] Therefore, one must be careful not to call "virtue" that which is perhaps only desire for glory. One too often judges the "heart" for its "countenance," and language itself encourages us to be fooled by "external appearances." Montaigne adheres fully to a nominalist criticism that denounces the false alliances between the language and the reality that it is supposed to represent.[33] We have already seen this: a person does not necessarily belong to an extremist party because he or she admires a certain personality trait of its leader. Once again, "distinguo" must be "the most universal member" of anyone's logic (II, 1, 242).

For Ronsard, the aim of political literature is to piece back together a France torn apart by the divisive forces of rebellion. Poetry is therefore placed in the service of power, in order to legitimize the political model of supremacy. Ronsard leaves it to history to reveal events as they really are, *without lying:*

> O historian, you who write the monstrous story
> Of our times in an *unlying ink,*
> Tell our children all this fatal misfortune,
> So that, by reading you, they may lament our evils
> And learn from their elders' sins,
> Lest they reproduce the same miseries.[34]

The distinction between the historian and the poet, so dear to rhetoricians from Aristotle to Quintilian, will become the object of long discussions in the *Franciade* prefaces of 1572 and 1587. Unlike the historian who searches for truth "without disguise or make-up" ("sans desguisure ny fard" [1572]), the poet "has as the most necessary maxim of his art never to follow truth step by step, but verisimilitude and possibility" ("a pour maxime tresnecessaire de son art de ne suivre jamais pas à pas la vérité, mais la vray-semblance, et le possible" [1587]). Ronsard defines this verisimilitude as "that which can be" or "that which is already accepted by public opinion" ("ce qui peut estre" or "ce qui est desja receu en la commune opinion" [1572]).[35]

Once again, nothing could be more foreign to Montaigne than this notion of a "feigning" poet who camouflages "the thing as it is" in order to valorize public opinion. One can see with what compulsion the essayist criticizes those who paint reality in false colors, veiling their true intentions with deceptive ornaments. How could he, the "sworn enemy of any falsification," accommodate "a turgid style, bubbling over with conceits, ingenious indeed, but farfetched and fantastic"—as he says of Aretino?[36] It is the search for *truth*, not *verisimilitude*, that concerns him; and this is never more important than when reflecting upon the political and social problems of his time.

Ronsard's and Montaigne's attitudes toward the French religious wars are also illuminated by the conception of the *subject* in sixteenth-century French society. For these two writers, as for Jean Bodin and most of his fellow jurists, the subject can only be public, in other words, the subject of the king. A private subject does not exist.[37] With Montaigne, however, we see the beginning of a conception of a proto-Cartesian subject who envisages the possibility of thinking from the standpoint of his own subjectivity. But this private subject is still the locus of "inconsistency" (II, 1), which Montaigne often addresses and which he identifies specifically as the space where *writing* is found.[38] In public affairs the true nature of signs is of little importance, and one can be satisfied with what is *seemingly true*. It is the realm of the "counterfeit," a necessary evil that is accepted and practiced by all lawgivers: "since men, because of their inadequacy, cannot be sufficiently paid with good money, let false be employed too."[39]

In his *Discours*, Ronsard raises the art of counterfeiting to exemplary heights—it is a work destined for the greatest glory of the king and his irreproachable subject. In contrast, outside this perverse and inflated world of public affairs, the private subject attempts to define the real world by means of his *Essais:* "I do not care so much what I am to others as I care what I am to *myself*. I want to be rich by myself, not by borrowing."[40]

It is in the "inner consciousness," the "inside," the "heart," where the true richness ("rich by myself") of moral conscience is found; and this has nothing to do with the obligations and the "countenances" of the public life. As Jean Starobinski has clearly shown, the movement toward interiority is also a movement toward the truth of signs.[41]

But for Ronsard, this search for interiority is fundamentally suspect. The valorization of the private subject who has privileged access to virtue and truth is detrimental to the public subject. In short, interiority is a revindication of the Reformers; it is another name for the monster called Opinion, the "daughter of imagination" ("fille de fantasie," 102, l. 255), whose dangers are well known. It is the very definition of uncontrollable change. Montaigne himself will condemn "Luther's innovations" ("nouvelletez de Luther"), citing Montaigne's father, who foresaw that "this incipient malady would easily degenerate into an execrable atheism." Thus, it is because they are based on verisimilitude rather than truth that these new opinions, nourished by the people, represent a real danger: "For the common herd, not having the faculty of judging things in themselves, let themselves be carried away by chance and by appearances."[42]

In other words, such new opinions might be admissible on the private level if they remained in the inner conscience of a person of judgment. But the problem is that they spread among the people; the "common folk" have taken them up, and these ideas have degenerated into a veritable crisis of public authority:

[The common folk] shake off as a tyrannical yoke all the impressions they had once received from the authority of the laws or the reverence of ancient usage... determined from then on to accept nothing to which they have not applied their judgment and granted their personal consent.[43]

From the perspective of literary theory, one might conclude that the *essai* distinguishes itself from the *discours* to the extent that the first form accommodates the general deliberations of a private subject, the "individual," whereas the second can only allow individual expression of public subjectivity. In the face of the "troubles" of the times, Ronsard's verse tries desperately to make us believe in the existence and coherence of a "subject of the king." Montaigne's prose, in contrast, refuses to obliterate the incoherence of subjectivity and liberates the inconsistency of the private subject, while at the same time warning of the risks of revealing the secrets of interiority to the people. Montaigne thus chose a literary genre that allowed him to expose the tension he felt between two worldviews at the end of the sixteenth century: one that still wanted to believe in the all-encompassing authority of the political body, and one that, wise to the state of public affairs, hoped to find "within" subjectivity some bases on which to construct a new order. This tension is expressed perhaps most clearly in the chapter "De l'institution des enfans," where Montaigne gives his opinion, in a late addition, on the choice of a "gouverneur" (tutor) for the future *honneste homme*:

> If his tutor is of my disposition, he will form his will to be a very loyal, very affectionate, and very courageous servant of his prince; but he will cool in him any desire to attach himself to that prince otherwise than by sense of *public duty*. Besides several other disadvantages which impair our freedom by these *private obligations*, the judgment of a man who is hired and bought is either less whole and less free, or tainted with imprudence and ingratitude.[44]

Ronsard conflates "public duty" and "private obligations." Montaigne attempts to separate them, though not without some hesitation. The poetics of the *Discours* and the *Essais* can be defined by parallel efforts, never easily realized, to express literary solutions to seemingly unreconcilable problems. Both writers, faced with the ideologies of their time, confront the literary dimensions of humanism in crisis and offer solutions that, in the final analysis, owe more to poetics than to politics.

NOTES

I wish to thank Kirk D. Read for his help in editing, translating, and typing this essay.

1. A companion version appeared in French in *Les Métamorphoses de Montaigne* (Paris: Presses Universitaires de France, 1989), 35–60. Except for those of Montaigne's *Essais* (see note 18), all the English translations are mine. About Ronsard's political ideas see, in particular, Michel Dassonville, *Grandeurs et servitudes*, vol. 4 of *Ronsard: Etude historique et littéraire* (Geneva: Droz, 1985), chap. 4. About Montaigne's attitude, see Géralde Nakam, *Montaigne et son temps: les événements et les "Essais"* (Paris: Nizet, 1982), 171ff.

2. See, on this subject, the study by Frieda S. Brown, "Interrelations between the Political Ideas of Ronsard and Montaigne," *Romanic Review* 56, no. 4 (December, 1965): 241–47. As we shall see, however, the two writers' attitudes differ significantly when one takes into consideration the literary dimension of their politics.

3. See Jean Plattard, *L'Oeuvre de Rabelais* (Paris: H. Champion, 1910), xii. One is of course familiar with McLuhan's famous phrase: "the medium is the message."

4. Etienne Pasquier, *Les Recherches de la France,* cited by Yvonne Bellenger in her edition of Ronsard's *Discours* (Paris: Garnier-Flammarion, 1979), 15: "Certes il [Ronsard] eut interest de faire ce coup d'essay, parce que les vers que l'on escrivit contre luy esguisèrent et sa colere et son esprit de cette façon . . . qu'il n'y a *rien de si beau* en tous ses oeuvres que les responses qu'il leur fit, soit à repousser leurs injures, soit à haut louer l'honneur de Dieu et de son Eglise." (Emphasis added.)

5. Du Perron, *Oraison funèbre,* ed. M. Simonin (Geneva: Droz, 1985), 89: "pour la defence et pour la propugnation de l'Eglise."

6. Claude-Gilbert Dubois, "Imitation différentielle et poétique maniériste," *Revue de littérature comparée,* no. 2 (1977): 147–48.

7. Agrippa d'Aubigné, "Lettres touchant quelques poincts de diverses sciences," in *Oeuvres,* ed. H. Weber, J. Bailbé and M. Soulié (Paris: Gallimard, Pléiade, 1969), 860: "c'est luy qui a coupé le filet que la France avoit soubs la langue, peut estre d'un stile moins delicat que celuy d'aujourd'hui, mais avec des advantages ausquels je voy ceder tout ce qui escrit de ce temps."

8. Ullrich Langer, *Rhétorique et intersubjectivité: les "Tragiques" d'Agrippa d'Aubigné* (Paris: Papers on French Seventeenth Century Literature, 1983), 81–82.

9. D'Aubigné, "Princes," in *Les Tragiques,* ll. 9–12: "Vous qui avez donné ce subject à ma plume, / Vous-mesmes qui avez porté sur mon enclume / Ce foudre rougissant aceré de fureur, / Lisez-le: vous aurez horreur de vostre horreur."

10. Ronsard, *Elégie à Loys Des Masures,* in *Oeuvres complètes,* ed. Paul Laumonier, 18 vols. (Paris: Didier, 1914), 10:364, ll. 30–31: "Je ne contraincts personne à mon vers poëticque, / Le lise qui voudra, l'achette qui voudra." See Langer, 81.

11. Brown speaks of the "savage tone" of these works (245) and attributes this to Ronsard's violent reaction against the Huguenots (he had advocated the use of force to exterminate the Protestants in the battles of Jarnac and Moncontour in 1569).

12. Marcel Raymond, *L'Influence de Ronsard sur la poésie française* (Paris: H. Champion, 1927), 1:362.

13. Daniel Ménager, "Le Combat des *Discours,*" in *Ronsard, le roi, le poète et les hommes* (Geneva: Droz, 1979), 253.

14. Ronsard, *Responce,* in *Discours des misères de ce temps,* ed. Malcolm Smith (Geneva: Droz, 1979), 157, l. 40: "Je suis maistre joueur de la Muse Françoise." All references to Ronsard's *Discours* are to this edition.

15. Ronsard, *Responce,* 205, ll. 1035–42: "Car de ma plenitude / Vous estes tous remplis: je suis seul vostre estude / Vous estes tous yssus de la grandeur de

moy, / Vous estes mes sujets, et je suis vostre loy. / *Vous estes mes ruisseaux, je suis vostre fonteine* / Et plus vous m'espuisés, plus ma fertile veine / Repoussant le sablon, jette une source d'eaux / D'un *surjon* éternel *pour vous autres ruisseaux*." (Emphasis added.)

16. David Quint, *Origin and Originality in Renaissance Literature: Versions of the Source* (New Haven, Conn.: Yale University Press, 1983), 24–30. On these questions see also Francis M. Higman's article, "Ronsard's Political and Polemical Poetry," in *Ronsard the Poet,* ed. Terence Cave (London: Methuen, 1973), 241–85.

17. Ronsard, *Responce,* 203–4, ll. 1019–26: "Adonques pour hausser ma langue maternelle, / Indonté du labeur, je travaillé pour elle. / Je fis des mots nouveaux, je r'appelay les vieux / Si bien que son renom je poussay jusqu'aux cieux: / Je fis d'autre façon que n'avoient les antiques, / Vocables composés, et phrases poëtiques, / Et mis la poësie en tel ordre qu'après, / Le François s'egalla aux Romains et aux Grecs."

18. Montaigne, *The Complete Essays of Montaigne,* trans. Donald Frame (Stanford: Stanford University Press, 1958), II, 18, 503 A: "Je ne dresse pas icy une statue à planter au carrefour d'une ville, ou dans une Eglise, ou place publique.... C'est pour le coin d'une librairie, et pour en amuser un voisin, un parent, un amy, qui aura plaisir à me racointer et repratiquer en cett'image." All subsequent English translations of Montaigne are taken from Frame's translation. The page number is followed by a letter (A, B or C) indicating one of the three major textual strata: 1580, 1588, or 1595.

19. See François Rigolot, "Montaigne en marge," in *Le Texte de la Renaissance* (Geneva: Droz, 1984), 221–52.

20. One must also refer here to the analysis done by Nakam in *Montaigne et son temps,* 171ff. See also Marianne S. Meijer's illuminating article on Montaigne's reproaches to the League, "Une Ambiguïté dans un essai de Montaigne," in *Mélanges à la mémoire de V. L. Saulnier* (Geneva: Droz, 1984), 491–99.

21. Montaigne, III, 10, 774 B: "Aux presens brouillis de cet estat, mon interest ne m'a fait mesconnoistre ny les qualitez louables en nos adversaires, ny celles qui sont reprochables en ceux que j'ay suivy."

22. Montaigne, III, 10, 774 C: "Je me prens *fermement* au plus sain des partis, mais je n'affecte pas qu'on me remarque *specialement* ennemy des autres, et outre la raison generalle."

23. Montaigne, III, 10, 774–75 C: "J'accuse merveilleusement cette vitieuse forme d'opiner: 'Il est de la Ligue, car il admire la grace de Monsieur de Guise.' 'L'activité du Roy de Navarre l'estonne: il est Huguenot.' 'Il treuve cecy à dire aux moeurs du Roy: il est seditieux en son coeur.'"

24. Montaigne, II, 12, 377 C: "va tousjours demandant et esmouvant la dispute, jamais l'arrestant, jamais satisfaisant, et dict n'avoir autre science que la science de s'opposer."

25. See Ménager, 238.

26. Ronsard, *Responce*, 199, ll. 921–28: "Ny tes vers ny les miens oracles ne sont pas, / *Je prends tanseulement les Muses pour ébas.* / *En riant* je compose, *en riant* je veux lire, / Et voyla tout le fruit que je reçoy d'escrire./ Ceux qui font autrement, ils ne sçavent choisir / *Les vers qui ne sont nés sinon pour le plaisir.* /Et pour ce les grands Roys joignent à la Musique / (Non au Conseil privé) le bel art Poëtique." (Emphasis added.)

27. Erasmus, "Ad Fratres," in *Opera*, cited by Ménager, 212 n. 148.

28. Montaigne, III, 13, 818 B: "J'ay veu en Alemagne que Luther a laissé autant de divisions et d'altercations sur le doubte de ses opinions, et plus, qu'il n'en esmeut sur les escriptures sainctes."

29. Montaigne, III, 13, 818 B: "Nostre contestation est verbale. Je demande que c'est que nature, volupté, cercle, et substitution. La question est de paroles, et se paye de mesme."

30. Montaigne, III, 13, 818 B: "Il y a plus affaire à interpreter les interpretations qu'à interpreter les choses, et plus de livres sur les livres que sur autre subject: nous ne faisons que nous entregloser."

31. Montaigne, III, 13, 817–18 C: "C'est signe de racourciment d'esprit quand il se contente, ou de lasseté. Nul esprit genereux ne s'arreste en soy: il pretend tousjours et va outre ses forces; il a des eslans au delà de ses effects; s'il ne s'avance et ne se presse et ne s'accule et ne se choque, *il n'est vif qu'à demy.*" (Emphasis added.)

32. Montaigne, II, 16, 468 A: "Il y a le nom et la chose; le nom, c'est une voix qui remerque et signifie la chose; le nom, ce n'est pas une partie de la chose ny de la substance, c'est une piece estrangere joincte à la chose, et hors d'elle."

33. This is the subject of Antoine Compagnon's book *Nous, Michel de Montaigne* (Paris: Editions du Seuil, 1980).

34. Ronsard, *Discours*, 68, ll. 115–20: "O toy historien, qui d'*encre non menteuse* / Escris de nostre temps l'histoire monstrueuse, / Raconte à nos enfans tout ce malheur fatal, / Afin qu'en te lisant ils pleurent nostre mal, / Et qu'ils prennent exemple aux pechés de leurs peres, / De peur de ne tomber en pareilles misères." (Emphasis added.)

35. See François Rigolot, "L'Imaginaire du discours préfaciel: l'exemple de la *Franciade*," in *Studi di letteratura francese* (Florence: Leo S. Olschki, 1986), 12:231–48.

36. Montaigne, I, 40, 186 C: "l'ennemy juré de toute falsification"; I, 51, 223 A: "une façon de parler bouffie et bouillonée de pointes, ingenieuses à la vérité, mais recherchées de loing et fantasques."

37. I follow Timothy J. Reiss's forceful argument in his "Montaigne and the Subject of Polity," in *Literary Theory / Renaissance Texts,* ed. Patricia Parker and David Quint (Baltimore, Md.: Johns Hopkins University Press, 1986), 115–49.

38. With remarkable clarity, Timothy Hampton locates this space in Montaigne's "écriture," in *Writing from History: The Rhetoric of Exemplarity in Renaissance Literature* (Ithaca, N.Y.: Cornell University Press, 1990).

39. Montaigne, II, 16, 477 A: "Puis que les hommes, par leur insuffisance, ne se peuvent assez payer d'une bonne monnoye, qu'on y employe encore la fauce."

40. Montaigne, II, 16, 474 A: "Je ne me soucie pas tant quel je sois chez autrui, comme je me soucie quel je sois *en moy mesme*. Je veux estre riche par moy, non par emprunt."

41. See Jean Starobinski, *Montaigne en mouvement* (Paris: Gallimard, 1983). See also Marc Fumaroli, "Montaigne et l'éloquence du for intérieur," in *Les Formes brèves de la prose et le discours discontinu (XVIe–XVIIe siècles)*, ed. J. Lafond (Paris: J. Vrin, 1984), 27–50.

42. Montaigne, II, 12, 320 A: "ce commencement de maladie déclineroit aysément en un execrable atheisme"; and "Car le vulgaire, n'ayant pas la faculté de juger des choses par elles mesmes, se [laisse] emporter à la fortune et aux apparences."

43. Montaigne, II, 12, 320 A: "[Le vulgaire] secoue comme un joug tyrannique toutes les impressions qu'il avoit receues par l'authorité des loix ou reverence de l'ancien usage, ... entreprenant dès lors en avant de ne recevoir rien à quoy il n'ait interposé son decret et presté particulier consentement."

44. Montaigne, I, 26, 114 C: "Si son gouverneur tient de mon humeur, il luy formera la volonté à estre très-loyal serviteur de son prince et très-affectionné et très courageux; mais il luy refroidira l'envie de s'y attacher autrement que par un *devoir publique*. Outre plusieurs autres inconveniens qui blessent nostre franchise par ces *obligations particulieres,* le jugement d'un homme gagé et acheté, ou il est moins entier et moins libre, ou il est taché et d'imprudence et d'ingratitude."

The Idea of Meaning and Practice of Method in Peter Ramus, Henri Estienne, and Others

Timothy J. Reiss

When the works of Scotus first came out, they were carried to a certain library, and had lodgings appointed them; but this author was no sooner settled than he went to visit his master Aristotle; and there both consulted together to seize Plato by main force and turn him out from his ancient station among the divines, where he had peaceably dwelt near eight hundred years. The attempt succeeded, and the two usurpers have reigned ever since in his stead: but to maintain quiet for the future, it decreed that all *polemics* of the larger size should be held fast with a chain.
—Jonathan Swift, *The Battle of the Books*

To note that the second half of the French sixteenth century was a time of profound and debilitating upheaval in politics, religion, education, economic and social order, and just about every other area of human practice is scarcely original. The more arcane realms of philosophy and philology did not escape this disarray. In some ways they would be central to its solution: not because philosophers or philologists intervened practically in concrete events (although as government officials, lawyers, publishers, ecclesiastics, and even soldiers, many did), but because their disciplines eventually provided the analytical tools that enabled those events to be described and understood. They made new concepts and practices of meaning, and consequently of action.

Scholars have usually considered "the Method" developed by Peter Ramus, his colleagues, and their successors, to be fundamental to the creation of these tools and the establishment of such new thought. Rightly so. Yet the recognition has always been at least ambivalent, and that same method condemned as logically weak, confused, incompetent, and even nonsensical.[1] In itself so violent a contradiction must give pause. Worse, it inhibits explanation of Ramism's immense pedagogical success in displacing older school curricula, and prevents any understanding at all of its enduring effect on Western philosophy (unless we defy scholarly consensus that considers Ramism to have been enabling of Descartes's work).

I wish to argue that the contradiction arises from mistaking the means for its end. What follows will therefore make a threefold case: (1) from the social and conceptual context within which Ramus and his colleagues were working; (2) against—or at least adjusting—a nowadays common interpretation of their work (including my own in *The Discourse of Modernism*);[2] and (3) about the nature of that work itself. For Method actually developed from the effort to resolve a problem that appeared wholly philosophical (or philological): that of meaning, or, more precisely perhaps, those of denotation and reference. The Method had not itself been the aim, but was more or less a side effect of the endeavor to set the relation between idea, word, and thing on some firm philosophic and linguistic ground. The issue was not new, of course. The medieval speculative grammarians, for example, had placed it at the center of their studies. But by the mid-sixteenth century there was a new sense of urgency about the matter.

"Man was endowed with language in order to proclaim truth," Erasmus could still write in 1523, as if little had changed since the height of the Christian Middle Ages.[3] Yet the difficulties were by this time manifest in a statement of this kind. In the colloquy just quoted a certain style of trade and commerce, for instance, was taken to militate against such a claim. While ecclesiastical writings on those subjects had always lamented the prevalence of cheating and usurious practices, Erasmus seemed to be implying that such practices were now general. Probably more immediately important was an already habitual understanding of the rhetorical arts—that they taught "the art of lying," as Pseudocheus observes in the same colloquy: "clever lying is a large part of eloquence." Since rhetorical skills were increasingly held to form the basis of civic life and social order, the implications were evidently immense. Indeed, they already provided matter for a debate over the role of rhetoric in civic life, education, and letters, a debate that grew ever sharper and was to last well into the seventeenth century.[4] Of still greater moment was the feeling that the divine guarantees beneath that "truth," "speech," and "man," terms used almost glibly by Erasmus's Philetymus, were rapidly losing their familiar ground—if indeed they had not already done so. It would not much longer be possible, as it still was for a late scholastic vernacular author like Thomas Wilson, to claim that the task of logic was "to finde out the trueth," that "perfeicte" knowledge naturally available to humans "before the fal of Adam" by "the secret woorking of God."[5]

The profound questioning of ecclesiastical authority had cast doubt on the relation between the human and the divine and thus, in the present context, on any divine confirmation of an assured relation between mind and world and its presentation in language. Reason and knowledge, their place, order, reliability, and indeed their very nature, were in serious question. Further, the mere fact of questioning theological authority made humans willy-nilly responsible for defining such matters and therefore effectively responsible *for* them. The development and ever wider use of vernacular languages would no doubt of themselves have provoked closer attention to language and its functioning. As it was they simply emphasized the urgency of the need for a stable concept and practice of meaning. So too did political debates about the relation between monarch and subjects, about the nature of sovereign authority, and about the subject's rights with regard to such authority. The rediscovery of Greek, and to a lesser degree, Roman arguments on these subjects added new material to an already volatile mix. Finally, the humanist and then the Reform desire for direct access to biblical and patristic texts and commentaries resulted in new explorations in the three languages—Latin, Greek, and Hebrew—whose study eventually affected all the disciplines.[6] Small wonder, therefore, that the sixteenth century saw so huge a production of "rational" and normative Latin and vernacular grammars.[7]

This was the method's general context. Ramus's questioning of Aristotle focused both on the philosopher's authority in the schools, authority that impeded all novelty of thought, and on his concepts of the human, of rationality, and of knowledge. Ramus's simultaneous interrogations of Cicero's theoretical rhetorical work and of Quintilian were aimed at the nature of the relation between reason, knowledge, and language. The Method was gradually elaborated from that debate—apparently in the ten years after his M.A. defense of 1536. It was not consolidated until the publication of the *Dialectici commentarii tres* in 1546, which appeared under the name of his colleague Omer Talon,

Ramus himself being still under royal ban. There he provided explicit definitions of method, genesis, and analysis.

Method in general, as he wrote in the 1555 *Dialectique,* was "a disposition according to which among several things the first noted is disposed in the first place, the second in the second, the third in the third and so on."[8] He divided it into two kinds. The first was that "of art" or "of nature," "by which whatever is absolutely most evident and clearest is set first." Such method was of art because it was traditional doctrine and "corresponded in quality of judgment to necessary utterance and properly concluded syllogism."[9] It was therefore also of nature, deploying principles from "universal reason" to explain singulars. It set out a clear taxonomic relationship between universals and particulars: from clear definition of rule, to right distribution of parts, to final explanation of particulars through singular cases. The second kind of method lacked such universality and clarity. It was that of "prudence," constrained by the requirements of social communication, dependent on contingent conditions, even substituting "suitability" and "probability" for certainty.[10] In practice this was virtually the same method adjusted to the Ciceronian civic virtue of *prudentia* (notably explored in one of Ramus's favorite Ciceronian works, the *De officiis*).

Analysis entailed the examination "of our own or others' examples in which invention and composition are to be looked into." It was where "the argument, enunciation, syllogism, method, in short...the whole art of logic" were to be examined. The deployment of argument from universals to particulars was there thoroughly analyzed. It was a procedure common to all arts, said Ramus, not only logic. Genesis reversed the process: it explained the development of an argument from singular instance to its generalization.[11] The method "was to govern all subjects" and let Ramus "reorganize the entire curriculum under the rule of *technologia,*...the logic or science of the arts themselves."[12] Indeed Ramus "himself undertook to apply his method to nearly all the academic fields of knowledge."[13] So, said Ramus, *Dialectique* taught "the art and judgment of the syllogism, whether simple or complex, whose proposition ordinarily belongs to a particular art, such as Grammar, Rhetoric, Logic, Mathematics, Mechanics, Physics, Ethics, Politics, those of divine and human laws, and generally of all the arts."[14] The similarity of these efforts, claims, and procedures to the later and more popularly known Cartesian method hardly requires further elaboration here.

So stated, and except for its taxonomies, there is nothing very new or even complicated about Ramus's method. Its scandal and influence remain inexplicable (setting aside its not altogether new organization into logic of *inventio* and *dispositio,* themselves corresponding no doubt to the question of reason on the one hand and heuristic display on the other). To understand these we need to look behind the method itself: not simply to its development—a matter made much easier since Nelly Bruyère's study—but to the work on meaning going on simultaneously both in Ramus's own writing and in that of certain contemporaries. Among these one could choose many, but Henri Estienne was a contemporary and a friend who fought many of the same battles. At the same time, because he situated his own thinking on these matters within both a philosophical and a political context, mention of some of his writings will at least hint at some of the connections indicated at the outset. For behind the simplicity, even naïveté, of the method lay a profound unease as to the very status of the elements essential to it, or indeed to any logical system whatever.

This discomfort echoed the general dread of dissolution and decay deplored by Erasmus in 1526:

> King Christian of Denmark, a devout partisan of the gospel, is in exile. Francis, King of France, is a "guest" of the Spaniards.... Charles is preparing to extend the boundaries of his realm. Ferdinand has his hands full in Germany. Bankruptcy threatens every court. The peasants raise dangerous riots and are not swayed from their purpose, despite so many massacres. The commons are bent on anarchy; the Church is shaken to its very foundations by menacing factions; on every side the seamless coat of Jesus is torn to shreds. The vineyard of the Lord is now laid waste not by a single boar but at one and the same time the authority of priests (together with their tithes), the dignity of theologians, the splendor of monks is imperiled; confession totters; vows reel; pontifical ordinances crumble away; the Eucharist is called in question; Antichrist is awaited; the whole earth is pregnant with I know not what calamity.[15]

In the 1529 *Charon,* Alastor comments that the "Furies" have set to work with a fine zeal: "not a corner of the earth have they left unravaged by hellish disasters, dissensions, wars, robberies, plagues." Yes, replies Charon, "I've hopes of a splendid slaughter in the near future."[16] We will not be surprised therefore that later in the century Henri Estienne explored the purity of the French language following and in conjunction with scathing attacks on current political and social conditions. The need for assurance of meaning and certainty of comprehension paralleled the demand for social and political stability.

Certain contemporaries of Erasmus, such writers on linguistic, grammatical, and rhetorical matters as Geoffroy Tory, John Palsgrave, and Pierre Fabri, for example (to take only vernacular writers), were already confronting the serious problem of expressed meaning and truth. They found themselves multiplying what one might call "places of meaning." They still worked on the basis of a theory of the sign as a place of repeated "readings," of continuing "glosses," as it were. For them, words were signs of signs of signs.... So long as this process could remain grounded in some authority, whether divine or secular, there was no very serious dilemma. The distanced relationships of God, humans, and the world; of truth, concepts, and signs; and of knowledge, language, and reference remained assured. So long as the assumption survived that the structure and use of words had in some way been created from objects in nature, however mediated, one could rely on linguistic *causas* (as Scaliger still called them in 1540): explicable origins of language and confirmable meanings.[17] But once guarantees of such fixed relations between concept and linguistic sign, between referent and concept, and between sign and denotation had been removed, then urgent and profound difficulties arose.

Without such certainties how was any knowledge or action, of whatever kind, possible? Without external guarantees, how could the questioned relations be defined? How could they be stabilized? Who or what could be responsible for them? The indications of uncertainty multiply. In Fabri, for instance, one finds a remarkable accumulation of vocabulary seeking to define and stabilize "places of meaning": *chose, significat, signifiance, signification,* (*significat*), and *terme* appear as so many words attempting to introduce and grasp distanced relations of meaning, enabling analysis, knowledge, and ultimately action. But Fabri was never able to affirm any final "anchor" that would assure the possibility of some "scientific" rationalism.[18]

This inability produced a widespread feeling that no kind of truth could be expressed, so that social action was entirely contingent, disordered, and indeed without ground. In the mid-1540s the Scottish humanist George Buchanan wrote two tragedies exploring these very dilemmas. Montaigne recorded that he performed in them at school,[19] and the essayist's own sense of the inconstancy and disorder of "inner life" may well have owed much to these debates. In 1562 Henri Estienne was asserting that if words lost their meanings, however conventionally established, the whole processes of language and learning became nonsense and degenerated toward madness:

> Similar absurdity (indeed, even more) is found in certain other locutions, which nonetheless please many, and for no other reason than that they are spoken against all reason. And it is the case that if this idiotic (indeed, insane) desire for novelty continues to gain ground, overturning everything wherever it goes, I fear that in the end we will have to call head foot and foot head. Especially will this be so once such a desire has entered the heads of ignorant people, be they courtiers or others.[20]

Estienne linked this unreason directly to political conditions, asserting that bringing Machiavellian political practices into France had crucially sapped linguistic and therefore conceptual certainties (*Apologie, Dialogues, Discours merveilleux*).[21] Not by chance did he assign blame in the matter to those who frequented the Medici-controlled court.[22] (A century later a successor to that same court was to be extolled as the source of the most excellent use of language.) Estienne's upside-down world of "fantaisie," where people function "sottement," "à tort et à travers," where indeed the "fou" has taken over language (to use a few of the terms used elsewhere in the preface to his *Conformité*), corresponded precisely to the fear of political and social dissolution. His 1566 *Apologie pour Hérodote* had already satirized much of this, and one might well read Ramus's own curious 1559 treatise on the "ancient Gauls" as inspired by like concerns.[23] By the 1570s and 1580s these writers were no longer alone in relating civic catastrophe to linguistic and conceptual incapacity. François de Belleforest, Louis Le Roy, François de La Noue, Montaigne, Etienne Pasquier, and Michel Hurault were but a few of those who echoed and embroidered upon Thucydides' well-known claim that linguistic decay was largely responsible for the civil war in Greece.[24] Most of these were high in government council, and one, La Noue, was judged perhaps the most considerable soldier of his time.

Earlier in the century people were possibly less conscious of the enormity of the stakes. Yet there was no doubt but that the deep sense of philosophical discomfort was already associated, however imprecisely, with a feeling of more general disquiet, even dread. The method publicized by Ramus was part of the quest for a solution to such anxiety in one area of (philosophical) activity. As we have seen, however, it depended on ideas of universal reason, of the real, of particulars, of words and meanings, of concepts and signs, that were themselves very far from clear and still less generally accepted. They required redefining. And they required redefining freed from any primacy of the Word. Some other, new grounding seemed necessary. That was why Ramus argued the need to start afresh. His dismissal of authority was partly a heuristic gesture in the case of "external guides," philosophers or others; it was wholly genuine where "authoritative" concepts were concerned. He had proposed, he wrote, to use new principles, now derived from "universal reason" and particular "experience." Only after "finding out for [him]self such principles and rules" could he then arrange "all this matter" according to the method.[25] He left no doubt, therefore, that he saw the method as an ordering device secondary to the actual discovery of principles.

The pictorial presentation of the method's taxonomies clearly emphasized a visual dimension. One major consequence has been that visualization has itself been taken as Ramus's attempt to recapture that lost ground. Spatial dimensions, color perceptions, and so forth seemed to offer ready closure for analysis, for meaning and understanding, in a way the accumulation of sign levels never could. At the same time they corresponded to at least one important dimension of what *we* think of as "scientific knowledge":

> Ramism specialized in dichotomies, in "distribution" and "collocation," (*dispositio* rather than judgment or *judicium*), in "systems" ..., and in other diagrammatic concepts. This hints that Ramist dialectic represented a drive toward thinking not only of the universe but of thought itself in terms of spatial models apprehended by sight. In this context, the notion of knowledge as word, and the personalist orientation of cognition and of the universe which this notion implies, is due to atrophy.[26]

According to this argument such visual models provided a firm distancing device, even that new ground whose lack posed such difficulties for Ramus's immediate predecessors. For the Ramists, thought itself had now become an object to be visually grasped. Words were no longer simply signs to be read under threat of an infinite regression, but were containers of such thoughts, themselves in turn containers of the reality to which they referred.[27] It is certainly the case that visualization played an important role in Ramist argument. Even its metaphors reveal such a slant:

> The truth of the things understood in our arts is thus naturally presented to the mind [in dialectics] as colors are to sight, and what we call teaching is not to inculcate knowledge but simply to turn and direct the mind to contemplate what it could itself have perceived had it turned and directed itself in that direction.... Just as the eyes of bats are blinded by daylight, so the point of our understanding blinks and closes before things whose nature is very clear and most evident.[28]

Rejecting Aristotle's demand for "two Logics," one for true knowledge the other for opinion, Ramus couched the dispute in the same terms. "As sight is the same for seeing all colors, whether immobile or changing," he wrote, "just so is the art of knowing, that is to say Dialectic or Logic, one and the same doctrine for perceiving all things." Or, as he said of its very foundations, "just as colors visible in themselves, so principles in themselves intelligible are clearer the ones than the others."[29] Antoine Fouquelin, in his 1555 translated version of Talon's *Rhetorica*, asserted that even the Philosopher gave in to such temptations: "Aristotle praises above all others those metaphors that strike the eye by the clarity of their meaning."[30] One can readily offer a myriad other examples. No one can question that the presence of visual metaphors, diagrams, and similar devices in Ramist writings is impressive. Yet we should beware.

First, the implications of such metaphors are evidently ambiguous at best (as the juxtaposition of these citations for and against Aristotle shows). Second, even so convinced a Ramist as Fouquelin remained ambivalent. The translation of the 1548 *Rhetorica* in the passage just cited was exact, but very frequently Fouquelin changed Talon's visual metaphors into auditory ones.[31] That would suggest a "return" to discussions of the relation between *voces, notae,* and *notiones* (spoken words, written signs, and denoted concepts) that had always been a part of the tradition. I will shortly show that in fact these notions always remained essential in Ramism, as did their conceptual implications.

Third, visual devices of one kind or another had always been important to *teaching* (hence Aristotle's remarks about metaphors). Early in the sixteenth century certain grammars and rhetorics for schoolchildren had already emphasized such aids. Mathias Ringmann's 1509 *Grammatica figurata* and Thomas Murner's *Chartiludium logicæ,* published in Warsaw in 1507 and Strasbourg in 1509, taught grammar as a card game.[32] Tory's 1529 *Champ fleury* depended upon its emblematic figurations, and may well have played a role in the development of Everard Digby's emblematic theory of knowledge published in his 1579 *Theoria analytica*. All this suggests that at least until considerably later we need to distinguish (as did Ramus himself) between logic as a teaching process and logic as a procedure for understanding reason and acquiring knowledge. The one made much use of visual devices. The other had little to do with them.

Dialectic or logic as an instrument of rationality was, Ramus insisted, first and foremost a matter of understanding order: both that of the rational elaboration of meaning within a given single level of argument, and that of the relation between different levels. More important for this than any visual aid was the connection he made between dialectic and mathematics. He was not alone. Many writers linked linguistic and mathematical questions and often wrote on both subjects. Charles de Bouvelles, the best-known French mathematician of his time, first published on mathematical subjects as early as 1510, but he was most active in mid-century. In 1533 he had published on linguistic matters as well. Claude de Boissière and Jacques Peletier Du Mans were also writing on both.[33] The association seemed entirely ordinary, and Catherine Dunn is not altogether right to imply that Ramus "turned to mathematics" in 1544–45 because he was no longer allowed to profess philosophy.[34]

In 1555 Ramus published his *Arithmetica* (defining the subject as the doctrine of reckoning well "doctrina bene numerandi") and his *Dialectique*, or "art of disputing well" ("Dialectique est art de bien disputer").[35] In the French text he went out of his way to relate the two: "So the first humans, who already knew Mathematics before the Flood, also thought of Dialectic."[36] Actually none of them was doing more than giving the Greek term *mathema* its etymological face value: that which is learned, or ordered knowledge itself (the mathematical sciences particularly, but as a special case). Nelly Bruyère has shown how important the matter really was. She argues that in Ramus's earliest extant writings (all from 1643: a manuscript and two printed works) the terms *mathema* and *mathesis* were clearly derived from Plato. *Mathesis,* she observes, retained its Greek sense of knowledge in process of acquisition. This dynamic mathesis "constituted the fundamental definition of Ramist dialectic, inspiring the method and fulfilled within it." *Mathesis* was a faculty of mind, a dynamic process bound in some way to the very sources of knowing; *mathema* was knowledge ordered. As levels of rational judgment they preceded those of the method itself and of syllogism (invention, the search for tropes, and so forth).[37]

A discussion of mathematics as simultaneously primary in reason and connected in some profound way with the very order of things did not, however, require Plato as its source (whatever Ramus's own strategic needs may have been). These claims were so widespread that even in a practical arithmetic such as Claude de Boissière's of 1554, the author instinctively noted that his "art of arithmetic" was connected first to the regulatory ordering of "this machine of the world" by the "Creator."[38] Over thirty years before, Estienne de La Roche had made similar remarks, also in a practical arithmetic.[39] For a more sophisticated writer like Bouvelles, neither a Christian divinity nor a Platonic idea was needed to furnish an ultimate source of ordered rational force, although he leaves it unclear as to just what was needed. The earliest known printed book, the *Treviso arithmetic* of 1478, had in fact already used the trope without claims of authoritative origin: "all things which have existed since the beginning of time have owed their origin to number." A century later, in his 1598 *Arcadia,* Lope de Vega repeated Alfonso de la Torre's fifteenth-century *Visión delectable de la Philosophia e de las otras sçienças* in calling arithmetic the "source and origin from which all good is born, which constructed all things."[40]

All agreed that arithmetic was the first of the mathematical disciplines (the other three being music, geometry, and astronomy). Arithmetic and geometry, wrote Bouvelles, differed from one another "as the soul from the body" ("pareille difference comme entre lame & le corps"). The former was "devoted to numbers, which lie and are situated within the soul" ("lesquelz sont gisans & situez en lame"). That is why arithmetic came first "in excellence of dignity and in natural perfection" ("en excellence de dignité & de naturelle perfection"). For arithmetic dealt with the concealed properties of things:

Arithmetic is comprised in but four principles: that is to say in one, two, three, and four, which joined together make the number ten:

according to Pythagoras's opinion, and that of all philosophers, this is most mystical and of great perfection. For in it as well, through the four numbers mentioned above, is based the whole science of Music, and all its consonances and harmonies. In imitation of Arithmetic, Geometry is also founded upon and contained by only four principles, in Latin called, *Punctum, Linea, Superficies, Corpus:* i.e., point, line, plane or surface, and body. And there is nothing to consider and contemplate other than these four, which are the measure of all things firm and solid, whether celestial or beneath the skies.[41]

Bouvelles remarked that mathematical sciences echoed the Holy Trinity in having but three dimensions: length, width, depth. Only the point was "exempt," resembling "arithmetical unity, just as unity is not a number, but the beginning and principle of all numbers."[42] Peletier would note in his 1552 *Arithmetique* that "however much unity may be indivisible, inasmuch as it is the beginning of whole numbers, ... yet we imagine it capable of infinite division."[43] In the 1554 *Algebre* he added that "One" was the "true image of the divinity."[44] More generally, Thomas Sebillet spoke in his 1548 *Art poetique* of all the arts as referring to an ultimate order of things hidden in "the profound celestial abyss where is the divinity."[45]

In fact, however, a sense of some divine presence was no longer altogether necessary. In the body of the work just cited, Bouvelles asserted that the need for mathematics lay simply in their coincidence with the order of things and indeed of all practice. That order lay otherwise hidden ("occulté," as Peletier put it in the "Proëme" to his *Algebre*), and where it came from was indifferent to the mathematician in particular or to the certainty of knowledge in general:

Nor is it at all possible for the human mechanism to profit well in philosophy and the sciences of natural things, without the help of the mathematical arts. These contain several mystical ones, upon which the ancient philosophers based themselves and by which they were guided in finding and describing the occult properties of all natural things. For as the philosophical proverb says, *Species rerum sunt, ut species magnitudinum & numerorum.* That is to say, the kinds of natural things are like the kinds of quantities and of numbers.[46]

The Idea of Meaning and Practice of Method   137

For "what is there in the world," Peletier was to ask, "that is not signified by numbers?" This "delectable abyss and ordered confusion" of numbers "represents the face and figure of the universe, wherein all Beings are in their order and hold an invariable rank":[47] words surely derived from Sebillet's *Poétique*.

Such statements found their counterparts in almost every treatise having to do with linguistic questions, whether grammars, poetics, rhetorics, or logics. Words and their order correspond, wrote Louis Meigret in his 1550 grammatical work, to concepts and judgments; so too wrote Robert Estienne in his Latin grammar of 1558.[48] *Ratio* and *oratio* may be identified with one another. In his 1555 *Art poëtique*, Peletier compared words in language, numbers in arithmetic, and stones in masonry. The year before he had spoken of arithmetic as providing the foundation of all judgment, without which we are like a mason having stones, lime, and sand but no knowledge of how to combine them. Numbers, he had written in the 1552 *Arithmetique*, were like an alphabet, a genuine language whose order signified and corresponded to mental concepts and judgments.[49] Three years later Ramus put this equation the other way around:

These two words [*logism* and *syllogism*] properly signify counting and enumerating. And from this signification arithmetic is called Logistic. It would seem these words have been translated out of mathematics into dialectic because just as the good reckoner, in addition and subtraction, sees with certainty the remainder in closing the count, so dialecticians, adding the proposition and subtracting the supposition, see in their conclusion the truth or falsity of the question.[50]

Much earlier, in his 1540 *De causis*, Julius Caesar Scaliger had already gone beyond relations between "languages" or mere metaphors of material things:

For things are as if double: either material or immaterial. And immaterial things are either outside the intellect, as God, or in the intellect, as concepts (I call concepts kinds of things understood in the mind) for as the hand acts on matter so the intellect acts on concepts.... And utterance is a sign of such notions as are in the soul. They have three conditions: formation, composition, truth. Truth is the adequation of a proposition to the thing of which it is the sign.[51]

Sebillet followed up on this eight years later by remarking that once "a foundation has been laid by invention, and the project for the future building set by calculated order [économie], a search follows for the stones or bricks to build and shape it. These are propositions, words or terms, among which as careful a choice and discretion exists as among things."[52] This passage clearly recalls Bouvelles's assertion of analogy between "kinds of natural things" and "kinds of quantities and of numbers."

Mathematics, words, and things furnished three systems, able to refer to one another, "adequate" in denotation (Scaliger's word was *aequatio*), and capable of being grasped in reasoned judgment. Bouvelles emphasized that numbers related to what rules the *system* of things. They revealed, we saw, the "occult properties of all natural things." They guided us toward their true meaning. What was shown was not things themselves but what made them meaningful to us. That may be why Bouvelles evoked not only Pythagoras, Archimedes, Euclid, and other ancients but, alone among the moderns, the Neoplatonic and politically ecumenical Nicholas of Cusa, "a man inferior to none in all knowledge, [who] cultivated geometry so studiously that he discovered very many things unknown to geometers before him."[53] Here we have the divine once again, but represented in a *deus absconditus*, under whose benign rule humans had to take responsibility for their knowledge and actions (as they might use them to develop a more peaceful and stable political process). The French language, wrote Meigret, had now reached such perfection as to be able to contain "even high theology" ("cete tant haote theolojie"), for that language "has in itself such order as to let us distinguish the parts of which all languages are composed." The language "of human reason" ("de la rézon humeine") may differ from "the authority of divine wisdom" ("l'aothorité de la sapiençe diuine"), but its French language can now contain such divinity.[54]

Such mathematization clearly had nothing at all to do with visualization, and very little to do—at least directly—with spatial figuration. The "mathematical" order discussed here did assure certain kinds of conceptual elements, certain modes of representation, certain kinds of reasoning processes. It had to do with some logic of rationality (although it may not yet be "ours"). But it remained very much a verbal order. If arithmetic was the doctrine of reckoning well, dialectic was the art of disputing well, and it was so because the one was developed from the other (as we saw Ramus claim). In that sense, Ramus continued in his definition, dialectic "is named logic, for both are derived from *logos,* that is to say, reason."[55]

He had long since written in the 1643 *Dialecticæ institutiones* that "dialectica virtus est disserendi": "the force of dialectic is that of discoursing precisely." *Disserere* connoted a carefully analytical use of language, and we need not therefore be surprised to see Ramus say that *disserere* was the same thing as to reason. Dialectic had to show a process, as he was to put it clearly in the 1566 *Dialectica,* that "continually proceeds from universals to singulars" ("ab universalibus ad singularia perpetuó progreditur").[56] That was the way of reasoned judgment itself, not just of the language bearing it. He would thus write in the 1569 *Schola* that reason and discourse were the same.[57] He said he had found this in Plato: "getting from his Socratic dialogues the equation that to discourse (*disserere*) is the same as to use one's reason (*ratione uti*), and hence that the distribution of dialectic which I had come across applied to the whole mental apparatus (*logica*)."[58] Thus the art of "bene disserendi" was also one of thinking well. Such an art could not help but depend upon a precise comprehension of how words and syntax mean, and upon a fixing of language as to terminology, grammar, and syntax: that was no doubt why so strong a fear of madness ran through the writings of so many who dealt with language—and why, too, such madness was associated with the social dissolution and political disarray of the time.

Logic, dialectic, and the proper use of words do allow us to get at meaningful truths. But they are truths of relationship and practical truths of manipulative action (of one domain upon another). There may be still some hidden origin of order, but our discourses have no longer any access to it. "Notation," Ramus wrote, the revelation (by etymology or other means) of the meaning of a word ("nom") in some representation of reality—easy when languages were "en leur entier" ("whole," as he remarked in various places)—could now only be used with great care. When we do so, we find not some external origin but a process of rational judgment: as when, for example, examining conjugate terms we find "a symbol of causes and effects to whose discovery we are often directed thanks to this conjugation of substantives, for the primitive term contains the cause of its conjugates, as Justice is the cause by which humans are just and live justly."[59] But any "final origin" for all this has disappeared, remaining, if at all, only as the distant God of Descartes's *Meditations.*

Words, thought Meigret, might well once have shown their first cause, but if so they no longer do. A word is but the "image" of a sound and a concept, "an assemblage of letters" ("un assemblement de lettres") whose meaning comes from its relation to other such images. Communication is a matter of customary usage. To believe otherwise is to adopt "a false principle" from which "follows an abyss of errors and confusion: so much so that when I consider the mistakes and flaws entertained by these poor superstitious people, I am reminded of a proverb common in Lyon, that 'mal avizé a prou peine.'" Indeed, such beliefs can come only from "great ignorance and superstition" ("d'vne grand' ignoranç' e superstiçion").[60]

Henri Estienne was even more violent in his rejection of such claims of this kind as were still published. In the 1562 edition of his *Conformité*, for example, he included a strong attack on Joachim Périon's etymologies. He railed that among them many were entirely "fantastic" ("phantastique"), or they were "stupid and inept, and so clumsy and asinine, that had this poor monk left no other evidence of his clumsiness and asininity one might think this work to be a forgery."[61] Léon Feugère attributed what he referred to as Estienne's "bad temper" to the fact that Périon was a monk (and the incident is curious, to say the least, if it is actually the case that the *Conciones*, a school anthology published only eight years later and still reprinted into the nineteenth century, was indeed compiled by them both).[62] More to the point here, I think, were the friendship and evident affinities between Ramus and Estienne. Ramus's dispute with Périon dated back to 1543 and the latter's anti-Ramist defense of Aristotle, and to 1547 and the debate over Cicero. Yet more important was the rejection of the very premise behind etymologizing of this kind. That was clearly in question here.

Discourse was no longer backed by some founding origin. The relation of orders sufficed—plus the judgment that a proposition was "clear and manifest" ("clere et manifeste"). "If," wrote Ramus, "a simple proposition is certain and credible, it is adjudged true, by a judgment of science if from necessity, of opinion if contingent."[63] Such assertions appear similar to the Cartesian axiom, and its "proofs" were no less nebulous: for how could one make a *jugement de science*? Science and necessity, opinion and contingency were given as axiomatic: one should "learn Dialectic to dispute well because it teaches us the truth, and therefore falsity of all reason, whether necessary, which is science, or contingent, i.e., what may both be and not be, which is opinion." Or again: "The judgment of absolutely true disjunction will be science, that of supposed or contingent disjunction will merely be opinion."[64] The argument was circular. It was about the internal coherence of a system of logic. Nonetheless, the claims went further. Ramus insisted that such judgment is as natural to animals as to humans and is thus defining of all animate life. It follows, since animals do not verbalize, that the simple proposition *is* the order of phenomena received via the senses; or, at least, that it is an axiomatic ordering of "sensible things":

> Judgment of the simple proposition is wholly natural and indeed common in part to animals as for instance of sensible things in the proposition itself.... Every animate being has in itself a natural power of judging that we call sense, also called in [Aristotle's] second Topics, species of judgment. And certainly sense is the true judge of things properly subject to its jurisdiction, as the eye of color, the ear of sound, the olfactory of smell.... Thus the judgment of the simple proposition is not wholly proper to humans, whereas the understanding of the universal proposition is, even though it appears that animals have some small part of reason.... Yet certainly this judgment is nothing else in animals than the phantasm of sensible notions, and animals do not have any conception of the universal.[65]

This argument implied not only that the word corresponded to the thing in some way beyond an association of their systems of order (as it did in Sebillet, in Scaliger, in Bouvelles), but also that certain relationships were "natural," able to be understood by some kind of innate *sensible union* between *fantasie* and phenomenon. Such relations were essential and in no way merely dependent on some symbolic system. Beyond them, however, remained the universal, approachable only by the rational understanding: "And by so much as it knows the universal, by so much is it more excellent and honorable than sense, understands better cause and principle, and is more scientific." To that extent, method revealed the divinity of humans, just as intelligence, "the syllogistic faculty," placed them above animals. Such a supposition sought perhaps to "justify" the entire absence of any explanation as to how a coherence theory of truth might yet provide knowledge of the world.[66]

Axiomatic knowledge became, then, as we have seen, the origin and source of the mathematical processes of logic. These immediately intelligible axioms of universal principles were unique to human reason. They relied upon those ordered systematic relationships of mathematics, language, reason, and things, whose very interplay bore witness to their truth. This reliability made possible the subsequent derivation of truths, "theses," through those "sensible notions" that permitted propositions and judgments to be commensurable with the structures of phenomena.[67] These ordered relationships allowing a knowledge of material (and immaterial) things were thus themselves thought of as a coherent system of logic. Later, correspondence, theories of truth, and knowledge (dependent to an increasing degree on spatialization and visualization) were not yet at all in question. The world and our reason were a logic, a precisely structured discourse—an arithmetic.

By the time he was writing the *Conformité* in 1562, therefore, Henri Estienne was very clear that what made for linguistic perfection was twofold. It consisted, first, in the proper ordering of the system within itself (as a *mathema*, we might say). In this it was more than merely analogous with arithmetic or any other mathematical order. Second, such perfection consisted in the quantity of clearly and separately defined words a language contained for naming things.[68] With the use of such a language, Estienne could write in the much later *Précellence* (1579) that humans had the great advantage "above all other animals" of "expressing their conceptions to one another by means of language."[69]

For Henri Estienne this was also a political claim, one put forward after his savage attack on Catherine de Medici (1575: let us not forget that the St. Bartholomew's Day massacre, in which Ramus had been murdered, had happened only three years before) and after his scathing satire on the distortion of the French language.[70] It seemed clearly to announce an end to the debate insofar at least as it concerned the connection of linguistic and conceptual order and knowledge. There yet remained a long way to go before they could be converted into a Cartesian kind of *mathesis*, which did appear to depend upon that spatial visualization Ong sought to ascribe to Ramus. As he himself wrote of Murner's *Chartiludium*, republished in 1629, and of the emblematic theory of knowledge advanced in Digby's 1579 *Theoria*, both books "reveal some of the stresses and strains which put in their appearance as the spatialized world apprehended by vision came to be more and more exploited to aid thinking. In both authors the stresses were particularly great because spatial models were being pressed into service to deal not merely with reality but with thought itself."[71]

Perhaps. But the tardiness of this insecurity suggests rather that a visual and spatial reordering of thought had yet to occur. We remain still in a world where reason was predicated upon an interrelation of conceptual, "linguistic" processes in which a still rather imprecise concept of (mathematical) "order" had replaced any other notion of "origin." Common to these mid-century texts were, above all, the ambivalence of their effort to ground reason and its judgment, their clear sense of discomfort with social, political, and educational conditions, and their disquiet concerning philosophical certainties. The Ramist method provided a teaching device that started to simplify the issues, by allowing them to be readily ordered and set out. But security of rational definition, stability of linguistic order, and asserted adequacy of conceptual reference had always been necessary before the method's very foundations could be at all defined. We begin to see this in later Ramist texts, but above all in still later writings such as Henri Estienne's *Précellence*. Even so, many years were to pass before a coherent theory of truth and knowledge would be articulated upon a theory of correspondence. Only then could modern epistemologies and an instrumental science be elaborated—with whatever success. This suggests, I think, a rather different history from the one with which we have grown familiar in recent years, one that implies a more complicated and slower change in mental life and explains (if need be) why drastic cultural struggle and debate went on for at least a century and a half.

NOTES

1. Walter J. Ong, *Ramus, Method, and the Decay of Dialogue: From the Art of Discourse to the Art of Reason* (Cambridge, Mass.: Harvard University Press, 1958). Ong noted that the royal ban forbidding Ramus from teaching philosophy owed more to "his demonstrated incompetence" than anything else; his opponents urged that his work not only contained things "faulses et estranges," but also misrepresented "the very meaning of what it pretends to comment on" (24). Carl von Prantl, I. M. Bochenski and Norman E. Nelson support this judgment, as does James J. Murphy (introduction to Peter Ramus, *Arguments in Rhetoric against Quintilian*, translation and text of *Rhetoricae distinctiones in Quintilianum (1549)*, trans. Carole Newlands [Dekalb, Ill.: Northern Illinois University Press, 1986], 57 n. 90). On Ramus, apart from the texts mentioned in subsequent notes, I have consulted Philippe Desan, *Naissance de la méthode: Machiavel, La Ramée, Bodin, Montaigne, Descartes* (Paris: Nizet,

1987); R. Hooykaas, *Humanisme, science et réforme: Pierre de La Ramée, 1515–1572* (Leiden: J. Brill, 1958); Wilbur S. Howell, *Logic and Rhetoric in England, 1500–1700* (Princeton N.J.: Princeton University Press, 1956); Walter J. Ong, *Ramus and Talon Inventory: A Short-Title Inventory of the Published Works of Peter Ramus (1515–1572) and of Omer Talon (ca. 1510–1562)* (Cambridge, Mass.: Harvard University Press, 1958); Wilhelm Risse, *Die Logik der Neuzeit, I: 1500–1640* (Stuttgart-Bad Canstatt: Friedrich Frommans, 1964); and Charles T. Waddington, *Ramus (Pierre de La Ramée): Sa vie, ses écrits et ses opinions* (Paris: Ch. Meyrueis, 1855).

2. Timothy J. Reiss, *The Discourse of Modernism* (Ithaca, N.Y.: Cornell University Press, 1982), 25.

3. Desiderius Erasmus, "Pseudocheus and Philetymus," in *Colloquies* [1518–33], trans. Craig R. Thompson (Chicago: University of Chicago Press, 1965), 134.

4. See Marc Fumaroli, *L'Age de l'éloquence: Rhétorique et "res literaria" de la Renaissance au seuil de l'époque classique* (Geneva: Droz, 1980); Daniel Javitch, *Poetry and Courtliness in Renaissance England* (Princeton, N.J.: Princeton University Press, 1978); and Timothy J. Reiss, "1640, The Jesuit Pedagogue Pierre Le Moyne Publishes *Les Peintures morales:* Problems in Logic and Rhetoric," in *A New History of French Literature*, ed. Denis Hollier et al. (Cambridge, Mass: Harvard University Press, 1989), 258–62.

5. Thomas Wilson, *The Rule of Reason Conteinying the Arte of Logique* [1551], ed. Richard S. Sprague (Northridge, Calif.: San Fernando Valley State College, 1972), 8–9.

6. In the early 1500s several schools for the study of these languages were set up in western Europe. They included the Collegium Trilingue at the University of Louvain, founded in 1517 through a bequest from Jerome Busleiden, Erasmus's and Thomas More's friend; Corpus Christi, Oxford; Christ's and St. John's Colleges, Cambridge; the trilingual college at the new University of Alcalá; the College of St. Nicholas at the University of Vienna; the Collège Royal in Paris (now the Collège de France). See Thompson, in Erasmus, *Colloquies*, 224.

7. G. A. Padley, *Grammatical Theory in Western Europe, 1500–1700*, 3 vols. (Cambridge: Cambridge University Press, 1976–87).

8. Peter Ramus, *Dialectique* [1555], ed. Michel Dassonville (Geneva: Droz, 1964), 144: "méthode est disposition par laquelle entre plusieurs choses la première de notice est disposée au premier lieu, la deuzième au deuzième, la troizième au troizième et ainsi conséquemment." Unless otherwise specified, all translations from the French and Latin are mine.

9. Ramus, *Dialectique*, 145: "Méthode de nature est par laquelle ce qui est du tout et absolument plus évident et plus notoire est préposé." Also called "méthode d'art parce qu'elle est gardée en la tradition des ars et doctrines et

respond en qualité de jugement à l'énonciation nécessaire et syllogisme deüement conclu."

10. Ramus, *Dialectique,* 150: "en laquelle les choses précédentes non pas du tout et absolument notoires, mais néantmoins plus convenables à celluy qu'il faut enseigner, et plus probables à l'induire et amener où nous prétendons."

11. Ong, *Ramus,* 245–46, 263–64; see also Nelly Bruyère, *Méthode et dialectique dans l'oeuvre de La Ramée: Renaissance et âge classique* (Paris: J. Vrin, 1984), 205–310.

12. Peter Ramus, *Scholae in liberales artes* [1569], intro. Walter J. Ong (Hildesheim: Georg Olms, 1970), v.

13. Peter Ramus and Omer Talon, *Collectaneae, praefationes, epistolae, orationes* [1577, 1599], intro. Walter J. Ong (Hildesheim: Georg Olms, 1969), viii.

14. Ramus, *Dialectique,* 142: "Voylà l'art et jugement du syllogisme, tant simple que composé, duquel la proposition est ordinairement de quelque art, comme de Grammaire, Rhétorique, Logique, Mathématique, Méchanique, Physique, Ethique, Politique, des loix divines et humaines et générallement de tous ars."

15. Erasmus, "The New Mother," in *Colloquies,* 269–70.

16. Erasmus, "The New Mother," 390–91.

17. See Manuel Breva-Claramonte, *Sanctius's Theory of Language: A Contribution to the History of Renaissance Linguistics* (Amsterdam: John Benjamins, 1983), 73.

18. Timothy J. Reiss, "Meaning in Early Sixteenth-Century Grammar and Rhetoric: Palsgrave, Fabri, Tory," typescript, 1987. The works in question are: Pierre Fabri, *Le Grant et vray art de pleine rhetorique* [1521], ed. A. Héron (Rouen: Lestringant, 1890); John Palsgrave, *L'Eclaircissement de la langue française*... [1530], ed. F. Genin (Paris: Imprimerie Nationale, 1852); and Geoffroy Tory, *Champ fleury ou l'art et science de la proportion des lettres* [1529], ed. Gustave Cohen (Paris: Bosse, 1931).

19. Timothy J. Reiss, *Tragedy and Truth: Studies in the Development of a Renaissance and Neoclassical Discourse* (New Haven, Conn: Yale University Press, 1980), chap. 2.

20. Henri Estienne, *Conformité du langage françois avec le grec* [1562], ed. Léon Feugère (Paris: Delalain, 1853), 27: "Autant se trouve d'absurdité (voire encores plus) en quelques autres locutions, lesquelles touttefois plaisent à plusieurs non pour autre raison que pource qu'elles se disent contre toute raison. Et de faict, si ce sot (voire enragé) désir de novalité va tousjours gagnant pays, & renversant tout par où il passe, i'ay grand peur qu'en la fin il ne faille appeler la Teste le Pied, & le Pied la Teste: & principalement quand un tel désir sera entré au cerveau de gens ignorans, soyent courtisans, ou autres." There is not a lot on Estienne (although all books on the growth of printing include discussions of him and his relatives). The standard biography remains the now dated work

of Louis Clément: *Henri Estienne et son oeuvre française (étude d'histoire littéraire et de philologie)* (1898; reprint, Geneva: Slatkine, 1967).

21. Henri Etienne, *Apologie pour Hérodote, ou traité de la conformité des merveilles anciennes avec les modernes* [1566], ed. Paul Ristelhuber, 2 vols. (Paris: Liseux, 1879); *Deux dialogues du nouveau langage françois italianizé et autrement desguizé, principalement entre les courtisans de ce temps* [1578], ed. P. Ristelhuber, 2 vols. (Paris: Lemerre, 1885); and *Discours merveilleux de la vie, actions & deportemens de Catherine de Medicis royne mere. Auquel sont recitez les moyens qu'elle a tenu pour vsurper le gouuernement du royaume de France, et ruiner lestat d'iceluy* (Geneva, 1575). This last text was probably written by Estienne with Innocent Gentillet.

22. Estienne was by no means the first to assert the quality of his own language by rejecting others. Most recently Pietro Bembo and Etienne Dolet had done so, while Dante and Machiavelli were among divers eminent precursors. Most important of all for sixteenth-century scholars was the scorn poured on Greek affectations by Cicero in *De finibus*. Bembo's and Dolet's eventual turn against Ciceronianism had its source in Cicero himself (Kees Meerhoff, *Rhétorique et poétique au XVIe siècle en France: Du Bellay, Ramus et les autres* [Leiden: J. Brill, 1986], 6–8). Like Ramus, what they were rejecting was not a style per se, but a theory and a slavish imitation of style. Imitation might be necessary at the moment of creating a new language, but its ultimate goal was to free the imitator from all dependence and allow the writer to "sound," depict, and work out "son naturel," as Du Bellay wrote. The poet was clear (this in 1549) that proper language use necessarily accompanied individual "jugement," as well as knowledge of one's "forces" and abilities ("combien ses epaules peuvent porter"). He was evidently approaching the idea that language and meaning now involved the responsibility of some "subject" (Joachim Du Bellay, *La Deffence et illustration de la langue françoyse* [1549], ed. Henri Chamard [1946; reprint, Paris: Didier, 1970], 107).

23. Peter Ramus, *Traitté des meurs et facons des anciens gavloys, traduit du latin ... par Michel de Castelnau ...* (Paris: Denys du Val, 1581). This is a reprint of the translation first published in 1559, the year in which the first Latin edition was also published.

24. Timothy J. Reiss, "Montaigne and the Subject of Polity," *Literary Theory / Renaissance Texts,* ed. Patricia Parker and David Quint (Baltimore, Md.: Johns Hopkins University Press, 1986), 115–49.

25. Ramus, *Dialectique,* 52–53: "Certes, la voye mesme [to acquire knowledge] nous est proposée par laquelle ilz debvoyent tous cheminer et marcher, partie de principes, qui est la raison universelle, partie d'experience, qui est l'induction singulière.... Et puis, après avoir faict ceste recherche et eslite, j'ai tasché à disposer toute ceste matière en manière et façon qui nous est monstrée par la méthode artificielle."

26. Ong, *Ramus*, 8–9.
27. Ong himself assigned the change to Rudolph Agricola's work but saw Ramus as his proximate successor (*Ramus*, 121).
28. Ramus, *Dialectique*, 61–62: "la vérité des choses comprises ès ars est ainsi naturellement proposée [in dialectic] à l'esprit comme est la couleur à la veüe, et ce que nous appelons enseigner n'est pas bailler la sapience ains seulement tourner et diriger l'esprit à contempler ce que de soy-mesme il eut peu apercevoir s'il se fut là tourné et dirigé.... Tout ainsi que les yeux des chauves souris s'eblouissent en la clarté du jour, semblablement que la poincte de nostre entendement se mouce et rebouche aux choses de leur nature trèsclaires et trèsmanifestes."
29. Ramus, *Dialectique*, 62 and 124: "tout ainsi que la veüe est commune à veoir toutes couleurs, soyent immuables, soyent muables, ainsi l'art de cognoistre, c'est-à-dire Dialectique ou Logique, est une et mesme doctrine pour apercevoir toutes choses"; and "comme les couleurs par soy visibles, ainsi les principes par soy intelligibles sont plus clers les uns que les autres."
30. Antoine Fouquelin, *La Rhétorique françoise*... [1557] (Paris: André Wechel, 1557), 15v: "Parquoy Aristote loüe entre toutes les autres, ces Metaphores, lesquelles frapent les yeus, pour la clarté de leur signification." On Fouquelin, see also Walter J. Ong, S.J., "Fouquelin's French Rhetoric and the Ramist Vernacular Tradition," *Studies in Philology* 51 (1954): 127–42.
31. Roy E. Leake, Jr., "The Relationship of Two Ramist Rhetorics: Omer Talon's *Rhetorica* and Antoine Fouquelin's *Rhetorique françoise*," *Bibliothèque d'Humanisme et Renaissance* 30, no. 1 (1968): 85–108. This commentary is on page 101.
32. Jean-Claude Margolin, "Mathias Ringmann's *Grammatica figurata*; or, Grammar as a Card Game," *Yale French Studies* 47 (1972): 33–46.
33. I will be referring to: Claude de Boissière, *L'Art d'arythmetique contenant toute dimention, tres-singulier et commode, tant pour l'art militaire que autres calculations* (Paris: Annet Briere, 1554), and "Autre art poetique reduit en bonne méthode," in Thomas Sebillet, *Art poetique françois: pour l'instruction des ieunes studieux, & encor' peu auancez en la poésie françoise. Auec le Quintil Horatian*... (Paris: veufve Jean Ruelle, 1573), 263–305; Charles de Bouvelles, *Geometricum opus, duobus libris comprehensum* (Paris: Michaelis Vascosanus, 1557), *Liber de differentia vulgarium linguarum, et Gallici sermonis varietate*...; *Que voces apud Gallos sint factitiae et arbitrariae, vel barbariae*...; *De hallucinatione Gallicanorum nominum* (Paris: Robertus Stephanus, 1533), and *Livre singulier et utile, touchant l'art et practique de Geometrie, composée nouuellement en Françoys* (Paris: Simon de Colines, 1542); and Jacques Peletier du Mans, *L'Algebre*... (Lyon: Ian de Tournes, 1554), *L'Aritmetique*... (Poitiers: Ian de Marnef, 1552), *L'Art poëtique* [1555], ed. André Boulanger (Paris: Belles Lettres, 1930), *De l'usage de la géometrie*... (Paris: Gilles Gourbin,

1573), and *Dialogue de l'ortografe e prononciation françoese*... (Poitiers: Ian Enguilbert de Marnef, 1550).

34. Peter Ramus, *The Logike*..., trans. Roland MacIlmaine [1574], ed. Catherine M. Dunn (Northridge, Calif.: San Fernando Valley State College, 1969), xii.

35. Peter Ramus, *Arithméticae libri tres*... (Paris: Andreas Wechelus, 1555), l, and *Dialectique*, 61.

36. Ramus, *Dialectique*, 50: "Or doncques les premiers hommes, qui avoyent jà congneu les Mathématiques devant le déluge, ont pensé de Dialectique."

37. Bruyère, 55.

38. Boissière, *L'Art*, fol. 4v: "ceste machine du monde."

39. Estienne de La Roche, *L'Arismethique nouuellement composee*... (Lyon: Constantin Fradin, 1520).

40. Frank J. Swetz, *Capitalism and Arithmetic: The New Math of the Fifteenth Century, including the Full Text of the "Treviso Arithmetic,"* trans. David Eugene Smith (La Salle, Ill.: Open Court, 1987), 41; Lope Félix de Vega Carpio, *Arcadia*, ed. Edwin S. Morby (Madrid: Castalia, 1975), 414, 406 n. 66.

41. Bouvelles, *Livre singulier*, fols. 3v–4r: "L'arithmetique est comprise sur quatre principes seulement: cestascauoir sur vng, deux, trois, & quatre, lesquelz conioinctz ensemble font le nombre de dix: lequel selon lopinion de Pythagoras, & de tous philosophes, est fort mystique, & de grande perfection. Car aussi en luy par les quatre premiers nombres dessusdictz, est fondee toute la science de Musique, & toutes les consenances & harmonies dicelle. La Geometrie par limitation de Larithmetique est pareillement fondee & contenue sur quatre principes seulement, nommez en latin, Punctum, Linea, Superficies, Corpus: Cestadire le poinct, la ligne, la plaine ou suffice, & le corps. Et na aultre chose à considerer & à contempler que ces quatre, lesquelles sont les mesures de toute chose ferme & solide, soit celeste, ou soit contenue soulz le ciel."

42. Bouvelles, *Livre singulier*, fol. 5r–v: "Le poinct (qui 'ressemble à lunité en Arithmetique. Car comme lunité nest pas nombre, mais est le commencement & principe de tous nombres...') de ces trois dimensions est du tout exempt."

43. Peletier, *L'Aritmetique*, fol. 28v: "Or est-il que l'Unité combien qu'elle soit indiuisible autant qu'elle est le commencement des Nombres entiers,... nous imaginons aussi l'Unité se pouoir [sic] diuiser en infinies particules."

44. Peletier, *L'Algebre*, 123: "l'Un [est la] Vrey image de la Diuinite."

45. Thomas Sebillet, *Art poetique françoys* [1548], ed. Félix Gaiffe (Paris: Cornély, 1910), 7–8: "ce profond abyme celeste ou est la divinité."

46. Bouvelles, *Livre singulier*, fol. 55v: "Et nest aulcunement possible, que lengin humain puist bien prouffiter en la philosophie & sciences des choses naturelles, sans laide des ars mathematicus: esquelles sont contenues plusieurs mystiques, sur lesquelles se sont fondez & reglez les antiens philosophes, pour inuenter & descripre les occultes, proprietez de toutes choses naturelles. Car

comme on dit en prouerbe philosophique. Species rerum sunt, ut species magnitudinum & numerorum. Cestadire que les especes des choses naturelles, sont comme les especes des quantitez & des nombres."

47. Peletier, *L'Algebre*, 124: "Qui a il au Monde qui ne soèt sinifié, voere conduit par Nombres? ... cet abime delectable [des nombres], e cete ordonnee confusion, represente la face e figure de l'Vnivers dedans lequel tous Etans, sont an leur ordre, e tient un ranc inuariable."

48. Louis Meigret, *Le Tretté de la grammere françoeze* [1550], ed. Wendelin Foerster (Heilbronn: Henninger, 1888), 3. Estienne's Grammar was translated into French by his son, Henri: Robert Estienne, *Traicté de la grammaire françoise* (Paris: Robert Estienne, 1569), 14–15. See also Louis Meigret, *Traicté touchant le commun usage de l'escriture françoise* ... (Paris: Jehan Longis, Vincent Sertenas, et Denis Ianot, 1542). Robert Estienne wrote copiously on linguistic matters. I have referred especially to *Les Déclinaisons des noms et verbes* ... (Paris: Robert Estienne, 1583); *Dictionnaire francoislatin, autrement dit les mots françois, avec les manieres duser diceulx, tournez en latin, corrigé & augmenté* (Paris: Robert Estienne, 1549); and *Dictionarium, seu latinae linguae thesaurus, non singulas modo dictiones continens, sed integras quoque latine & loquendi, & scribendi formulas* ... (Paris: Robertus Stephanus, 1531).

49. Peletier, *L'Art poëtique*, 116; "Proëme," in *L'Algebre;* and *L'Aritmetique*, fols. 2v–3r (cf. fol. 28v).

50. Ramus, *Dialectique*, 126: "tous ces deux motz ["logisme" et "syllogisme"] signifient proprement compte et dénombrement. Et de ceste signification arithmétique est nommée Logistique. Et semble que ces vocables soyent traduictz de mathématique en dialectique car comme le bon compteur en adjoustant et déduisant veoit certainement en la closture du compte le reliqua, ainsi les dialecticiens en adjoustant la proposition et déduisant l'assomption, voyent en la conclusion la verité ou faulseté de la question."

51. Julius Caesar Scaliger, *De causis linguae latinae libri tredecim* ...[1540] (n. p.: Petrus Santandreanus, 1583), 2: "Res autem quem duplices sint: aut materiales, aut immateriales: & immateriales, aut extra intellectum, vt Deus, aut in intellectu, vt notiones (notiones appello rerum species mente comprehensas) quod vtique manus agit in materiam, hoc intellectus in notiones. . . . est enim vox nota earum notionum, quae in anima sunt. Vocis affectiones tres: Formatio, Compositio, Veritas. Veritas est orationis aequatio cum re cuius est nota." I have also made use of Scaliger's *Poetices libri septem* ... [1561], 2d. ed. (n.p.: Petrus Santandreanus, 1581).

52. Sebillet, *Art poetique françoys*, 29: "Ce fondement jetté par invention, et le projét du tout le futur bastiment pris par l'economie, suit la queste des pierres ou briques pour l'élever et former. Celles sont les dictions, mós ou vocables: entre lesquelz a autant bien chois et élection, comme entre lés choses".

53. Bouvelles, *Geometricum*, fol. 3v: "Nicolaus Cusanus. . . . Uir in omni

scientiae genere nulli inferior, tanto studio Geometriam excoluit, ut plurima ante eum Geometris ignota adinuenerit."

54. Meigret, *Grammere*, 3: "ell' a en soe qelq'ordre, par le qel nou' pouuons distinger le' parties dont sont composez tou' langajes, e la reduir' a quelqes regles."

55. Ramus, *Dialectique*, 61: "Et en même sens est nommée Logique, car ces deux noms sont dérivez de *logos*, c'est-à-dire raison."

56. Peter Ramus, *Dialecticae libri duo, Audomari Talaei praelectionibus illustrati* (Paris: Andreas Wechelus, 1566), 367.

57. Ramus, *Scholae in liberales artes*, cols. 155–56. I should perhaps indicate that apart from those works of Ramus and Talon already noted, I have also referred to: Peter Ramus, *Dialecticae Institutiones . . . ; Aristotelicae Animadversiones . . .* (Basel: Sebastianus Henricpetri, 1575), *Gramere . . .* (Paris: André Wechel, 1562), *Grammaire* (Paris: André Wechel, 1572), *Institutionum dialecticarum libri tres . . .* (Paris: Ludouicus Grandinus, 1554), *Rudimenta grammaticae . . .* (Paris: Andreas Wechelus, 1559), *Scholae grammaticae* (Paris: Andreas Wechelus, 1559); Omer Talon, *Dialecticae commentarii tres . . .* (Paris: Ludouicus Grandinus, 1546) (actually by Ramus), *Institutiones Oratoriae . . .* (Paris: Jacobus Bogardus, 1545), and *Rhetorica . . .* (Paris: Andreas Wechelus, 1562); *Rhetorica, e P. Rami regii professoris praelectionibus observata* (Paris: Andreas Wechelus, 1572).

58. Ong, *Ramus*, 42.

59. Ramus, *Dialectique*, 89: "un symbole des causes et effetz à l'inuention desquelz souvent nous sommes conduitz par l'indice de ceste nominale conjugaison car le nom primitif contient la cause de ses conjugués, comme Justice est cause par laquelle l'homme est juste et qu'il vit justement."

60. Meigret, *Grammere*, 4–7: "Voela coment d'vn faos princip' il s'en ensuyt vn abime d'erreurs e confuzion': tellement qe qant je considere le' faotes e inconueniens q'encouret çe' pouures superstiçieus, il me souuient d'vn comun dit de' Lionoes, qe *mal avizé a prou peine.*"

61. Henri Estienne, *Conformité*, 203 n. 1: "sottes et ineptes, et si lourdes et asnieres, que n'estoyent les autres tesmoignages que ce pauvre moine nous a laissez de sa lourderie et asnerie, on pourroit penser cest [sic] oeuvre estre supposé."

62. Henri Estienne and Joachim Périon, *Conciones sive orationes ex graecis latinisque historicis excerptae* (Paris: Henricus Stephanus, 1570).

63. Ramus, *Dialectique*, 123: "Si l'enonciation simple nous est certaine et credible, elle est jugée pour vraye, par jugement de science si elle est necessaire, ou d'opinion si elle est contingente."

64. Ramus, *Dialectique*, 61–62: "apprendre la Dialectique pour bien disputer à cause qu'elle nous déclare la verité, et par conséquent la faulseté de toute raison, soit nécessaire, dont est science, soit contingente, c'est-à-dire qui peult et

estre et non estre, dont est opinion"; 123: "le jugement de la disjonction absolument vraye sera science, de la supposée et contingente sera seullement opinion."

65. Ramus, *Dialectique,* 118: "Le jugement de la simple énonciation est fort naturel mais voyre commun de quelque part aux bestes comme des choses sensibles en l'enonciation propre. . . . tout animant a en soy une puissance naturelle de juger qu'on appelle sens, lequel est pareillement nommé, au deuziesme des Topiques, espèce de jurisdiction, comme l'oeil de la couleur, l'ouye du son, l'odorement de l'odeur. . . . Ainsi le jugement de l'énonciation simple n'est poinct propre de toute part à l'homme, mais bien l'entendement de l'énonciation universelle, combien toutesfois qu'il semble que les bestes ayent quelque petite parcelle de raison. . . . Mais certes ce jugement n'est autre chose aux bestes que la phantaisie des notions sensibles et la beste ne conçoit poinct l'universel."

66. Ramus, *Dialectique,* 118: "Et jà d'autant qu'il cognoist l'universel, d'autant est-il plus excellent et honorable que le sens, et comprend plus la cause et principe, et est plus scientifique." The remark about intelligence as the "syllogistic faculty" is on p. 153.

67. Ramus, *Dialectique,* 124.

68. Henri Estienne, *Conformité,* 19–25.

69. Henri Estienne, *La Précellence du langage françois* [1579], ed. Edmond Huguet, pref. L. Petit de Julleville (Paris: Colin, 1896), 10: "Entre les beaux et grands auantages que Dieu a donnez aux hommes pardessus tous les autres animaux, cestuy si estant un, qu'ils peuvent s'entreposer leurs conceptions par le moyen du langage." For Estienne, I have also used the recent reprint volume containing *Traicté de la conformité du langage françois avec le grec* [1566], *De latinitate falso suspecta* [1576], and *Projet du livre intitulé: De la précellence du langage françois* [1579] (Geneva: Slatkine Reprints, 1972).

70. Henri Estienne, *Deux dialogues.*

71. Ong, *Ramus,* 91.

The Crisis of Cosmography at the End of the Renaissance

Frank Lestringant

Cosmography (or universal geography), according to Ptolemy's canonical definition, differs from *chorography* (or topography) in that it describes the world according to the circles of the sky and their projection onto the earth (i.e., ecliptic, equator, colures, parallels, meridians), and not according to the morphology of the areas under consideration (i.e., islands, continents, mountains, basins, etc.). In addition, cosmography places more importance on an area's quantity (*quantitas*) than on its quality (*qualitas*). It encompasses the entire globe divided into small sections and covered by a projection system network. For each point of terrestial space that it describes, cosmography indicates the latitude and the longitude, and establishes the "climate" and the length of the longest day of the year. Unlike qualitative topography, which is interested only in the particulars and is attached to the picturesque aspect of the earth, including such details as the changing colors of the fields, cosmography, at least in its beginnings, falls within the discipline of mathematics. Precious to the sailor who consults it while navigating his route by instruments, cosmography is also the ideal and universal form that allows the scientist to distribute the totality of "natural philosophy" into vast compilations arranged by continents and zones. The cosmographical model was revived and revised in 1544 by the German cosmographer Sebastian Münster, himself a tributary of Grynaeus and Vadianus, and then about thirty years later, with the publication in 1575 of the twin works of André Thevet and François de Belleforest, it underwent a crisis from which it never recovered.

The signs of this crisis were numerous. As early as 1580, Montaigne, at the beginning of the chapter of his *Essais* devoted to the "cannibals" of Brazil, heaped shame on the cosmographers, who, "because they have over us the advantage of having seen Palestine," "want to enjoy the privilege of telling us news about the rest of the world."[1] Instead of this doubtful and presumptuous science, he preferred the testimony of simple and unrefined men, the so-called *truchements,* accustomed to living in the wild, and of sailors and merchants—in short, of all people who did not go beyond the limits of their own experiences. Echoing Montaigne, Richard Hakluyt "the Younger" saw in the cosmographer a sort of universal liar whose productions were similar to the fiction of poets. Thus, following in Ptolemy's footsteps, in the introductory epistle of the *Principal Navigations* he contrasted the *Peregrinationis historia,* which leads to a certain and complete knowledge of the world, with "those wearie volumes bearing the titles of universall Cosmographie... beyng indeed most untruly and unprofitablie ramassed and hurled together."[2]

It is of course proper to consider the individual circumstances of a disrepute that had become general by 1580. The author implicitly referred to by Hakluyt as well as by Montaigne was André Thevet, great voyager and cosmographer of the last of the Valois, whose boastings were legendary and who claimed to exercise from Paris a veritable monopoly on the geographical knowledge of his time. But beyond his particular case, which is all the more enlightening since it borders on caricature, indeed the discipline as a whole was at stake.[3]

How did it come to that?

Distant Causes: Mathematical Geography and Regional Description

Cosmography claims straightaway a double patronage: that of Ptolemy and that of Strabo. From the former the discipline derives its mathematical and theoretical side; from the latter, its descriptive and empirical side. Ptolemy's *Geographia* is first and foremost a commentary on tables of coordinates. Renaissance cosmographers found in it the latitudes and longitudes of the areas they covered, and they borrowed from it a formal framework and a descriptive order. Ptolemy's lists are indeed based on the map, and they link consecutive areas in the form of a catalogue. As for Strabo's *Geographica,* its influence on Renaissance thought is even more evident, in that Renaissance cosmography often lapsed into history, with its cartographical origins quickly forgotten. Rather than a geogra-

The Crisis of Cosmography 155

phy in the strict sense of the term, it is a "geographical history"—in the sense of natural history—that develops in the rather loose contours of the different continents. Inside each continent, the description follows the natural forms of the land, moving gradually from one country to another. It goes from the Pillars of Hercules toward Russia in the case of Europe, and in the opposite direction from Egypt and Tunisia toward Morocco in the case of Africa.

There is a complete hiatus between these two complementary conceptions of cosmography. The necessity of making such a distinction was evident to Ptolemy himself, who, as we have seen, schematically opposed cosmography and chorography, as quantity is opposed to quality. Before him Eratosthenes and Poseidonius had succeeded in safeguarding the unity of geographical knowledge by placing observations on geology, climatology, and hydrology in the interval between cosmography and chorography. With Ptolemy, then with Strabo, who was hardly inclined to consider general problems, these physical bases disappear, leaving face to face the empty sphere—an abstract framework of mathematical theory—and the picturesque and disorderly mass of local descriptions. Thus, although they represent opposing and even contradictory tendencies, Ptolemy and Strabo appear to agree on essential matters. In their respective enterprises one finds no transition and no link between mathematical geography and local description. In both cases, the break is accentuated in order to emphasize one part of the cosmographical science more than the harmonious totality of its composing elements. In the work of Ptolemy, synecdoche serves to underline the mathematical bases, while it highlights the concrete details and chorography in the work of Strabo, who, moreover, mentions the astronomical preliminaries only for the record.[4]

Renaissance cosmographers consequently inherited a divided knowledge, one that had been cut in two by the scholastic opposition between *quantitatim* and *qualitatim*. Their task, which they carried out more or less successfully, was to try to join together the disconnected pieces of the ancient science. It was a task all the more delicate since the knowledge of the world had been enlarged and the slack *ecumene* had now overflowed into the two hemispheres.

The difficulty arose when, concerned with pedagogy, yet at the same time wanting to base their teachings on the most eminent authority, the modern geographers unanimously adopted the dichotomy dear to Ptolemy. From Sebastian Münster to Pierre d'Avity, including Belleforest and

Thevet, the introductions to all cosmographical works religiously repeat the distinction between mathematical geography and descriptive chorography. It is almost always in order to dispose elegantly of the former, which is reduced to a couple of introductory pages, thereby allowing the cosmographical program to be devoted in its entirety to the latter. The eviction of the mathematical part is compensated, it is true, by an increase in its dignity. It is said that it rightfully comes first, and that the arrangement of the materials confirms this hierarchy, since the sphere precedes the particular regions and places. In reality, however, what results from this loudly proclaimed preeminence? Quickly formulated in some ritual definitions at the beginning of the work, the mathematical exposition has difficulty in counterbalancing the thousands of profuse pages that contain the many-hued descriptions of countries, regions, towns, and islands.

Consequently, instead of searching for the missing link between cosmographical quantity and chorographic quality, Renaissance geographers proceeded in the simplest manner possible: by juxtaposition and collage. One chapter from Ptolemy—the first chapter of the *Geographia*, giving the canonical definitions—was followed by several books in the style of Strabo. Such was the method of Sebastian Münster. The organization of his works consisted in pasting onto the general cartographical framework of the reinvented world map a linear descriptive history, embellished with *mirabilia*, and nourished with chronologies and lists of more or less legendary dynasties.[5]

Indeed, in spite of its title and the cartographical elements contained within it, Münster's *Cosmographia* remain rather traditional. Laid out from the outset, the mathematical framework is filled with material from the *Epitome topographica* of Joachimus Vadianus, whose title clearly designates its subject matter, or from Joannes Boemus's *Omnium Gentium Mores*. Sacred topography and moral history of nations inadequately fill the astronomical framework, which is forgotten as soon as it is established. In addition, Münster does not always attempt to synthesize his information. In order to remain honest and to respect the rules of exchange and recognition that govern the *respublica litteraria*, of which he was an active member, he presents in their original form the documents that his humanist colleagues and his close friends have sent to him, including maps, individual descriptions, and memoirs of towns and countries. Among the excerpts of his correspondence presented to the readers, there is a letter from Louis Vergerius on Istria, which begins:

"From my Istria where I was born";[6] a description of Lüneburg addressed to him from "his uncle Joseph Munster, docteur és deux droictz," accompanied by a letter;[7] and the most significant passages from a "booklet published in Constantinople," in which the Jews give their opinion on Prester John and which Münster translated himself from the Hebrew.[8] In fact, Münster's *Cosmographia* often resembles a simple collection of documents. Thus, in spite of an ambitious title and a real effort toward unification, it is similar to a collection of voyage narratives such as *Novus orbis regionum,* edited in 1532 by Simon Grynaeus.[9] Münster, who moreover had helped prepare a world map for Grynaeus's book, reused some of its disparate elements in the *Cosmographia,* such as voyages of Marco Polo, Cadamosto, Columbus, and Cabral, and a letter of Maximilian Transylvanus on the circumnavigation of Magellan.

Apparently falling short of even Strabo's work, which unified the various first materials of geographical inquiry in a single rewriting, the cosmographical plan of Münster appears to be fundamentally a failure. Nevertheless, what Münster tried to do is in no way negligible. In fact, he tried to substitute the two-dimensional space of cartographical representation for the linear development of annals and histories, as illustrated by the historical culture of the Middle Ages.[10] Cosmographical "history" is inseparable from a primary cartography: the world map laid out right away at the beginning of the book. A map is the complete opposite of an illustration; it is the foundational structure of an area of knowledge, and it outlines the compartments of a taxonomy.

Münster simply did not have the practical means to carry out his ambitions, and the "poorly assembled marquetry" seen in the *Cosmographia* of 1544 did not live up to its unifying plan by which the "quantity" of the world would serve as a framework for the classification of its "quality." The geographers and historians after him who tried to systematize his method of description based on cartography fell into either approximation or caricature.

The famous "theory of climates," also called the theory of mesological determinism, as systematized by the jurist Jean Bodin in the *Methodus ad facilem historiarum cognitionem* (1566) and in *Les six livres de la Republique* (1576), is none other than a cosmographical reading of the political and moral history of the people.[11] Doubtless, it has nothing in common with the crude accumulation or the intinerary list as seen in the works of Joannes Boemus or Joachimus Vadianus. The cartographical structure orients the description along a double axis of comparison:

vertical oppositions and antagonisms follow the axis of the latitudes, which governs the contrast between the North and the South, and lateral equivalences follow the scale of the longitudes, going from East to West. Such a spatial systematization is possible only at the price of flagrant distortions. The elasticity of the cosmographical model lends itself to artificial symmetries obtained by the transfer of objects and discrete strokes of the pen. Bodin's South brings together Italy and Brazil, and his North brings together Canadians and Bretons, Slavs and Scandinavians. Southern melancholy is seen both in the cannibals of Rio de Janeiro and in the Neapolitans unrelenting in their vengence.[12] The somewhat earlier treatise of Guillaume Postel, entitled *Des merveilles du monde* (1553), applied a similar procedure by making the Orient of the Superi contrast with the Occident of the Inferi. The opposition, in this variant of the cosmographical model inspired by the Christian Cabala, governs the relationship of the two hemispheres cut longitudinally along the meridian of Jerusalem.[13] The accordian of the world map, at a time when the longitude could not be precisely determined, made the Holy Land equidistant from the Molucca Islands and Portugal. It also allowed one to consider the *manucode,* the famous bird of paradise of the eastern isles, and the *bradypod* of Brazil, a night bird, as two creatures placed in a relation of inverse symmetry, diametrically opposed on the parallel.

Such geometrical simplifications do not resolve the initial problem—already mentioned in regard to Ptolemy, Strabo, and Münster—of the mounting of descriptive chorography onto mathematical cosmography. In order to cut the Gordian knot, François de Belleforest, the French follower of Münster, chose to do away with the sphere and the numerical references that allow one to assign a latitude and a longitude to each place. Convinced that he was living in the time of sublunar degeneracy, and also taking into consideration the antiquity of Ptolemy, who was the witness of a younger earth and of a cosmic order whose decline was less advanced, he concluded that such a model could not be applied without the risk of making errors:

> Given that, in the many hundreds of years that have passed since the time of Ptolemy, there have been different eclipses and other accidents seen in the astral rules, it is sure that the sun's course has slowed down, and that consequently the degrees limited by it have been modified.[14]

According to Belleforest, the numbers are not certain, and, in addition, trying to discover the hidden arithmetic would violate divine secrets. Furthermore, astronomical calculation nourishes political controversies and rekindles antagonism among rivaling forces. The proof of this was seen in the debate between Spain and Portugal over the Molucca Islands, that floating archipelago that hired cartographers would unscrupulously place toward the West or the East, according to the desires of their respective princes.[15] Belleforest thus denied the right to err, and hence he challenged the cosmographical model in its very principle.

His intimate enemy André Thevet, cosmographer to the kings of France from 1560 to 1589, fostered higher ambitions. Hoping to go beyond a timid revision of Münster's work, he mounted history point by point onto the map. He did this in the most elementary way, by giving the position in degrees for each country, town, or village mentioned. In doing this, Thevet recopied—or had scribes recopy—an already existent description, and glossed it by means of the numerical data taken from Ptolemy's tables. In one of the rough drafts of the *Cosmographie universelle* that have been conserved, these arithmetical notations appear in the form of marginal or interlinear additions made by the author himself, as opposed to a text reworked by a copyist.[16] However, such a rudimentary construction evidently could not be called a system, and the unity of cosmography could not be reestablished by multiplying the stitches between the mathematical framework of the world map and the descriptive diversity of the regions.

Secondary Causes: World Map and Portolan Charts

We now arrive at the second difficulty posed by cosmography: the cartography on which it was based was not homogeneous. In it, theory coexisted with practice, antique tradition with modern experience, and the science of the laboratories with the savoir faire of simple sailors. To be sure, the word *cosmography* was extremely fashionable during the Renaissance. It appeared in the works of uneducated technicians of nautical science who expressed themselves in a vague French, such as the Portuguese sailor Jean Alfonse "de Saintonge,"[17] as well as in the works of learned reformers of the ancient geographical science, such as Waldseemüller, Petrus Apianus, and Sebastian Münster. The discredit that later came upon this concept was due in part to the fact that it was not socially discriminating. It brought together pell-mell, on an equal level, uncultivated pilots and "bargemen," who knew how to sail by dead reckoning and could draw portolan charts and sometimes even world maps, with authentic scientists who, in the shadowy light of their studies, working with documents, controlled new discoveries by the old ones and tried to update the authorities.

A significant example of the confusion between practical and theoretical cosmography can be seen in the letter of dedication of Guillaume Le Testu's *Cosmographie universelle,* an atlas illuminated on vellum paper, dated 1556. In it, the pilot from Le Havre recopies, while addressing himself to Admiral Gaspard de Coligny, a large excerpt from André Thevet's dedication of the *Cosmographie de Levant* to Francis III de La Rochefoucauld.[18] These two homonymous works have almost nothing in common. The *Cosmographie de Levant,* which does not have a map, seems to be the fruit of a hasty compilation that mixes together ancient and modern authors from Pliny, Herodotus, and Diodorus to Erasmus, Vadianus, and Münster. The pretext of the work is a pilgrimage to the Holy Land, during which moral and rhetorical commonplaces are dutifully reproduced in the correct places of the successive compartments of a sort of geographical "snakes and ladders." As a small portable encyclopedia with a geographical base and a heterogeneous content, the *Cosmographie de Levant* is similar in its descriptive design to the *Polyhistor* of C. I. Solinus and is addressed to simple inquisitive persons, i.e., amateurs of curiosities rather than specialists, and half-scientists rather than accomplished humanists.

Le Testu's *Cosmographie universelle,* on the other hand, is the work of a seaman and a practitioner. It is essentially a nautical atlas containing, in addition to six different projection maps of the universe, fifty portolan maps, painted and illuminated on large folio paper. Each map is accompanied by a brief handwritten commentary on the opposite page. Existing in a single copy and addressed to a single person, Admiral de Coligny, head of the French navy, this very elaborate work associates firsthand technical information from the Portuguese school of cartography with the exaltation of the expansionist and conquering politics of Henry II's minister. On all the globe's seas, the French ships bombard and sink the Spanish and Portuguese vessels. The French flag flies over Brazil and Canada, while in the middle of the ocean Coligny's coat of

The Crisis of Cosmography   161

arms, placed on a triumphal chariot, is drawn along by sea monsters led by Neptune and Amphitrite.[19]

In spite of the flagrant disproportion that exists between the two *Cosmographies*, the same rhetorical *topos* introduces both of them, led by the following question: "Who is this new Cosmographer who, after several well-known authors, both ancient and modern, has tried to invent new things?"[20]

In recopying Thevet, Le Testu suppressed only the scholarly reference to Anacharsis, the Scythian whose long voyages made him wiser than the wisest of Greeks. The answer, which is just as commonplace, is borrowed word for word from Thevet, who optimistically evoked immense Nature, recreated from generation to generation by a generous Providence, whose action is always ahead of the timid efforts of human knowledge. The praise of cosmography gives rise to a hymn to Nature and to the expansion of the knowledge of the world:

I will answer them, that Nature has not restrained itself nor is it subject to the writings of the Ancients in such a way that it has lost the power and virtue to produce new and strange things, in addition to the things that they have described.[21]

The interest of such a borrowing is twofold. It shows first of all, as noted above, that the title *cosmographer* was common to two distinct professions, that of a copyist, who popularized or updated, in the best of cases, the knowledge of the ancients, and that of an expert navigator. Furthermore, it proves that cosmography was not an immutable, fixed knowledge or a finished science closed in itself, but that it necessitated constant revision because of its subject matter. Since the cosmos is superabundant and varies with time, its description must try to embrace its movement and continual creation.

It fell to the experience of Renaissance men to adapt man's knowledge to the reality of a world that was no longer exactly the world of Ptolemy or Strabo. The sacrosanct principle of experience, already celebrated by Aristotle, assumed from this moment on a new meaning, clearly marked by a polemical spirit. "Master of all things" ("omnium rerum magistra"), experience became the convenient pretext, especially for Thevet, to demolish the sovereign authority of the ancients in the most diverse domains of natural philosophy. In view of the results of recent explorations that proved the existence of the antipodes and the inhabitability of the torrid and the glacial zones and suggested the immensity of unsuspected continents, they denounced with equal harshness the laziness, complacency, and intolerable presumption of the Greeks and Romans, including even Aristotle, Plato, and Pliny.

The Renaissance crisis of cosmography was born of the absence of a satisfactory answer to two questions: How could one reconcile the practical cartography of deep-sea navigators with the erudite geography of the humanists? And how could one proclaim the primacy of "autopsy"— or personal observation—while at the same time claiming to modernize and revise a scientific tradition that was over fifteen hundred years old? As a result of this double contradiction—practice against theory, autopsy against tradition—cosmography perished in its new form established by Münster and his followers.

The grafting, hazardous by definition, of practical observation onto theoretical hypothesis is the effect of a general constraint that weighed heavily on cartography at the dawn of modern times. The geographer needed to assure an arbitrary link between a geometrically constructed whole—the armillary sphere, whose form was said to be first—and the parts that became integrated into it, at the variable rhythm of the progress of navigations and their divulgence. In other words, the geometric framework of the world map had to incorporate partial accounts, drawn up at diverse times and by diverse pilots, without worrying about the coherence of the scales.

In addition, the portolan charts differed, in the way they were constructed, from the geography of Ptolemy, which borrowed its base from astronomy. Destined for the practical use of pilots, at first they were constructed by "route and distance," without reference to the celestial circles. The North indicated by the portolan charts was not the geographical North of the world map, but the magnetic North that moved the navigator's compass. The portolan charts did not have an explicit system of projection, but, insofar as they conserved the angles, they were similar to conformal projection maps. The network of the portolan charts, based on rhumbs that radiate out of *marteloios* and become entangled like a spider's web, did not at all coincide with the grid of the parallels and meridians of the world map. In addition, the vain attempts during the sixteenth century to determine longitude by means of hourglasses, eclipses, lunar distances, and the magnetic variation of the compass[22] made the representation of linear distances and their transfer onto a uniform skeleton map difficult, to say the least.

The erudite cartography thus had difficulty in incorporating the empirical data of the geography of the portolan charts. Conversely, the portolan charts and the nautical maps had to come to terms with the astronomical construction of the globe, whose data they eventually adopted in part. Drawing up navigation maps by angles and distances, with a mariner's compass and a pair of dividers being the privileged instruments of the sailor, presented some notable inconveniences. For example, in order to compensate for the anomalies of magnetic declination, which increases as one moves westward and reaches its highest point in the region of Newfoundland, certain cartographers, such as the Spaniard Diego Guttierez in 1550, resorted to representing two equators separated by an interval of two or three degrees. This invention, whose logical outcome was the representation of four tropics, was in fact impracticable and was fought against as early as 1544 by Sebastian Cabot, who was at the time pilot-major of the Casa de Contratacion in Seville. One variant of the previous procedure consisted in representing, in the vicinity of Newfoundland, a scale of auxiliary latitudes at a twenty-two-and-one-half degree angle with respect to the magnetic meridian. Finally, the transition from navigation by dead reckoning to astronomical navigation was accompanied, in Portuguese sea maps around 1500, by a beginning of cosmographical construction: the portolan charts integrated a scale of latitudes, a north-south line graduated in equal degrees, an equator (sometimes doubled, as seen above), the tropics, and the polar circles. This astronomical skeleton was supplemented from 1529 on by a scale of longitudes, where the value of the degree was taken as constant for every latitude considered.

The crisis of cosmography during the Renaissance originated for a large part in what William G. L. Randles calls the "crisis of cartography,"[23] which resulted from the fact that it was technically impossible for geographers, whether theoreticians or "mechanics," to join the empirical space of the portolan charts, whose new information was precious, with the astronomical geography inherited from the ancients and revised by Renaissance men. The unity of cosmography was a postulate gladly accepted and repeated by seamen as well as scholars, but it remained a pious wish as long as the portolan charts and the world maps pursued parallel and concurrent developments. Because of the lack of sufficiently precise measuring instruments and of complete and coherent

164 *Humanism in Crisis*

information on the globe, the separation was inevitable, and it lasted until the end of the seventeenth century. However, it was not an absolute divorce, because of the few clever attempts discussed above, which, in bringing together the work of a cartographer and that of a handyman, erected numerous bridges between theory and practice, and between the savoir faire of the ports and the science of colleges and academies.

Guillaume Le Testu's metaphor, which he borrowed from Thevet, makes this clear: Like generous and fruitful Nature, the representation of the world cannot be stabilized. The map does not show a definitive state of the world, but a mosaic, assembled within a floating space, of fragmentary accounts whose chronology can be spread out over centuries. From these spatial and temporal drifts come both dynamism and prospective value. Not only are the lands that are already well known represented, but also those still to be discovered. Like Aristotle's Nature, cosmography detests the void.

During the Renaissance, a map rarely had holes. It hid them, in the worst of cases, under a cartouche, or filled them with drawings of mythical creatures. The ever-expanding portolan chart and the universal world map were both characterized by this graphic plenitude. Cosmography did not only anticipate its own theory by arbitrarily "mounting" accounts of seamarks and capes onto an empty structure; it made up territories in order to fill in the lacuna of the sphere.

Thus, following many others, Le Testu, whose imagination was probably nourished by the *Schedelsche Weltchronik,* populated the depths of Asia and Africa with *blemmyae, sciopods,* and other *arimasps.* In that respect the *Cosmographie universelle* of 1556 was a descendant of medieval world maps. At the beginning of the twelfth century, the canon Lambert of Saint-Omer, in the world map illustrating the *Liber Floridus,* filled Asia, a traditional "wonderland," with a mythical bestiary borrowed from the *Physiologus* and from Isidore of Seville. In it, the elephant lives side by side with the lion and the phoenix, figure of the risen Christ. The most repulsive of these legendary creatures are confined to the uninhabited world, such as the ferocious Amazons who haunt the northern extremities of Scythia, or the serpents, dragons, and "cocodrilles" (crocodiles) that overrun the torrid wastes of Africa, a continent fertile in monsters and which, it is known, always produces something new.[24] For Le Testu, who claims the authority of Marco Polo and of the more recent Vespucci,[25] Africa also contains grass snakes seven hundred feet long, capable of swallowing goats and cattle, basilisks that kill men by looking at them, satyrs, blemmyae or "headless men," dog-faced baboons, and colopedes.[26] The battle of the *pigmies* and the cranes is placed in "India extra Gangem," while *sciopods* and *cynocephali* prance about near the Himalayas.[27] But in this modern nautical *Cosmographie,* these traditional wonders do not play exactly the same role that they did in the theological and moral cartography of the Middle Ages. Le Testu's world has lost symbolic coherence and geographical closure. With him, the mythical creatures of the universal atlas regain in the picturesque what they lose in allegorical meaning, and they pay their tribute to the cosmographical principle of *varietas.*[28] In addition, they mark places to conquer in a New-France inhabited by men with the heads of dogs or boars, or in the "Isles of Griffons" near the "Terre Australe" (*Terra Australis*).[29]

This applies especially to the ocean, the area that most interested the seaman Le Testu. Strewn with whales spurting streams of water, and covered with ships that display the French flag or the Admiral de Coligny's coat of arms, the ocean bathes imaginary lands and receives in its bosom the mythical austral continent established by Portuguese cartography.[30] Le Testu by no means tried to hide the fiction that governs in many instances his representation of the world. "However, that which I noted and depicted is only by Imagination," he declared concerning the austral continent, because "there is no man who has yet made any definite descovery of it."[31]

The key term *imagination* returns as a leitmotiv in Le Testu's writings. The strength of his imagination was such that it created islands and empires ex nihilo. In the twelve maps—out of the fifty that make up the atlas—where he tried to describe the extent of this fictive geography, Le Testu in a way preempted the future progress of the nautical science. While "waiting for more certain knowledge," he marked and named capes that were possibly not at all the edges of vast territories, but rather the sporadic emergences of reefs and atolls.[32] Thus, explorers would be able to "be aware when they think they are approaching the said land."[33] The fiction was prospective, but it also served an immediate practical use: it would spare the navigator the chance of shipwreck, by enjoining him to advance with caution in the regions of the sea that hid the always possible surprise of an abrupt and continuous coast.

This heuristic role assumed by the cartographical imagination was not an absolute novelty. Ptolemy had already placed, on his own, the

Island of Thule at sixty-three degrees of northern latitude, halfway between the parallel of Rhodes and the North Pole. The result of earlier contradictory hypotheses, such an invention was destined to leave the path open for all future research, while at the same time responding to "a need for symmetry and simplification."[34] As an island boundary mark closing the ecumene in the north, Thule also had the merit of being equidistant, in longitude, from the prime meridian of the Fortunate Islands and the meridian of Rhodes and of Alexandria, cutting the inhabited world into two equal halves.

This function, both heuristic and taxonomic, is also found in Le Testu, who, although possibly indifferent to the spirit of geometry that lived in the cosmographer of Alexandria, was equally anxious to arrive at a complete, if not exact, representation of the terraqueous globe. The imaginary cartography that he recommended to his contemporaries made it possible, in the final analysis, as he said and repeated in his Norman patois, to "assemble the pieces" of the universal atlas.[35] Filling in the lacuna of the world map, the island and continental fictions—the Grand Java lengthened to the South Pole and joining the Tierra del Fuego—suppressed any solution of continuity among the heterogeneous fragments of an atlas in book form. The "joining together" of the reported pieces was in this case facilitated by the very evidently floating character of the imaginary spaces that could be made to drift at leisure, in order to find the optimal location, at the junction of two maps whose scales did not correspond and whose orientation left something to be desired. In one of the twelve tables consecrated in his atlas to the "Terre Australe," Le Testu mentions the enigmatic Cape of More in the East, while specifying that it is "only marked in order to make the pages of this book correspond with each other."[36] One sees thus how the cosmographical fiction served as a hinge inside "real" cartography, so long as one could clearly distinguish between the two. It was no longer a simple means of filling in, but a veritable structure that articulated the successive sections of the world's description.

At this stage, the difference between Ptolemy and the legacy hunters Le Testu and Thevet is obvious. Le Testu's patching up of the map did not aim solely at creating the "good form" of the world, this *eusunopton* dear to the cartographers of antiquity.[37] The notion of universal harmony certainly had not deserted the language of the geographers during the Renaissance. But, more than the geometrical perfection of the universal body, what was important for a practitioner like Le Testu were the cracks that made the ancient representation of the cosmos collapse from all sides. However, cosmography acquired dynamism and mobility from these unstable borders, which resembled loosely sewn seams and which varied according to both the imagination of the one constructing the maps and the progress of navigations. In this sense one sees how the crisis of cosmography could become fruitful. From the play between the geometrical whole of the sphere and the empirical fragments of hydrography, and between the parts of the world themselves, a moving space was born, in which conquering efficiency and the imaginary were closely related. The approximations in the map left room for the invention of new territories. For Le Testu, as for his Portuguese predecessors, the immense "Terre Australe," promised to the dreams of future conquistadors, was the concerted fruit of technical error and strategic calculation, one serving as a beginning for the other. The king of France, Henry II, and his minister Coligny were the new beneficiaries of a prospective fiction destined at first for the House of Portugal.

New Causes: A Polemical Autopsy

Cosmography, like history according to Herodotus, is based on the direct view of things. There was no commonplace repeated more often in the Renaissance than the one depicting the cosmographer as a traveler and an eyewitness. "Cosmography is a science that no man has been able to learn or know except by experience," declared for example the doctor Leonardo Fioravanti in the chapter of his *Universal Mirror* devoted to this discipline.[38] The task of the cosmographer is consequently "to go first and go over with a fine-tooth comb all the parts of the world that can be seen."[39] It is an infinite project, one for which a human life is not enough. Nevertheless, cosmography needs this authority of immediate sight to establish the authority of its teaching. "The eye writes":[40] such a methodological summary is demanded by the undisputed principle of autopsy.

As Fioravanti also said, if at night one contemplates all things with the eye of understanding, during the day one sees them with the physical eye. It is the same for cosmography, "because by science and study, one sees it with the eye of the mind, but afterwards when a man sees it for real, he sees it with the physical eye, and it seems to be something quite different from the first."[41] From this dialectic between theory and practice, it is easy to slide into the Manichean opposition of shadows and light, and to contrast the sleep of dogmas to the vigilant and lucid activity of experience.

The difficulty was quickly overcome by the new scholars of the Renaissance, who claimed to contrast the fruit of unprecedented experiences with the stale certainties of the ancients. A navigator like Duarte Pacheco Pereira of Portugal, the author of the *Esmeraldo de situ orbis,* willingly claimed the authority of "experience which is the mother of all things," a formula similar to the one found around the same time in Leonardo da Vinci's *Notebooks.*[42] Three-quarters of a century later, the potter and architect Bernard Palissy took pleasure in creating a dialogue, in his *Discours admirables de la nature des eaux et fonteines,* between wise Practice and stupid and pompous Theory.[43]

Being an eyewitness was the supreme argument of authority that the cosmographer André Thevet threw in the face of his precursors as well as his most fierce enemies. Since he himself had traveled "in the four parts of the world" and had gone to the Levant and then to Brazil when he was young, he confidently denied the teachings of all his rivals and of all those who came before him. From the very beginning of the monumental *Cosmographie universelle* of 1575, the tone is set, and the fact that the author has personally observed that which he is discussing establishes his tyrannical and discretionary power:

> I can certainly say that I have observed some stars fixed over Brazil, which I never would have come to know even after listening for ten years to a doctor laboring over an astrolabe or a globe.... If the Ancients had seen and known them, they would not have forgotten them any more than the others that they have seen here in our lands.[44]

The univocal polemic against the authorities and their systematic destruction in the name of sacrosanct autopsy were not without danger. First, they amounted to denying any idea of progress, in favor of a revolution of knowledge that necessarily would result from the ubiquitous and totalitarian experience of the writer-voyager. Following the rather passionate declaration just cited, Thevet comes to contrast, in a very arbitrary manner, the naked eye of the observer with the nevertheless indispensable instruments of the astrolabe and the globe. The claim of a unique and "naive" experience borders on the most obvious obscurantism. One mysticism is replaced by another: the absolute credit enjoyed by authorities such as Aristotle, Pliny, or Ptolemy is substituted by a no-less-blind confidence in ocular perception, liberated from any bookish hindrance.

In doing this, Thevet deliberately confuses the scales of representation. He sins in fact by incoherence, imagining that only autopsy can guarantee the truth of a synthetic—and, as such, second—vision. Unless one adopts the ideal sight of the world's Creator, and unless one transports oneself to the moon like Menippus, or, in other words, if one is on either of the two privileged access roads of ecstasy and satire, it is impossible to make the myopia of the human observer coincide with the intellectual and encompassing vision of the cosmos. These two extreme and contrasting dimensions of geographical investigation could not both be contained in the immediate and concrete moment of experience. In other words, if topography, this "particular narration" valued by Montaigne,[45] results from the experimentation of an individual subject, cosmography on the other hand supposes the mediation of a theoretical model and the recognition of a scientific tradition and of conventions of analysis. Facing the landscape-object that he evaluates on the spot, the topographer is alone. However, in order to fully comprehend the world-object, the cosmographer needs assistants and precursors. His occupation places him at the end of a chain of operators, each with an individualized task. Tributary of the history of the discipline, he also depends on his field-workers and on a network of informers whose observations he must blend together.

Instead of respecting this division of the geographical work, Thevet, on the contrary, multiplies the telescopic shortcuts by which he claims to be an eyewitness of data that have nothing to do with the visual experience of the voyager. If, for example, it is a matter of proving that the ocean is surrounded by land and not the opposite, as the ancients thought, claiming the authority of his peregrinations is enough for Thevet to overcome, or so he thinks, twenty centuries of cosmographical tradition. It is by exercising—in the sense of "experience" or "test" evoked by Montaigne—his faraway navigations that he can affirm that the ocean is not an aquatic belt that borders the ecumene, but rather a second and larger Mediterranean, reuniting scattered peoples on its borders: "And since in my navigations *I experienced* that not only is there land, but also that the sea is so restricted by it that one can no longer see any water, as near Antarctica."[46]

At the price of a spatial and temporal ellipse, the fleeting moment of the voyage opens to a completely abstract evidence, usually impossible to understand without the help of the world map and astronomical instruments, and without the usual distance of theoretical reflection carried out by the scholar in his study: "Since I have found such large lands, why would I say that it is the ocean that surrounds the land, seeing that, on the contrary, *I saw the ocean with my own eyes*, twirling and turning in circles from East to West."[47] The confusion of the scales is evident and makes the sight of the pilot, scrutinizing at a slight distance the curvature of a gulf or the inflection of a line of seamarks, suddenly coincide with that of the cartographer in his room considering the great masses of emerged lands, simplified by the miniaturization of the globe.

In fact, short of adopting the ubiquitous point of view of the Creator, who "has hands so big that in one he holds the whole world, and with two or three fingers he turns the whole earth,"[48] it is difficult to understand how the practice of navigation, with the eye riveted on the horizon or lifted toward the stars, could deliver coherent, uniform, and general information about the terraqueous globe. It means not taking into account the incidents of journeys, the subjectivity of the observer, and, even more, the limited capacity of the sensory organs.

However, Thevet needs a fiction that is both particular and general, personal and nonetheless objective, in order to ruin the claims of the ancient geography. The triumphant autopsy of the pilot "sitting on his ship, following the lesson of the winds,"[49] serves to condemn the dreams of the ancients as well as the speculations of Thevet's bothersome contemporaries. In a significant way, the discussion found at the beginning of the *Cosmographie universelle* of the land encircling the ocean follows upon the criticism, which could not be more traditional during the Renaissance, of *vana gloria*. The double exemplum of Aristotle and Empedocles killing themselves by pride and foolish love of glory, the first by throwing himself into the Aegean Sea, the second into the crater of Etna, denounces, according to the proven topic of Christian humanism,[50] the presumptuousness of a discipline incapable of establishing human limits for itself because of its encyclopedic vocation.

However, the anti-authority argument turns inside out like a glove, and Thevet experiences this reversal at his own expense. Immediately following the publication of the *Cosmographie* in 1575, the Catholic François de Belleforest and the Protestant Ludwig Camerarius unite their voices to condemn the blasphemies "against God and man" that they claim the work contains. In proclaiming the solitary sovereignty of his

The Crisis of Cosmography   171

personal experience, Thevet is questioning not just the secular authorities, but the sacred authority of the Bible.

First, he commits the sin of pride, insofar as he boasts of a superhuman experience and claims qualities of longevity, endurance, and omniscience that greatly exceed those that one could rightly attribute to a sinful man. In him appear, joined and to the highest degree, *vana gloria* and *cupiditas sciendi,* the twin vices that belong particularly to intellectuals and that doctors of the Church and theologians, since the time of Saint Augustine, had vied with each other in denouncing.

Second, his faith in experience leads him to a long series of propositions that openly contradict Scripture and the exegetical tradition. According to Thevet, Jerusalem, in spite of the teaching of the Church, is not in the middle of the world.[51] In Bethlehem, the crib where the baby Jesus was born is a cave.[52] The present-day limits of Palestine do not correspond to the choronomy of the Gospels.[53] There are no lions near the gates of Gaza nor in Arabia, which makes the story of Samson seem unlikely.[54] Nobody has ever seen a whale in the Mediterranean, and thus the story of Jonah loses its credibility.[55] As an intrepid tourist, Thevet visited the tower of Babel, although the story in Genesis tells that it collapsed, having never been finished.[56]

These careless and repeated attacks against the reigning dogma seem inevitable, given that personal experience has been raised to the status of an absolute value. The fact remains that the "cosmographical heresy" developed by Thevet goes against a movement in the history of natural sciences that began during his lifetime. As François de Dainville reminds us in his *Géographie des humanistes,* one of the notable effects of the Council of Trent was the reconciliation of the domain of sensory experience with the principle of authority. Without being able to speak plainly of a theoretical regression, and without the control of ecclesiastic authority forbidding all progress of observation, it tied the scientist to an elementary prudence. Sometimes this prudence had beneficial consequences. The restoration of Aristotelianism, the Church's official doctrine for physical science, and the attachment to the system of Ptolemy, which Copernicus's sacrilegious hypothesis had not been able to shake, were in a way compatible with the investigation of natural facts. The return to an intellectual discipline, which Thevet always stubbornly refused, could promote further research in the specialized domains of botany and astronomy, for example.

The retreat went thus from a general science, whose principles were no longer discussed for the moment, toward particular, individual, and practical knowledge, thoroughly developed within the limits of each art. This specialization, which favored what Father de Dainville called "the motions of Christian humanism,"[57] ran counter to a clearly premature plan: the dream of a universal science had provisionally gone out of style in the sad beginning of the classical age.

The End of Cosmography

The crisis of cosmography manifested itself in these stages. In the beginning it resulted from the solution of continuity that existed between the astronomical geography and the chorographical description of the inhabited regions of the earth. Second, during the Renaissance the hiatus was encountered again and became visible in the disparity between the renovated scholarly cartography of Ptolemy and the practical cartography of the portolan charts. It is true that from the unequal marriage of these two traditions some fruitful errors could result, such as those exploited by the Portuguese, Spanish, and Norman cartographers for strategic ends and for the profit of their respective kings. The most enlightening example is the "Terre Australe," reinvented, according to Lusitinian portolan chart information, by Guillaume Le Testu, pilot from Le Havre. Finally, the crisis of cosmography became moral and theological, when the sovereignty of autopsy, as dear to Thevet as it was to Herodotus, clashed head-on with the truths taught by tradition.

The end of cosmography had become inescapable by the twilight of the Renaissance. The restoration of the principle of authority under the alternating pressure of the Reformation and the Counter-Reformation, and the division of scientific work, which became more common with the progress of specialized knowledge, demolished the demiurgical claims that a universal science could be constructed on the sole basis of experience, thus making a *tabula rasa* of all anterior traditions. It would take all the efforts of Sebastian Münster and Richard Hakluyt, acting in the perspective of the German and Anglican Reforms, and later those of Mercator and Hondius in the Netherlands of the Catholic reconquest, in order to Christianize this discipline that had sinned in its excess of self-confidence. Next came the establishment of the fruitful tradition of "cosmographical meditations," which, from Vadianus to Mercator,

The Crisis of Cosmography   173

made the contemplation of the atlas the privileged access road to the understanding of the Scriptures.[58]

"From the Mappe he brought me to the Bible."[59] By this striking summary, Hakluyt describes his conversion to geography, under the aegis of his cousin Richard Hakluyt the Elder, who, having received him one day in his study, guided his reading from the planisphere to the *Psalms*. The commentary of the map is a spiritual exercise like any other, and it offers in addition the merit of not separating the interior reflection of the believer from his practical activity in the world. The admiration aroused by the sight of Creation miniaturized in the map goes hand in hand with the examination of the "conveniences" that the geographer's apprentice discovers in it. The beauty of the cosmos resides in its practical value and in the profit that the Christian can derive from it. Spontaneously the young Hakluyt discovered that the service of this generous God whose humble chaplain he would be and the plan for a larger England constituted the two sides of a single duty.

The same submission of geography to the transcendental truth of Christianity is proclaimed at the beginning of Pierre d'Avity's *Monde*, whose success did not waver throughout the seventeenth century. The first definition given of the world is theological: "The World is sometimes taken for God; but it is by associating this word with that of Archetype and Intelligible, because of the forms and models of all things, which are in the divine understanding."[60] The angelic world is evoked next, "in order to express the three Hierarchies and the nine Orders of the Angels." Finally, the world treated exclusively by cosmography is evoked, that of "the assembling of the Heavens, of the Elements, and of the things which they contain, created by the omnipotence of God, for his glory and the good of men."[61] The order of the presentation and the descending hierarchy that it presupposes, from the heavens toward the earth and from the unity of the Creator to the complexity of the creation, indicates an attitude of strict obedience to the Church and the humility of a descriptive design that confines itself to the realities of this lower world. D'Avity goes back to the sources of the cosmographical genre in its modern avatar. Like Sebastian Münster, he takes up and abundantly comments upon the biblical narrative of Genesis, before coming to the description of the universe and its parts.

Nevertheless, a fundamental difference contrasts him with his predecessor. D'Avity, as his son Claude (author of an apologetical preface) says from the outset, neglected the general, theoretical, or "common

Philosophy," in favor of the applied, political, or "practical Philosophy"—the one that most interests legislators and governments. At a time when the world was witnessing the "explosion of the geographical discipline,"[62] d'Avity attempted, in face of the centrifugal forces that were threatening its existence, an ultimate synthesis. But, in spite of the scope of his undertaking, he was unable to keep himself from yielding to the tendency to specialize. This new style of cosmography moved toward statistics, and no longer bore the name of cosmography. In a Europe in which nations were experiencing a first apotheosis as political entities, the description of the resources, "riches," and "strengths" of the states overrode the interest in the general form of the world.

Concurrently, cosmography was made obsolete by the success of the collections of voyage narratives, whose fortune, from Simon Grynaeus and Giovanni Battista Ramusio to Richard Hakluyt and Theodore de Bry, was European. Unlike the cosmographer, the editor of collections gave up trying to unify the disparity of the materials of the collection in the name of an all-powerful subjectivity. On the contrary, he presented them as they were, under the plural responsibility of authors unequal in merit and in style. Eventually supplemented by atlases, these collections, in which judicial documents were presented side by side with the accounts of large navigations, defined an open form, theoretically capable of unlimited growth. Inasmuch as these vast collections reunited the regularly updated elements of a geographical and strategic debate about the sharing of the world among great powers, it can be said that they prepared the way for colonial expansion of England, Holland, and France. Unlike cosmography, which proudly rested on the illusory totality of a universal knowledge, the collections of voyage narratives and documents reconciled the materials of a discipline in the throes of a crisis of growth with the plane of practical efficacy.

NOTES

This essay was translated by Alan Savage.

1. Montaigne, "Of Cannibals," in *The Complete Essays of Montaigne,* trans. Donald M. Frame (Stanford: Stanford University Press, 1958), I, 31, 152 A: "pour avoir cet avantage sur nous d'avoir veu la Palestine, ils veulent jouir de ce privilege de nous conter nouvelles de tout le demeurant du monde." All subsequent English translations of Montaigne are taken from Frame's transla-

The Crisis of Cosmography   175

tion. The page number is followed by a letter (A, B or C) indicating one of the three major textual strata: 1580, 1588, or 1595.

2. Richard Hakluyt, "Richard Hakluyt to the favorable Reader," in *The Principall Navigations, Voiages and Discoveries of the English nation* . . . (London: George Bishop and Ralph Newberie, 1589), fol. 3v.

3. For more information on André Thevet (1516–92), see my biography, *André Thevet: cosmographe des derniers Valois* (Geneva: Droz, 1991).

4. Concerning this, see Germaine Aujac, *Les Sciences du monde*, vol. 1 of *Strabon et la science de son temps* (Paris: Les Belles Lettres, 1966), 305–6.

5. See in particular Numa Broc, "Sébastien Münster, l'apogée du genre descriptif," in *La Géographie de la Renaissance (1420–1620)* (Paris: Bibliothèque Nationale–CTHS, 1980), 77ff.

6. Sebastien Münster, *La Cosmographie universelle* (Basel: Heinrich Petri, 1568), 833: "De mon Istrie en laquelle je suis nay." The first Latin edition dates back to 1544.

7. Münster, 870–71.

8. Münster, 1396.

9. Regarding Grynaeus's undertaking, see Broc, 29–30, as well as Michel Korinman, "Simon Grynaeus et le 'Novus Orbis': les pouvoirs d'une collection," in *Voyager à la Renaissance* (Paris: Maisonneuve et Larose, 1987), 419–31.

10. For more information on this historiographical heritage, see Bernard Guenée's fundamental *Histoire et culture historique dans l'Occident médiéval* (Paris: Aubier, 1981).

11. Concerning this point, see, in addition to Philippe Desan's recent work *Naissance de la méthode: Machiavel, La Ramée, Bodin, Montaigne, Descartes* (Paris: Nizet, 1987); Frank Lestringant, "Jean Bodin, cosmographe," in *Jean Bodin: actes du colloque interdisciplinaire d'Angers (24–27 mai 1984)*, 2 vols. (Angers: Presses de l'Université d'Angers, 1985), 1:133–45.

12. See Frank Lestringant, "Rage, fureur, folie cannibales: le Scythe et le Brésilien," in *La Folie et le corps*, ed. Jean Céard (Paris: Presses de l'Ecole Normale Supérieure, 1985), 49–80.

13. Guillaume Postel, *Des merveilles du monde, et principalement des admirables choses des Indes et du Nouveau Monde* (Paris: J. Ruelle, 1553). Regarding this treatise, see Frank Lestringant, "Cosmologie et *mirabilia* à la Renaissance: l'exemple de Guillaume Postel," *Journal of Medieval and Renaissance Studies* 16, no. 2 (1986): 253–79.

14. François de Belleforest, *La Cosmographie universelle de tout le monde . . . Auteur en partie Munster . . .* , 2 vols. (Paris: N. Chesneau et M. Sonnius, 1575), 1:iij-r: "eu esgard que depuis tant de centaines d'ans qu'il y a que Ptolomée vivoit, y ayant eu divers Eclipses, et autres accidents remarquez par les reigles Astrales, il a fallu aussi que le cours solaire ayt esté retardé, et par consequent les degrez limitez par sa course."

15. Belleforest, 2: cols. 1743–45.

16. This partial draft of André Thevet's *Cosmographie universelle* (Paris: P. L'Huillier and G. Chaudière, 1575) is entitled *Le Livre contenant la description de tout ce qui est comprins soubz le nom de Gaule fait et observé par André Thevet Cosmographe du Roy et chevallier de Jherusalem,* MS. fr. 4941 (Paris: Bibliothèque Nationale, c. 1566 and 1572). On the verso of folio 10 one finds, for example, the following marginal note, written crosswise, concerning the town of Angoulême: "town that lies at 17. degrees longitude 23. minutes and at 45 degrees longitude [mistake for *latitude*] /44/ minutes. Its longest day is /15/ hours /23/minutes according to my calculations ["on the spot" is crossed out], given that it is my birthplace."

17. For more information on Joâo Afonso, pilot of Portuguese origin, "bought" by Francis I and a naturalized French citizen, see Luís de Matos's decisive study, *Les Portugais en France au XVIe siècle: études et documents* (Coimbra: Acta Universitatis Conimbrigensis, 1952), 1–77. For an evaluation, in general rather severe, of Afonso's (or Alfonse's) cosmographical work, refer to Luís de Albuquerque's article, "Joâo Afonso (ou Jean Fonteneau) e a sua 'Cosmographia,'" in *Les Rapports culturels et littéraires entre le Portugal et la France* (Paris: Fondation Calouste Gulbenkian, 1983), 101–21.

18. André Thevet, *Cosmographie de Levant,* 2d ed. (Lyon: Jean de Tournes and Guillaume Gazeau, 1556; reprint, Geneva: Droz, 1985), 3–4: "A Monsigneur, Monsigneur François, Conte de La Rochefoucaud." See Guillaume Le Testu, *Cosmographie universelle selon les navigateurs, tant anciens que modernes. Par Guillaume Le Testu pillotte en la Mer du Ponent, de la ville Françoyse de grace,* atlas of 58 manuscript plates (including 50 maps) illuminated on 530 x 370 mm. paper (Vincennes: Bibliothèque du Service Historique de l'Armée de Terre: DLZ 14, in folio, 1556 [1555 old style]), fol. 1r.

19. For the description of Le Testu's atlas, see A. Anthiaume's study, which to this day has not been replaced: "Un pilote et cartographe havrais au XVIe siècle: Guillaume Le Testu," *Bulletin de géographie historique et descriptive,* nos. 1–2 (1911): 28–29.

20. Le Testu, fol. 1: "Qui est ce nouveau Cosmographe, qui aprez plusieurs autheurs tres-renommes, tant anciens que modernes: a voullu entreprendre d'inventer chozes nouvelles?" See Thevet, *Cosmographie de Levant,* 3–4: "Who is this new Anacharsis or Cosmographer, who after several ancient as well as modern Authors, can invent new things?"

21. Le Testu, fol. 1: "Mais je leur respondray, que Nature ne s'est tant astrainte, ou asubjetie aux escrips des Anciens, qu'elle aict perdu le pouvoir et vertu de produire chozes nouvelles et estranges: oultre les chozes dequoy ilz ont escript."

22. Regarding these different means of measurement, all inadequate, see William G. L. Randles, "Portuguese and Spanish Attempts to Measure Longitude

The Crisis of Cosmography   177

in the Sixteenth Century," *Boletim da Biblioteca da Universidade de Coimbra* 39 (1985): 1–21.

23. William G. L. Randles, "From the Mediterranean Portulan Chart to the Marine World Chart of the Great Discoveries: The Crisis in Cartography in the Sixteenth Century," in *Géographie du monde au Moyen Age et à la Renaissance* (Paris: Bibliothèque Nationale-CTHS, 1989). Regarding the difficult marriage of the portolan charts and the ancient geography, consult the reference work of Monique de La Roncière and Michel Mollat du Jourdin, *Les Portulans: cartes marines du XIIIe au XVIIe siècle* (Freiburg: Office du Livre, and Paris: Nathan, 1984), as well as Michel Mollat's article, "Le témoignage de la cartographie," in *Le Monde de Jacques Cartier,* ed. Fernand Braudel (Paris: Berger-Levrault, and Montreal: Libre-Expression, 1984), 149–64.

24. This medieval world map was analyzed by Danielle Lecoq in "La Mappemonde du Liber Floridus ou la vision du monde de Lambert de Saint-Omer," *Imago Mundi: The Journal of the International Society for the History of Cartography,* no. 39 (1987): 9–49. Cf. David Woodward, "Medieval Mappaemundi," in *Cartography in Prehistoric, Ancient, and Medieval Europe and the Mediterranean,* vol. 1 of *The History of Cartography,* ed. John B. Harley and David Woodward (Chicago: University of Chicago Press, 1987), 330ff.

25. Le Testu, fol. 19r: "as the Florentine Amerigo de Vespucci tells, in his Cosmography of the New World, of a grass snake which eats cattle and goats" ("ainsy que tesmoigne Emeric de Vespuce Florentin en sa Cosmographie du nouveau monde, laquelle Couleuvre mengent les beufz, et chievres").

26. Le Testu, fol. 21r, opposite the map of southern Africa (fol. 20v).

27. Le Testu, fol. 28v, map representing the Bay of Bengal and the Malacca Peninsula. In the corresponding commentary (fol. 29r), he claims the authority of "Marc Vénitien" (Marco Polo).

28. For more information on the theme of varietas during the Renaissance, see Jean Céard, *La Nature et les prodiges: l'insolite en France, au XVIe siècle* (Geneva: Droz, 1977).

29. Le Testu, fol. 34v. Commentary on fol. 25r.

30. Anthiaume, 45. See Roger Hervé, *Découverte fortuite de l'Australie et de la Nouvelle-Zélande par des navigateurs portugais et espagnols entre 1521 et 1528* (Paris: Bibliothèque Nationale–CTHS, 1982), 27.

31. Le Testu, fol. 35r: "Toutefoys ce que Je en ay marqué et depainct n'est que par Imagination"; "il n'y a encor eu Homme qui en aict faict descouverture certaine." Commentary on the map of fol. 34v, representing the "Illes des Grifons" and, below, the "Terre Australle," with a battle of naked and bloody savages.

32. Le Testu, fol. 35r: "en atendant que cognoissance en soit plus certaine."

33. Le Testu, fol. 37r: "se donner garde lorsqu'ils auront oppinion qu'ils approcheront ladicte terre." Commentary on the map of fol. 36v: "Mer oceane de l'Inde orientale."

34. Germaine Aujac, "L'Ile de Thulé, de Pytheas à Ptolémée," in *Géographie du monde au Moyen Age et à la Renaissance:* "un besoin de symétrie et de simplification."

35. Le Testu, fol. 35r, concerning the "Terre Australe": "radresser les pièches."

36. Le Testu, fol. 40r: "n'est marqué que pour radresser les feuilletz de ce livre."

37. For a definition of this concept, whose literal meaning is "which the glance [le regard] can grasp easily," see Christian Jacob, "La Mimésis géographique en Grèce antique: regards, parcours, mémoire," in *Sémiotique de l'architecture: espace et représentation: penser l'espace* (Paris: Editions de la Villette, 1982), 67. On the notion of universal harmony, see Leo Spitzer, *Classical and Christian Ideas of World Harmony: Prolegomena to an Interpretation of the Word "Stimmung"* (Baltimore, Md.: Johns Hopkins University Press, 1963).

38. Leonardo Fioravanti, "De la cosmographie et de ses effects," in *Miroir universel des arts et sciences, divisé en trois livres* (Paris: P. Cavellat, 1584, 1586), 167: "La Cosmographie est une science, que jamais homme n'a peu apprendre ny sçavoir, sinon par le moyen de l'experience." The original edition appeared in Venice in 1564 under the title *Lo spechio di scienza universale*.

39. Fioravanti, 169: "d'aller premierement voir et esplucher par le menu toutes les parties du monde qui se peuvent voir."

40. François Hartog, *Le Miroir d'Hérodote* (Paris: Gallimard, 1980), 275: "L'oeil écrit."

41. Fioravanti, 168: "car par science et estude, on le voit de l'oeil de l'esprit, mais quand l'homme est puis apres sur le faict, on le voit alors de l'oeil corporel, et semble autre chose fort differente de la premiere."

42. See Joaquim Barradas de Carvalho, *A la recherche de la spécificité de la Renaissance portugaise: l'"Esmeraldo de situ orbis" de Duarte Pacheco Pereira et la littérature portugaise de voyages à l'époque des Grandes Découvertes. Contribution à l'étude des origines de la pensée moderne*, 2 vols. (Paris: Fondation Calouste Gulbenkian, 1983), 2:677ff.

43. Bernard Palissy, *Discours admirables de la nature des eaux et fonteines* (Paris: Martin le Jeune, 1580).

44. André Thevet, *La Cosmographie universelle*, 2 vols. (Paris, 1575), 2:5v: "Je peux bien dire avoir observé quelques estoilles fixes en ceste terre Australe, que quand j'eusse esté dix ans à ouyr un docteur, se tourmentant sur un Astrolabe, ou sur un Globe, je n'en eusse eu autre cognoissance.... Si les Anciens les eussent veuës et congnuës, comme j'ay fait, ils ne les eussent oubliées, non plus que les autres qu'ils ont veu par deçà."

45. Montaigne, I, 31, 152 A: "narration particulière."

46. Thevet, *Cosmographie universelle*, 1:6v: "Et toutefois depuis par mes navigations j'ay essayé, non seulement qu'il y avoit terre, mais que encores la

mer en estoit tellement bornée, que on ne voyoit plus d'eau, comme du costé de l'Antarctique." (Emphasis added.)

47. Thevet, *Cosmographie universelle*, 1:6v: "à present que j'ay trouvé terres de si grand traict, pourquoy diray-je que c'est l'Ocean qui environne la terre? attendu que au contraire j'ay veu de mes yeux l'Ocean, faisant comme une virevouste et retour en soy d'Occident à l'Orient."

48. Thevet, *Cosmographie universelle*, 1:â v-r: "a les mains si grandes qu'en une il contient tout le monde, et entre deux ou trois doigts tourne toute la terre." See Isaiah 40:12 (Vulgate).

49. Thevet, *Cosmographie universelle*, 2:906v (second pagination).

50. For more information on Empedocles, refer to the suggestive work of Gérard Defaux, *Le Curieux, le glorieux et la sagesse du monde dans la première moitié du XVIe siècle* (Lexington, Ky.: French Forum, 1982), 119–28. Diogenes Laertius's *Vita* is the source of this negative legend.

51. Thevet, *Cosmographie universelle*, 1:174v–75r.

52. Thevet, *Cosmographie universelle*, 1:177r and v.

53. Thevet, *Cosmographie universelle*, 1:164r and v.

54. Thevet, *Cosmographie universelle*, 1:165v.

55. Thevet, *Cosmographie universelle*, 1:168v and 243v–44r. Regarding the tricky question of the whales, Thevet later fights back in the *Cosmographie universelle*, 2:1016v, and in the *Histoire de deux voyages*, MS. fr. 15454 (Paris: Bibliothèque Nationale, c. 1586), 150v.

56. Thevet, *Cosmographie universelle*, 1:354v.

57. François de Dainville, *La Géographie des humanistes* (Paris: Beauchesne, 1940), 84ff.: "les motions de l'humanisme chrétien."

58. Gérard Mercator and Josse Hondius, *Gerardi Mercatoris Atlas, sive Cosmographicae Meditationes de fabrica mundi et fabricati figura. Iam tandem ad finem perductus . . . a Iudoco Hondio* (Amsterodami: sumptibus C. Nicolai and J. Hondi, 1607, in folio).

59. Richard Hakluyt, letter to Sir Francis Walsingham Knight, in *The Principall Navigations, Voiages and Discoveries . . .* (1589), fol. 2r.

60. Pierre d'Avity, *Le Monde ou la description generale de ses quatre parties, avec tous ses empires, royaumes, estats et republiques* (Paris: Claude Sonnius, 1637), 2: "Le Monde est pris quelquefois pour Dieu; mais c'est en couplant ce mot avec celuy d'Archétype ou d'Intelligible, à cause des formes et modelles de toutes choses, qui sont en l'entendement divin." This vast compilation, whose first title was *Les Estats et empires du monde*, was printed eleven times between 1614 and 1635. It was expanded, after the death of its author, by Ranchin and Rocoles, and was used as a reference work until the end of the eighteenth century.

61. D'Avity: "l'assemblage du Ciel, des Eléments et des choses qu'ils contiennent, créé par la toute-puissance de Dieu, pour sa gloire et le bien des hommes."

62. Broc, 95.

The Crisis of the Science of Monsters

Jean Céard

Interest in monsters does not die out with the end of the Renaissance. One could even maintain, judging from the abundance and variety of publications that treat them, that in a certain manner interest in monsters intensifies and, in any event, grows increasingly diverse. Without counting republications of works, such as the numerous republications of Ambroise Paré's *Des monstres et prodiges*,[1] there is available a great quantity of work by physicians, reflections by commentators of Aristotle on the second book of the *Physics* or the *De animalium generatione*, and works by naturalists, the most voluminous of these latter works, Aldrovandi's *Monstrorum historia*,[2] being for our purpose very worthy of interest. But there are still other books that address themselves to a less specialized public. At the forefront of these one must place the *Histoires prodigieuses* by Boaistuau and their numerous continuations,[3] without forgetting the *Thresor d'histoires admirables et memorables* by Simon Goulart,[4] nor the many periodical publications, the *canards*, eager to relate the birth of monsters.[5] Thus, there is no shortage of available material for trying to ascertain whether or not the European crisis of humanism extended to this field.

It would undoubtedly be suitable to begin by defining the idea of humanism. If one understands by this an interest in human letters and, above all, in philology, to employ the full sense of the term, teratology is certainly not foreign to these interests. But the philological approach to the problems that teratology raises bears nothing specific to them; and the crisis within humanism, if it does exist, has many other stakes. If, on the other hand, one attaches to the idea of humanism an *épistémè* and a "worldview"—to have recourse to an older term—then teratology certainly constitutes an excellent observation post for viewing the crisis that rocks humanism taken in this larger though perhaps more elusive sense.

One might even say, in examining the subject's bibliography, that there is justification for the historian's thinking that teratology constituted one of the locales where humanism first portended and formulated the crisis that it underwent. Indeed, to the mass of publications from the end of the Renaissance that were indicated earlier, the preceding era has few works to compare. It is Ambroise Paré who first distinguishes the problems associated with monsters from the larger problems of the generation, even if in their first edition (1573) the two works are still considered complementary; and the preceding period offers nothing comparable to the *Monstrorum historia memorabilis* by Johann Goerg Schenck (1609)[6] or, to take a very different example, to the *Tractatus de monstris* of Arnaud Sorbin (1570).[7] What at first characterizes the late Renaissance is a very distinct tendency to distinguish and isolate the problems particular to monstrosity. We would like to show here that this effort comes about in response to a number of deeply underlying causes that, in the final analysis, must be ascribed to a crisis in the idea of nature, and that it is this crisis that renders obsolete the systems of interpretation elaborated and employed by the preceding age.

Let us sum up first of all the problematics of monstrosity at issue in the late Renaissance. Gathering and reshaping an antique and medieval heritage in which the first places were assigned to Aristotle, Pliny, and Saint Augustine, the Renaissance has not forgotten any more than its predecessors that *monstrum* was originally a term belonging to the vocabulary of divination.[8] The Renaissance even readily employs divination's rich lexicon, which, to *monstrum,* adds notably *prodigium, ostentum,* and *portentum.* The title of Ambroise Paré's book suffices to prove that even for a man with a medical education this tradition remains alive. The crisis in teratology, then, will express itself notably in the works that, in whole or in part, will undertake a philological examination of these terms.

The preceding facts can be viewed, however, in two different lights: in the sense of divination, one can understand monsters as *presages;* in contrast, one could consider their unusual, unwonted character as one manifestation of the variety of things, of this *varietas rerum* that constitutes one of the key notions of the *épistémè* of the Renaissance.

From this derive two systems of interpretation that must quickly be described. The first comes out of divination and remains closely associated with it. It is certain that ancient divinatory procedures were wholly modified by Christianity, which, since the Apostolic era, has shown strong reservations vis-à-vis all divination.[9] Yet it must be noted that in the Renaissance, what one calls the vanity of divination does not designate its false character, but rather its danger; even if the numerous refutations of divination can establish the unsubstantiality of certain practices, they devote themselves less, on the whole, to destroying divination than to avoiding it as a condemnable "curiosity." In such a context, monsters have a singular status that partially excludes them from the mistrust surrounding divination. Indeed, in accordance with the *De divinatione* of Cicero, one continues to distinguish two main kinds of divination; the first, called natural, i.e., spontaneous, is the type that the dreamer experiences; the other, called artificial, requires, as its name indicates, an art in order to recognize the signs that it interprets.[10] The adversaries of divination have not failed to point out that these signs are often questionable, if not fabricated: one need only think of the ass's head, the cheese, or simply the lines of the hand in which, in Rabelais's *Tiers livre*, Her Trippa unhesitatingly discerns the sure signs that Panurge will be unhappy in marriage.[11] Such is not the case with monsters, which force their obvious singularity, their provocative strangeness, upon one's attention. If attentive, on the whole, to the reservations of the Church, the Renaissance carefully avoided the restoration of an art of interpreting monsters, or rather of a teratomancy (and still there are imposing exceptions, as the work of H. C. Agrippa shows),[12] it did not abstain from attaching to monsters some degree of meaning. The theologian Arnaud Sorbin, in his *Tractatus de monstris* of 1570, is quite careful to indicate that he does not intend "to attribute to such things some sort of power or some sort of efficacy,"[13] but he does leave the door wide open to view them as signs and denounces as an impiety any tendency to think that, since these realities have natural causes, they would not have sign value.

The Reformers, for their part, also demonstrated an interest in the idea that monsters have a signifying power: Luther and Melanchthon devoted themselves to educing the significance of two monsters, the Calf-Monk and the Ass-Pope, which remain indebted to their commentators for their celebrity; and Calvin gave his approval to the French version of their opuscule.[14] It is also known that at the time of the religious wars, Catholics and Protestants disputed the favors of heaven by giving warrant to the authority of monsters (like the one that was born in Paris,

Rue des Gravellers, in 1570)[15] and of various marvels, like the hawthorn that blossomed again suddenly in the cemetery of the Holy Innocents[16] and the windstorm that let loose at the moment of the Cardinal de Lorraine's death.[17] Finally, there was also the new star of 1572, which long held the attention of Guillaume Postel and which, in 1590, the Ligueurs connected to the conduct and fate of Henry III.[18]

These strange signs, to which is being attached a divinatory value or, if one prefers, a presagious value, are not only monsters, in the current usage of the term; they can also take the form of an earthquake or a flood, an eclipse, or a comet. One need only page through the imposing *Prodigiorum ac ostentorum chronicon* of Lycosthenes (1557) to verify this statement. Apparent from the title of the book, this work is a catalogue of the prodigies that, from the beginning of the world to the present, "announce to men the severity and the wrath of God against crimes, as well as the great changes affecting the world."[19]

It is among these greatly varying signs that monsters are given a place: language has not yet—precisely due to the nature of the interest shown to monsters—fixed their name in the sense that we attach to it, and it would be imprudent to isolate them too much from the other strange realities among which they have been placed. After all, if the *monstrum* has as its function to *monstrare*, the *ostentum* is destined to *ostendere*, the *prodigium* to *porro dicere* and the *portentum* to *portendere* or *praeostendere*. These etymologies, taken from Cicero, Saint Augustine, and Isidore,[20] suffice to prove that the nuances of meaning that philologists are able to detect in these various terms do not preclude the terms from designating realities that signal, that are signs.[21]

This feature of the first system of interpretation is in keeping with the second, which includes not only monsters but also floods and earthquakes in its list of prodigies. Indeed, within this second system, all these realities are equally *rare*, even if they are so in differing ways: as a two-headed child is rare among men, the magnet's virtue of attracting iron is rare in the mineral order. If one defines the marvel by its rarity, monsters are marvels. As with any marvel, they provoke our amazement, that amazement that reminds us that basically all of nature is a marvel. Therefore, far from renouncing them as occupying a place outside of nature, one must see them rather as the extreme in nature's activity, the remarkable indication of its inventive ingenuity. Notably, it is by the creation of marvels that nature's activity, instead of being a monotone repetition of the same, is one of incessant diversification.

It is perhaps Ambroise Paré who most precisely developed this thesis; even if he did not completely theorize it, he did at least clearly formulate its orientation. He did this upon examination of a certain number of monstrous productions that occur in the human body, broadening the question in the following way:

> In apostemas (abscess), one finds very strange bodies, such as stone, chalk, gravel, snail shells, blades of wheat or grass, hay, horns, hair and other things, together with several different animals, both living and dead. The generation of these things (accomplished through corruption and diverse alteration) should not surprise us much if we consider that, since fecund Nature has proportionately in the excellent microcosm every sort of matter in order to make it resemble and be like a living image of the big world [the macrocosm], so she plays at representing in it [i.e., the microcosm] all her actions and movements, never being idle, so long as she is not lacking in matter.[22]

So, not only is nature constantly active, but its activity is precisely oriented. That is, the productive activity of nature is conducted by *analogy*, as the adverb *proportionately* clearly indicates, the French equivalent of the Greek ἀναλογία; the chief figure of the analogy being that of the macrocosm ("this big world") and the microcosm. As Paré states in the same treatise, man is the "small portrait of the big world, abridged,"[23] whence he receives his eminent dignity.

To guard against over-abstraction, Paré does not hesitate to provide detail in his thesis, offering lengthy comparisons of rainshowers and floods to the "aqueous apostemas," eclipses to syncopes, fruits to birthmarks, mountains to humps and to enormous growths,[24] and the two eyes to the "two great lights, to wit, the sun and the moon,"[25] of the big world. These examples show clearly that, for our surgeon, the normal and the abnormal, as we would call them, are equally fruits of nature's activities and that, if the abnormal amazes us more, it is only because familiarization blunts our admiration for the normal. The "fabric" of the human body, like that of all of nature, is a marvel, and its meaning is already lost by making the distinction, even in passing, between the normal and the abnormal. When Paré specifies that the generation of these strange bodies takes place "through corruption and diverse alteration,"[26] he simply wants to recall that in the world here below we know, since Aristotle, that generation and corruption are two inseparable facets of one and the same activity; the ways of nature that produce "strange bodies" are the same ones that assure the production of all beings. If it is nevertheless fitting to consider strange bodies in particular, it is because they permit us, so to speak, to surprise nature at work busily modeling ever more closely, the one on the other, the big world and the little world, the microcosm and the macrocosm. If one defines nature essentially by this incessantly inventive activity, then nothing must appear to us as being more profoundly natural than these "strange" productions. Enriched certainly by the thematic of the analogy, though still recognizable, Ambroise Paré's thought thus reflects the Augustinian doctrine of monstrosity. In a celebrated page of the eighth chapter of the sixteenth book of the *De civitate Dei*—a page to which we will have cause to return later—Saint Augustine wrote: "For God is the creator of all things, and he himself knows at what place and time a given creature should be created, or have been created, selecting in his wisdom the various elements from whose likenesses and diversities he contrives the beautiful fabric of the universe."[27]

These, briefly summarized, are the two systems elaborated by the Renaissance to explain monsters. They might appear contradictory to us, as the first reflects an underlying *disorder*—it is because the ordinary course of things is disturbed that the manifestations of this disturbance are read as presages—while the second implies an *order*—it is because nature strives in an orderly fashion toward an ever more perfect uniformity that it produces things that are "strange" to us.

It should be noted, however, that these two explanatory systems did not cease to coexist during almost the whole of the Renaissance, a fact that does not fail to astound the historian. Oddly enough, for a long time, their contrariness didn't strike anyone. It even seems that there was not much difficulty when expounding upon the one to give place to the other. Already, in the preface of *Des monstres et prodiges*, Ambroise Paré unquestioningly ratifies the divinatory thesis in a parenthesis: "Monsters are things that appear outside of the course of Nature (and are usually signs of some forthcoming misfortune)."[28] Furthermore, it is not rare to see a single example travel from one book to the next, illustrating first the one and then the other thesis. Luther's Calf-Monk turns up again in the collection of Paré, but in this instance it is no longer, charged with the task of denouncing the deception and the depravity of the monastic state, but rather with illustrating the power of the imaginative virtue, one of the ways by which nature reproduces the big world in the little world.[29]

Can one be satisfied with accusing the Renaissance thinkers, whose compilatory method hastily juxtaposes two irreconcilable systems, of mere conceptual weakness? This is an all-too-easy explanation that does not stand up to examination. Do we have the right to totally oppose, as we have done, order and disorder? This opposition suggests that to natural effects one would have to oppose their contrary, which would be effects considered to be against nature. Furthermore, the two explanatory systems are both averse to the idea that any effect whatever can in fact be against nature. If we observe that those who interpret an earthquake as a presage are not necessarily disclaiming the explanations that physicists give of the event, we have to admit that it is perhaps not by mere lack of theoretical rigor that those who connect this earthquake to the analogical activity of nature—Paré thus makes the connection between these effects and the quakes that shake the fever-stricken—are not by the same token rejecting the idea that, being rare, it could assume in addition some particular significance and in fact be a presage. When, in 1607, the revisers of Ambroise Paré's *Oeuvres* introduced into his *Des monstres et prodiges* interpolations that tended to present some of the monsters that he had analyzed as signs of the changes that had occurred in the world, they obviously were not respecting the intention of the author, but it is not clear that they made him contradict his main argument.[30]

One must consider as a new given the sense, which dawned at the end of the Renaissance, of the contradiction presented by the two explanatory systems. It first manifested itself in a remarkable manner among writers who, not possessing great speculative powers—and for this very reason—disclose to the historian the signs of the crisis in gestation. Thus we find Claude de Tesserant, who in 1567 published a continuation of the *Histoires prodigieuses*, debating with the idea of the variety of things, which he doesn't reject, but which seems to him to be incapable of accounting for the irreducible singularity of certain monsters. None of the "alterations" of which Ambroise Paré, after some others, will enumerate the causes (for the physical etiology of monsters changes little over the course of the Renaissance)—an excess of seed, the indisposition of the womb, the imagination of the mother, etc.—can explain the monster of Arles: "All these reasons however cannot provide sufficient proof of why our monster was born in the form in which one sees him painted."31 A little later, in 1575, another continuator of the *Histoires prodigieuses,* François de Belleforest, contrary to the notion of the monster-sign, uses the idea of analogy: that a fisherman had brought in a sea lion in his nets "gives us no wonder, knowing that there are very few animals on the earth that the sea, like a monkey, doesn't imitate in its depths."32 Inversely, one finds him citing the extreme strangeness of an event in order to refrain from attributing it solely to an activity of nature and to ascribe it rather to divination. Great crosses were seen imprinting themselves on a tree: "Notwithstanding that nature's effort is noble, and its diversity admirable, how is it that these crosses appeared on this tree in such a size, that being a foot in length, without some mystery and marvel of uncommon significance."33

With a view to dispelling the belief that these are but the objections of lightweight thinkers, let us invoke once again the testimony of Montaigne, who entitles one of the chapters of his *Essais* "Of a Monstrous Child" (II, 30). Even though he describes with great precision the double monster that he saw—descriptions of the kind are not rare, and a person would have to be misinformed to award to it any special merit—he announces straight off that it should be left to the physicians "to discourse of it." In reserving this task for the physicians, Montaigne thus deposes the soothsayers, later consecrating to them these mocking remarks: "This double body and these several limbs, connected with a single head, might well furnish a favorable prognostic to the king that he will maintain under the union of his laws these various parts and factions of our state. But for fear the event should belie it, it is better to let it go its way, for there is nothing like divining about things past."34

Does this mean that Montaigne is making "rationalist"35 remarks, as some have asserted? This vague term, seemingly intended to designate a certain philosophy of nature that leaves no room for miracles, would be equally fitting for those who hold that monsters are signs without in any way rejecting the "physical" explanations of the phenomena under consideration: Camerarius is ready to make any concessions to the physicists that they would like on this point.36 In other words, to oppose the natural and the supernatural, as is so often done by the historians of "rationalism" is to neglect the complex history of the notion of nature and, by lending our own logic to the men of the Renaissance, to commit the sin of anachronism.

Montaigne, for his part, takes exception to the diviners only in order to side more closely with the Augustinian thesis and, like Saint Augustine, whom he very accurately recalls, to attribute this monster that he described to God, who, he says, "sees in the immensity of his work the infinity of forms that he has comprised in it." It is "for us to believe," continues Montaigne, "that this figure that astonishes us is related and linked to some other figure of the same kind unknown to man,"[37] in the same manner that Saint Augustine, cited above, observed: "But one who cannot see the whole clearly is offended at the apparent difformity of a single part, since he does not know to what it is related and linked [quoniam cui congruat et quo referatur ignorat]."[38] The formula seems so pertinent to Montaigne that later on he translates it a second time: "We do not see its assortment and relationship."[39] The author of the *De civitate Dei* wanted to combat those who sought to deny the wisdom of God by suspecting Him—when, for example, a child is born among us with six digits—of having made an error in the calculation of the fingers, as Saint Augustine amusingly puts it. Montaigne likewise affirms: "From his infinite wisdom there proceeds nothing but that is good and ordinary and regular."[40] Like Saint Augustine, Montaigne concludes that this explanation through an appeal to nature's order suits all monsters without distinction. They are therefore in no way "against nature," even if they are "against custom." Or, to adopt his words, it is "this universal and natural reason" that makes it possible to explain the monster that he described as well as all the others.

Contrary to what has been alleged by some, there is here no appeal to "*the* natural reason," no affirmation whatsoever that science will one day be more able than today to account for monsters and that this finally satisfying explanation will eventually reduce the monster to a pure effect of mechanical causes, thereby exempting it from divination. It is already possible to challenge the soothsayers by alleging the thesis of the complex order of the world, such as it proceeds from the wisdom of God. As for this complex order, there is no reason to think that it can ever be completely grasped; even the physicians, who are doubtless in a position to elaborate an etiology of monstrosity, are themselves no more capable than anyone else of ever achieving an understanding of the order of the world.

Montaigne, citing Cicero without crediting him, calls for a distinction between the act of looking itself and the rarity of an unusual effect. This was, indeed, what Cicero was saying, that it is the rarity of an event that makes us cry prodigy or, rather, attribute to an event the value of being a sign and a presage, while in fact its rarity is entirely relative to the narrowness of our own observations. But in taking it up in an Augustinian context, Montaigne solicits us not to reduce the rare effects to what are for us ordinary effects, but to attribute them to the totality of natural effects, which, for God, are all ordinary; that is to say that they are all in conformity with the order of his creation: "What we call monsters are not so to God."[41]

If, at the end of the sixteenth century, so many minds, both great and small, thus opposed the two systems for explaining monstrosity, which had gotten along so well together for so long, it is without doubt because the idea of nature itself was undergoing a profound transformation. The representation of nature that tolerated the two explanatory systems during the High Renaissance authorized both of them and allowed between them the articulation of a physics and a theology of monstrosity.

As far as monstrosity is concerned, the two points of view were distinct and even of different orders, but were in no way mutually exclusive. Nature was, indeed, imbued with divinity. By that, let us understand not only that nature is the work of God (creationism is not really put into question, and the thesis of the eternity of the world, discussed at great length, does not necessarily challenge it),[42] but, more important, that nature actively collaborates in God's designs. When, in order to give us a sign, God inscribes it in nature, nature is not merely a malleable lump of clay that, in the hands of God, is molded to his liking; endowed with what scholasticism called an obediential power, nature actively collaborates in the expression of the will of God. By dint of considering the regularity of nature's effects, we can be tempted to forget it. The function of monsters is precisely to invite us to remember it. Their irregularity is the sign that nature is not a mere machine, that its diverse procedures—"corruption" and "diverse alteration" included—are but the ways by which it goes about its task, which is, according to the words of Paré, to be the "chambermaid of the great God."[43] This is what makes it permissible to call nature divine; what is so improperly called the pantheism of the Renaissance is most often only this feeling that nature actively collaborates in the work of God: it is actively his chambermaid.

Monsters appear, then, in order to awaken the feeling of the "quid diuinum" of nature. This is what Paré means when he writes: "There are divine things, hidden and to be wondered at, in monsters."[44] When Chateaubriand, in the *Génie du Christianisme,* wants to draw from his reflection on monsters an apologetic argument in favor of divine providence, he can do no more than treat them as the empty traces of the latter: "In our opinion, God has permitted this distortion of matter expressly for the purpose of teaching us what the creation would be *without Him*. It is the shadow that gives greater affect to the light—a specimen of these laws of chance which, according to the atheists, brought forth the universe."[45] The Renaissance, on the other hand, interpreted the monsters not as the traces of an absence, but as the indications of an intimate presence.

Two consequences follow from this representation of nature, one relative to causes and the other to signs. First, in regard to causes, let us recall that physical causes are subordinate to metaphysical causes. When some say that in his book Paré frames ten natural causes (a too large or too small quantity of seed, narrowness of the womb, etc.) by three supernatural causes (the glory of God, the wrath of God, and the action of demons), they poorly summarize the work as they lead the modern reader to believe that, overflowing the bounds of medical discourse, Paré outlines causes to which one would have to directly attribute certain monsters—without mentioning the fact that they unduly place on the same level both God and demons, demons being hardly anything more than impostors or counterfeiters. Moreover, Paré is too convinced that nature is God's chambermaid not to consider that physical causes are the means by which God manifests his glory or his wrath. It suffices to state that in the chapter "Of the Wrath of God,"[46] Paré takes into account various examples that will later illustrate a "natural" cause of monstrosity: the "fusing together of strange species."[47] Let us add right away, however, that Paré does not fetter God to his creation, and that he readily admits that God is not held to making use of physical causes, as he states precisely: "There are other causes that I leave aside for the present, because beyond the human reasons, one cannot give any that are sufficient or probable."[48]

Let us note here the significant expression "human reasons," meaning reasons that are accessible by the intelligence of man. If this reserve places limits on medical discourse, it does not prevent the causes to which the latter has access from belonging to the order of "second causes." Consequently, the attribution of a particular monster to the indisposition of the womb of the mother or to the quality of the seed is not a complete explanation of it. So medical discourse, which examines the physical etiology of monstrosity, does not reduce the monster to a pure effect of physical causes; it does not reject the possibility or even the legitimacy of another discourse on monstrosity. Paré is not alone in thinking this way. Joachim Camerarius, in his *De ostentis* (1532), well knows that the physicists have at their disposal an entire arsenal of physical causes to account for comets or monsters, and he does not reject their science. But, he says, they put forward only the "inferior" (and therefore second) causes, and one has the right to continue to wonder "what assuredly greater and more powerful force than these inferior causes was able to set them to work in order to produce such effects at this time, in this place, at this precise moment."[49] One can very well render a physical account of simple eclipses; all the same, they are not reducible to pure effects of physical causes. The problem of knowing according to which criteria one recognizes the effects of nature that have a particular power to signify is another question that we will not tackle here; it suffices to have noted that these thoughts refuse reductionism.

If this is so—and here we touch on the second consequence, relative to signs—it is because, in a nature imbued with divinity, everything is more or less a sign. Actual miracles are only the most eminent of the signs: their voice does not explode in an otherwise silent world. One of the reproaches made to divination is precisely that it makes an arbitrary choice among the signs and forgets that in a certain sense all is a sign. If certain signs have a greater value than others as "presagious" signs, it is by this quality of being presages that they distinguish themselves, not by a special privilege to signify.

From this point of view, we have to take up once again what we said earlier regarding order and disorder. A disorder supposes and requires an order, as Cardan incessantly makes it understood—Cardan being the philosopher who is possibly the most representative or in any case the most influential of the Renaissance, notably in France. He is the great authority on the order of natural sciences; even Bernard Palissy read him.[50] The philosophy of Cardan is all the more worthy of interest as it is he who most rigorously theorized the notion of the variety of things and as at the same time all his preoccupations led toward divination; for him, these are two intimately related interests. In order to manifest itself, the variety of things is in need of a complex apparatus of hierarchized causes organizing an order. But these causes that Cardan, profoundly marked by Neoplatonism, conceives as *forces* are closely interrelated, and any weakening of one of them affects the others. For example, were a political power guilty of committing crimes, this would result in a diminution in the divine force penetrating the world; the inferior causes feeling the effects of it, an earthquake or the birth of a two-headed calf might occur. One could therefore relate this earthquake or this birth to the changes affecting the political power, of which they would be found to be the signs.[51] In the same way, there is nothing better attested to and nothing more explainable than the showers of stone, "but, since their natural causes are joined to superior causes, these showers are terrible presages and bring with them grievous disasters."[52]

Cardan is without doubt the philosopher who most forcefully theorizes this approach, authorizing at once a physics and a theology of unusual occurrences. But he is far from being the only one to do so. One could just as well focus on Cornelius Gemma who, in a book with the significant title *De naturae divinis characterismis* (1575), proposes the creation of a new art, cosmocriticism, an art of the critical signs that crop up in the world, permitting one to portend and, if necessary, to forestall the changes they warn of. This Neoplatonist, who showed a particular interest in the new star of 1572 and who owes to that event the conception of this work, is infused with the idea that all the parts of the world intimately "conspire" between them. A divine force—the soul of the world, if you will—travels through all of creation and assures it a tightly knit cohesiveness; it follows that if this order is in some way perturbed, the perturbation is at once the effect of a cause and the sign of other foreseeable effects. It is by taking as his basis the notion of the analogical order of the world, which itself is hierarchized, that Gemma undertakes to elaborate the science.[53]

One need no longer be versed in philosophies of this sort to put at odds the two readings of monstrosity that were up until this point wholly reconcilable. This is indeed what is established at the end of the Renaissance. Two new, coordinated visions develop confusedly, accommodating themselves badly to the coexistence of the two readings. One of them, it is suspected, deals with causes, and the other with signs. Even if the attribution of monsters to God is not foregone, there is a tendency no longer to attribute them to God, except in an indeterminate manner, as equal to other creatures. The idea of a natural order endowed with a certain autonomy is gaining ground. So it is that in 1605 the physician Jean Riolan takes advantage of the birth of a monster in Paris to challenge the divinatory thesis, comparing nature to an artist. If the comparison is old, the reflections to which it lends itself under Riolan's pen are remarkable: an architect, he says, is a man who has received from God a mind capable of architecture and to whom nature provides the materi-

194 *Humanism in Crisis*

als to put it into practice; it remains that the house he constructs is, properly speaking, his work, and can only be attributed to God and to nature in an indirect and indeterminate manner. In the same way, when a monster is born, if examination of the natural causes of its production allows for its explanation and if it is possible to perceive just how nature was prevented from achieving its end and committed an "error," it is useless to attribute this monster to God, except indirectly and indeterminately.[54] Despite strong resistance, but seeing henceforth that the mere play of natural causes suffices to explain an effect, minds grow accustomed to the thought that it is unnecessary to resort to higher causes.

The *canards*, who during these years multiply the accounts of monstrous births, appear informed of these reflections, even if they are dispensed by their purpose from discussing them and encouraged instead to reject them without examination. But if they now so brusquely sweep away the objections of the "naturalists," of the "philosophers," it is because they accept the idea that if a monster can be explained by the mere play of second causes, one might well have to forego attributing it to a higher cause. Such was the crux of the debate provoked by the Parisian monster of 1605;[55] one of the *canards* reporting on it issued to philosophers this interesting challenge:

> Philosophers, who hold the key to nature's cabinet, and who by the brilliance of your minds attain knowledge of all things, and provide an explanation of the ordinary and extraordinary actions of this common mother, teach us how it can be that she, who tends only toward the good, sometimes dozes off, indeed so neglects her duty, that we are unable to see what she intended to do.[56]

The objection is thus made to the philosophers that the notion of nature's autonomy stumbles on the obstacle of the monsters, the admission being made implicitly that the play of natural laws suffices to account for ordinary effects. By isolating nature's "errors" from the whole of nature's effects, this concession amounts to denouncing the thesis of the world's ordered diversity in an attempt to salvage the thesis maintaining that monsters have the value of presages: the two theses have become irreconcilable.

Let us add in passing that it is not only in the field of teratology that the idea of nature's autonomy gains its ground; demonology records it as well. It is increasingly thought that for it to be permissible to attribute this or that effect to a demon, it must first be proven that the demon exceeds the order of natural causes. The physician Jourdain Guibelet, in the third of his *Discours philosophiques* (1603), draws up a narrow list of operations that, being "extraordinary," might be imputed to Satan; if Satan wants to reveal himself, he knows what he must henceforth do to be recognized. He no longer has the right to conceal himself behind nature.[57]

In the order of signs, a comparable and concomitant change is taking form. The miracle proper tends no longer to be simply the highest of the signs; and, despite the identity of names, Father Richeome emphasizes in his *Discours des miracles* in 1598 that the miracle, an "evident effect produced beyond the common course and forces of nature, possessing its extraordinary and hidden cause," is essentially different from those effects that are "commonly baptized miracles of nature, because God gives them through the intervention of the latter working naturally through a fixed and common course."[58] Laurent Joubert, in his *Erreurs populaires*, already formulates this distinction with an equal clarity. Joubert no longer makes mere rarity the criterion of the sign: "We continue to think that there are very strange and rare things that come about by natural means, also rare. These we call natural miracles or miracles in nature, unlike super-natural and divine miracles, for which nature is not employed, and which have no foundation in nature."[59] Father Lenoble maintained that it was the desire to restore the notion of the miracle that drove Mersenne to mechanism:[60] the work of Joubert shows that this desire dawned as early as the time of the crisis of Humanism, and that even if he did not yet have available to him the intellectual tools that mechanism would provide, he had at least already laid down as a prerequisite the necessity of conceiving the order of nature as being invested with a certain autonomy. This represents a considerable revolution in thinking.

The teratological literature of these years reflects this change, as the list of the productions composing it will show.

First of all there are the inventories and the dossiers. Since the old teratology is threatening to collapse, let us bring together the teratological facts. C. Bauhin, in 1610, conducts a vast lexicological investigation, first by underlining the differences between authors, and collects the opinions of theologians, jurisconsults, physicians, philosophers, and rabbis on monstrous childbirths.[61] The physician Johann Schenck consecrates two ample volumes to the gathering of observations; the very diversity of the adjectives he retains to characterize the collected facts shows his desire to abstain from all theories of monstrosity: "Observationum medicarum, rararum, novarum, admirabilium et monstrosarum tomus unus et alter."[62] Let us note, however, that this undertaking is not totally without theoretical significance. By ordering the retained facts according to the parts of the human body, Schenck submits them to a purely medical inspection. Further, by isolating them from the mass of marvels, with which they have been placed until this point, the authors establish them as objects of a separate branch of knowledge.

Next are the treatises that, to a hasty reader, might appear quite traditional but which are in fact new in their silences and their denials. In twenty years, Weinrich in Germany (1595), Riolan in France (1605), and Liceti in Italy (1616) give to the new teratology three remarkably concordant treatises.[63] All three decide first off to reserve the appellation *monster* for the bodies of the animated beings that, at birth, are of a different species than their parents or that present a notable deformity. They dispense themselves from having to speak of the other realities that, along with monsters, formerly constituted the mass of marvels, by stating simply that this is not their subject. They refuse next to consider monsters as presages, not that it is not theoretically possible, says one or the other, but because they choose not to talk about monsters, except as physicians; in this way Liceti completely neglects all questions that touch on divination; if Weinrich does not follow suit, he only speaks of divination in order to establish its falsity. Finally, they resolve to consider teratology as a part of physiology; physiology gains from taking interest in monsters in the way that the logician gains from taking interest in sophistic reasoning. That is to say, as Weinrich well observes, that the monster is no longer called upon to contribute to the beauty of the world; by this, Weinrich openly acknowledges that he is rejecting the venerable thesis of Saint Augustine. For, he asks, who would dare to say that a crooked beam contributes to the beauty of a house, or that a barbarism adds to that of a text?[64]

Anyone considering the etiology of monstrosity that these authors propose will most likely find that it is by no means new; but its newness lies elsewhere—that is, in the desire of the authors to be no more than *physici*. Their books record the birth of the spirit of specialization: a specialist has the right only to discuss his specialty, without being obliged to address everything. Following this new spirit, our new teratologists resolutely decide to carry on a "profane" discourse on monsters; in their own way, they illustrate the change that Montaigne witnesses: "In my time I have also heard certain writings reproached as being purely human and philosophical with no admixture of theology."[65]

The less specialized literature reflects this new state of mind in its own way. It is to edifying literature that the genre of the prodigious story, inaugurated by Boaistuau in 1560, became connected; for almost forty years this genre remained quite fashionable. Monsters and portents, Boaistuau used to say, are supposed to incite us to retire into ourselves and "to hammer at our conscience."[66] However, as we saw earlier in citing Tesserant and Belleforest, this genre was also the site where important issues were once again put into question. Were these questionings extended, or were they to open themselves completely to the new state of mind, the genre itself would be destroyed—or totally transformed. This is precisely what the last continuator (1598) very clearly stated: the notion of prodigy is extremely uncertain and, in any case, very confused and composite. As far as monsters are concerned, they surely elude qualification as prodigies, since even if nature strays from her ordinary course in creating them, most of the time they are by no means to be considered presages. What remains then is the pleasure of relating some enjoyable stories and of counting on readers who will sample them. This pleasure is substituted for the desire for edification, or at least changes its meaning in a profound way: one will perhaps want to inspire a sense of the limits of knowledge, but one will no longer seek to make the signs legible.[67]

Must scholarly literature be henceforth forbidden from embracing these marvels? The exemplary case of Aldrovandi shows both that scholarly literature does not easily abandon them and that continuing to embrace them now exacts a price. The *Monstrorum historia,* left in the rough-draft stage by Aldrovandi and completed by his disciple B. Ambrosini, is unaware of none of the recent developments in teratology and is acquainted notably with the works of the new teratologists. But the work is careful not to follow them, because it would become necessary for the author to choose—that is, exclude—and he makes it no secret that he does not want to have to do so. After having examined a host of definitions for *monstrum,* he retains the definition given by Donat, who gave the appellation *monster* to all that is "praeter naturam." Here is why: "We will thus be able to extend the definition in such a way as to include many more objects, by supposing to be a monster any sublunary creature that does not conform to the usual standards of Nature and which, because of this, is capable of powerfully arousing the admiration of those who contemplate her."[68] Here then, once again counted among the monsters, are the numerous effects of nature, comets, eclipses, celestial marvels of all sorts, that Liceti had worked so vigorously to expel. Summoned to explain himself, the author does not, like a classical Aristotelian, refuse to admit that monsters are errors of nature, *naturae errata,* but he recognizes, and we with him, that these errors possess the means to surprise and entertain the gaze. For anyone considering them carefully, these errors of nature are, in fact, nature's sport: like the animal forms, the various shapes of plants or those of inanimate objects, the monstrous forms are attributable to the playful activity of nature. The idea of nature's play is not new: we need only recall that Cardan willingly had recourse to it. But, for Cardan, nature plays by seeking the greatest diversity in her productions without interfering with the order that governs them. If, for example, certain beasts are crowned with oar-shaped antlers, it is because, having created various sorts of horns, nature "perfected all the parts within a division insofar as it was allowable: otherwise she would not have been acting wisely."[69] The idea of play, under the pen of the author of the *Monstrorum historia,* is much less philosophical than aesthetic; he has no fear of maintaining the paradox that nature imitates the artist as much as the artist imitates nature:

> One must contemplate nature's paintings. Because if art, through sculpture and painting, competes with nature in everything, nature in its turn, as if trifling in art, seems to imitate the sculptor and the painter when, on the branches and trunks of trees and sometimes on rocks, like with brushstrokes, she so artistically arranges certain features that she imprints in them the images of various objects.[70]

Monsters are only the extreme form of this playful activity, and, so to speak, the most beautiful fruits of the artistically inventive imagination of nature. The author claims that he must first describe man in his perfection in order to establish a norm; yet what is his description if not an ever-expanding narration of infinite human diversity? To the diversity of lifestyles, climates, languages, eating habits, customs, etc., monsters add, by diversifying man again, the diversity of appearances. One might be amazed that as receptive as the author is to all of the strangest accounts, he rejects on several occasions the idea of monstrous human races; but it is because at bottom this idea would imply the existence of different species and would thus limit the inventiveness of nature. He prefers to think that nature endeavors to diversify man's form indefinitely, that in the manner of the painter or the sculptor, with one piece of clay, she models figures that always succeed, by their novelty, to surprise. Moreover, the art of nature, like that of the artist, is an art of shaping appearances. Thus the author does not believe that *astomes* really exist, and only admits that it is possible for men to have such small mouths that, hyperbolically speaking, those who observed them would say they were mouthless. This does not prevent him, though, from providing a full-page representation of an *astome:* illusion is a part of art.

Why then, under these conditions, waste one's time delving into the definition of the monster? Doing so would be to attempt to measure the astonishment and the admiration that we owe to the art of nature. This is the reason for which the author is writing not a treatise but a *historia,* in the old and classical sense of the term.

In one sense, no other work is further from the new scientific spirit elaborated by the seventeenth century. Posterity was not mistaken: in the nineteenth century, it was not Geoffroy Saint-Hilaire who read the *Monstrorum historia,* but Flaubert. For us, the work is to an extent the sumptuous field of ruins of Renaissance teratology as well as the most voluble witness (the work numbers 748 pages in folio) to the crisis of the science of monsters. As luck would have it, Aldrovandi died in 1605, leaving behind an unfinished work that remained unpublished until 1642. So it was that in the mid-seventeenth century he erected the funerary monument of a definitively defunct teratology. We have sought to show here that what destroyed it was, in the last analysis, the crisis and the disappearance of the representation of nature that had prevailed during the Renaissance. It would be worthwhile to show, as we have suggested, that other domains of knowledge such as demonology make it possible to confirm these analyses.

NOTES

This essay was translated by Constance Spreen.
  1. After the first edition, entitled *Deux livres de chirurgie,* vol. 1, *De la génération de l'homme...,* vol. 2, *Des monstres tant terrestres que marins...* (Paris: A. Wechel, 1573), the book *Des monstres et prodiges* continued to be

republished in the *Oeuvres* of Ambroise Paré (1575, 1579, 1585, 1595, 1607, etc.). *Translator's note:* All quotations in English from Paré's *Des monstres et prodiges* have been taken from Janis L. Pallister's translation of the work, *On Monsters and Marvels* (Chicago: University of Chicago Press, 1982). However, it has been necessary on occasion to modify Pallister's translation slightly, as it did not always correctly reflect the sense of the French. These modifications will be indicated in the notes.

2. Ulisse Aldrovandi, *Monstrorum historia* (Bononiae: N. Tebaldini, 1642).

3. See R. Schenda, "Die französische Prodingienliteratur in des Zweiten Hälfte des 16. Jahrhunderts," *Münchner Romanistische Arbeiten* (Munich: Heft 16, 1961); Ambroise Paré, *Des monstres et prodiges*, ed. Jean Céard (Geneva: Droz, 1971), 205–6.

4. Simon Goulart, *Histoires admirables et memorables de nostre temps, recueillies de plusieurs auteurs*, 2 vols. (Paris, 1600–1610); *Thresor d'histoires admirables et memorables de nostre temps*, 4 vols. (S. Crespin, 1610–14).

5. See Jean-Pierre Seguin, *L'Information en France avant le périodique* (Paris: Maisonneuve et Larose, 1964); Jean Céard, *La Nature et les prodiges* (Geneva: Droz, 1977), 468–83.

6. See Céard, 441.

7. Arnaud Sorbin, *Tractatus de monstris* (Paris: Marnef et Cavellat, 1570); French. trans. François de Belleforest, in *Histoires prodigieuses* (1582).

8. See Céard, 3–30.

9. See in particular S. Jérôme, *ad Michée*, 3.11: "Numquam diuinatio in Scripturis in bonam partem accipitur"; Guillaume de Paris, *De uniuerso*, 2.3.18; Gratien, *Décret*, Causa XXVI. A good summary of the condemnations of divination by Scripture, the councils, the canons, the popes, and the fathers of the Church is found in J. M. Maraviglia, *Pseudomantia veterum et recentiorum explosa* (Venice: Valvasensem, 1662).

10. Cicero, *De divinatione*, 1.6.11–12 and passim.

11. Rabelais, *Tiers livre*, chap. 25.

12. H. C. Agrippa, *De occulta philosophia*, 1.56.

13. Sorbin, dedicatory epistle in *Tractatus de monstris* (1570): "attribuer à de telles choses quelque pouvoir ou quelque efficace."

14. *Deuttung des czwo grewlichen Figuren, Baptesels czu Rom und Munchkalbs czu Freyerberg ijnn Meysszen funden* (1523); letter entitled "Jean Calvin to the Christian reader," dated November 15, 1549, in *De deux monstres prodigieux, à savoir, d'un Ane-Pape ... et d'un Veau-Moine ...* (Geneva: Jean Crespin, 1557).

15. Paré, *On Monsters and Marvels*, 17. See *Des monstres et prodiges*, 16, 159 n. 27; Céard, 216–17.

16. See François de Belleforest, *Discours sur l'heur des presages advenuz de nostre temps* (Paris: Robert, Le Mangnier, 1572), fol. 30v; *Le Resveille-matin*

des François et de leurs voisins (Edimbourg: Imprimerie de Jacques James, 1574), 70.

17. See Pierre de L'Estoille, *Journal pour le règne de Henri III*, ed. L.-R. Lefèvre (Paris: Gallimard, 1943), 54, 62; Agrippa d'Aubigné, *Les Tragiques*, ll. 1005–14 and ll. 1035–65.

18. See Jean Céard, "Postel et l' 'étoile nouvelle' de 1572," *Guillaume Postel (1581–1981)* (Paris: Guy Trédaniel, 1985), 349–60.

19. Conrad Lycosthenes, *Prodigiorum ac ostentorum chronicon, quae praeter naturae ordinem, motum et operationem, et in superioribus et his inferioribus mundi regionibus, ab exordio mundi usque ad haec nostra tempora, acciderunt. Quod portentorum genus non temere euenire solet, sed humano generi exhibitum, seueritatem iramque Dei aduersus scelera, atque magnas in mundo vicissitudines portendit* (Basel: H. Petri, 1557), fol. 24r: "annoncent aux hommes la sévérité et la colère de Dieu contre les crimes, ainsi que les grands changments affectant le monde."

20. Cicero, *De natura deorum*, 2.3.7, and *De divinatione*, 1.42.93; Augustine, *De civitate Dei*, 21.8; Isidore, *Etymologies*, 11.3.

21. In regard to the efforts of ancient and modern lexicographers to distinguish these terms, see Jean Céard, *La Nature et les prodiges*, 39–40, 439.

22. Paré, *On Monsters and Marvels*, 60: "Aux apostèmes [abcès], il se trouve des corps fort étranges, comme pierre, craie, sablon, coquilles de limaçon, épices, foin, cornes, poil et autres choses, ensemble de plusieurs et divers animaux, tant morts que vivants. Desquelles choses la génération (faite par corruption et diverse altération) ne nous doit étonner beaucoup, si nous considérons que, comme nature féconde a mis proportionnément en l'excellent microcosme toute sorte de matière pour le faire ressembler et être comme image vive de ce grand monde, aussi elle s'ébat à y représenter toutes ses actions et mouvements, n'étant jamais oisive quand la matière ne lui défaut point"; *Oeuvres complètes* (Paris: J.-F. Malgaigne, 1840–41), 3:38. Pallister's translation of Paré has been slightly altered as she translates the verb *s'ébattre* as "to struggle" rather than "to play."

23. Paré, *On Monsters and Marvels*, 53: "petit portrait du grand monde accourci"; Paré, *Oeuvres complètes*, 3:33.

24. Paré, *On Monsters and Marvels*, 54–55: "apostèmes aqueuses."

25. Paré, *On Monsters and Marvels*, 53: "deux grandes lumières, à savoir le soleil et la lune."

26. Paré, *On Monsters and Marvels*, 60: "par corruption et diverse altération."

27. Augustine, *City of God*, trans. E. M. Sanford and W. M. Green (Cambridge, Mass.: Harvard University Press, 1988), vol. 5, bk. 16, chap. 8, p. 45: "Dieu, créateur de tous les êtres, connaît le lieu et le temps où il faut ou a fallu créer un être, lui qui sait par quel assemblage de parties ou semblables ou différentes tisser la beauté de l'univers." In the original Latin, *De civitate Dei*, 16.8: "Deus enim creator est omnium, qui ubi et quando creari quid oporteat

vel oportuerit, ipse nouit, sciens uniuersitatis pulchritudinem quarum partium vel similitudine vel diversitate contexat."

28. Paré, *On Monsters and Marvels*, 3: "Monstres sont choses qui apparaissent outre le cours de Nature (et sont le plus souvent signes de quelque malheur à advenir)."

29. Paré, *Des monstres et prodiges*, 36–37, 165 n. 67.

30. Paré, *Oeuvres* (Paris: N. Buon, 1607), 1007, 1011, 1076.

31. Claude de Tesserant, *Histoires prodigieuses* (Anvers: G. Janssens, 1594), 284: "Toutes ces raisons toutefois ne peuvent faire preuve suffisante pourquoi notre monstre a été né de la forme dont on le voit peint." Tesserant's continuation dates from 1567.

32. François de Belleforest, *Histoires prodigieuses* (Anvers: G. Janssens, 1594), 456: "ne nous donne aucunes merveilles, sachant qu'il y a fort peu d'animaux en la terre que la mer, comme un singe, n'en ait de tels et semblables en ses abîmes."

33. Belleforest, *Histoires prodigieuses*, 438: "Nonobstant que l'effort de la nature est grand, et sa diversité admirable, si est-ce que ces croix ne sont venues en cet arbre en telle grandeur, que d'avoir un pied de long, sans quelque mystère et prodige de signifiance non vulgaire."

34. Montaigne, "Of a Monstrous Child," in *The Complete Essays of Montaigne*, trans. Donald M. Frame (Stanford: Stanford University Press, 1958), II, 30, 539 A: "Ce double corps et ces membres divers, se rapportant à une seule tête, pourraient bien fournir de favorable pronostic au roi de maintenir sous l'union de ses lois ces parts et pièces diverses de notre Etat; mais, de peur que l'événement ne le démente, il vaut mieux le laisser passer devant, car il n'est que de deviner en choses faites." In this and subsequent references to Montaigne, a letter (A, B, or C) following the page number indicates one of the three major textual strata: 1580, 1588, or 1595.

35. This is the term used by Villey in *Essais* (Paris: Presses Universitaires de France, 1965), 712; he in turn owes it to Henri Busson, and it recurs under the pen of various critics.

36. Joachim Camerarius, *De ostentis* (Basel: Oporin, 1552). See Céard, *La Nature et les prodiges*, 170–74.

37. Montaigne, II, 30, 539 A: "voit en l'immensité de son ouvrage l'infinité des formes qu'il y a comprises"; "à croire que cette figure qui nous étonne, se rapporte et tient à quelque autre figure de même genre inconnu à l'homme."

38. The Sanford and Green translation has been altered here in order to insist upon the direct influence of Augustine on Montaigne. In the original Latin, *De civitate Dei*, 16.8: "Qui totum inspicere non potest, tanquam deformitate partis offenditur, quoniam cui congruat et quo referatur ignorat. Pluribus quam quinis digitis manibus et pedibus nasci homines nouimus; et haec leuior est quam ulla

distantia; sed tamen absit, ut quis ita desipiat, ut existimet in numero humanorum digitorum errasse Creatorem, quamuis nesciens cur hoc fecerit."

39. Montaigne, "Of a Monstrous Child," II, 30, 539 A: "Nous n'en voyons pas l'assortiment et la relation." The Frame translation used in the text has been modified here.

40. Montaigne, II, 30, 539 A: "De sa toute sagesse il ne part rien que de bon et commun et réglé."

41. Montaigne, II, 30, 539 A: "Ce que nous appelons monstres ne le sont pas à Dieu."

42. See Etienne Gilson, *La Philosophie au Moyen Age*, 2d ed. (Paris: J. Vrin, 1962), 535.

43. Paré, *On Monsters and Marvels*, 125: "chambrière de ce grand Dieu"; *Des monstres et prodiges*, 117.

44. Paré, *On Monsters and Marvels*, 73: "Il y a des choses divines, cachées et admirables aux monstres"; *Des monstres et prodiges*, 68.

45. Chateaubriand, *The Genius of Christianity*, trans. Charles I. White (Baltimore, Md.: Howard Fertig, 1976), 5:144: "Il nous semble que Dieu a permis ces productions de la matière pour nous apprendre ce que c'est que la création *sans lui:* c'est l'ombre qui fait ressortir la lumière; c'est un échantillon de ces lois du hasard qui, selon les athées, doivent avoir enfanté l'univers."

46. Paré, *On Monsters and Marvels*, 5: "De l'ire de Dieu."

47. Paré, *On Monsters and Marvels*, 5: "confusion d'étranges espèces"; *Des monstres et prodiges*, 7, 66–67.

48. Paré, *On Monsters and Marvels*, 4: "Il y a d'autres causes que je laisse pour le présent, parce qu'outre toutes les raisons humaines l'on n'en peut donner de suffisantes et probables" (translation altered); *Des monstres et prodiges*, 4.

49. Camerarius, 295: "quelle force assurément plus grande et plus puissante que ces causes inférieures a bien pu les mettre en oeuvre pour produire de tels effets en ce temps, en ce lieu, en ce moment précis."

50. See Céard, *La Nature et les prodiges*, chap. 9.

51. Cardan, *De rerum varietate* (Basel: H. Petri, 1557), 14.68.533. See Céard on "La notion de *miraculum* dans la pensée de Cardan," in *Actus Conuentus Neo-Latini Turonensis*, 2 vols., (Paris: Vrin, 1980), 2:925–36.

52. Cardan, *De rerum varietate*, 14.70.539: "mais, puisque leurs causes naturelles sont conjointes aux causes supérieures, ces pluies sont de terribles présages et apportent de très graves calamités."

53. Cornelius Gemma, *De naturae divinis characterismis* (Anvers: Chr. Plantin, 1575). See also Jean Céard, "Postel et l' 'étoile nouvelle' de 1572."

54. Jean Riolan, *De monstro nato Lutetiae A.D. 1605. Disputatio philosophica* (Paris: O. Varennaeum, 1605), 25.

55. On this debate, see Céard, *La Nature et les prodiges*, 476–77.

56. "Philosophes, qui avez les clefs du cabinet de nature, et qui par la vivacité de vos esprits parvenez à la connaissance de toutes choses, et rendez la raison des actions ordinaires et extraordinaires de cette mère commune, apprenez-nous comme il se fait qu'elle, qui ne tend jamais qu'à un bien, s'endort quelquefois, voire s'oublie tellement en son devoir, que nous refusons de voir ce qu'elle a pensé bien faire."

57. See Jourdain Guibelet, *Trois discours philosophiques* (Evreux: Ant. Le Marié, 1603), 283b-84a. See also Jean Céard, "Folie et démonologie au XVIe siècle," *Folie et déraison à la Renaissance* (Paris: Presses Universitaires de France; Brussels: Presses de l'Université de Bruxelles, 1976), 140.

58. Louis Richeome, *Trois discours pour la religion catholique, des miracles, des saints, des images* (Bordeaux, 1598), 14–15: "effet évident produit au dessus le cours commun et forces de la nature, ayant sa cause extraordinaire et cachée"; "communément baptisés miracles de nature, parce que Dieu les donne par l'entremise d'icelle oeuvrant naturellement par cours arrêté et commun."

59. Laurent Joubert, *Des erreurs populaires* (Bordeaux: Simon Millanges, 1578), 98–99: "Nous recevons toujours qu'il y a des choses fort étranges et rares, qui adviennent par moyens naturels, lesquelles aussi sont rares. Et appelons miracles naturels ou miracles en nature, à la différence des miracles supernaturels et divins, auxquels nature n'est employée, et n'y a aucun fondement en nature."

60. Robert Lenoble, *Mersenne ou la naissance du mécanisme*, 2d ed. (Paris: J. Vrin, 1971).

61. Caspard Bauhin, *De hermaphroditorum monstrosorumque partuum natura et Theologorum, Jureconsultorum, Medicorum, Philosophorum et Rabbinorum sententia, libri II hactenus non editi* (Oppenheim, 1614). One reads, however, at the bottom of the title page: "Francofurti excudebat Mathaeus Becker impensis Io. Theo. et Io. Israel de Bry, frat. M.D.C."

62. Friburgi Brisgoiae, 2 vols. (1596; reprint Francofurti, 1600).

63. Martin Weinrich, *De ortu monstrorum commentarius* (M. Osthesii, 1595); Riolan, *De monstro* . . . ; Fortunio Liceti, *De monstrorum caussis, natura, et differentiis libri duo* (Padua: G. Crivellari, 1616); French trans. (Leyde, 1708).

64. Weinrich, fol. 86.

65. Montaigne, "Of Prayers," I, 56, 234 A: "J'ai vu aussi de mon temps faire plainte d'aucuns écrits, de ce qu'ils sont purement humains et philosophiques, sans mélange de théologie."

66. Boaistuau, dedicatory epistle in *Histoires prodigieuses* (1560): "frapper au marteau de notre conscience."

67. On this little-known continuation, see Céard, *La Nature et les prodiges*, 462–68.

68. Aldrovandi, *Monstrorum historia*, 321–22: "Nous pourrons ainsi étendre la définition de façon à englober beaucoup plus d'objets, en posant qu'est monstre

toute créature sublunaire non conforme à la norme habituelle de la nature, et par là capable de susciter grandement l'admiration de ceux qui la contemplent."

69. Cardan, *De la subtilité* [French trans. of *De rerum varietate*] (Paris: G. Le Noir, 1556), fol. 218v: "a parfait tous les membres de sa division, tant qu'il lui a été licite: autrement elle n'eût été sage."

70. Aldrovandi, 673: "Il faut contempler les peintures de la nature. Car, si l'art, par la sculpture et la peinture, rivalise en tout avec la nature, à son tour la nature, comme en se jouant de l'art, semble imiter le sculpteur et le peintre lorsque, sur les branches et les troncs des arbres et parfois sur les pierres, comme au pinceau, elle ajuste si artistement certains traits qu'elle y imprime les images de divers objets."

The Erosion of the Eschatological Myth (1597–1610)

Claude-Gilbert Dubois

A physically tangible observation and an objectively constructible analysis can lead to the hypothesis of decline or decay. But to assert decay is to express an ideological position supported by the imaginary. Such an assertion brings into play a mythology of history and the interpretation of observed events as signs of the approach of a radical transformation—an end, in the sense both of *termination* and of *finality*. These observed events set up as symptoms and converged in such a way as to establish the diagnosis of decay constitute one of the elements of the eschatological syndrome, one way in which the historical imaginary is structured.[1]

In the Christian West, decadence as a sign of the approach of the end was perceived at the same time as the expectation of a renewal. Once again we encounter both meanings of the word *end*. The decline was the last phase of an evolution and at the same time heralded an impending revolution. Its scriptural foundations were the eschatological texts contained in the Gospels (Mark 13, Matt. 24–25, Luke 21), the Pauline conception of anthropological metamorphosis (Rom. 6), and a few apocalyptic fragments incorporated into John's Revelation.[2]

Since it would be impossible to tackle the entire eschatological myth within the religious and political context of the sixteenth century in France, I will content myself with following the trail of one of the premonitory signs of the end of time. I will show, to use the terms of Pierre Viret, an author of that period, "the birth, the building up, and the consummation of the mystery of the Antichrist."[3]

In accordance with the theme of the colloquium, I will stress the last phase, the decline of the myth in the circumstantial interpretation imparted by the sixteenth century. But since it is not, strictly speaking, a matter of a figure peculiar to the French Renaissance but to the age of the Reformation, exclusively theological to begin with, and characteristic of a period of rupture and of conflict, it is conceivable that this decline actually constituted a revival or in any case a reintroduction of more peaceful times. In the 1970s I had the chance to take up this problem in another research context.[4] I am happy to have been granted a new opportunity, in a different context, to bring up to date, to develop, and to refine what I had written somewhat naively or in any case with overconfidence in my previous inferences from the texts consulted. In the meantime I have learned to be if not suspicious, then at least cautious.

A legend of the Antichrist was formed in the Middle Ages from a corpus of disparate texts.[5] The word *Antichrist* appears only three times in all the canonical books, in the Epistles of John (1 John 2:22, 1 John 4:3, and 2 John 7), texts of minor import and of evident meaning, where it is said: οὗτός ἐστι ὁ ἀντίχριστος, ὁ ἀρνούμενος τὸν ηατέρα καὶ τὸν υἱόν ("He is antichrist, that denieth the Father and the Son").[6] The prefix has a solely adversative value: he who is opposed to the Christ. The ingenuity of the glossarists who followed was to play on the two meanings of the prefix αντι, which means not only *against* but also *in the place of:* from the opponent of God, we move to the idea of usurpation, he who wrongfully puts himself in the place of God, a shift in meaning that authorized a shift in identification. As for the French form *Antéchrist* (French was one of the few languages to coin this neologism), it was achieved by the hybrid prefixation of the Latin *ante,* he who comes before the Christ, in reference to a passage from Saint Paul that we will talk about presently.

In the Second Epistle to the Thessalonians, Paul warns the Christians of Thessalonica against excessive impatience or credulity that would make them believe in the imminent return of the Christ (actually a basic belief of the first disciples): "for *that day shall not come,* except there come a falling away first [ηρῶτον, translated as *primum* in the Vulgate which is the origin of the form *Antéchrist*], and that man of sin [ὁ ἄνθηω ηοςτῆς ἀνομίας, translated as *homo peccati*] be revealed, the son of perdition; Who opposeth and exalteth himself above all that is called God, or that is worshipped; so that he as God sitteth in the temple of God" (2 Thess. 2:3–4; emphasis added). In order not to disappoint their expectations for too long, Saint Paul adds: "For the mystery of iniquity [τὸ μυστήριον τῆς ανομίας, translated as *mysterium iniquitatio*] doth already work: only he who now letteth *will let,* until he be taken out of the way. And then shall that Wicked [ὁ ἄνομος, translated as *iniquus*] be revealed, whom the Lord shall consume with the spirit of his mouth, and shall destroy with the brightness of his coming: *Even him,* whose coming is after the working of Satan with all power and signs and lying wonders" (2 Thess. 2:7–9; emphasis added). Most of the themes that would be used to develop the character of the Antichrist can be found in this text. However, nowhere is the word itself pronounced [the only reference to it is that of the ἀνόμια], and, since the neuter alternates with the masculine, nothing indicates that a choice between an identifiable person and a collective force is possible.

Apocalyptic literature provided, moreover, an imagery for the construction of the legend: in particular, the great dragon defeated by Saint Michael (Rev. 12) and the beast born of the earth, which works wonders and makes the earth's inhabitants worship another monster (Rev. 13:13–17). The imagery of John's Revelation refers to other apocalyptic texts, notably to a rather long passage from Daniel (11:21–45), which would be another source for establishing the details of the reign of the Antichrist. This text, the content of which was ascribed by modern exegesis to the Maccabean period, and more precisely to the Seleucid Antiochus IV (Flavius Josephus had already interpreted the passage thus), was disengaged from its context—as was John's Revelation—and became an eschatological prophecy.

The medieval apocalyptic and sibylline traditions, likewise nourished by a phantasmagoria of impatience and persecution, influenced this belief,[7] and thus from scanty references was developed the legend of the Great Antichrist, an individual who will be born of a prostitute in a Jewish environment and who will rise very high in the political hierarchy. His reign, placed at the end of time, will be marked by wonders and miracles, which will inspire belief in his divinity. It will be a period of war. He will set himself on the throne of the Church (the temple of Jerusalem), but will be defeated by Saint Michael, or by a prince with the help of Saint Michael. Before his fall, two messengers (associated with Enoch and Elias) will have denounced the usurper. The reign of the Antichrist will last several decades (since it will come during a man's lifetime) and will precede the Second Coming of Christ and the end of time.[8]

Thus, through this construction based essentially on apocalyptic texts and on the apocrypha, the Antichrist appeared as a mythical character, projected at the end of time, rather extraordinary, akin to such other great figures of orthodox or heterodox eschatology as the Last World Emperor, the Angelic Pope, the Scarlet Woman, or the Four Horsemen. But this imaginary character, located in an indefinite future, could take on a presence and a historical actuality: when unrest, arising from misery, joined forces with the awareness that disorder or scandal was reigning over the Church, the temptation was great to see in the mighty of the world, especially in the Church, the marks of an incarnation of the Antichrist, a temptation augmented by eschatological impatience when it was the only form of hope left to misery. These apocalyptic beliefs fomented movements inspired by Joachism, and by John Wycliffe's and John Huss's first demands for reform, which became inflammatory, particularly with the Taborites. However, one could not go so far as to speak of a systematic application of the myth to the ruling power.

The beginning of the Reformation witnessed an awakening of eschatological impatience, accompanied by a feeling of decay, symptomatic of the approach of the end of time. The idea that the reign of the Antichrist was imminent, that he "doth already work," to use the biblical term, entered into the general pattern of exacerbated rebellion and hope. During the years 1519–20, Luther asserted his own particular conception of the Antichrist. In 1519 in a letter to Spalatin (George Burckhardt), he admitted: "And, confidentially, I do not know whether the pope is the Antichrist himself or whether he is his apostle, so miserably is Christ (that is, the truth) corrupted and crucified by the pope in the decretals." In 1520, again to Spalatin, he wrote, "I hardly doubt that the Pope is the Antichrist, which the world at large expects." And on August 18 of the same year he said, "We are here persuaded that the papacy is the seat of the true and genuine Antichrist."[9] How did we get to this point; how did this mythical character, who nourished an iconography steeped in the fantastic and a dramaturgy set in allegory and fiction, become a historical figure, if not ordinary, then rendered commonplace, whose actions inscribed in history have but little to do with medieval apocalyptic imagery?

At the outset, there was a denunciatory passion: "It is difficult to deal seriously with a matter," wrote Florimond de Raemond, who participated on the Catholic side in the Antichrist quarrel, "without some degree of fervor and intellectual strife, says someone in Plutarch. The dispute is only better, truth shines brighter when words fly, when arguments are stirred up, and when disputes spur each other on like two knives sharpening each other."[10]

Knives grew sharp and arguments intensified throughout the next century. Treatises about the Antichrist multiplied and gave free rein to the following "truth": the Pope was the Antichrist; it was he who was the usurper who had taken his seat in the temple of God and who had worked wonders in order to deceive the masses. Lutheran dialectic applied to the interpretation of history—the purity of primitive Christianity, an internal corruption brought on by the reign of the Antichrist, a recovery of the original light in modern times (note the affinity between this and the principle that Vasari later applied to the history of the arts in the secular domain)—inspired the ecclesiastical history written by Carion and Melanchthon (1532) and that by Flacius Illyricus, which was known under the name *Centuries de Magdebourg* (1558).[11] *De anatomia Antichristi*, by John Huss, was published in Strasbourg in 1526. *Byrthe and Lyfe of Antechryste*, published by Wynkyn de Worde (1528), can also be placed in this line of thought. In 1528, Luther openly denounced the *Bulla Antichristi*. *La Comédie du Pape malade*, by Conrad Badius (1561), depicted the pope as the Antichrist.[12] England experienced a similar spread of this "truth." In his *Meditationes in Apocalypsin*, John Foxe developed the theory according to which the Antichrist referred not to an individual, but to an institution. And in his *Christus Triumphans* (1556), in which Pornapolis represents the false Church, the character Europus asks his mother Ecclesia if the Antichrist could only be Asian and Muslim. Ecclesia answers that the Church has other enemies and that the Antichrist cannot be identified with Asia and Islam alone. William Fulke (1538–89) expounded the Reformed theory of the Roman Antichrist, which led to a reaction by the Jesuit Nicholas Sanders. We should also point out Thomas Dekker's *Whore of Babylon*, Thomas Becon's *The Acts of Christ and of Antichrist*, and the work of Spenser himself, whose character Archimago, in *The Faerie Queene*, displays the kindred spirit that unites him with the Antichrist—he works miracles on behalf of Duessa (from the church of hypocrites) who wears the triple crown of the papacy. In the French language, the quarrel of the Antichrist was entrenched in Reformed commentaries on the Book of Daniel and the Apocalypse, and in writing coming out of Geneva. In 1553, Louis Des Masures, under a pseudonym, published *Babylone ou la ruine de la grande cité et du règne tyrannique de la grande paillarde;* Pierre Viret's *Naissance, bastiment et consommation de la Messe et de la Papauté et du mystère de l'Antéchrist* appeared in 1554; in 1555, Simon Du Rosier published *Antithesis Christi et Antichristi, videlicet*

212 *Humanism in Crisis*

Papae, which was republished and translated into French in 1561 with the title *Des faicts de Jesus Christ et du Pape avec la description de l'image de l'Antéchrist*; Lambert Daneau published *Tractatus de Antichristo* in 1576; a French version appeared in Geneva the following year.[13]

Enough enumeration. Let us try to synthesize all of this information. What became of the medieval image of the Antichrist at this point in history? From the moment the Antichrist was perceived as a manifest historical reality, the problem lies in getting the historical facts to coincide with the clues contained in the texts. A comparison of the starting and ending points brings to light five antitheses.

1. The medieval Antichrist was embodied in a man whose origin and identity could be defined. The Reformation Antichrist referred to a doctrine or to an institution that took on an abstract and collective character and was embodied in a multiplicity of actors whose function transcended them.

2. The medieval Antichrist's existence was set in the future. The Reformation Antichrist was present in actuality or had already been revealed in the past.

3. The medieval Antichrist was imaginary and his existence potential. The Reformation Antichrist was real and historical.

4. The history of the medieval Antichrist did not exceed a man's lifetime (his reign was set between twelve and one hundred and twenty years). The history of the Reformation Antichrist spanned several centuries.

5. The medieval Antichrist was defeated by a political and human force: his fall should be understood as a military defeat. The Reformation Antichrist was vanquished by a return of the evangelical spirit; the denunciation of the Antichrist put an end to the usurpation. The role of the messengers of God—Enoch and Elias interpreted as metonymies of the Christian conscience—was more important than the Antichrist's political defeat.

This metamorphosis was obtained by a particular semantic treatment of the fundamental apocalyptic texts, a treatment that can be described both as symbolic, by which an allegorical or symbolic reading was substituted for the literal reading, and as referential, since it was a matter of establishing a connection between the texts and the events that had occurred. Let us take as an example the text from Daniel that has already been cited, in which we find the following prophetic and enigmatic phrases: "Neither shall he regard the God of his fathers, nor the desire of women, nor regard any god: for he shall magnify himself above all. But in his estate shall he honour the God of forces."[14] Modern exegesis, which incorporates facts put forward by Porphyry and Saint Jerome, understands the text in the following way: Antiochus Epiphanes will reject the Syrian gods, particularly the women's worship of Tammuz or Astarte ("the desire of women"), in order to urge worship of the Greek gods. "The God of forces" is an allusion to Jupiter Capitoline, representing military force, to whom Antiochus sent offerings—we have Livy's account of this—and in honor of whom Antiochus may have built a temple in Antioch. In his commentary on Daniel, Luther acknowledges that the historical allusion to Antiochus is evident, but in his opinion this monosemic reading is insufficient. Into the name Antiochus should be read all the political and military powers that tend toward autocratism to the detriment of the love of God. To Luther, the most important phrase is "he shall magnify himself above all." From there he gets more specific: "The Pope is depicted in his vivid and true colors, he roars, bellows and neighs impudently in his Decrees, glorying in the fact that he is judge of all, and that he is not subject to the judgment of others.... And if he had reigned longer, if God had not hushed him up, if He had not stopped his tyranny, if He had not put up his sword, he might well have banned spitting, nose blowing and farting."[15] Not to regard "the desire of women" means to refuse to marry (befitting Catholic priests), and "the God of forces" refers to "the temples, cathedrals and monasteries" for which he has a liking and which he orders to be built in Rome. Luther even suggests a consonantal affinity between *Maozim,* which designates the forces, and *Missa,* "mass."

From 1560 on, the idea that the pope was the Antichrist was not only accepted, but was deemed to be unquestionable among Reformed circles. It was even an article of the confession of faith of the new churches. In a situation of conflict, in which priority is given to arms, the ideological armament must not be neglected. When the Reformation was victorious, the principle of the pope as Antichrist was maintained in order to avoid any retreat and to justify the argument for the final defeat; such was the case in Elizabethan England. When the fight remained uncertain, this weapon incited men to action; it was an essential postulate of holy war, expressed in the following terms: "It is a great advantage to know our enemies, but a greater encouragement to know that our enemies are God's enemies."[16] As long as the conflicts remained undecided, this thesis was wielded as a weapon to superimpose a psychological action on a practical one: when the moral intentions were not apparent in day-to-day concrete action, the ultimate theological affirmation was there to remind all concerned that the enemies of the day were ever the same because they were "God's enemies."

Where does the matter stand in the period of French history that is of particular interest to us, and which I will consider to coincide with the reign of Henry IV? Let us remember first of all that this idea was not a Renaissance idea, both for chronological reasons—it was an invention of the age of the Reformation—and because the Renaissance was associated with a cultural syncretism, whereas the political myth of the pope as Antichrist conveyed a symbolism of rupture and of purification. While this period witnessed the myth's decline, to use a term of the colloquium, this decline coincided with a relative appeasement and a temporary reconciliation. It is true that the ideological fighting continued and that each side stood its ground; the problem of the Antichrist remained at the heart of the debates, but it was confined to discussion among the clergy. In the quarrel itself, there was a lessening of passion, for de facto or for tactical reasons. Florimond de Raemond, whose militant remark we have already cited, ended his conclusion thus: "It is difficult to deal seriously with a matter without some degree of fervor.... but in that [the meaning of texts pertaining to the Antichrist] there must be moderation; there should not be an all-out fight."[17]

Initially, the Catholic counteroffensive went through a phase of moderation. This counteroffensive consisted essentially in demythologizing and in turning the argument against the adversary.

1. The revision of ecclesiastical history and of biblical commentaries took into account the grievances introduced by the controversy and consisted in reducing each of the incriminating facts to strictly human proportions. The collapse of the signs led to a reduction in their meaning and hence to an easing of tension. In the same way, it was a matter of demonstrating textual inconsistencies or improper textual extrapolation on the part of the adversary. The Jesuits in particular—Viegas, Ribera, and Pereira—restored the texts to their historical context and rejected the referential polysemy that amalgamated distant facts.

2. The argument consisted in demonstrating that the Church had remained faithful to her original foundations, and, consequently, in substituting the concept of continuity and of linear historical development—

which does not lend itself to impassioned assertion—for the Lutheran dialectic of rupture.

3. One offensive, although not widespread, consisted in turning the argument back on the adversary and in proving by the intrigues of the Reformed that, if there were indeed an Antichrist, it was on their side that he should be sought. The argument was essentially linked to the metaphysical prerogatives attributed to unity. This inability to conceive of pluralism in other than negative terms was of a tactical but also of an ideological nature. (Indeed, authoritarian centralism and one party, or in any case a single ideological armament, would remain the foundation of papal politics long after the Wars of Religion.) It played the same demobilizing role as the continuity argument: whoever fought or debated showed by those very actions that he was renouncing the unitarian and totalitarian principle that all is one and that nothing must escape this unity, a metaphysical principle considered to be as evident as it was undeniable.

4. There was a return to the traditional, medieval notion of the Antichrist as found in Florimond de Raemond and in the works of literary authors, particularly Spanish playwrights.

The main protagonists of this counteroffensive, which was rather a defensive, were the Jesuits. The propositions *quod Papa non est Antichristus ille insignis,* by Nicholas Sanders (1530–81) were published in London in 1583, and the treaty *De visibili monarchia ecclesiae,* containing a chapter on the Antichrist, was published in Würzburg in 1592. Francisco de Ribera's *Apocalypsin commentarij* appeared in 1603, and those by Brás Viegas in Cologne in 1603 and in Lyon in 1606. The *Disputationes...de Controversiis Christianae fidei, adversus huius temporis haereticos,* by Robert Bellarmine, were published between 1586 and 1593, and the *Annales ecclesiastici,* by Caesar Baronius, between 1588 and 1607. Laymen participated in the debate as well. Florimond de Raemond, a counselor in the Bordeaux *Parlement* and a friend of Montaigne, published in 1597 a *Traité de l'Antichrist,* which he took up again and expanded in 1599, at the very moment when Henry IV succeeded in proposing a temporary means of reconciliation by the Edict of Nantes.[18] Undoubtedly the conversion of the king played a role in the debate in which the virulent mythology of the past years was deflated. Raemond's argument was in fact based on a misunderstanding: history, for him, proved the inanity of the accusations brought against the papacy, since the papacy endured, a phenomenon that was not consistent with the prophecy of a lightning reign and of a dizzying fall. The Church was still doing well, and in an already baroque triumphalism, Raemond enumerated her successes in the field of evangelization. Moreover (and this was yet another misunderstanding), Raemond took up the argument for unity: "One always has the upper hand." Raemond's position developed into an apology, also baroque, for unitarian systems, a development that cleverly succeeded in comforting the French monarchy. From there we thus return to the traditional notion: the Antichrist had not yet arrived; by its perseverance and by its preservation of unity the Church's history denied that the pope was the Antichrist. Nor was the Antichrist the Reformation, which was not in any way new or exceptional, and which could be considered one of the cyclical movements of permanent opposition to the glory of the triumphant Church, the specter of which kept consciences on the alert. The Antichrist would come later, exactly as had been foretold, and those for whom he had not yet come would be better prepared to confront him. In sum, in a style often cluttered with metaphors, with baroque themes and tropes, the content of the work displayed a relative moderation and adapted itself easily to the circumstances of the time. In short, it became necessary to prove that the king could not have joined the Church if she had been the Antichrist's, and that those who accepted her sovereignty would do well to lower their voices.

Indeed, if the assertion continued to make itself heard resolutely among the Reformed circles of France, the voice was lowered: the *Antichrist,* by Nicolas Vignier, (1610) and Philippe de Mornay's *Le Mystère d'iniquité* (1611) kept their distance from the political action and the militant function of the idea, a distance that gave them an occasionally academic tone. In 1603, the Synod of Gap decided to retain in the confession of faith an article worded thus: "We believe and maintain that [the pope] is properly the Antichrist, and the son of perdition foretold in the word of God."[19] Henry IV intervened, and the article was withdrawn. While the positions remained, they were confined to an intellectual domain and did not call for resorting to arms to fight the usurper. Nicolas Vignier replied to Raemond that there was no need for a military defeat to make the fall of the Antichrist known; the fact that he was unmasked was sufficient. It was therefore not necessary to rise up in arms, and his preface confirms it: "Let it not be thought that this Theater of the Antichrist challenges to some new fight. Which is far removed from those who entrusted me with the job of drawing it up."[20] The political circumstances did not lend themselves to stirring up passions. Ever since the king, of Reformed origin, had gone over to the other church, the rules of the game had been changed. It was no longer in the interest of the Catholics who had advocated reconciliation to revive quarrels implicating the king's origins, and it was not in the interest of the Reformed to say that the king's new religious affiliation meant he was siding with the Antichrist. There would be no theological renunciation, but there would be a political rallying, which implied a certain amount of accommodating and a partial overlapping of attitudes. This lowering of voice was a mark of a willingness to coexist without compromise, but without provocation.

If in France the doctrine of the pope as Antichrist went unexpressed except in small intellectual circles and was not publicly stated without all sorts of precautions, this was due to political circumstances. As an antithetical point of reference, it would be interesting to note how it all happened in a neighboring country. In England, the notion of the pope as Antichrist acquired a certain "respectability," to use Christopher Hill's phrase, that served the interests of the Elizabethan monarchy. Following Martin Bucer and John Foxe, Robert Abbott and Thomas Beard proposed new rehashes of the idea.[21] In 1615, Thomas Brightman published *The Revelation of St. John Illustrated,* in which he predicted the imminent end of the two horns of the Antichrist, the Ottoman Empire and the papacy. Nevertheless, the fever dropped, and at this point once again the debate turned academic, for different reasons: the idea of the pope as Antichrist was considered to be accepted. Yet in 1622 James I reprimanded a preacher who made too much of this idea. In his reply to Bellarmine, Lancelot Andrewes spoke of "probability" rather than of "certainty." This was because other Antichrists had been denounced in the meantime, and in particular the Anglican church, which would bear the cost as the target in the fighting of the more radical religious groups: English royalty and Anglican bishops became the henchmen of the Antichrist.

Thus, the sixteenth century witnessed the birth, the explosion, and the irreversible decline of a circumstantial idea, a decline that began in France with the return to civil peace, and which would occur elsewhere as politico-religious givens changed. This idea remained alive among fundamentalist and integralist groups, and would make us smile nowadays if tragic circumstances did not occasionally rekindle the tension as a result of conflicts of another sort into which religious signs of differentiation have been introduced.[22]

But beyond specific circumstances that made the Church of Rome the target of this phenomenon, there is something permanent about the myth of the Antichrist, which is rekindled in every period of rupture and conflict, and whenever demands for regional, national, or cultural identity are stirred up. This is because the Antichrist is the chosen form in the Christian civilization for the phantasmagorical representation of the Other. When coexistence with the Other is no longer tolerated, the Other becomes the enemy: we then witness the confusion and blending of the political interests of the moment with the cultural imaginary to constitute a myth that is an ideological weapon. But considering all that has been revealed to us about the specular mechanism and about the manner in which alterity splashes back onto identity (for stirring up the image of the Other leads to states of schizophrenic delirium that constitute a loss of identity), the reflection of the Other onto the Self results in the Antichrist argument turning itself around and becoming a reply to the sender.

The myth of the Antichrist was taken up again during the nineteenth century by the clergy to describe both the French Revolution and modernist and scientistic movements,[23] although it is true that the movements in question had themselves used arguments that brought into play a mythology of blackness—obscurantism, ravens—as a symbol of negativity opposed to the Goddess of Reason or to the Angel of Light. As we all know, *Antichrist* is the title retained by Ernest Renan for his study of the Roman Empire in his *Origins of Christianity,* and by Nietzsche for a denunciation of the debilitating attitude, in his opinion, of Christian culture; Dmitri Merezhkovsky, in his *Christ and Antichrist* (1904), took up this theme and applied it to Peter the Great; the decadent themes of the invasion of the barbarians, the great apocalyptic upheaval, and the expectation of a new savior played a sure role at the end of the nineteenth and the beginning of the twentieth centuries, before the subsequent major cataclysms. These themes are in fact eschatological.

Nazism presented itself as a crusade driven by an apocalyptic phantasmagoria and a mythology of purity: "If, with the help of the Marxian creed, the Jew conquers the nations of this world, his crown will become the funeral wreath of humanity.... Therefore, I believe today that I am acting in the sense of the Almighty Creator: *By warding off the Jews I am fighting for the Lord's work.*"[24] Through the effect of the specular reflection of the image on its model, Nazism was considered one of the two fundamental manifestations of the Antichrist in the twentieth century. The other one is obviously socialism, particularly in its Soviet version. Norman Cohn remarked how much the view of capitalism sold by Leninism-Stalinism corresponded to an Antichrist image.[25] Capitalism, in return, treats the Antichrist the same way. Very recently, for circumstantial reasons, we heard a president of the United States of America speak of "the evil empire." We also recently learned of a non-Christian country speaking of its political adversaries in terms of "small" and "great" Satans.

The myth of the Antichrist—in this cultural form or in any other form in other cultures—linked to the representation of the Other will persist as long as the antithesis of the Self and the Other remains unresolved. On the other hand, its application to reality assumes a less consistent approach. When the image of the Antichrist looms, it is because there is a storm somewhere. When it is on the decline (which is the case at the end of the sixteenth century in France), this waning is the sign of its opposite: I would not say of what is called dawn, but at least of what is called a bright spot.

NOTES

This essay was translated by Alice Musick McLean.

1. Claude-Gilbert Dubois, "Décadences," *Eidôlon* 9 (1979): 229–35.

2. Besides Daniel 11, Ezekiel 38–39, and Zechariah 9–14, the importance assumed by the apocrypha in the sixteenth century should be taken into account, in particular the Second Book of Esdras, presented as an appendix to the holy books by the Fathers of the Council of Trent.

3. Pierre Viret, *La Naissance, le bastiment et la consommation de la Messe et de la Papauté, et du mystère de l'Antéchrist* (Geneva, 1554).

4. Claude-Gilbert Dubois, "Le mythe de l'*Antéchrist* et son contexte apocalyptique," in *La Conception de l'histoire en France au XVIe siècle* (Paris: Nizet, 1977), 501–73.

5. Richard Kenneth Emmerson, *Antichrist in the Middle Ages: A Study of Medieval Apocalypticism, Art, and Literature* (Seattle: University of Washington Press, 1981); Klaus Aichele, *Das Antichristdrama des Mittelalters der Reformation und Gegenreformation* (The Hague: Martinus Nijhoff, 1974). Alfred-Felix Vaucher's short work, *Antichrist* (Collonges sous Salève: Bibliothèque Nationale, 1972).

6. The same generality can be found in the other two occurrences: "And every spirit that confesseth not that Jesus Christ is come in the flesh is not of God: and this is that spirit of antichrist" (1 John 4:3); 2 John 7 contains the same idea.

7. On these traditions and their relationship to the elaboration of the legend of the Antichrist, see Norman Cohn, *The Pursuit of the Millennium: Revolutionary Millenarians and Mystical Anarchists of the Middle Ages*, rev. ed. (New York: Oxford University Press, 1970), 29–36.

8. Medieval iconography illustrated these various episodes, sometimes drawing a parallel between them and the life of Christ (e.g., *Fatti dell'Anticristo*, painted by Signorelli in Orvieto Cathedral, and illustrations in the *Liber Chronicarum* by Hartmann Schedel [Nuremberg, 1493]). In literature, the *Tournoiement de l'Antecrist*, an Old French allegory by Huon de Méry, details a battle between the armies of Christ and Antichrist; the work is mentioned by Nicolas Vignier in an ironic reference to Raemond. The *Jour de Jugement*, the only extant play in Old French about the Antichrist, is summarized in Aichele. This inspiration regained its vigor in the theater of the Counter-Reformation, after the period of passional excitement of the sixteenth century, notably in *El Antichristo* by Juan Ruiz de Alarcón (1581–1639) and in another play of the same title attributed to Lope de Vega. In the *Mystère de l'Antéchrist et du Jugement de Dieu*, staged over three days at Modane, the Antichrist is a man born of a prostitute, according to the traditional medieval interpretation. (These examples are cited from Emmerson.)

9. The first letter can be found in Helmut T. Lehmann, ed., *Luther's Works*, 55 vols. (Philadelphia: Fortress Press, 1963), 48:114; the second in Preserved Smith, trans. and ed., *Luther's Correspondence and Other Contemporary Letters*, 2 vols. (Philadelphia: Lutheran Publication Society, 1913), 1:291; and the third in Preserved Smith, *The Life and Letters of Martin Luther* (Boston: Houghton Mifflin, 1911), 86.

10. Florimond de Raemond, *L'Antichrist* (Lyon: Jean Pillehotte, 1597), 836: "Il est malaisé de traiter une chose sérieusement sans quelque chaleur et contention d'esprit, dit quelqu'un chez Plutarque. La dispute n'en vaut que mieux, la vérité reluit plus quand les raisons se pressent, les arguments se piquent, et les disputes s'aiguillonnent comme deux couteaux s'entr'aiguisent affilés l'un contre l'autre."

11. Dubois, *La Conception de l'histoire en France au XVIe siècle*, 393, 424–38. The French translations of the collective work by Carion, Melanchthon, and Peucer were published from 1552 to 1611. In the last edition (1640), the following can be read: "Besides the idolatries and superstitions of the second age [which lasted until the reign of Emperor Henry IV], the worship of the god *Maozim* was introduced into the Church, which god was worshipped instead of the true God, and drew to himself the eyes and hearts of everyone" ("Outre les

idolatries et superstitions du second âge [qui va jusqu'au règne de l'Empereur Henri IV], fut introduit en l'Eglise le service du dieu *Maozim,* lequel a été adoré au lieu du vray Dieu, et a tiré à soy les yeulx et les coeurs de tout le monde"), a banal rendering of the Reformed interpretation of the god of forces mentioned in Daniel 11.

12. Emmerson, 204–37.

13. The content of this last work has already been analyzed in Dubois, *La Conception de l'histoire en France au XVIe siècle,* 510–16.

14. Dan. 11:37–38.

15. Martin Luther, *Le Commentaire de Martin Luther sur Daniel le prophète* (Geneva: J. Crespin, 1555), 378, 384: "Le Pape est despeint en ses vives et vrayes couleurs, lequel rugit, beugle et hennit impudemment en ses Decrets, se glorifiant qu'il est juge de tous, et qu'il n'est subject au jugement d'autrui.... Et s'il eust régné plus longuement, si Dieu ne luy eust couppé la broche, s'il n'eust arresté sa tyrannie, s'il n'eust fait reboucher sa poincte, peut estre qu'il eust interdit à tous de cracher, de se moucher et de péter."

16. Alexander Leighton, *Speculum Belli Sacri* (Amsterdam: 1624), 304–5, cited in Christopher Hill, *Antichrist in Seventeenth-Century England* (London: Oxford University Press, 1971), x.

17. Raemond, 837: "Il est malaisé de traiter une chose sérieusement sans quelque chaleur..., mais en cela [la signification des textes relatifs à l'Antéchrist] il y faut de la modération; il ne faut pas que ce soit un combat à outrance."

18. An analysis of this can be found in Dubois, *La Conception de l'histoire en France au XVIe siècle,* 516–33. My judgment about this text has changed. Today I am rather sensitive to his wish to demythologize and to play down the drama, in keeping with the requirements of the time, in a vocabulary that remains very vivid all the same.

19. Synod of Gap, 1603: "Nous croyons et maintenons qu'il [le Pape] est proprement l'Antéchrist, et le fils de perdition prédit dans la parole de Dieu."

20. Nicolas Vignier, *Antichrist* (1610): "Qu'on ne pense donc point que ce Théatre de l'Antéchrist porte un défi à quelque nouveau combat. Ce qui est du tout esloigné de ceux qui m'ont chargé de le dresser."

21. Robert Abbott, *Antichristi demonstratio* (1603); Thomas Beard, *Antichrist the Pope of Rome* (1625) (works cited by Hill), Andreas Helvigins's *Antichristus Romanus* (Wittenberg, 1612) continued this polemic tradition in Germany. In this tradition, but in the opposite camp, *De Antichristo libri undecim* (1606), by the Spanish Dominican Thomas Malvenda, suggested that the Reformation could be a form of the Antichrist.

22. I have not found convincing indications of this in the integrist Catholic discourse that followed Vatican II. On the other hand, on two occasions, the last on August 22, 1988, I heard these assertions: "the Catholic Church, the church

of the Antichrist" (on the French Antenne 2 evening news at 8:20); and "there are no mixed marriages with Catholics among us, because we are chosen and they are damned." These remarks were made by extremist Protestants from Ulster. Yet everyone is aware of the churches' role in attempting to quell passions during this conflict.

23. The notes written by Canon Crampon in his translation of the Apocalypse (the translation of the Bible took from 1894 to 1904) are quite characteristic: the first beast of the Apocalypse represents the spirit of protest born in the street, in ungodliness, and the second beast, which comes to the rescue of the first, represents the intellectual movements that put "false science" in the service of "ungodliness." The absence of any reference to current events does not rule out an allusion to social and intellectual problems at the end of the nineteenth century. Vaucher, moreover, furnishes examples of the application of the Antichrist myth to the French Revolution, in particular the application of *Maozim* to the Goddess of Reason. A more recent work, Hadès, *Le Mythe de l'Antéchrist* (Paris: Albin Michel, 1979), takes as its target the technocratic societies of the twentieth century.

24. Adolf Hitler, *Mein Kampf*, ed. John Chamberlain et al. (New York: Reynal and Hitchcock, 1940), 84. (Emphasis added.)

25. Norman Cohn, *The Pursuit of the Millennium* (Fairlawn, N.J.: Essential Books, 1957), 308–10. In the conclusion of the second edition of his book, Cohn does not specifically address this issue, although he does say: "But one may also reflect on the left-wing revolutions and revolutionary movements of this century.... Those who are fascinated by such ideas [emotionally charged fantasies of a final, apocalyptic struggle or an egalitarian millennium] are, on the one hand, the populations of certain technologically backward societies which are not only overpopulated and desperately poor but also involved in a problematic transition to the modern world, and are correspondingly dislocated and disoriented" (285–86). And: "During the half-century since 1917 there has been a constant repetition, and on an ever-increasing scale, of the socio-psychological process which once joined the Taborite priests or Thomas Müntzer with the most disoriented and desperate of the poor, in phantasies of a final, exterminatory struggle against 'the great ones'; and of a perfect world from which self-seeking would be for ever banished" (286).

Fin de Siècle Living: Writing the Daily at the End of the Renaissance

Marc E. Blanchard

The issue I want to raise here has to do less with literary history or the problematics of genre in the Renaissance than with a basic question: Why do people write? I will argue that at a time when humanism is in decline, the writing activity is characterized less by faithfulness to established canons than by a new, irrepressible desire to express oneself in modes that, because they eschew literary tradition, raise the question of their own literariness. At a time when literature frees itself from the canon (Montaigne confesses that his Greek is poor and his Latin now shaky), the authors I have chosen shun intellectual abstractions the better to concentrate on the stuff of daily life. In the midst of one of France's most troubled periods, with very little support from a humanistic tradition and with no pretentions to scholarship, they feel compelled to take up the pen and record their impressions on their *escriptoire*. Two of them, Gilles de Gouberville and Pierre de l'Estoile, chose the diary form; a third, Blaise de Monluc, that of the memoirs.[1] I have elected to write about these three not because they represent three distinct social types, although, in each case, the writer's social and economic status is important and helps situate his narrative. De l'Estoile is a middle-class urban dweller who sees his city of Paris as the site of a show that the monarchy puts on for the benefit of the Third Estate; Gouberville is a country gentleman who seems to care only about his land; and Monluc is a professional soldier of the lower nobility who knows nothing but arms, battle, and service to his king. Yet all three are also impelled to write by an ongoing desire to testify that they are a part of their time, that they *are here,* and, at least in Monluc's case, to ensure that posterity will remember their deeds. In a century known for its poets, its humanists, its historians, we have here three testimonies of daily narrative.[2]

Some preliminary remarks. First, in the traditional humanist context from Rabelais to Montaigne, the writer is someone both active in the affairs of state and conversant in the classics. There is no contradiction between an interest in politics and a thorough knowledge of the history of Athens and Rome. Anyone writing about the state or about himself is expected to fashion his literary persona after the image of antiquity and to clothe a private discourse with the guise of a public discourse. It is only by writing the *Discorsi* or the *Principe* that Machiavelli hopes to attract the Medici's attention. In this sense the private model of the person is a public historical model.

Second, there is toward the end of the sixteenth century a proliferation of memoirs, personal histories, the so-called *Livres de Raison,* where the diarist simply chronicles life in the same vein and sometimes on the same page with his accounts of the day. While this proliferation of *Livres de Raison* is well known and has been the object of intense historical research, it has not yet been sufficiently pointed out how these histories constitute on their own a form of literature and contribute not only to what has now been identified as the genre of self-portraiture,[3] but also to what I am calling here the *writing of the daily* at the end of the Renaissance, as the writer, free from the weight of a classical canon he doesn't or can't recognize, searches in the center of things for a form of writing more attuned to his everyday life. It is the authority of a writer fixed upon his own persona, his own things, his vision of the world, that now guarantees history. The chronicler, the diarist, writes no longer to imitate or to preserve an ideal but to substantiate the individuality of his own existence. To be sure, the three authors I have chosen are not the first to have kept a diary or written a memoir, but that they write in their time and explore their contemporaneousness in novel ways makes their work distinctive. They write in order to keep track of the time that passes, to keep, like Gouberville, a check on their property or to chronicle, like Monluc, the events of which they have been a part. But they also write because of an irrepressible desire to express themselves, and to say their piece about the times they have lived.

While the end of humanism is generally associated with someone like Montaigne, whose knowledge of the classics is deficient but whose *Essais* at least continue to discuss life in the context of reading the books of antiquity and thus put him at the beginning of a long line of detached observers of worldly routine (Pascal, La Bruyère, Saint Simon, Chamfort), my authors have a commitment to the daily routine that they see as their lot. Paraphrasing Montaigne himself, I could say that it is not the life of others they write, but their own. They face up to the monotony of the quotidian. They indicate that for every day recorded in their memoirs, a writer has something to say that makes his involvement in that day very clear.

The Battlefield

One of the most moving moments in the *Commentaires* occurs when Monluc, in the midst of the siege of Siena, heroically rouses himself from his bed to exhort the city fathers not to surrender despite the famine and the increasingly restive populace. As a good joke to play on women and cowards ("les peureux"), he decides to wear the splendid finery he keeps for amorous assignations, and he totters up to the mirror as his officers unexpectedly enter the room. All burst out laughing. Neither they nor he recognize the picture in the mirror: "I swear to you that I did not recognize myself and it seemed to me that I was still in Piedmont, in love as I then was. I could not keep from laughing, as it seemed to me that all of a sudden God had given me a totally different face."[4] Once on the street, Monluc passes equally unrecognized among the populace. To their queries, he replies that the real Monluc is dead and that he is someone else. This passage is representative of the *Commentaires* because it indicates that the book is, after all, also a book about self-knowledge. In the midst of a repetitious narrative of battles, sieges, skirmishes, injury, and death, the author finds time to play with his own image. Displaying not only the common warrior's prejudice against women but a sense of playfulness and mischief—"We had a period of leisure time in our garrison, and having nothing to do, this time was given over to the ladies.... At that time I was wearing grey and white for the love of a lady whom I was attached to when I had spare time"[5]— he simply decided to give the lie to all the rumors that he was dying, and thus he prevented a surrender. To a reader familiar with the problematic of Self and Other in the Renaissance, the episode antedates Montaigne's enterprise of capturing his own self in the mirror of his writing and his discovery that the enterprise ends with something unexpected: the image in the mirror or the portrait is more a grotesque monster than a real semblance of the sitter. To be sure, the context of the two works, the *Essais* and the *Commentaires,* is different. Montaigne, who often praises the military profession, writes, nonetheless, from the point of view of someone who has for a long time been retired from public life and who only wishes to use his leisure to adjust the picture of himself. Monluc, disfigured horribly by a harquebus shot and prevented by age from continuing to charge at the head of his troops, writes an exemplum of military conduct from the professional point of view. Montaigne begins his *Essais* with a foreword, "To the Reader," in which he states that his book is only for the benefit of family and friends. Monluc, who has lost three male children at war and friends all died in battle, asserts throughout his book that he is writing for those who might learn from his exemplary career.[6]

The difference is also about culture. It lies in the presence, on one hand, and the absence, on the other, of the knowledge transmitted by a cultural tradition. Montaigne's book of self would not have been written had it not been for his reading of, and his endless writing of commentaries on, others' books as well as his own. Throughout the *Essais,* the author recalls that his work is simply a makeshift aggregate of quotes, reflections, memories, and commentaries on his readings. Monluc, on the other hand, knows nothing and professes to know nothing: he states, shamelessly, that he hasn't read a book in thirty years. His Latin doesn't go beyond a few prayer words and the phrases of the Mass.[7] For him, no Cicero, no Plutarch. A bit of Livy, perhaps, and, of course, Julius Caesar, from whose book he has borrowed the idea of his own: his only literary debt. Although Monluc did go over his text between 1571 and 1576, adding and correcting with the help of an editor, whose name remains unknown to us, he doesn't consider himself a man of letters: "This is not a book for scholars, there are historians enough, but rather for a soldier, captain, and perhaps one from which a lieutenant could learn something."[8] It is not so much the physical act of writing (like Montaigne later, he dictates his *Commentaires* to a secretary) that costs him as the thought of having to compose something literary. Having to send letters to all the nobility in Guienne to exhort them to stay faithful to the king during the civil wars, he confesses that he hates the whole business. It reminds him of staying at home in one's office, a *cabinet,* instead of being on the battlefield. And although he knows that his contempt for the leisurely belles lettres is exaggerated, he would still much rather build trenches, climb walls, and fight hand-to-hand than to have to write a single line.

And yet the man writes on. He writes to be remembered.[9] In this he is no different from the rest of the writers of the Renaissance. Monluc's search for posterity and fame is not unlike Ronsard's and Du Bellay's "honneste desir de l'immortalité." To be sure, writing is not his *mestier*. He proves himself on the battlefield. His book is the book of his life, in which he has done nothing but go to war: "le discours de ma vie." Yet the book is not, like Léry's *Histoire d'un voyage faict en la terre du Brésil* or d'Aubigné's *Sa vie à ses enfants,* an apology *pro domo*. It is not, like Montaigne's *Essais,* a discourse on reading. It is not, like so many other books of the time, a topical discourse on a moral theme.[10] He speaks only for himself.

> The greatest captain that ever was, Caesar, showed me the way, having himself written his commentaries, writing during the night what he executed during the day. Accordingly, I wanted to train my unruly men, as emerging from a soldiers's hand, and even from that of a Gascon, who is always more concerned with doing well, rather than thinking well. Even though I be a gentleman, I have nevertheless arrived step by step, as would have the poorest soldier who had spent a long time in the kingdom.... And as I was the oldest of six brothers, as was the case, it was necessary that I make known the name of Monluc.[11]

It is this testimonial aspect that sets Monluc's book apart from the other works of his generation and offers a glimpse into what might have been one of the more pressing issues of the time. As the Renaissance is waning and the civil wars are raging, the question is: How can an individual still speak for himself? How can he point to himself as someone who wants to be known individually? Montaigne provides one answer: The man who wishes to identify himself is the man who, with time on his hands, is willing to search the culture in order to trace, in the books that he reads, something approximating his own image. Monluc offers a different, perhaps more traditional, answer. The individual is he who, totally committed to what he is doing, can define his life in terms of how well he remains in the field of vision. People will talk about him. He will have fame and be known exactly, no more and no less, for what he has done from the beginning to the end. Hence the idea of recounting one's life entirely—not because one needs to know all the exact details. Monluc admits that he may have made mistakes, that his memory (he is so old) may have failed him. He wants to tell all because, by doing so, he remains ever present to the reader. There is not, as in Montaigne, the fear that he will not be able to communicate. Communication is transparent. When Monluc says that the writing (*l'escriture*) of the book will convince anyone, he is not referring to the process of sorting ideas through composition. He simply means that the book, as the written (*l'escriture* means "what is now written") monument of his life, bears witness that he tells the truth; that in the operation of a certain *escriture*, which is not that of the humanists nor that of Montaigne, any reader can retrieve the stuff, the dailiness of a private experience. The *escriture* is true because Monluc was always there, both in the literal sense—he was where he said he was—and in the metaphorical sense—he was entirely and exclusively where he said he was: through pain, close to death, on the front line, always.

However, if the testimony is so strong and Monluc never wavers in his determination, it is because he refers to particular political events. Monluc is devoted to the king and the kingdom. To serve the king and to acquire fame are synonymous. The preservation of the monarchy provides, in the turbulent setting of the *Commentaires*, one of the few possible rules of conduct; and it can be argued, following Foucault, that the power that emanates from *raison d'état* is what fuels the text of Monluc, the faithful servant of the king endlessly battling to defend monarchic authority. For the author of the *Essais*, who has decided to retire from public business early, to write is to appropriate a singular authority. While Montaigne's writing is the locus of a search for a self unconstrained by political authority, Monluc's parameters are well defined. His existence is governed by the commissions he has received from the king and defined by his uninterrupted war service.[12] Not being able to pursue his service, he must find other ways to make himself useful. For him writing is a way not only of showing the world his valor and his dedication to the king, but also of showing his role in a history that some will claim is not his own, since everything he has accomplished was exclusively for the king's and the kingdom's greater glory.

The fact that Monluc constantly uses an injunctive relation to his reader ("Listen to me" ["Escoutez moy"]) indicates more than simply the paranoia of someone afraid of not being heard. It suggests a desire for what I would call, for lack of better words, *obsession with locality:* pointing to a place one occupies in the history and geography of the world, a place where one is, where one belongs, where there is no question that one has lived and functioned. Addressing other people as if one had something of the utmost importance to teach them, calling upon the highest authorities to warrant one's truth, is part of one general attempt at establishing historical authority for oneself. One doesn't need the Livy, the Tacitus, the Machiavelli, the Guicciardini. One can be one's own historian. Monluc can be seen as representative of the attempt to protect the foundations of a private/public historical authority. The old tradition from Joinville, Froissart, and Commines—that one knows because one is close to those who know—is now modified to read that only those who have directly participated on their own have the right to speak and teach. Toward the end of the century, as popular historical and cosmographical publications proliferate in which the author is often no more than the editor of the chronicles and travelogues of others, which he reproduces without investigating them, Monluc's work, addressing not simply the curious but those who sincerely want to learn, strikes a chord: "Take instead this one, rather than one who never lost nor won, and who never served in a camp, except as a witness. I am not writing this without experience; I learned these lessons under fire."[13] To have been there, which Montaigne would have required from every informant with whom he came in contact, and certainly from all the authors whose books he had read, is especially important in the *Commentaires*. It is not simply a question of speaking truthfully, but of appropriating the authority relinquished by the individual who has entirely committed himself to the king's service. Monluc writes of having been there because it is important to local history and because he thus retrieves for himself the authority, the prestige, that his years of unconditional service to the king have overshadowed. One can juxtapose two textual strategies in the *Commentaires*. The first one is self-denial: Monluc lived only for his king and the defense of the kingdom. The other is self-assertion: he was there all the time, by himself. That those strategies are not specifically Monluc's but also part of the project of developing a practical theory of *raison d'état* in the Renaissance is clear. Works like Hotman's *Francogallia* or Hurault's *Second discours sur l'estat de la France* indicate the writer's preoccupation with power and representation, and suggest that the political system has evolved from a concept of reliance on monarchy as the model of divine reason to another where monarchy is founded on the more rational motivation of preserving order and stability in a troubled world.[14]

Shall we decide that Monluc has lived entirely for the king, or for himself? What is at issue at the end of the Renaissance is not simply the question of how the writing self is derived from an accommodation of the political self, but something rather more personal and *tactical*. The question is now of the relevance of one's narrative, after all entirely personal, of pain and joy and suffering and, one would want to think, of private thoughts and fantasies as well, to a historical, public narrative with which everyone else is familiar; the question is also of the respective relevance of each to a writing enterprise that constitutes them both in the first place. Clearly Monluc wants to be identified in a familiar historical setting: he sees himself as sharing in the glory of the French kings. And yet he also wants attention for himself as better and more truly the soldier than anyone else—more truly himself: "One will still have to admit that I have found myself in as many combats, battles, skirmishes, undertakings, during the day and the night, assaults, captures, defenses of towns, as any man today in all of Europe."[15] The question is the extent to which authority from *above* can alone legitimize an experience that shows the subject continuously exercising delegated power from *below* at a time (the civil wars in France) when this authority is being contested. The narrative that tells of this laborious and underhanded practice suggests the opening of an internal distance in the text whereby the author calls attention to an intangible rule governing him and underlying all history, while it also suggests an internal resistance to the ideal of an overarching, de-individualizing authority. In the latter case, Monluc's repeated calls for attention and his admonitions to the reader represent an effort to protect attempts at self-definition and the delineation, however difficult (even dreams are for Monluc the occasion to wrestle with his worth), of a private daily space where he can say to himself that he has indeed been part of history: he has made his own.[16]

While it is true that the main object of the *Commentaires* is to garner honor, there is also a paradigm of knowledge in the book. To the extent that the art of war is practiced well and that the practitioners are doing what they are supposed to do, then the whole world is functioning well. This is not entirely new. Machiavelli in his *Arte della guerra* had already asserted that the full exercise of strategy with an army of citizens allowed one to protect one's state but also to better one's worldview. War becomes a procedure that regulates the world gone awry, as the way you comport yourself in war is also the way your opponents will treat you. Monluc's *Commentaires* are indicative of the writer's coup, which Monluc practices just as well as Machiavelli. The reader of the *Commentaires* well understands the object of war and of service of one's prince: to acquire a good reputation; but by reading, he also participates in the exchange. Granting Monluc his fame, he acquires indirectly, like the grandchildren and the commanders in the field by whom Monluc hopes to be read, the virtue, in its Machiavellian sense, and the knowledge that justify the reputation in the first place. Just as in war, where the face you present to the enemy is that by which the enemy interprets you, the text you offer readers in a book is the means by which they understand you and constitute you. In this sense the circulation of reputation, virtue, and knowledge in the *Commentaires* contributes to the world's equilibrium while serving individual needs. To write about one's own life in the military makes perfect sense: it is not only to write about your own exploits in order to acquire more honor and reputation but also to reflect other people looking at you throughout your life, since by being a good commander in the field, the military leader also arranges for people to see him to his best advantage. For Monluc, to write about war is, already before his death, to inscribe inside the book the process of other people looking at him and reflecting his image. To this extent the Siena episode is central to the book: the *Commentaires* are full of self-reflecting mirrors in which the writer/warrior looking at himself constitutes the world of his king, his battles, and, last but not least, his readers.

The City

At first glance, Pierre de l'Estoile's case is different from Monluc's, because de l'Estoile is a man of culture who can read and write Latin and quote the classics. Yet his diary, the *Journal-Registre,* could hardly be called learned. Most of the Latin in it is not de l'Estoile's own but comes from the pamphlets he has collected and which he has copied alongside his own entries. The real difference between Monluc's *Commentaires,* Gouberville's diary, and de l'Estoile's *Journal* is in the *escriture:* the *Journal's* writing process. While Gouberville and Monluc are interested in recording in their own words the happenings of their time, their deeds, and the state of the world, de l'Estoile's manuscript, by itself quite extensive, is supplemented, sometimes even supplanted, by an avalanche of extraneous materials. Entire parts of the diary are made up of collections of news items, newspapers annotated by de l'Estoile, which he calls *Ramas:* an odd assortment of written and pictorial material that he offers as context or illustration for his diary. It is not surprising, therefore, that up to now de l'Estoile has been known mostly to Renaissance historians who have found him a mine of information on late Renaissance Paris. De l'Estoile himself had no doubt about the value of his labors. Besides satisfying his yearning to express the day-to-day history of his time, he was also conscious of the immense service he was performing for future generations, and in this sense he too, like Monluc, can be said to have worked for posterity, except that de l'Estoile's preoccupation is not fame but historical truth. Intending to restore some balance to a perspective so heavily weighted against Henri III, he criticizes the ultraconservative *Ligue,*

> of which no other evidence is needed than the defaming writings and the libelings, professed and published in Paris, against the memory of this unfortunate prince. The following are taken from the quantity of these ... which I have extracted from my inventory, and which I have kept and am keeping as evidence of these tenets for posterity, a doctrine by which they sell their places in paradise to assassins, as naively as a merchant would sell the seats at a fair; nevertheless, such a sale is easier here below than up above.[17]

Beyond those similarities and dissimilarities, I will argue that de l'Estoile should be of interest to literary critics and historians of culture because, like the other two authors I am discussing here, he is obsessed with the recording process. All his life he narrates, he compiles and edits a collage of notices, papers, and pamphlets, which he continues to review and annotate, sometimes incorporating into the manuscript the suggestions of friends who have borrowed a portion of the *Journal.* Displaying the skills of the archivist, the bibliographer, and the commentator, he writes on current history and meticulously and sometimes humorously explains and comments on each of his entries. In the end the question about de l'Estoile is: What possessed a regular, upper-class bourgeois literally to live for his *Journal,* recording, with remarkable effectiveness, the state of the world he was living in? In real life a low-level administrator at the Paris parliament, de l'Estoile ranks among the most original *curieux* of the sixteenth century. Not interested in a quarrel with the

Sorbonne, the Church, or his king, and representative of the growing class of bourgeois concerned with stability and law and order but also desirous of civil and political liberties, he is also a chronicler of history in the making and the heir to a long line of chroniclers, of which the previous Bourgeois of Paris, living and writing in the fifteenth century, was an illustrious example.[18] Despite his culture, he really is the man on the street. One imagines him, as he describes himself, picking up pamphlets lying in the street or slipped under his door, going around Paris overhearing casual conversations, listening to rumors and jokes, and coming back to his study to write what he has learned. What he hears compounds what he sees and helps him reconstruct at home not only the event, but a whole culture of the street. Many pages thus read like small human-interest stories complete with moral tales and parables of folklore. Commenting on the shortsightedness of the Parisian mob, he states that it acts like those stupid creatures one can read about in the *History of the Druids,* which used to complain that they had been beaten senseless, and when asked who had abused them so, could only answer that they had done it to themselves.[19] There is much talk of domestic quarrels, forbidden erotics ("paillardise"), crimes of passion, and petty thefts, reminiscent of Boccaccio, except that what the narrator reports is true: the tales are events. De l'Estoile's peripatetic reportage and home editing provide a microscopic view of the world where history is daily, trivial, and proximate: things happen close by.

However secure his place in history as one of the premier historians of sixteenth-century Paris, de l'Estoile's meticulous, if not obsessive, brand of archival preservation is also extraordinary to us because it reminds us of a modern collector's behavior. The collector gears part of his professional life and generally all of his libidinal life to the acquisition of complete series of objects. Because the series are rarely complete and objects are missing, the incentive, or rather the drive, to complete the series is always present. Although de l'Estoile does not systematically enter thoughts or materials every day, the finished *Journal* is only the last part of an awesome editorial process (the *Recueils* representing the raw notes and documents that, much like an anthropologist in the field, he collects routinely) that sifts the daily. The process is twofold. On the one hand, de l'Estoile is always outside hunting information, observing, gathering evidence, making mental notes, and, like Borges's famous Funes, always filing away for reference, living his life in the historical mode. On the other hand, he also lives inside, a man of the *cabinet,* reading, arranging, very literally cutting and pasting, and, last but not least, writing in his study. This suits him fine, since he has no lost love for the mob, and his bourgeois instincts keep him out of mischief and on the defensive. Obviously, he can't have it all. There are things he misses, events he has not witnessed, explanations he is not privy to, and in this sense, perhaps, he is not as obsessive as our modern collector. But he is fully committed to his task. There is not a piece of news he can't improve in the privacy of his home—not that he embellishes or distorts, but he is intent on noting, commenting, and explaining. And since his field is the daily, the trivial, the historical undigested, he makes it complete by incorporating it, giving it body and texture, in his testimonial. The collector's series has become the narrator's story and all entries are part of the story. It is not enough to have the event, the scoop. It must be arranged, put in context. This obsession with writing extends to all aspects of the work's production.

Why does one write, if not because things appear more clearly in ink than in spoken words, or even than in pictures? Having collected a series of satirical portraits on the main characters in the civil war, de l'Estoile goes so far as to provide the reader with references, comments, or explanatory notices under each figure. His description of "a drawing made with a crayon" exemplifies his commitment to articulated representation.[20] The writer can make the world memorable and understandable. He is the one who knows the difference between what can and what should be observed. Precisely because de l'Estoile is not a simple *flâneur* he is able to make the distinction between life as survival and response (to nature and authority) and culture as the symbolic context that regulates daily existence. This is mostly where de l'Estoile is different from his medieval predecessor. Perfectly capable of editing and condensing, he also knows when to give ample latitude to the different *voices* in his narrative, allowing the most diverse opinions to be heard. Precisely because the *Journal* testifies to moderation and good sense, the reader is allowed to form his own opinion from the most extreme views. Thus, while abhorring the excesses of the ultraconservative *Ligue,* de l'Estoile doesn't mind, and one suspects he rather enjoys, reproducing their wildest speeches and sermons. While using the fragmentary format of the chronicle, he is fully the narrator, arranging scenes, dispensing judgments, extracting the symbolism, and evaluating the consequences of an event, a fact, and, more often than not, a rumor. When it rains, he lets us know the damage to the harvest. When the king and his *mignons* (his male favorites) roam through Paris, de l'Estoile notes the damage to persons and private property. When France is at war with itself and Paris is besieged, he notes both the high cost of feeding him and the human misery visited on his fellow citizens. Although the story is proximate, the plot and its consequences are global and systemic. Hence also the extraordinary importance given the written and pictorial material he collects for his *Recueil* and his *Ramas*. An event is only as important as what people make of it, and a rumor, while extravagant, says more about the state of things than an official decree. By composing a dialogue where he shows Catherine de Medici wrongly firing one of her field marshals on the strength of mere gossip, he can show that politics is indeed the art of juggling fame and managing reputations.[21] He also demonstrates vividly the extent to which the historian now functions at the intersection of chronicling and full-fledged narrative practices. De l'Estoile is neither completely outside nor completely inside the story he narrates. He is present and, as Monluc wanted it, always as close as possible to the event. But how can one be *there,* be present and understand this present? Chroniclers deal with the present, but piecemeal, precisely because they do not have enough distance from it. Historians understand only the past. By reconstructing the *raw* happenings in the privacy of his cabinet the next day, or even, à la Montaigne, years later, de l'Estoile establishes in writing, through the process of his *escriture,* the mediations by which we become aware of the historical process: from the routine and variances of our days to the long view that constitutes our horizon and enables us to situate ourselves in the times in which we live.

On this, the chronicler turned historian is exceedingly clear. The times are confusing, the passions run high, and there are few people with enough sense to act and think in a way beneficial to the commonwealth. How does one, how *can* one, communicate what constitutes a life? Monluc, speaking for himself, and anxious to speak for himself under a monarchy that he still sees in a feudal context, claims with a rigid Realist argument that to prove that one had been *there* is the memorialist's ultimate duty in what remains largely a one-way communication. For de l'Estoile, things are more complex, and the dailiness of life experience is conveyed in another mode. It is not to have been *there* that counts, since the reader will himself never be able to experience the personal, the emotional, richness of this locale. What the journalist wishes is to place the event in context; and in order to do that, he must reconcile two values, especially to the middle class, which he represents: first, a political value, that peace can only be attained within the framework provided by stable institutions; and, related to the former, a cultural value, that history is too complex to be simply the making of one group, one person, one ideology. To be sure, there is no discussion in the *Journal* of the theoretical issues raised by its editing and formatting, but the ongoing care and detachment with which documents are inserted and stories entered testifies to de l'Estoile's understanding of the need to *read* the daily, however incongruous or nonsequential its representation may prove. This de l'Estoile achieves twice: by managing to remain detached from the events that he so meticulously records and by seeking in a universal humanistic perspective the transhistorical, moral, or psychological law regulating specific daily practices.

If, as has been argued, the *Journal* so distinctively casts its author as representative of the parliamentarian bourgeoisie, the preoccupation with economics and things concrete has replaced the intensity of religious feelings prevalent in a broad section of the urban upper-middle class. The emerging bourgeoisie plays a leading role in this new development; it mistrusts all manners of intolerance and extremism. While a good Catholic, de l'Estoile doesn't conceal his hatred of religious zealotry and his skepticism about religious rituals. Reporting a ritual in which the populace has been called to pray for rain, he comments acidly that the prayer seems to have alleviated the present drought.[22] In his distaste for religious and political extremism de l'Estoile is akin to Montaigne, who in the *Essais* states the need for conservatism. However, whereas Montaigne's conservatism is the guarantee of his personal independence as a writer free to investigate at a remove his own place in the history and culture of his time, de l'Estoile's own brand of political conservatism functions much closer to day-to-day affairs. It is often argued that Montaigne's work at the end of the French Renaissance is essential to the constitution of a moral discourse that runs the course of French literature to Proust and beyond, on the margins of the major established genres (epic, drama, poetry, novel), but de l'Estoile's *Journal* may prove more relevant to the growing theoretical shift of which the specific genre of the Moralist discourse is a part. While Montaigne's discourse harks back to the discussion of *otium* at the very beginning of the Italian Renaissance and proudly proposes a reasoned exemplum of cultured withdrawal, de l'Estoile's proximate, albeit ironic, position on the threshold of the political daily is important for the evolution of the relations of

Fin de Siècle Living   237

private and public discourse, as the monarchy establishes its absolute hegemony with Henri IV and the Bourbon dynasty. To be sure, with its combination of diligent reporting and careful editing, the *Journal* makes short shrift of the writer's self and cannot begin to compare with Montaigne's enterprise of self-portraiture—although it could be shown that the ongoing rereading and editing process, which goes on through the length of de l'Estoile's life, in fact colors the material that the author affects to present to us in a neutral way, and constitutes, more liberally as it were, the lineaments of the cultural order to which Montaigne always seeks to give his own private stamp. Nor does it treat the culture of its time in the fictional mode, which, for other writers, like du Fail, allows the production of stereotypes essential to the circulation of symbols and the constitution of specific styles, although it could be shown that de l'Estoile's decision to stick to facts and documents effectively communicates, still unprocessed, the complex relations between power and representation that a specific fiction, say Noël du Fail's *Balivernes,* chooses to articulate only in a very limited context. Precisely because it chooses to deal exclusively with the daily in a time when the processes of power and cultural strategies have not yet been clearly established (civil wars, problems of succession, geopolitical instability, cultural hegemony of Italy and Spain), de l'Estoile offers to the postmodern reader an archaeological insight into the problematic of the literary versus the historical and political, and a *terminus ab quo* in the ongoing debate about the writer's place in the society he remains intent on describing. After the *Journal,* two paths remain open to the writer desirous of giving meaning to the culture in which he lives: either he addresses the problems confronting the individual from the perspective that this individual is only modeled after the exemplum, the persona that the regime needs to sustain itself (this is what is accomplished by the playwrights of the *School of 1660,* the historiographers and the novelists who strive to render, in a discourse emanating from a portrait of the monarch, the political unity of all cultural processes), or, either unable or unwilling to compete for attention and more interested in examining the consequences of such a homogenization for everyday relationships, the writer withdraws to observe the scene the better to fashion stereotypes, what we still consider today as eternal *characters*. In both cases, the perspective on the daily has jelled into literary topics. On the one hand, by engineering historical representation as a spectacle in which characters are but the marks and the signs of representation, the playwright seeks to give full weight to the power principle underlying his system (*Le Cid*);[23] on the other, by taking into account the effects of a politics of representation on a society at large where the individual has become but the sum of his social practices, the portraitist and Moralist evidences the rules by which individuals seek to avail themselves of the system (*Les Caractères*). Written in a period that, for about a half-century (roughly from Henri III to the end of the Fronde), constitutes the historical prelude to such cultural productions, the *Journal* suggests a possible third or middle way. Writing as a member of a defined class, choosing openly and factually to articulate his own presence vis-à-vis the events he selects for inclusion in the *Journal,* the journalist, seeking to combine involvement with critical detachment, refuses the privileges of fiction or the solace of rhetoric and insists on making do with every day that becomes part of his memoirs. As a politician, a legislator, and a recorder of the trivia that add up to a human existence, de l'Estoile is not a poor brother to Montaigne or a weak predecessor of Pascal or La Bruyère. He is, as it happens, by the privileges and, more important, the tastes of the class he serves, a true parent to Saint Simon and Retz.

Writing from the perspective of someone living in the city and walking its streets as others write about the salons they frequent, he has a peripatetic view, adjusted to the changing landscape he observes or reconstructs for us. His elaborate description, actually a dramatic reconstruction, of the separate murders of the de Guise brothers in public and of Henri III in private is an excellent instance of the way in which de l'Estoile, combining historical information with psychological insight, can position himself close to an event so sudden and so awesome as to make it appear inexplicable, fated, while at the same time recasting it in the ordinary context of a daily routine that it has interrupted, and thus show it to be but the last development in a long series of causes and effects.[24] People do things, e.g., organize the Saint Bartholomew's Day massacre, appropriate royal authority, and they end up murdered in the course of the life they thought they could live. What changes is what one notices, and if one notices enough, one will see that things do change every day. It is to this connection of routine and change that de l'Estoile's consciousness testifies: the extent to which historical events are not simply social phenomena but are the subtle way in which the arrangement of people and things, the semiotics of daily life, can be altered in the course of one single day or hour, and a mere existence, or the lack of it, enter the realm of the symbolic. Barthes' *notable* is apprehended everyday. Like Montaigne who cumulates exempla under the influence of the medieval topic, de l'Estoile is not averse to the *monstrum,* that which must be displayed because it is not in order and contradicts custom: the boy arrested and tortured for having fornicated with a cow, the alleged result being a monster half beast, half man;[25] a baby born with a gigantic penis in the middle of the stomach;[26] a priest suddenly become mad while preaching and having to be forcibly removed from the pulpit and tied.[27] Yet the bizarre is not bookish, nor does de l'Estoile have any use, as does the early Montaigne, for extensive compilations running the gamut from the pseudo-Aristotle to the cosmographers of his time. His bizarreries he can live with—he lives close to them, a block, a conversation, a rumor away. He too, like Monluc, has been there. He mentions himself in relation to his family, his connections, his sources of information: "a lady I know" ("une dame que je connais"); his son, gone to war (in these bad times the only thing people can think of to better their lot is to go and fight in some religious dispute); his mother, who happens to live next door to one of his informants; his friends, who have died during the siege of Paris because of their religious convictions and whose life had been morally outstanding in these times of turpitude.

Situating himself in the context of his family and social practices (including his dreams of how others view him) allows him to delineate, almost naturally *de soi,* the moral field of historical experience. In one instance, he mentions a freak accident: a piece of marble fell on him while he was working at renovating his study, and he says it almost killed him.[28] Although de l'Estoile is not, as Pepys will be, obsessed with egocentric surroundings, the private always ends up creeping into the public domain, inexplicably: in the same passage we read of other incidents (a young man died of "hot" fever; there was a terrible frost). We are at the point where the observer begins to look at himself. But the pull of the outside world and, as in Monluc and Gouberville, a commitment to the task, what Montaigne calls his "registering and counter-registering" ("role and contrerolle"), keep the subject from internalizing reality.[29] Surprised by death, the weather, or hunger in besieged Paris, de l'Estoile the passerby is brought to confront his past, his tradition, his culture. To understand oneself is to understand the way history is being made: not simply by recounting what happened, but by being able to find the *punctum,* the relevance of life, as in the case of the young "picklock" (*crocheteur*) who knew his trade so well that he managed to make a lot of money.[30] With de l'Estoile we come to understand that daily occurrences are not singular, heroic events but parts of historical movements to be retraced in the long haul and whose reception must be interpreted. Narrating the daily excesses of Henri III and Monsieur's *mignons,* he follows their history and their quarrels, and to make us understand how they were received, he reproduces the tracts denouncing them all over Paris.[31] Finally, if there is room for personal experience in all this, it is indeed to the extent that the *Journal* helps clarify the connection between recording and living the experience, between theory and practice. If for the *journaliste* writing is of the essence, there comes a point where he must appreciate the difference between books about life and life itself. De l'Estoile lives his times intensely. He feeds the hungry during the siege of Paris;[32] he can't always eat ("my governess bought me four eggs for one crown");[33] like everyone else he buys because of a panic—only to comment, when the panic is soon over, that one never learns one's lesson.[34] Or does one?

The Country

The case of Gilles de Gouberville offers us a third, very different model of daily life. Gouberville was a gentleman farmer in the uppermost northwestern part of Normandy who wrote his diary probably for longer than fifteen years, entering into it his activities, his expenses, and, to a very limited degree, an account of the world around him.[35] On the face of it, his *Journal* is not very different from the famous *Livres de Raison,* whose popularity is established during the period.[36] Yet the size of the work, its scope, and the dogged perseverance with which the author continues to record the most trivial of occurrences suggests that the *Journal* is also something else. What compelled a man like Gouberville to keep a diary of his everyday actions? Perhaps nothing else than what compels Monluc and de l'Estoile—except that the gentleman farmer is neither a soldier nor a parliamentarian. He doesn't build trenches or collect pamphlets. His interest in the outside world is limited. When compared to the siege of Siena by Gianjacomo de Medici or the siege of Paris by Henri of Navarre, the future Henri IV—both described from the perspective of the besieged, the former by Monluc, the latter by de l'Estoile—the routine of keeping the manor of Gouberville going appears trivial and boring. But it is precisely the limited scope of the account and the gesture of the chronicler entering his record into the book day after day that catch our interest. Instead of an attack on a citadel, or a riot in the street, we read about a servant injured in the performance of a task ("Maillard ripped his arm on his fork"),[37] a woman giving birth, the weather turning nasty, a deal being struck at the market, or day workers being paid. The master is always there, not, like de l'Estoile or Monluc, to bear witness to and be part of a glorious history in the making, but to take care of urgent business, to supervise and to assist. The point is, a farmer's work is never done and something always happens.

Besides taking care of the land (planting, cutting, harvesting), the park (pruning, raking), and the house (fixing walls, furniture), there is the accounting. Every day in the diary the sales, purchases, and trades are recorded, and it is clear that money and currency are scarce even as the silver from America reaches Europe. There is no silverware in the manor and part of the tin has already been traded. But Gilles de Gouberville is also a civil servant. His charge as *Lieutenant des Eaux et Forêts*, cumulating administrative and judicial responsibilities for an area roughly the size of a county, has him criss-cross the neighborhood, hearing complaints, seeing to it that judgments are served and regulations respected, tracking poachers, and keeping the peace. In an area that is both private and public, he makes a point of attending the rituals of the live and the dead: celebrating births, going to weddings and funerals, being present when wills, especially those of his relatives, are read and safes opened. In general, the diary records that the squire is available and busy, and sometimes the chronicler is meticulous enough to note that when there is nothing to do, that too is worth remembering: taking a walk, sleeping, eating. He leads a full life, then, with servants galore, relatives (many illegitimate half-brothers and -sisters among them) and friends, visitors, both known and unknown, that one lodges for one night or longer, clerics, merchants and doctors, as well as the tailor-shoemakers who cut and fit garments and shoes for the whole household in a day or two. Finally, albeit outside all those concentric circles, there is the history we know and are familiar with: Henri II and Catherine de Medici, the sumptuous travels of the court from Paris to Blois and other places, and, last but not least, the religious wars. Of all that, Gouberville seems to have tasted little. He travels throughout his province of Cotentin on business, even when this business is less than legitimate, as when he takes his party cattle rustling on one of the islands off the Normandy coast.[38] He went to Blois once to solicit from the king a promotion to *Maître des Eaux et Forêts*. After several days of living on the cheap and eating in the king's kitchens to save money, he returned to Gouberville empty-handed. We can infer from the *Journal* that he quickly became interested in the Calvinist doctrine newly propagated in Normandy; but, cautious and fearful of retribution, much like Montaigne insistent on watching the years of trouble from a distance, he keeps his faith to himself, remaining outwardly a Catholic and a devotee of the king and making sure he is not implicated in anything. Minding his own business and that of his household, being involved in the business of others only to the extent he has to, the author of the *Journal* tells us only about his world.

What does this add up to? The *Journal* is a private document, so private that it was never published and would never have been found, had its first editor, the abbot Tollemer, not discovered it in an attic about a century ago. This is not to say that the *Journal* is introspective. There is no mention of moods, of a love life, of the hopes and fears that fill a daily existence. And yet to say this is to say too little too fast. To read the diary from beginning to end, one needs patience and one must be alert. Events are noted in passing, and what would under another writer's pen be a meditation or a dissertation, even a fantasy, is here only a quick sentence, a few words, often concealed by the innocuous "I did not move from here" ("Je ne bougé pas de céans"). Here and there, Gouberville uses the Greek alphabet to transliterate what he likely wants to keep to himself, some of it so trivial that the practice appears to be for pleasure only. At other times, the matter is more serious, but the Greek, quickly written over in a lapidary French, remains tucked away under the rest of the trivia. One thus learns, *en passant*, from the exact accounting of money and requests for money, that the uncle turned him down on a loan, so that he "could get married."[39] Gouberville never did get married, but continued to live a bachelor on his country estate, with only an occasional tryst here and there—as we can infer from another notation: Hélène, a woman (his servant? his mistress?), "was now pregnant."[40] One reason the squire is so cagey about himself is that living at the manor means being around other people continuously; what little private life he should have is in fact restricted by the space and the time he shares with others. Gouberville's illegitimate siblings live with him, and every day sees him directing work on his property: tending his apple trees that will produce cider, or feeding the few cattle he will sell at the market, or dealing with the peasants, adjudicating, collecting, and imposing retribution.

Obviously, the *Journal* is a mine of information. Of all the Renaissance texts, it is perhaps the one that has, since its recent discovery, most fascinated historians, precisely because very little happens in it: from the mass of data strung along its fragmented, albeit repetitious, narrative line, the reader can reconstruct areas of daily life, thematically organized. Cumulating and arranging data into preordered categories, he can derive a fragmentary vision of what it must have been like *to be there*. Reviewing Gouberville's meticulous account of everything he earns and, mostly, spends, it is not difficult for us to understand, by inference, what the life of a cash-poor country gentleman must have been. The interest of the *Journal* lies in the extent to which the self is involved with others: Gouberville being rarely alone, the text is not very introspective. Much has been made of the fact that he seemed to have remained single, but the *Journal* makes clear that in the manor there is always something for the squire himself to do or to manage. This is the main difference between de l'Estoile and Monluc. Because Gouberville is involved with the stuff of daily life, his writing is not, like Monluc's, predicated on making his prowess known and teaching others. No thought is given to posterity.[41] Instead, the author derives pride from recalling his activities of the day and listing the names of the people he has met or worked with. Accompanied by his *factotum*, the indefatigable Chantepye, his illegitimate brother, and a few close servants, the squire attends to his tasks and to his guests not in the grand manner, but in the simple medieval tradition of the lord giving food and shelter without expecting anything in return. Things are always done together with other people, because one needs their help, their knowledge, and their presence, and because one has camaraderie with them.

From Tollemer to Le Roy Ladurie to Foisil, the *Journal* has been the object of two kinds of study, both exclusively historical: one in the diachronic mode, the other in the synchronic mode. On the one hand, by tabulating all data extracted from the *Journal*, one can always delineate the various practices of Gouberville, and, by comparison, one can safely arrive at an estimate of the ways of doing things; one can determine the value of things and derive a fairly accurate idea of the social hierarchies in place. On the other hand, the new historian, seeing the limitations of this approach, is also interested in deriving from all those data an idea of the *rhythm* of life, of its flow.[42] One of the more attractive aspects of this kind of study is that it derives its synchronic data from a literary approach to texts, where the choice of vocabulary, of phrases, of words, and even of adjectives becomes significant. For instance, Foisil tabulates the moments of the day, and this allows her to delineate the *Journal*'s *natural* time between functions: sunup and arising, *disner* and the midday, *soupper* and sundown. In other words, the text, in its coding, holds the key to a simple, transparent relation between words and things. A study of this type (Le Roy Ladurie's, Chaunu's, Foisil's), aims at retrieving, beyond themes and categories (food, clothing, expenses, agricultural economics) the *rhythm* of the days of the *chatelain* and the rural community he leads. Yet, in applying literary criteria to this reconstruction of the *mentalité*, the historian fails to ask the *writerly* questions on which his or her reconstruction is based. What kind of reality (its level of narrative and character involvement) does the text produce? What kind of writer would be interested in the *rhythm* of things, instead of pursuing the heroic or the picaresque?[43] And what kind of historical consciousness is the writer's, given his extremely narrow and limited view of the world? Following Tollemer, we will easily be convinced by Le Roy Ladurie that the work is important, albeit unreadable.[44] Yet the *Journal* says something about the writing practices and the operation of the writing subject within a field already loosely defined by the *Livre de Raison*.

Roland Barthes reflected in various ways and at different times in his work on the question of the relevance of writing to the writer's self. He confessed, quite late in life, that he had thought of writing a diary but had never executed the thought, probably because he considered a diary essentially unprocessed; he also argued that the routine of daily recording inhibits what Jakobson used to call language's poetic function, the interplay of code and message in the text.[45] However, it is likely that when Barthes speaks of writing a diary, he has in mind the *intimiste* tradition of autobiography that Stendhal and the Romantics made famous: to think of a diary that would not be reflective is unthinkable today. In a tradition that extends from Descartes's *Discours* to Camus's *L'Etranger*, the writer defines himself outside of the world where he lives, whether he seeks to interpret this world or has given up understanding it. In Descartes and Camus, the discourse or confession addressed to the reader is based on the writer's security about his own critical position. However, things are different in the Renaissance, and especially the late Renaissance, when the writer still sees himself in a monist relation to the world, to the culture in which he or she lives. And when the Reformation strikes, the significance of this change is as much political as it is religious: Protestants question the authority of the king and the pope, but they continue to want to live alongside their Catholic brethren. Individuation through religion is not the norm. For the Catholic Ronsard of the *Discours* and the Protestant d'Aubigné of the *Tragiques,* the religious question is a question of the relation to nature, because it is still in the context of something larger than the individual that the individual defines himself.[46] This helps understand the peculiar writing operation at work in the *Journal.* Gouberville never talks about himself, as has been pointed out by all, and leaves to others, the historians, the task of reconstituting his fields of activity. However, what distinguishes the *Journal* is less the absence of self and the lack of private data, of erotic fantasies and secret revelations, than the peculiar effects produced by the definition of a public or a semiprivate world, in which the writer is the accountant, the controller of acts and exchanges. Instead of lamenting the extent to which Gouberville's reflexive self is missing, it might be worthwhile to consider the extent to which his individual persona is defined within the circle of his acquaintances, in the context of his everyday work, as a *figura*, albeit not in the sense given this word by Auerbach.[47] For Auerbach, the *figura* is an individual representation that illuminates the individual on the scene of world history. The Goubervillian subject emerges in a patch of daily notations from an ongoing self-interpretation of his own history, his own surroundings.

The effects of such a hermeneutic process are several. First, and as in Monluc, the writer of the memoir asserts his presence in a particular place at a particular time and in a particular type of weather. As I have said, time follows daylight; but in fact, it is not as important as the practices *(disner, soupper)* that *take* time; the place is essentially defined as *here (ceans),* in contradistinction to *there,* and this other place is in relation to a specific practice as well, usually a trip: an opportunity for trade or for administrative duties. The subject's actions, his comportment, are entirely determined by the environment that the *Journal* takes great pains to record: they are functional. The famous and ritual "je ne bougé de ceans," which might be interpreted precisely as recording no activity, is rather the occasion for recording activities that could not be performed if the squire had taken a trip. When Gouberville goes on a trip, he can't attend to his manor. When he is at home, he entertains the people who otherwise wouldn't have found him. What gives the *Journal* its specificity is precisely Gouberville's delineation of an existence in which the subject sees himself at the nexus of functional relations. The *Journal* records that every action is in response to a certain necessity—

mostly that one needs to work and sell the product of one's work in order to eat. But there are also other things one needs to do in order to escape death or injury, simply to survive. In few texts is the writing activity so intent on recording this implicit, sometimes tacit, necessity to which one must respond, with which one can perhaps negotiate. The squire works with the elements: when the weather is good, for instance, it is time to separate the wheat from the chaff and to prepare it for grinding; when the weather is not good enough to plow, one can at least gather wood. And he works with people: he must always supervise his servants and attend to his guests. In the end, however, this necessity also becomes the writer's own. There is hardly a moment when the thought of coping, of making do, of working, and of finishing what has to be done does not intrude on the writer's reflective space. Gouberville cannot live without his *Journal*. It becomes his companion, his *alter ego*, perhaps. Once on a trip, he notes once that he has forgotten his *escriptoire:* and he sends for his writing materials, his quill and paper, from wherever he is.[48] If he has to live, he has to write as well. While other sixteenth-century texts may be more synthetic and therefore more useful to the historian—I am thinking in particular of parish priest Haton's Troyes diary[49]—the *Journal* is more interesting precisely because the narrative includes all the functions through which the writer continuously justifies his text. Each recording instance becomes the opportunity to recapitulate the history of which this instance is the product in the first place. In an archival or foundational sense, this recapitulation defines the diarist: with each new instance certifying the subject's place and role in his world, the *Journal* reasserts a tradition.

The second Goubervillian effect is related to the comptrolling and the mercantilization of day-to-day existence. To the extent that the *Journal* is essentially a *Livre de Raison*, to the reader who reads it cursorily it can only appear as the recording of trades, of exchanges. The self, however anachronistic this notion might be in the Renaissance, is the result of putting a value on actions and responses and articulating this value in the context of a narrative that records the sale or the purchase, justifies it, and thus makes the particular act subject to review. In that sense, the recording function is directly linked to the economic activity, or, Montaigne would say, to the essaying activity, to the extent that individual life results not only from trades and interpersonal exchanges, but also from the ability to evaluate, to review, and to memorize. Memory plays here its economic, social, and interpersonal role in constituting the writing subject.[50] The difference between Montaigne's *Essais* and Gouberville's *Journal* is that the latter was written on the *Ephemerides* model, and devoid of the culture with which the author of the *Essais* interrogates the life of people he reads about. And yet, to a chatty, expansive Montaigne and a reserved, tight-lipped Gouberville, *comptrolling*, keeping track of one's acts as one would of one's expenses, remains equally important, as both call their culture and agriculture to account, *essaying* them (etymologically, "weighing" them) in order to know how much they own and who they are. Montaigne's "je me contrerolle" is echoed by the title of the first of Gouberville's original *cahiers:* "Order and receipts made myself, Gilles de Gouberville, since Saturday (this day included), March 25, 1553, with no record of any of the following days since said day, this being the case for my affairs as for those of others, which, if there had been any, would have been found with mine, one for each day, month and year, as they will hereafter."[51]

The third effect produced by the *Journal* on its readers is the illusion of its author's complete availability. If Gouberville records all entries into his log book with great care, it is mostly because approximating one's expenses to the nearest penny is a necessity at a time when the monetary order is in chaos (many different currencies are recorded); currency is scarce ("I did not pay Landès or Bérot because I had not the money, as it was three days late in coming"),[52] and a man must watch what he does with it, the reflex of the merchant counting one's expenses only shadowing the gesture of the chronicler quoting the most important events of the day, the month, or the year. The *Journal* presents an interesting combination of the accounting mode and something else that I propose to call the *twaddling* mode (*radotage*), where the author's discourse, in addition to itemizing the sum of what has been accomplished in a day of his life, sketches for each of the items the choices implied, the routes traveled, and the strategies employed, as well as the inconsequential, the funny, the rare, and the comic.[53] Unlike a Montaigne or a Haton, Gouberville is able to notice the weather, the moon in the sky, or, on the occasion of a hike, flowers, trees, and even the strangest of objects, such as "elephant's teeth" brought back from Africa and left on the beach by mariners.[54] He can also catch himself gossiping at church, discussing the civil wars, or listening, as he must often do ex officio, to quarrels and litigations between peasants. All this doesn't make up a narrative. It suggests an incomplete one, made up of false starts, incidents, vignettes that are, however, complete in themselves and that illustrate the perspective of someone uninterested in the grand narrative but careful to articulate his thoughts about the events and the characters of the moment. Gouberville and the people surrounding him are profoundly historical, not because they are representative of a particular class or culture, but rather because they offer an image of what it means (and must have meant) for subjects to interpret history on a day-to-day basis. Because the *Journal* is the great recorder, it forces its author to use the established terms to make his entries. Yet the *Journal* is more than simply a book of accounts. It not only speaks of private and public practices, but, sometimes blurring the line between fact and interpretation, it also sketches the human contours of a social world. It suggests an array and an intensity of emotions that the accountant can barely keep to himself. In one particularly moving passage, Gouberville recalls how on a particular outing he frightened the parish priest riding ahead of him, who believed that the squire and his party were Protestant rebels ready to kill him. This little vignette of the country priest, frightened out of his wits and whipping his horse to flee those he feared were about to murder him, remains one of the most moving testimonies to the *petite histoire* of the Wars of Religion.[55] How did people whose business it was simply to survive, and who had no connection to the grand designs now laid out for us in history books, interpret the events that we think we know so well today? The *Journal* opens the door on this world.

These three effects define Gouberville's *Journal* as a book of necessities and strategies, of memory and observation, and as a testimony to the writer. The accountant is also the historical subject, the participant, the agent, who has not yet, like his Romantic successors, caught his own reflection in the web of his own daily life, who does not feel he must disentangle it from his own text, and who can thus derive the most satisfaction from delineating the limits of his world. But he treats himself as he does others. His own game is simply that in writing, he is simply showing why he must write. The first *écrivant* is also the first *écrivain*.

In conclusion, I would like to make three very brief points. First, while a certain literature of the end of the Renaissance cannot be understood without reference to the end of humanism and the erosion of literary and linguistic canons, it is likely that this erosion is, to a great degree, compensated for by the development of a style unhampered by classical references. What is striking in this development is the authorial shift that accompanies the leveling, or what I would call the *routinization,* of texts which now make it possible to access a lived, practical experience for which the narratives of the past are no longer so useful. Where in the past an epic structure would have been necessary to configure *and teach,* here a new form of writing, the memoir, makes possible a relationship with a life history in which the memory of things past is mediated by a progressively more intense present. The literary experience, in other words, is more immediate. And as one moves from Monluc to de l'Estoile to Gouberville, one notices that the overall narrative perspective, to which a humanist subject would have been used, shrinks more and more to the dimensions of a descriptive discourse whose references are more and more proximate to the writer.

Second, as the subject becomes more and more fascinated by his immediate past, the magnum opus becomes a text in which the narrator ceases to plot his sequences to please an imaginary reader, and instead doubts (like Monluc or Gouberville) that he will ever be read and accordingly despairs of ever being published. This new writer, however, is learning progressively, albeit awkwardly, as can be seen from Monluc's somewhat pathetic summons to his unattentive readership, to respond to his own needs: to establish for himself, *proprio sensu,* that he has been part of a tradition.

Third, in this turn from a grand narrative to a descriptive discourse where facts and events are progressively replaced by practices, and where the articulation of choices (what to do and how to do it?) is as important as the succession of sequences (when to do it?), the communicative format also undergoes change. Occurrences, while continuing to be listed on the sequential model—which is why Le Roy Ladurie thought the cursory reading of Gouberville utterly boring—are now considered a matter for discussion and appreciation. It is no longer a matter of finding, and much less of holding, the truth. It is one of stating what is true for oneself. The format of enunciation is no longer that of an anonymous, unlocatable *topic* conferring authority on the narrator as soon as he begins writing. It is, rather, that of a *locutor* of a new *sermo,* a conversation in the original sense of the term, who knows, and sometimes doesn't, that his views are merely opinions about himself and the world. It is, ultimately in this fragile context, and perhaps only in this context, that a life is worth being written about.

NOTES

1. Actually, Monluc's memoirs are his *Commentaires*. The difference between *memoir* and *diary* is minor to the extent that both are records of personal experience. But the difference is in the perspective: a diary's prospect is successive and fitted to the calendar. A memoir, while often made up of the recording of individual events, is geared to the long haul. The diary encompasses days in the life; a memoir, a whole life or a slice of life.

2. The dates set us firmly in the latter part of the sixteenth century. Monluc dictated his *Commentaires* after 1577; Gouberville must have been writing between 1554 and 1570; de L'Estoile, between 1574 and 1600. Because *daily life* is my theme and because Gouberville is, perhaps, the most striking instance not of a historical life but of a life in history, not of a *res gesta* but rather of a life gestuary, I will end this study with him and use a chronological order for the other two authors.

3. The standard book on the genre of self-portrait is Michel Beaujour, *Miroirs d'encre* (Paris: Seuil, 1979). The best book on the *Livres de Raison* is by Elisabeth Bourcier, *Les Journaux privés en Angleterre de 1600 à 1660* (Paris: Imprimerie Nationale, 1976). See the introduction, "Les journaux et leurs auteurs."

4. Blaise de Monluc, *Commentaires*, ed. Paul Courteault (Paris: Gallimard, Bibliothèque de la Pléiade, 1964), 395: "Je vous jure que je ne me cognossois pas moy-mesmes, et me sembloit que j'estois encore en Piemont, amoureux comme j'avois esté. Je ne me peus contenir de rire, me semblant que tout à coup Dieu m'avoit donné tout un autre visage."

5. Monluc, 294: "Nous estions lors de loisir en nostre garnison, et n'ayant rien à faire il le faut donner aux dames.... En ce temps là je portois gris et blanc, pour l'amour d'une dame de qui j'estois serviteur, lorsque j'avois le loisir."

6. Never does Monluc show more than occasional chagrin that he has lost all his sons and that only grandsons remain, about whom he can only say that he fervently hopes that they will grow to be soldiers of distinction like their grandfather. There is in Montaigne a mention of "Monsieur de Monluc" in the chapter "Of the Affection of Fathers for Their Children" (II, 8). Montaigne recalls having met Monluc, who told him how saddened he was by the fact that he had just lost a son and that he felt he had never shown him the love and affection he should have. Montaigne comments that the best thing that can happen to us when our friends or relatives die is to know that we haven't forgotten to show them our love.

7. Curiously, he has learned a smattering of foreign languages: some German, English, and mostly Italian that, characteristically, he has pickpocketed on the run and in one-to-one combat.

8. Monluc, 23: "Ce n'est pas un livre pour les gens de sáavoir, ils ont assez

d'hystorien, mais bien pour un soldat, capitaine, et peut estre qu'un lieutenant de roy y pourra trouver de quoy apprandre." Paul Courteault, the editor of the *Commentaires,* distinguishes between an original, which was a copy of the first version, and the published 1592 text of the "final" version by Florimond de Raemond. It is likely that both versions, as we have them today, postdate Monluc's dismissal from the stewardship of Guienne. (He resigned because of his harquebus injury, only to find out that he had been cashiered by Charles IX two months before. "Remontrance au Roy," now a part of the final version, was actually sent to Charles IX in 1571. The king published a reply in which he defended his dismissal of Monluc. Monluc was later made marshal of France.) While it can be argued that the two-step process of publication of the *Commentaires* is reminiscent of that of the *Essais,* the modifications are only interesting to the extent that they testify to Monluc's desire to appear more learned and to reach a wider audience with a more readable text. Moreover, even if de Raemond is to Monluc what Mademoiselle de Gournay is to Montaigne (the posthumous publication of Monluc's *Commentaires* is almost contemporary with that of Montaigne's *Essais* in the Gournay edition) and, accordingly, if Monluc is only partially the author of his *Commentaires,* the issue of authorship is not my business here. Whether Monluc is entirely or partially responsible for his text, it remains a testimony to the relation between a collective and individual imaginary of the daily at the end of the Renaissance.

9. If only Monluc's family had not let the manuscript rot away until someone discovered it in an attic in 1592, the year of Montaigne's death and about twenty years after it had been written, the author of the *Essais* would probably have had the *Commentaires* in his "librairie." So much for writing for posterity.

10. See, for instance, Guillaume Chevalier's *Discours de la vaillance* (Paris: Robert le Fizelier, 1585). The success of professional or topical books is considerable in the sixteenth century. I have mentioned military matters, but the interest is just as strong in peaceful or pastoral matters. Didactic treatises, military or nonmilitary, all have one thing in common: their discourse is professional and uninvolved. The object of the author is to appear classical, the less personal, the better. Among the better known of such treatises are Charles Estienne's *La Maison rustique* and Olivier de Serres's *Le Théâtre d'agriculture.*

11. Monluc, 22: "Le plus grand capitaine qui ait jamais esté, qui est Cesar, m'en a monstré le chemin, ayant luy-mesme escrit ses Commentaires, escrivant la nuit ce qu'il executoit le jour. J'ay donc voulu dresser les miens, mal polis, comme sortans de la main d'un soldat et encor d'un Gascon, qui s'est tousjours plus soucié de bien faire que de bien dire.... Encore que je sois gentilhomme, si suis-je neantmoins parvenu degré par degré, comme le plus pauvre soldat qu'aye esté de longtemps en ce royaume.... Et comme j'ay esté le premier de six frères, que nous avons esté, il a fallu que je fisse cognoistre le nom de Monluc."

12. It is also true, however, that by writing mostly *after* having been cashiered

by the king from his governorship of Guienne, Monluc writes not only because he wants to but also because he has to. The king, realizing his mistake, soon elevates Monluc to the post of marshal of France and recalls him to active service, but it is too late. Now an invalid, he can no longer serve in the military.

13. Monluc, 571: "Prenez plustot celuy-là qu'un qui n'aura jamais perdu ny gagné, et qui n'aura jamais servi en un camp que de tesmoin. Je ne vous escri point ceci dans experience; j'ay appris ces leçons sous feu."

14. On this, see Timothy J. Reiss, "Montaigne and the Subject of Polity," in *Literary Theory / Renaissance Texts* (Ithaca, N.Y.: Cornell University Press, 1982), 115–49.

15. Monluc, 795: "L'on m'accordera tousjours que je me suis trouvé en autant de combats, batailles, rencontres, entreprinses, de nuict et de jour, assauts, prinses et deffenses de villes qu'homme qui soyt aujourd'huy en toute l'Europe."

16. The concept of an authorial voice echoing on either side of a public/ private fault line owes much to Stephen Greenblatt's "The Forms of Power and the Power of Forms in the Renaissance," *Genre* 15, nos. 1–2 (1982): 1–4; and Adrian Louis Montrose's "The Elizabethan Subject and the Spenserian Text," in *Literary Theory / Renaissance Texts*, 303–40.

17. *Journal de l'Estoile pour le règne de Henri III (1574–1589)* (Paris: Gallimard, 1943), 5: "dont il ne faut autres tesmoins que les escrits et libelles diffamatoires criés et publiés à Paris contre la mémoire de ce pauvre prince. Du nombre desquels sont ceux qui suivent . . . que j'ai extraicts de mon inventaire, et que j'ai gardés et garde pour tesmoins à la postérité de leur doctrine, par laquelle ils vendoient les places de paradis aux assassins, aussi naifvement que pourroit faire un marchant les siéges d'une foire: laquelle vendition toutefois se fait plus aisément dejà qu'elle ne se livre là hault." The various *Journaux* of Pierre de l'Estoile (*Journal du règne de Henri III*, which covers the years 1574–89; *Journal du règne de Henri IV*, 1589–1610; the *Journal* of the beginning of Louis XIII's reign, from 1610 to 1611) were written in many stages, as the author would constantly edit them and revise them, usually adding notes and commentaries. The history of the editing and publishing of the de l'Estoile manuscripts can be put together from three major sources: first, from the Moreau edition published in the Michaud and Poujoulat series in 1837; second, from the Lemerre twelve-volume edition (1875–96) by a group of scholars; and third, from the Lefèvre editions of 1943 and 1948 (portions of the *Journal* from 1574 to 1600 only), which establishes the text of the *Journal* from expanded, previously unknown sources and restores text previously rejected by editors on the basis that the style was at variance with the rest of the manuscript. The Henri III *Journal*, originally titled *Registre-Journal d'un curieux de plusieurs choses mémorables advenues et publiées librement à la française, pendant et durant le règne de Henri III, roi de France et de Pologne, lequel commença le dimanche 30 mai, jour de la Pentecôte 1574, sur les trois heures après midi et finit le mercredi 2 août 1589, à deux*

heures après minuit, was edited anew during the war by Louis-Raymond Lefèvre, who, after having discovered a new version, used it to put together a more recent, definitive edition of the entire *Journal: Journal de l'Estoile pour le règne de Henri III (1574–1589)* (Paris: Gallimard, 1943), and *Journal pour le règne de Henri IV (1589–1600)* (Paris: Gallimard, 1948), vol. 1. It is from these two versions (respectively *"Henri III"* and *"Henri IV"*) that I will be quoting de l'Estoile. Actually de l'Estoile's historical collecting boggles the mind. The *Registre-Journal* is only the last step in his awesomely complicated compiling and editing process. Most of his collected items go first into a *Recueil,* original fragments of which we still have (see a recent critical edition by Isabelle Armitage of one fragment, *Fragment des Recueils de Pierre de l'Estoile* [Lawrence: University of Kansas Humanistic Studies, no. 47, 1976]). One particular *Recueil,* "Les belles figures et drôleries de la Ligue," was published as vol. 5 of the Lemerre edition. When I quote from it, I will so indicate ("Les belles figures"). In addition to the *Recueils* and the *finished* versions of the *Journal,* we also have masses of documents and notes, the *Ramas,* and larger files and dossiers, some of which Lefèvre has preserved in the copious notes to his two volumes. By restoring the text, Lefèvre proves that de l'Estoile, although the most meticulous of archivists himself, was not always above jumping into the fray and giving a piece of his mind in the tone of the satirical material he was collecting. As the most recent editor of the *Journal* reminds us, de l'Estoile may have continued editing his work throughout his life in a Montaignean way, and only completed his task in the last years of Henri IV's reign and during the very beginning of Louis XIII's reign, just before his own death (see *Henri III,* 23). De l'Estoile does not stand alone in the memorializing enterprise. There are innumerable *Memoires* dealing with a particular event, a single period of history, a battle, a day in the life of the king, of a people (the famous *deductions* on the royal entries), of a city (*Henri IV,* 652). There is the example of a Simon Goulart's *Memoires de l'Estat de la France sous Charles Neuviesme,* which is a compilation of other *Memoires,* but Goulart limits his job by collecting only Catholic material (*Henri III,* 675). One can judge de l'Estoile's superiority by comparing him also to Belleforest, the author of a *Cosmographie,* who in his *Histoire des neuf rois Charles* admits that he is going to write mostly a "Charlaide." De l'Estoile is the most comprehensive and the most original, as well as the most objective, since most *Memoires* deal only with one period and only from one, usually highly partisan, side.

18. The earlier Bourgeois's work was published by Godefroy for the first time in 1654. However, some people, like Pasquier, knew it in the sixteenth century, and de l'Estoile had parts of his predecessor's *Journal* copied for his own use. While there are similarities between the two *journaux,* they are very general. De l'Estoile is a better observer, and his decisive advantage is that he is more interested in historical truth and, as I am arguing here, obsessed with the problematic of recording.

19. De l'Estoile, *Henri III*, 453.
20. De l'Estoile, *Henri III*, 396ff. and "Les belles figures," 5:417: "ung tableau faict au crayon."
21. De l'Estoile, *Henri III*, 74–75.
22. De l'Estoile, *Henri III*, 498.
23. Louis Marin, *Le Portrait du Roi* (Paris: Minuit, 1981), 130–43.
24. De l'Estoile, *Henri III*, 580–82.
25. De l'Estoile, *Henri IV*, 200.
26. De l'Estoile, *Henri IV*, 219.
27. De l'Estoile, *Henri IV*, 241.
28. De l'Estoile, *Henri IV*, 218.
29. Montaigne, *The Complete Essays of Montaigne*, trans. Donald M. Frame (Stanford: Stanford University Press, 1958), II, 17, 499 A: "I continually observe myself, I take stock of myself, I taste myself" ("je me considere sans cesse, je me contrerolle, je me gouste").
30. De l'Estoile, *Henri III*, 122.
31. De l'Estoile, *Henri III*, 181ff.; *Henri III*, 154 and passim.
32. De l'Estoile, *Henri IV*, 66–67.
33. De l'Estoile, *Henri IV*, 269: "ma chambriere m'acheta quatre oeufs un escu."
34. De l'Estoile, *Henri IV*, 184.
35. The *Journal* was discovered in the latter part of the last century by the Abbot Tollemer, who procured a copy as well as wrote a complete historical and thematic analysis of it. When Tollemer discovered it in a country attic, the *Journal* consisted of three large books. Parts of the beginning (before 1545) and of the end (after 1562) are missing. The *Journal* was subsequently printed in 1892 by the Société des Antiquaires de Normandie in Caen (Henri Delesques), and it is from that particular version that I will be quoting. Since then, Gouberville has become the toast of the *mentalités* historian. Three major historians have contributed to Gouberville's fame. Emmanuel Le Roy Ladurie wrote a lengthy preface, "La verdeur du bocage," to a reissue of Tollemer's analysis (*Un Sire de Gouberville, gentilhomme campagnard au Cotentin de 1553 à 1562* [Paris-La Haye: Mouton, 1972]). Le Roy Ladurie's essay was reprinted in his more recent book *Le Territoire de l'historien* (Paris: Gallimard, 1973). Madeleine Foisil has provided a new analysis of Gouberville's text, combining Tollemer's study with recent developments in geo- and ethnohistory (*Le Sire de Gouberville, un gentilhomme normand au XVIe siècle* [Paris: Flammarion, Champs, 1986]). Pierre Chaunu, himself a historian of the European Reform, wrote the preface to Foisil's study. Broadly speaking, Gouberville's *Journal* has been one of the main references for the historian concerned with the relation between the public and private sphere at the end of the Renaissance. The *Journal*

Fin de Siècle Living   255

has also been important for those interested in rural history, as it is one of the most continuous and complete accounts of works and days of the period. However, to my knowledge, precisely because his text is deemed so exact but so boring, Gouberville has not been discovered by literary critics.

36. For an analysis of the *Livre de Raison,* see in particular Roland Mousnier, *Les Institutions de la France,* 2 vols. (Paris, 1974–79), 1:48–49. It should be remembered that Montaigne had written, besides the *Essais,* a *Livre de Raison,* which deals essentially with events in his private life. The book was published as *Le Livre de Raison de Montaigne sur les Ephemeris historica de Beutler,* ed. Jean Marchand (Paris: Société des Amis de Montaigne, 1948). Strictly speaking, one should have compared Gouberville's *Journal* to Montaigne's *Livre,* but the comparison would have proven useless. Unlike Gouberville's *Journal,* Montaigne's *Livre* is very short, and one does not feel in it the rhythm of a whole life. Clearly, the author of the *Essais* reserved most of his energy for his main work.

37. Gouberville, 285.

38. This particular adventure is discussed by Le Roy Ladurie in his introduction, where he suggests that this lone occurrence underscores Gouberville's attachment to the land and his lack of interest in things maritime.

39. Gouberville, 295: "pour m'aller marier."

40. Gouberville, 127. The announcement is, as is the case for many private matters, written in the Greek alphabet.

41. In one of the few additional Gouberville papers still extant, there is a testament allocating the squire's meager resources. However, rather than a desire to vouch for himself vis-à-vis posterity, this should be construed as a desire to see to it, once again, that the resources of one are shared equitably in the community. Community is the word, not posterity.

42. In this, Foisil's quote of a sentence from another *Journal,* that of the Goncourt brothers, is extremely revealing of the historian's methodology: "Notre effort, écrivaient les Goncourt, dans la préface de leur journal, a été de chercher à faire revivre auprès de la postérité, nos contemporains, dans leur ressemblance animée, à les faire revivre... par la surprise physiologique d'un geste... par ce je ne sais quoi, qui donne l'intensité de la vie" (The Goncourt brothers wrote, "We have attempted to bring back to life for posterity, our contemporaries in animated likenesses, to make them alive through the physiological surprise of one gesture, though we know not what gives life its intensity,") (Foisil, *Le Sire de Gouberville,* 105).

43. On this point, it should be noted that Gouberville reads. We have a pretty good idea of the books at his disposal. He reads aloud to his household in the evening the adventures of *Amadis des Gaules.* Like Don Quixote, he believes in the old narratives, but unlike him, he limits his experience with them to reading them, for it is one of the things he does best with his household. It is clear,

256 *Humanism in Crisis*

however, that literature of imagination and fantasy has no direct bearing on Gouberville, and his own literary process, in turn, is not one of escaping but of taking stock of reality.

44. Since Gouberville's recent *recupération* by modern historians (Le Roy Ladurie had shown the way) on top of the exegesis already provided by the Abbot Tollemer, other texts have been discovered and studied (see Natalie Zemon Davis's work, *The Return of Martin Guerre* [Cambridge, Mass.: Harvard University Press, 1981]). In particular, much has been made from what I would call *conditional texts*—narratives reelaborated by the historian on the basis of judicial or administrative data, which call our attention not to the facts themselves, but to the cultural context in which those facts must be understood. Natalie Zemon Davis's work on Martin Guerre is one of the best examples of such reconstructive attempts, which the historian poses as ethnographer and storyteller as well. The question I am interested in raising is not that of the realism or reality of the life thus depicted but of the relationship between the writer and the facts or scenes he describes. In other words, what is Gouberville's writing practice? And to what extent can we still understand it?

45. "Tout cela n'a aucun intérêt," in *Roland Barthes par Roland Barthes* (Paris: Seuil, 1975), 81.

46. On this, see the chapter "Freedom and Necessity" in Ernst Cassirer, *The Individual and the Cosmos in Renaissance Philosophy*, trans. Mario Domandi (Philadelphia: University of Pennsylvania Press, 1972).

47. The notion of *figura*, which is used in *Mimesis*, to illustrate the conditions under which all representation is not simply an imitation of daily life, but a setting of the present on a stage, which is that of the history of the world, is not Auerbach's original creation. In his famous *Scenes from the Drama of European Literature* (Minneapolis: University of Minnesota Press, 1984), i–xviii. Auerbach shows the history of the concept of *figura*. From Lucretius to the Fathers of the Church, *figura* refers to a form both ideal and dynamic, and in constant motion. From the Christian period on, the term applies to any image the interpretation of which promises to reveal a truth, if not the Truth. In the context of this article, my use of the term *figura* implies the ongoing historicization of the interpretation in a culture attempting to constitute itself as culture by representing itself to itself.

48. Gouberville, 865.

49. Haton's diary is more learned and worldly. He has in mind the broader picture. The following passage is a good example: "L'an 1555, la France avoit prins un peu d'assoupissement par le benefice de la trêve faicte l'an passé entre l'empereur et le roy, qui fut ung peu de repos aux pauvres gens de Piccardie, la plus grande partie desquelz ne volurent s'en retourner en leur pays, ayans en eux ceste oppinion qu'elle ne dureroit pas le terme entier prins entre les princes" ("Last year 1555, France had become a bit quieter, thanks to the truce between

the emperor and the king, and that was some relief to the people of Picardy, most of whom refused to return to their land, because they were convinced that it (the truce) would not last the time agreed between the princes") (*Mémoires de Claude Haton,* ed. F. Bourquelot, in *Collection des documents inédits sur l'histoire de France* [Paris: Imprimerie Impériale, 1857], 1:15).

50. See Michel Beaujour, *Miroirs d'encre* (Paris: Seuil, 1979), 186–203.

51. "Mises et receptes faictes par moy, Gilles de Gouberville, d'empuys le sabmedy 25ème jour de mars (icelluy comprins) 1553, avecques le memoyre d'aulcunes choses qui d'empuys ledit jour se sont ensuyvies, tant pour mes affères que pour ceux d'aultruy, lesquels se seroyent trouvés avecques les miens ung chacun jour, moys et an, ainsy qu'il apparoystra cy-après."

52. Gouberville, 287: "Je ne payois poinct le Landès ni Bérot, pour ce que je n'avoye poinct de monnoye, qui avoyent fauché trois jours."

53. See Marc E. Blanchard, "Changer d'avis: Montaigne, histoire, radotage," *L'Esprit créateur* 27, no. 2 (1987): 30–41.

54. Foisil, *Le Sire de Gouberville,* 73.

55. Passage also commented on by Foisil, 73.

De Arte Rhetorica: The Gestation of French Classicism in Renaissance Rhetoric

Bernard Crampé

There are many pitfalls in using the notion of crisis for the discussion of rhetoric. Time and time again rhetoric has been presented as in a state of crisis, as ailing, degenerate, or languishing at death's door. And yet the symptoms that move us to infer the decline of rhetoric so often hide from view profound transformations that adapt it to novel situations, thereby invigorating it all the more. The risk of a false diagnosis might seem more remote in the Renaissance than in any other period. For though we may speak in certain respects of a crisis in humanism toward the end of the sixteenth century, nothing could be more misguiding than to seek a parallel crisis in rhetoric. Not only did rhetoric suffer no malaise during that period; it flourished as never before. In no other period since antiquity was there so much enthusiasm for eloquence, nor so much care lavished on the teaching of this art.

And yet paradoxically, though the art of oratory drew heavily on the humanist tradition, it was to play an important part, as far as the use of language is concerned, in the dissolution of beliefs and practices that were highly valued in the Renaissance. As Latin rhetoric, and in its wake vernacular rhetoric, found its place in the curriculum, there arose a conception of language and use of language radically different from that which prevailed in other areas during the same period. Rhetoric took shape and thrived in the schools, quite at odds, however, with the ideal of language current in the vernacular literature. Rhetoric, as it was conceived in academic institutions toward the end of the Renaissance, helped define the conception of language and letters that was to triumph in succeeding generations, and which culminated in French classicism. Historians of literature seem somehow to have overlooked the contributions of rhetoric on this score.[1]

Given the part oratorical training had to play in education during the Renaissance, and given the attitude toward language that it presupposed, it would be worthwhile to determine its impact on the conception of language and writing, an impact that was to prevail in the generations to come. To this end, we will especially take into account that treatise on rhetoric that circulated the most rapidly and the most widely at the end of the Renaissance, and which remained in use for many generations thereafter: the *De arte rhetorica* of the Portuguese Jesuit Cyprian Soarez.

In fact, in the sixteenth century, rhetorical instruction became what is doubtless an underestimated locus for the diffusion of new ideas about language. This resurgence of interest inspired by rhetoric, as well as the return of rhetoric to a place of honor in school curricula, is a fact that deserves to be fully integrated into sets of concepts that define the Renaissance. From the earliest moments of humanist endeavor, intellectuals accorded particular attention to the works on the theory or practice of public discourse. The flourishing of rhetoric is intimately bound with their project.[2] The most important writings of Cicero on eloquence, which had been available only in part (*De oratore, Brutus*) or had been completely unknown during the Middle Ages, were rediscovered during the course of the fifteenth century,[3] along with the works of Tacitus.[4] Among some of the very first printed texts appeared two editions of the fourth book of Saint Augustine's *De doctrina christiana*, under the title *De arte praedicandi* (Strasburg, 1466; Mainz, 1466 or 1467).[5] The newly established printers in Venice were quick to issue the no-less-celebrated *Rhetorica ad Herennium* in 1470.[6] A most noteworthy event in the history of letters was the preparation during the first half of the sixteenth century of Erasmus's great edition of Saint Augustine (Basel, 1529),[7] comprising once again the *De doctrina christiana* and replete throughout with innumerable thoughts and observations on the use of eloquence. Rhetoric supplanted dialectic in the schools within the traditional trivium; exercises in oratorical training took the place of exercises in the old Scholastic logic. Teachers in the many academic institutions that were cropping up at the time began to think of ways to renew the methods of instruction in the *ars oratoria*. During the Renaissance the praise of rhetoric was one of the most frequently exploited commonplaces.

Rhetoric requires and fosters an attitude toward speech altogether opposed to the wayward and disorderly enthusiasm that characterized the conceptions of language prevalent during the Renaissance, as they appear, for instance, in the works of Rabelais, Montaigne, and numerous schools of poets. As the greater number of sixteenth-century writers were to bear witness, the French language lent itself to anything. For example, Henri Estienne delighted in the versatility of this language, explaining, "There are so many advantages, for our language is so well suited to all sorts of mincing ways [*mignardises*] that we can do with it as we will."[8] Daring was often the rule in taking advantage of the vernacular. This word *daring,* or *hardiesse,* was used with its meliorative connotation, in all the poetic arts.[9] Such was hardly the case, however, in the field of rhetoric. Oratorical training always looked favorably on disciplinary measures. In the teaching of eloquence, one could expect to cultivate a student's natural abilities through knowledge and understanding of oratorical techniques. This could be accomplished in the end through study and close imitation of a well-defined body of texts, tried and true in the field of persuasion, whose aesthetic value had long been universally recognized. Moreover, such a venture could only be undertaken once solid foundations had been laid in grammar, that is, in Latin, having accustomed the student to purity (*latinitas*) and clarity of expression. There could be no question of leaving language to the mercy of "mincing ways."

We are dealing, of course, with two distinct subjects: poetics or French letters on the one hand and Latin rhetoric on the other (though rhetoric frequently made headway in the vernacular as well). But as history seems to have shown, the relationship between the two subjects was complex, the one not so impervious to the other. In fact, the "regratteurs de littérature" at the beginning of the seventeenth century and theorists of the classical age proved to be closer to the rhetors of the sixteenth century than to their forerunners in French belles lettres, if we are to judge by the positions they held and their conceptions of language. The break was already present synchronically, as well as in the diachronic evolution, in the diverse conceptions of the use of speech in the Renaissance.

Soarez's *De arte rhetorica* is one of the most complete, not to say typical, of the works making up the corpus of this rhetorical instruction then being established in such an imposing fashion. Teachers of rhetoric could use a variety of different materials in the classroom. Naturally they could choose from among the classical works newly issued to the public.

But certain people, such as Ramus, desired a more radical reorganization of the educational system and therefore sought a break with tradition; they hoped to redefine in this way the principles to put into practice and the tasks to assign to each discipline.[10] More often than not educators adopted a compromise solution, making use of both old and new. Thus new programs of study, at once exhaustive and coherent, were designed so that one might grasp the elements common to the works of the ancient rhetors; so that one might reformulate more systematically the basic ideas developed in these works.

De arte rhetorica of the Jesuit father Cyprian Soarez is characteristic of the last approach.[11] This work represents at once the ruck of general ideas on the oratorical art at the time and a model for instruction in the schools. First published in 1562, it was far and away the manual most often reprinted. It served as a school textbook and as the master's *vade mecum* in the Jesuit schools, and in many other academic institutions as well, for more than one hundred and fifty years. Even at Port-Royal it was held in high esteem.

Soarez's work comes of a major pedagogical preoccupation that appeared in almost all fields during the Renaissance: the elaboration of textbooks. Because none of the classics was suitable in itself to present the whole of the oratorical art, the need for textbooks was especially pronounced in rhetoric. The first task, then, was to see to this want, by designing an introductory manual in rhetoric such as had not really before been available in the Western tradition, a manual at once clear, systematic, and complete. Such was indeed the overriding concern of the Jesuit superiors as the order laid the foundation of its educational system, placing as it did a great emphasis on letters and eloquence. Soarez reverentially recalls the Jesuits' concern in the preface to his work: "Thus it was the wish of our teachers that all the parts of eloquence be explained by definitions and illustrated by examples from the opinion of Aristotle, and not just from the opinion of Cicero and Quintilian, but also using their very words; that they should be put together in some book, method and order."[12] Certainly, the writing of a manual necessarily requires clarity, rigor, organization, and method, qualities that were not always of concern in the sixteenth century, but which were of great consequence in the seventeenth. Though venerated as always, none of the traditional authorities, Aristotle, Cicero, Quintilian, and the rest, was to constitute by itself the main body of the new manual.[13] Indeed, all references and

De Arte Rhetorica   263

acknowledgments to those authorities were relegated to the margins of the page. It was vital to start afresh, beginning with a precise formulation of the definitions and moving on to the orderly presentation of the principles that govern the craft, so that the student could take on tasks of greater and greater difficulty. Nonetheless the new manual was to make frequent allusions to the ancient authors. Following the wishes of the Jesuit superiors, the treatise appropriated revered passages from Cicero and Quintilian, as well as the Latin translations of passages from Aristotle, though only as the opportunity to clarify or reinforce some point presented itself. It is abundantly illustrated with examples borrowed from Cicero's discourses and with fragments of poems by Virgil, Lucan, and even Juvenal and Ovid. The formula, systematic though eclectic, was intended to suit many. This in itself was to guarantee the work wide circulation for years to come.

Plainly Aristotle, Cicero, and Quintilian are especially well represented in the examples featured in *De arte rhetorica*. No doubt the honor is due to the authority that they exercise in so many areas, but it is also due to their perspective on the discipline itself. In accordance with the wishes of his superiors, Soarez highlights Aristotle of all the ancient rhetors, because his is the most analytical presentation of the oratorical art; he highlights Cicero and Quintilian because they had always been ready advocates of the alliance of rhetoric with philosophy and morals. Obviously, Soarez deliberately excludes the Sophists from the available body of ancient texts, and indeed all those who insist above all on stylistic embellishment. He includes rhetors who promote clarity and purity of language, who take tremendous care in organization of arguments, who stress precision of thought rather than excessive ornamentation: atticism, in a word, is the main model for Soarez.

De arte rhetorica was to help formulate a certain theory in oratorical instruction on the use of language, a theory quite different from the one that held sway among the advocates and promoters of the French vernacular. For its presentation of rhetoric depends on the notions of "reason," "judgment," "order," "clarity," and "measure;" that is to say, it depends on the paradigm later to be reclaimed and exploited by the theorists of classicism, who will often give very explicitly as counterexamples well-known literary pieces of the Renaissance.

Soarez highlights the close bond between discourse and thought right from the preface by means of commentaries that will find echoes in literary and philosophical movements of the seventeenth century, and upon which Descartes, at the College of La Flèche, had, no doubt, the occasion to meditate:

> Such is the likeness between thought and speech that the Greeks who were of the first rank not only in understanding, but in speaking as well, called them both by the same name.... For speech is a certain image of thought.... Reason guides our thoughts; speech changes the thoughts of others.[14]

Oratio must conform perfectly with *ratio*. Thus the first task of rhetoric is to teach us to draw a faithful portrait of thought using the medium of language. We must learn to communicate our thought if ever we hope to engage the reason of others. Soarez gives no further elucidation of the word *ratio;* and though he does not take this word in as strict a sense as it was to have for the rationalists of the seventeenth century, he already sets the tone and the framework for the debates to ensue. From the outset, then, Soarez seems closer to the theorists of classicism than to the writers in poetics of his own time. The notions of reason and judgment come to join forces at all the key junctures of the work. Soarez calls upon them to shed light on the various elements of discourse, whether they be the choice of materials, their arrangement, or their final form.

In the first book, which he devotes to invention and the choice of arguments, Soarez invokes these notions insistently. In their name, he calls for restraint, forbids vagaries and digressions in the use of topics, and teaches us to look upon excessive inventiveness with a wary eye:

> There is nothing more fertile than the mind, especially when it has been cultivated by education. But just as fertile fields produce not only useful harvests, but also bad weeds which harm them, so too frivolous, irrelevant and useless arguments come from these places.[15]

This argument, a sort of paradoxical vituperation of abundance, already found in Cicero,[16] was to be exploited again by French classical writers. It will be, for example, further developed by Lamy ("Abundance often causes sterility"),[17] who also adds some Cartesian flourishes to his request for a minimal reliance upon the technique of commonplaces:

The fecundity derived from it is inconvenient. Those things are trivial and by consequence the art of topics furnishes nothing that is fit to say. I am of the opinion that to persuade we need but one argument, if it be solid and strong, and that eloquence consists in clearing of that and making it perspicuous. All those feeble arguments derived from commonplaces are like ill weeds that choke the corn.[18]

Like the sections on invention, the sections devoted to *dispositio* in the second book develop further concepts, as essential to rhetoric as they will be cherished by the theorists of classicism: the search for uniform coherence as well as for harmony of the parts and the whole, each of the parts developed as the subject requires.

Though certain modern critics have been interested in rhetoric above all as a technique of elocution, and though others have been content to remind us that rhetoric was also a technique of invention, we must not forget that, since antiquity, only the last parts of the craft, *memoria* and *pronunciatio,* had in fact fallen by the wayside and that, during the Renaissance, the first three were still a matter of concern. Indeed, *De arte rhetorica* devotes a whole book to *dispositio.*

The metaphors that Soarez carefully chooses to convey the importance of *dispositio* are by tradition the most potent: that of combat and that of discourse as a body. It had always been the favored custom of rhetors to define their practice as a form of combative competition. The conceit resurfaces in *De arte rhetorica:* "The value of a great leader is nowhere more in evidence with the choice of the best and the most courageous soldiers than in the arrangement of the whole of the army for battle."[19] Likewise, the image of discourse as a body points out the need for cohesion of discourse, emphasizing its corporeal nature, as it were: "The least dislocation of our limbs destroys the activity which strengthens them."[20] These translations of the classical principles of coherence and unity into the standard registers of rhetoric are among the most forceful ways of establishing the point that weakness in arrangement is bound to be costly.

One of the most essential tasks of rhetoric has always been in fact to teach, in an orderly fashion, how to pose a problem, how to define the terms at issue, how to set the stakes, how to effect expedient divisions in the face of certain difficulties, how to dispose arguments in sequence according to the impact we can expect these arguments to have on our

266 *Humanism in Crisis*

audience, and how to make our case without violating the precepts of logic. In rhetoric, we always reprove unconditionally the illogical, the disjointed, and the disorderly. As Soarez observes in the introduction to his second book, nothing could be more unsettling to the auditor in the end than a discourse that breaks the rules of *dispositio:*

> Thus, a speech that lacks this quality will inevitably be confusing. Without a director it will waver, lacking coherence. I will repeat many points and skip others like a traveller astray at night in unfamiliar regions. Since neither beginning nor ending has been fixed, it will follow rather chance than design. For this reason, this book will be devoted to arrangement.[21]

About a century later, Boileau was to lay down the rules for organizing a poetical work:

> 'Tis not enough when swarming faults are writ,
> That here and there are scatter'd sparks of wit:
> Each object must be fix'd in the due place,
> Till by a curious art dispos'd, we find
> One perfect whole, of all the pieces join'd.
> Keep to your subject close in all you say;
> Nor for a sounding sentence ever stray.[22]

With such a formula, trite in appearance only, Boileau gives an abbreviated expression of a set of rules on which one might find whole chapters in the traditional textbooks on rhetoric. Order and direction of the subject were to be points of contention between poets and writers of prose during the Renaissance and their readers in the following century. The later theorists never fail, on these points above all others, to accuse their sixteenth-century predecessors of having fallen short of the rules. Thus so-called neoclassical thought defined itself largely by criticism of the literary practices of the sixteenth century.

It was on rhetorical grounds, for instance, that Chapelain and Balzac denounced Ronsard in the 1640s for being nothing more than a "commencement de poète." They complained that one finds in Ronsard, "as much natural talent, imagination and ability as one could wish, but little order, little economy and no skill in choice."[23] Hence *dispositio* was the ultimate target of their criticisms. But the tensions between poetics and rhetorical theory on this subject were already making themselves felt in the sixteenth century. In his *Quintil Horatian,* Barthélemy Aneau[24] had directly addressed Du Bellay to condemn him on analogous grounds:

> You are thus incoherent; the chapters and theses do not follow one from another, but are placed thus as they came from thought to pen, and from pen to paper; so much so that the whole work is without thought and sure consistency, without proposed and sure themes, without methodical order, without economy, without point or goal.[25]

Granted, Aneau's criticisms here do not concern poetry itself, but the discourse on poetry. But beyond that, Aneau has in view a whole literary practice that avails itself of language with no care for the rules of good rhetoric. Barthélemy Aneau goes so far in his *Quintil* as to envisage a rival defense of the French language, against the one undertaken by Du Bellay; a defense this time that would advocate the supremacy of the rhetor over the poet:

> Please God that these Sages and eloquent men, living or dead, whose names I need not mention so well known are they, should have wished to take the trouble to write out their beautiful, and good and prudent orations, diatribes, Actions, Counsels, Opinions, and words in such form or better, than they ever pronounced them in public, following the example of orators, Senators and Greek and Roman Emperors. For in this way the French language would be better defended and illustrated than by the clever juggling of most of the poets who are rightly blamed for this.[26]

Recall, by way of background, that Aneau, jurisconsult and orator, was himself professor of rhetoric at the Collège de la Trinité in Lyons. He became principal of the college at about the same time that Perpinian, the Jesuit father who edited the second and the most commonly consulted version of *De arte rhetorica,* came to teach there. Rhetoric already counted for a lot in the critique of the poetic movements of the Renaissance. For like reasons, classicism was to treat the verses of the Pléiade just as Aneau had treated their prose.

Following the chapters on invention and arrangement, the chapters Soarez devotes to style apply the same ideal of rigor and good judgment to the shaping of a discourse in all its detail. By and large, Soarez recommends that we avoid the esoteric and that we strive for accuracy and clarity. We must choose ways of speaking that hold the attention of our listeners, *sine satietate,* without committing excesses, which always run the risk of provoking disgust. Soarez devotes the greater part of the third book of *De arte rhetorica* to tropes and figures whose sole purpose is to render a discourse more clear and more beautiful. At the same time, they must ornament a discourse and express that to which ordinary language, because of its weaknesses and lacunae, can never do justice. Since these two goals are likely to conflict in practice, the fear is always that the search for embellishments might prevail over the search for clarity. *Restraint* and *moderation* are the key terms that qualify the use of these tropes and figures.

Soarez expounds the two fundamental rules governing the use of all tropes more specifically with regard to the metaphor, the object of the longest development (in four chapters), because, according to Soarez, it is of all the tropes "the most beautiful, and the one most widely in use." The first rule concerns theory: it requires that the likeness between the object we wish to designate and the object suggested in the ordinary sense of the metaphorical term be not too remote.[27] The second rule concerns practice, it requires that restraint be exercised in the use of the metaphors so that the transposed term "should easily find itself in a different place, without bursting on it" and so that "it should come on request, not by force."[28]

Beyond a certain limit, the use of many tropes goes too far. Excess produces results contrary to those that were thought to come from the *translation* of words. Enigma is the upper bound on the use of metaphor and thus allegory, i.e., the limit beyond which a discourse becomes hopelessly confused: "Though the metaphor can make a discourse more clear if the use of it be moderate and opportune, frequent use of it, on the other hand, makes a discourse dull and obscure. And the uninterrupted use of it leads to allegory and enigma."[29] Hence the practical rules for attenuating each of these tropes: that the metaphor be introduced as needed by formulas designed to lessen the surprise effect; that allegory should refrain from combining elements from different metaphorical registers; and that allegory should use obvious elements drawn from reality, for greater impact.

Use of the other tropes is not unaccompanied by risks of the same sort. Periphrase is an obstacle rather than an aid to discourse when it verges on perissology.[30] We must not even give free rein to hyperbole.

De Arte Rhetorica 269

As a contrived form of exaggeration tailored for diminishing as well as aggrandizing, hyperbole must avoid immoderation.[31]

Of course, the measure or degree of exaggeration effected by a figurative expression will itself vary, following *De arte rhetorica* and the whole rhetorical tradition, according to the type of discourse. The poet, who is not the focal point—plainly—of rhetorical teaching, may indulge in liberties that the orator must avoid. Nevertheless, this is but a question of degree. Most of the seventeenth-century writers on poetics would not accord greater liberties to the poet than treatises on rhetoric would grant the orator. In matters of style, classical poetics appropriated virtually unaltered the prescriptions of rhetorical teaching.

It is clear that the grievances concerning style that readers of the seventeenth century were to raise against the work of the Renaissance would turn, more often than not, on the transgression of the rules of rhetoric. Even if the poets of the Pléiade often invite us to "select words with judgment," and to "keep away from fantasies,"[32] they fall short of the mark in practice, if only in the estimation of the likes of Chapelain, Balzac, Malherbe, or Boileau. They are always called to task for their lack of judgment, their daring, their departure from well-trodden paths. Ronsard, leader of the rank and file, is always the target of choice. Chapelain declares his affinity to the taste of Balzac on this score:

> You blame him for the unbridled licence of his prosody, for his negligence of diction, for his daring choice of words and for his temerity in forcing the nature of figures.... In all this we agree.... I have noted almost all these faults, just like you.[33]

Aneau, who objects to confusion and extravagance, is no more indulgent toward Du Bellay:

> The whole beginning of the chapter is vicious and incoherent *translation;* it begins by eating, carries on by planting and finishes by building, yet always speaking of the same things; to which vice those capitulate ordinarily who wish to make metaphors where there is no need, and who wish to apply figures where propriety would be better suited. For they judge oration, figurative in every instance, to be more beautiful than that which is simple, equable, and seldom laced with such ornaments.[34]

270 *Humanism in Crisis*

On the subject of style, the common ground of rhetoric and poetics alike, many theorists of the preclassical and classical periods, as well as the rhetors of the Renaissance, were in complete agreement.

Whether *De arte rhetorica* played a part in educating contemporary tastes, along with the teaching of rhetoric as a whole at the end of the Renaissance, or is simply a mirror of those tastes, one thing is certain: it accords perfectly with the growing trend of the time. Rhetorical teaching has to be considered central to the destruction of literary practices developed in the vernacular language during the sixteenth century, and to the development of the French classical ideal. In this respect, it would be wrong to believe, merely because there was, for instance, a baroque style called Jesuit in architecture in the early seventeenth century, or because the Society violently opposed the Port-Royalists, who were certainly tightly linked to classicism, that Jesuit pedagogy made a meager contribution. At any rate, Soarez's *De arte rhetorica* answers to the aspirations of the period, to the efforts undertaken for the sake of methodical organization, to the desire for ornate but clear and rigorous expression, all which found voice in the teaching of rhetoric.

By its very nature, Soarez's work was destined to succeed. Moreover, circumstances were to favor it considerably. Because it was conceived, completed, and slightly revised at the very time when the Jesuits were compiling their various programs of study, its good fortune was tied very early to the polishing of the *Ratio studiorum*. Early drafts of the *Ratio studiorum* from 1575 allude to Soarez,[35] and the *Ratio* of 1599, the definitive program of Jesuit teaching, requires the use of *De arte rhetorica*.[36]

When one considers the tentacular network of institutions founded by the Society, as well as the concern for conformity and obedience that prevailed there, one little doubts the ease with which the treatise managed to circulate. But its dissemination was not restricted to the Jesuit schools. For though there were pronounced ideological differences, often concerning pedagogical methods and goals, among numerous teaching congregations, just about everybody was in agreement on the question of rhetoric in general, invoking the same references and recommending similar techniques. No doubt the list of grievances expressed by opponents against Jesuit education was long: excessive concern for formalism; disdain for speculative studies, for philosophy and science; little time taken for history; scant attention paid to the vernacular, etc. Many of the Jesuits' former pupils, not the least of them Descartes and Voltaire, for example, were to go to no trouble to shorten the list. And yet under no circumstance was one to charge the Jesuits with mediocrity in their teaching of eloquence. Though they might well have been criticized for spending too much of their time on the subject, never would they be criticized for wasting it. The courses that the Jesuits offered in rhetoric and in the humanities were often to serve as models.

The influence of Soarez's work was all the greater since virtually no contributions to the field of rhetoric were made in other educational institutions of the time. The university was quietly stagnating. Armed with statutes going all the way back to the fifteenth century,[37] the university was impervious to reform and innovations, as Ramus and his followers had discovered. Not until 1600 were new statutes to be promulgated. And unlike the Jesuit tradition, the statutes in the university tradition made much of philosophy and logic; but the new programs in the university resembled the *Ratio studiorum* on many points concerning letters and rhetoric. Nearly the same methods, authors, and sorts of exercises figured in the university curriculum as in the Jesuit curriculum. It is to be observed that Balthasar Gilbert, five times elected rector of the University of Paris in the eighteenth century, praised Soarez for the conception of rhetoric he proposed and for the virtues of his book.[38]

In the seventeenth century, even congregations such as the Oratory and Port-Royal, the most ideologically removed from the Jesuits, were not in complete disagreement with them on the question of instruction in rhetoric. Some have too closely identified the Oratory with Cartesian thought, no doubt because certain eminent historians of Cartesianism, education, and the Oratory itself tend greatly to favor Descartes and Port-Royal. Since the regulations of the Oratory were rather lenient, it could afford considerable liberties to the members of its congregation. It is precisely for this reason that so many Cartesians sought refuge there. It is also for this reason that many of them were free to propound divergent opinions. A certain number of them refused to oppose the Jesuits at the time of the conflicts that marked the century. Not everybody at the Oratory in the seventeenth century would take the part of, say, a Bernard Lamy, Cartesian and follower of Malebranche, who did not do the honor of citing *De arte rhetorica,* or at any rate included it without mentioning it specifically by name as one of "les traités de rhétorique ordinaires."[39] There is no reason Soarez should not have suited the needs and the taste of many of the Oratorians. As far as Port-Royal is concerned, we do not know very well the works used as textbooks, except for those that were written for Port Royal's own classes, such as the *Logique,* the *Grammaire,* and the *Nouvelles méthodes.* No program or curriculum seems to have been conserved or written down. We have only some remarks, the late *Mémoire* of Arnauld, and some observations of former pupils. Arnauld cites the work of Soarez on the very page where he recommends the reading of Sophocles, Aeschylus, or Livy for an education in letters.[40] That the treatise of Soarez should receive such an homage, more than a century after its publication, from one of the most determined adversaries of the Jesuits indicates how highly esteemed it was, the extent of the readership it had established for itself, and its fundamental accord with rationalist thought on the rules of discourse.

Soarez's work circulated largely in the various milieus of education, and it was to remain in use for a long time. In fact, the first attempt to replace it, the *Candidatus rhetoricae* of François Pomey, did little indeed to eclipse it.[41] Not until Joseph de Jouvancy at the beginning of the eighteenth century could one expect to find any significant novelty in the oratorical teaching of the Jesuits.[42]

Following a slightly different presentation (in the form of questions and answers, with the addition of numerous examples and model allocutions), Jouvancy elaborated the section on the passions, which Soarez had been reproached more than once for neglecting. At the same time, he made more room for tropes and figures. For it was the task of tropes and figures in classical rhetoric to give expression to disorders of the passions. But for all that, the balance of the three principal parts of rhetoric was not disturbed. Jouvancy voiced the same concern for the proper assimilation and the methodical use of the map of places, for the control of invention, and for expedient arrangement and appropriate expression.

De arte rhetorica is thus the original of a whole line of manuals that dominated for a long time. One need only crack open the archives to be convinced that the works of Soarez and his successors would endure. French translations of Pomey and Jouvancy were still issuing from the press in the last years of the nineteenth century. The criticism against the modes of Renaissance writing made by generations nourished on treatises of such a kind were in some way the unfolding by history of tensions between the poetic vernacular and Latin rhetoric that already marked the sixteenth century.

In the first decades of the seventeenth century, just as the works of the Renaissance writers were falling out of circulation or were being read only to be cited as bad examples, *De arte rhetorica* was reprinted and circulated widely in an impressive number of editions. Soarez's treatise is not unique for all that, or even original. But it is typical of rhetorical teaching in the Renaissance, of schoolwork prescribed for students at the time, and of efforts to enlist the works of ancient theorists in the service of the punctilious instruction of the moderns. Such a work carried weight in the development of the neoclassical doctrine. One cannot help but notice that the positions concerning the shaping of discourse held by writers on poetics in the age of neoclassicism frequently coincide with those held by the rhetors of the preceding century.

NOTES

1. Most of the critics of the twentieth century have neglected the role of rhetoric in the development of the classical ideal. René Bray is one of the most typical. In 390 pages of his *La Formation de la doctrine classique en France* (Lausanne: Payot, 1931), he considers one after the other the influence of the Italians, the Spanish, Aristotle and the ancients, and rationalism, but says not a word about the teaching of rhetoric, not even in the chapters on the influence of antiquity or on verisimilitude. In *Qu'est-ce que le classicisme?* (Paris: Nizet, 1964), Henri Peyre prefers to redefine classicism without the notions of imitation, model, approval of posterity and all others, "which for too long have encumbered our textbooks and our former classes in rhetoric." That is of course his choice, and his right. Plainly the question of the influence of rhetoric on classicism does not even come up from this perspective. Daniel Mornet is one of the few to take up this issue with force in his *Histoire de la clarté française, ses origines, son évolution, sa valeur* (Paris: Payot, 1929), 147–48: "One might have bestowed proper names on these powers which subjected the classical spirit to a reflective logic; they were called Malherbe and Balzac. They certainly played their role in the development of classical thought. But above all they were masters of expression, teachers of language and prosody. Their contemporaries had only to follow the rigorous directives of this rhetoric, supreme in the colleges, and without rival, in order to organise and to link their ideas effectively.... These directives enjoyed the most brilliant success in France. Though the discipline of the schools at the outset, they were to become the discipline of thought in general." Daniel Mornet, however, takes this as self-evident. He neither considers specifically nor mentions any work in rhetoric of the sixteenth and seventeenth centuries.

2. For a more complete panorama of rhetoric in the Renaissance see Morhof,

274 *Humanism in Crisis*

Polihistor (Lubeck, 1688); and the chapter entitled "Le Ciel des idées rhétoriques" in Marc Fumaroli, *L'Age de l'éloquence: Rhétorique et "res literaria" de la Renaissance au seuil de l'époque classique* (Geneva: Droz, 1980).

3. Until that time, of the works of Cicero on eloquence chiefly *De inventione* and *De oratore* were known, as well as the *Rhetoric to Herennius*, which was falsely ascribed to him until Valla called this attribution into question.

4. It was only at about the middle of the fifteenth century that a manuscript containing the *Dialog on Oratory*, together with *Germania* and *Agricola*, was discovered in the monastery of Hersfeld.

5. Augustine, *De arte praedicandi* (Strasbourg: Johann Mentelin, 1466; Mainz: Johann Fust, 1466 or 1467).

6. Edited by Nicolaus Jenson for the press of Omnibonus Leonicenus. The treatise was reedited at least twenty-eight times before the end of the fifteenth century.

7. Published in ten volumes in folio in Basel between 1528 and 1529 by the press of Froben.

8. Henri Estienne, *De la précellence du langage françois*, ed. Léon Feugère (Paris: Delalain, 1850), 97.

9. See Du Bellay, "Uses donques hardiment...," in *La Deffence et illustration de la langue francoyse*, ed. Henri Chamard (Paris: Nizet, 1970), 160. Ronsard suggests we understand certain grammatical categories "librement et hardiment" (*Abbrégé d'art poétique françois*, in *Oeuvres complètes*, ed. Gustave Cohen, 2 vols. [Paris: Gallimard, 1938], 2:1011); Peletier du Mans laments, like Ronsard, that he has yet to encounter "quelque hardi inuanteur," in *L'Art poëtique*, ed. André Boulanger (Paris: Belles Lettres, 1930), 121.

10. For instance, Omer Talon, *Institutiones oratoriae* (Paris: Bogart, 1547).

11. The first edition of 1562 at Coïmbra is exclusively the work of Soarez (1524–93). A second version, reworked by Perpinian (1530–66) was available already in 1565. It was often to be reedited, sometimes with still further minor modifications and synoptic tables. Abridged as well as more elaborate versions circulated. A complete compilation remains to be done. In an unpublished thesis for the University of Florida, "Soarez's *De arte rhetorica*," Lawrence Flynn gives a list of 135 editions that appeared between 1562 and 1735 in forty-six cities in Europe. This list is not exhaustive. Latin quotations will hereafter be given as they appear in the edition of Bartolomeo Zapata (Torino, 1661).

12. Soarez, 10: "His de causis cupiebant nostri praeceptores, ut omnes eloquentiae partes explicatae definitionibus, exemplis illustratae, ex Aristotelis sententia, Ciceronis vero, & Quinctiliani non sententia solum, sed plerunque etiam verbis aliquo libro, via, & ordine comprehenderentur."

13. Latin works on eloquence are enumerated one after another in the *Proemium* in order to demonstrate the inadequacies of each. The *Institutio oratoria* is too long and often obscure; the *Partitiones oratoriae*, too short and too con-

cise; the *De oratore,* inconvenient for teaching, and too difficult for novices; the *De inventione,* considered inadequate by Cicero himself; the *Topica,* too difficult, reserved for jurists; the *Orator,* too spotty.

14. Soarez, 13: "Rationis & orationis tanta est similitudo, ut Graeci, qui non intelligendi solum, sed loquendi etiam principatum tenuerunt, uno utra[m]que vocabulo, Latini Graecorum prudentiae aemuli eodem pene nominarint. Est enim oratio quasi rationis imago quaedam.... Ratio moderatur proprium animum. Oratio flectit etiam alienas."

15. Soarez, 49: "Nihil enim feracius ingeniis iis praesertim quae disciplinis exculta sunt; sed ut segetes foecundae, & uberes, non solum fruges, verum herbas etiam effundunt inimicissimas frugibus, sic interdum ex illis locis, aut levia quaedam, aut a causis aliena, aut non utilia gignuntur."

16. Cicero, *Orator,* 15.47.

17. Bernard Lamy, *De l'art de parler* (Paris: Pralard, 1675), 4–5: "L'Abondance cause souvent la sterilité."

18. Lamy, 241–42: "cette fécondité est mauvaise," because "pour persuader il n'est besoin que d'une seule preuve qui soit forte et solide."

19. Soarez, 76: "Excellentis ducis virtus non magis in deligendo fortissimo, & strenuissimo quoque milite ad bellum, quam in instruendo ad pugnam, & aciem cernitur."

20. Soarez, 76: "& artus etiam leviter loco moti, perdunt quo viguerunt."

21. Soarez, 76–77: "sic oratio carens hac virtute, tumultuentur necesse est, & sine rectore fluitet, nec cohaereat sibi, multa repetat, multa transeat, velut nocte in ignotis locis errans: nec initio, nec sine proposito, casum potius quam consilium sequatur. Quapropter hic liber dispositioni serviat."

22. Nicolas Boileau, *L'Art poétique,* trans. John Dryden, canto 1, ll. 175–81: "Il faut que chaque chose y soit mise en son lieu; / Que le débat, la fin répondent au milieu; / Que d'un art délicat les pièces assorties / N'y forment qu'un seul tout de diverses parties; / Que jamais du sujet le discours s'écartant / N'aille chercher trop loin quelque mot éclatant." One always notes that this passage comes from Horace. That's true. But it is also true that it also comes from all of the treatises on rhetoric.

23. Guez de Balzac, *Les Lettres de M. de Balzac* (Paris: Louis Billaine, 1665), 1:856, letter 20.

24. Barthélemy Aneau, *Le Quintil Horatian,* in Du Bellay's *Deffence,* ed. E. Person (Paris: Baudry, 1878), 193.

25. Aneau, 193: "Tu es ainsi inconsequent, les chapitres et propos ne dependans l'un de l'autre, mais ainsi mis comme ilz venoyent de la pensée en la plume, et de la plume au papier; tellement que toute l'oeuvre est sans propos et certaine consistence, sans theme proposé et certain, sans ordre methodique, sans oeconomie, sans but final."

26. Aneau, 199: "Et pleust à Dieu qu'iceux Sages et eloquens hommes tant

defunctz qu'encor vivans (desquels les noms assez nommez je tais) eussent voulu prendre le labeur de mettre par escript leurs belles et bonnes, et prudentes oraisons, harengues, Actions, Conseilz, Sentences et parolles, en telle ou meilleure forme d'escripture qu'ilz les ont prononcés à vive voix, ainsi qu'ont faict les Orateurs, Consulz, Senateurs, et Imperateurs Grecs, et Romains. Car par iceux seroit mieux defendue, et illustrée la langue Françoyse, que par la subtile jonglerie de la plus grande partie des Poëtes, qui pource à bon droict sont blamez."

27. Soarez, 121: "Videndum est ne longe simile sit ductum."

28. Soarez, 121: "Et enim verecunda debet esse translatio, ut deducta esse in alienum locum non irruisse, atque ut precario, non vi venisse videatur."

29. Soarez, 121: "Ut modicus autem, atque opportunus ejus usus illustrat orationem, ita frequens, & obscurat, & taedio complet: continuus vero in allegoriam, & aenigma exit."

30. Soarez, 131: "cum in vitium incidit, perissologia dicitur: obstat enim quicquid non adjuvat."

31. Soarez, 133: "Sed tam in augendo, quam in minuendo servetur mensura quaedam. Quamvis est enim omnis hiperbole ultra fidem, nom tamen esse debet ultra modum."

32. Pierre de Ronsard, *Abbrégé de l'art poétique françois*, in *Oeuvres complètes*, 2 vols., ed. Gustave Cohen (Paris: Gallimard, 1950), 2:999–1000: "mots choisis aveques jugement," "inventions fantastiques."

33. Jean Chapelain, letter to Balzac, dated June 10, 1640, in *Lettres*, ed. Tamizey de Larroque (Paris: Imprimerie Nationale, 1980), 537.

34. Aneau, 196: "Tout le commencement du chapitre est de translation vicieuse, et inconsequente, commençant par manger, moyennant par planter, et finissant par bastir, en parlant tousjours de mesmes choses; auquel vice tombent coustumierement ceux qui toujours veulent métaphoriser, ou il n'est besoing, et applicquer figures, ou proprieté seroit mieux convenante: estimans l'oraison par tout figurée, estre plus belle que la simple, et egale, et rarement entremeslée de telz ornemens."

35. The reading of it is recommended there. One may choose among the *De oratore*, the *Ad Herennium*, and the *De arte rhetorica*.

36. The treatise is mentioned on several occasions in the *Ratio*. Its use is prescribed as an introduction to the art of oratory in the class on humanities. It was also often to be used in more advanced courses on rhetoric.

37. The statutes of d'Estouteville.

38. Balthazar Gibert, *Jugemens des savans sur les auteurs qui ont traité de la rhétorique* (Amsterdam: Aux depens de la Compagnie, 1725), 230–32.

39. Lamy, preface.

40. Antoine Arnauld, *Oeuvres* (Paris and Lausanne: Sigismond D'Arnay, 1780). The manuscript was published in the nineteenth century, with notes by

Father Adry and A. Gazier, under the title *Mémoire sur le règlement des études dans les lettres humaines* (Paris: Armand Colin, 1886).

41. François Pomey, *Novus candidatus rhetoricae* (Paris, 1659).

42. Joseph de Jouvancy, *L'Elève de rhetorique*, trans. H. Ferté (Paris: Hachette, 1892).

Marie de Gournay and the Crisis of Humanism

Cathleen M. Bauschatz

Marie de Gournay, editor of Montaigne's *Essais* and author of numerous tracts on moral, social, and linguistic themes, was a reliable observer of the crisis of humanism in early seventeenth-century France.[1] Born in 1565, she lived on until 1645, and was able to comment on (actually to bemoan) the decline in classical education and the changes in perceptions of language and literature that accompanied this decline. As well as being a moralist and early feminist, Gournay was a perceptive sociolinguist, acutely aware of connections between language change and other forms of social change in the early seventeenth century. As might be expected, she was not happy about any of these changes. This negative, defensive posture is what earned her ridicule and derision at her time, but it also makes her work extremely useful as a sort of measuring stick for the changes which were in fact taking place around her.

I will discuss here the "Deffence de la Poësie et du Langage des Poëtes," written around 1619, but first printed in 1626 in *L'Ombre* and then reprinted in 1634 and 1641 in the second volume of her collected works, *Les Advis*.[2] The "Deffence" is concerned with bolstering an earlier conception of language and literature against what Gournay perceives as decline or even betrayal in her own time. Like all her work, this essay is not value-free: she states her own biases forcefully, but also allows us to perceive just what or who in her society she finds responsible for the assault on authors and conceptions of poetry she holds dear.

The "Deffence de la Poësie" begins with the famous exclamation "I have just left a house where I have seen thrown to the wind the venerable ashes of Ronsard and of his contemporary poets, as much as the impudence of ignorant people can do." The main objection she hears to these poets is linguistic—"their great and general refrain abuts on the poets' language, claiming: 'One doesn't talk like that any more.'"³

Language change, or perceived language change, is thus the first and one of the most important topics in the "Deffence." Gournay believes, in actuality, that French has not changed as much since the previous century as some think, for language always changes slowly—"it can only walk at a snail's pace."⁴ Gournay appears strikingly modern in her observation that this perceived change is just a "change of usage" ("changement d'usage"); actually, Ronsard, Du Bellay, Des Portes, and Du Bartas were not as different as they are being portrayed by theorists like Malherbe. The contemporary French seem in fact to want change, and may overemphasize it: "the appetite of the French who are gluttons for change."⁵

Gournay recognizes that we create language as we use it: "we are artisans in our language" ("nous sommes artisans en nostre langue"):

> Each artisan practices his trade according to the capacities of his intelligence, and we are artisans of our language: that is, we are not only obliged to deliver it as we have learned and received it, but also to mold it, form it, and build it, to intertwine goods with goods, and beauties with beauties.⁶

Gournay shows her sense that we have a responsibility toward language, to tend it and care for it. She accepts changes in usage that build on the past, but not those that tear it down. Language needs to progress in order not to go backward—"and languages seek out progress, as much as they avoid going backward or declining, which would lead to the decay of the fruits which they have produced." But what Gournay really objects to is arbitrary or frivolous language change: "Still this is always our triumphant refrain: one no longer talks this way, *the fashion has changed.*"⁷ Rather than letting usage govern a natural evolution in language, this current linguistic fashion appears to be arbitrarily or artificially imposed—much like changes in clothing fashion, which it is doubtful that Gournay followed, either.

In his *Language and Meaning in the Renaissance*, Richard Waswo has shown the significance of an awareness of language change to the emergence of the linguistic philosophy of the early humanists, particularly that of Lorenzo Valla and Juan Luis Vives.⁸ Waswo shows that once an observer sees that language changes, he is more aware of what language is, and of the fact that the same ideas can be expressed in a variety of different ways, with different words. Gournay anticipates many of these views, and like these early linguistic philosophers, as well as later scholars like Foucault or Waswo himself, she is also concerned about the *mots/choses* division in perceptions of language change. She thinks that those who hold to the belief that language has radically changed are overly concerned with *mots,* rather than *choses,* and do not look at the connection between the two as well as to syntax and construction—what we would call the structure of language rather than details of grammar and vocabulary.

Gournay probably became preoccupied with the *mots/choses* distinction while editing Montaigne's *Essais.* She shares his concern with the superficiality of much language use (and talk about language). The familiar statement at the beginning of "De la gloire" makes it clear that Montaigne is suspicious of words, which are not the same as the things they refer to: "There is the name and the thing. The name is a sound which designates and signifies the thing: the name is not a part of the thing or of the substance, it is an extraneous piece attached to the thing, and outside of it."[9] For Gournay, it is the "sweet language" ("doux langage") of her contemporaries that she mainly objects to: "it is to express an idea only by halves, that is to say the shell and not the thing, or to speak better, it is to whisper it and not to say it."[10] Contemporary speakers do not follow through in expressing their ideas, from superficial generalities to the point—"la chose":

> The reason is, that an idea can only be expressed by someone who comprehends it: and this sweet speaker or explicator after their fashion does not care about understanding ideas or making others understand them: his understanding giving only a soft and feeble attempt at the surface of subjects, which cannot pierce to the marrow, as is required to express ideas fully, by a strong and powerful attempt: but in this kind of attempt the tip of the tongue of such a man, as timid as it is flabby and thin, does not care to give it to them because it does not attempt to pierce, for fear of getting the tip stuck.[11]

As in many of Montaigne's discussions of language, there are some unmistakably sexual overtones in this discussion of the weakness and softness of current language and its speakers, as well as in the suggested relationship between speaker and listener, who waits to be penetrated by a more vigorous tongue or sword.[12] Gournay does not generally follow through on the implications of these metaphors, nor does she ever seem to consider their incongruity for a woman writer. But they certainly do contribute to a picture of earlier usage as vigorous, heroic, and male, while contemporary usage is weak, trivial, and, for want of a better analogy, female.

Strong language can maintain its connection with thought, here portrayed explicitly as a sort of male bonding and containing theological overtones as well: "what a marvel, since language is the son of the spirit, that most of its riches are abstract and profound in imitation of those of its father!"[13] Metaphors, forbidden by the "grammarian poets" (*poëtes grammairiens*), provide one of the ways to maintain the connection between language and thought.[14] The need to make the connection between language and thought—between linguistics and epistemology—is then developed by Gournay with a series of striking metaphors for writing and reading, reminiscent of Rabelais, Montaigne, and earlier classical authors:

> To conclude, it is necessary to break the kernel with effort, to break the bone, and bite crisply the apple, not to lick them or suck them softly, for whoever wants to extract the nut, the marrow, and the good substance which they hide.[15]

The end of this development repeats and spells out what Gournay believes to be the proper relationship between language and thought, again making an opposition between firmness and softness: "speech being exactly an image of spirit (so that accordingly as language is firm and solid, or slack and soft, it shows which of these two characteristics the idea holds)."[16] But the "nouveaux maistres" have banished strong, forceful writing, replacing it with their "tendres douceurs." Once again, it is clear that Gournay is using male sexual metaphors, probably borrowed from Montaigne, and through him from ancient authors, to describe forceful writing.

She closes the "Deffence" with the hope that she has converted the reader to an appreciation of ancient poetry—she has gone on at such length because she feels that this defense was needed. Curiously, by the end of the treatise, it is no longer Ronsard and his contemporaries who are being defended, but the ancients:

Can I insist too much on the defense of ancient and legitimate poetry, against the furious aggression of the new poetry, its parricidal daughter, so that she puts this illustrious mother in danger of destruction.... I would be happy and glad, Reader, if I could lead you to love antiquity, because being myself of that date, I would hope to glean in the process some particle of your good graces.[17]

Gournay defends the ancients, and also explains why she is such a strong defender—she herself is ancient! Interestingly, we see modern poetry represented here as a female—"sa parricide fille"—who has killed her parents, ancient poetry and rhetoric. Gournay, on the other hand, "covenant daughter of Montaigne" ("fille d'alliance de Montaigne"), defends and supports her literary ancestors.

In reading the "Deffence," we are first introduced to language change as the reason the poetry of Ronsard and Du Bellay is no longer valued as it once was. But as the treatise develops, it is evident that Gournay is not just talking about language change. Rather, she reveals a whole constellation of related issues: changing views of the role of the poet and of poetic language, and, behind that, declining respect for the ancients, their language, and their humanistic conception of literature. Gournay tries valiantly to defend all these things, but throughout the "Deffence," as in her other works of literary theory, we sense the reasons that have brought her to write in the first place. Often in a rhetorical and declamatory manner, she documents pedagogical, political, religious, and social factors that account, in her opinion, for this changed perception of Ronsard and Du Bellay, as well as for a changed definition of language and literature themselves.

Occasionally Gournay makes comments about the political and religious climate of the early seventeenth century, which she feels is not conducive to great language and literature, either prose or poetry.

Early in the "Deffence," she offers an explanation as to why France has not produced its own Cicero:

And I would add, that if we regard Cicero as the supreme Orator, such people don't occur in a Monarchy, where superiority in thought and letters is always transferred to the other functions of the Muses, if these Goddesses deign to honor such states with their favors at all.[18]

Anticipating some eighteenth-century analyses of the cultural impact of different forms of government, Gournay seems to be telling us that not until France becomes a republic will serious oratory flourish. The muses appear to have been co-opted by the need for frivolous occasional poetry celebrating the monarch and his family.

Not only the form of government but also the direction of religion is harmful to language. The "nouveaux Docteurs" are among those who have imposed a new prudery on language, to which Gournay objects. They have also forbidden the use of diminutives, which, she points out, are used extensively in the Bible.

Gournay does find exceptions to these linguistic trends, however, and cites the king himself, the Cardinal Richelieu, and several "Prélats" as authorities on language use, which she feels political and religious leaders should be:

> So I can't abstain here by exception, from turning once more my eyes toward the writings of the Most Eminent Cardinal the Duke of Richelieu to see whether his style follows the laws of the new doctors.... And how also this Cardinal, pillar of the State, and whose name the highest Crowns can't hear without fear, if they are enemies of France; wouldn't he also be a pillar of language, which is a part of the same state, and of the stability of which he has such need for the conservation of his writings.[19]

Gournay is clearly searching for a source of authority in linguistic matters, and feels that she cannot go wrong in selecting the cardinal and the king—political authority figures. They do not speak "the language of the Court" ("le langage de la Cour"), but actually use "some of the terms most severely forbidden by our correctors" ("aucuns des termes les plus sévèrement deffendus par nos correcteurs"). She concludes this section in a triumphant manner, having proven that the court is at fault, not the king and his councillors, who still use the "old words" ("vieux mots"). Authoritative male institutions are those to which Gournay appeals in her attempt to stem the tide of frivolous "salon" usage.

Most of Gournay's wrath is reserved, however, for the frivolity and ignorance of young people at court. They seem to have no education, nor are they interested in getting any—they change linguistic fashion the way they change fashions in dress. Appearance is all that counts—not substance. Clearly, these arguments about the superficiality of a world of appearance at court are closely related to the statements about the superficiality of language itself, and the fact that "they"—her enemies— are misled by appearance to think that language has changed more since the sixteenth century than Gournay believes that it actually has.[20] The "Deffence" is filled with attacks on the "young curly heads" ("jeunes frisés"), who now seem to legislate language use with a "touch of the comb" ("tour de pigne"), and who appear, oddly enough, to be in league with the *poëtes grammairiens,* in dethroning Ronsard, Du Bellay, and the ancients.

Both groups seem to feel that by eliminating old, ugly, or awkward words, language can be polished and perfected—but "a parrot can say or not say as much, and will become the Homer of the century at this price when it pleases him." Since these people don't read, their vocabulary is not enriched with the resources of the past. In one of her pungent physical metaphors about language Gournay suggests that "they would have given her a kick in the stomach to make her abort."[21]

The ignorance of the *poëtes grammairiens* is appalling: "Still there is no boy of fifteen at school, who would not know how to teach them to speak and write." Fashion, rather than education, dictates language, which can change from breakfast to dinner: "unfortunate that we are if we don't go to the dressing of these lords and ladies every morning, to learn in what language we will order dinner." Language changes from day to day: "more flighty and changeable than those feathers that they wear on their heads."[22]

With this emphasis on ignorance, frivolity, and fashion, it is not surprising that Gournay attacks as well the role of women in language change. Despite her feminist inclinations, as well as the fact that the "Deffence" is dedicated to a woman, Gournay does find women largely at fault in the degeneration of language, and in the lack of respect for the great authors she holds dear.[23] Throughout the "Deffence," she takes great pains to distance herself from the women of the "cabinets et ruelles," who seem to support the *poëtes grammairiens* like Malherbe, and who are the first to reject Ronsard and Du Bellay on the basis of their old-fashioned language.[24]

Living language is being stifled by the removal of perfectly good words, at the request of women, so that the very people who forbid these words are forced to admit that the common people use them, the councils of the king, preachers, parliament, even the court, except for a small number of dried out wits, mostly female, whom they have roped in to their way of thinking.[25]

Not only do women have permission to decide which words they do and don't like, but now "they" have decreed that nothing should be written or said that women could not understand:

> I am afraid that those who invented the rule which holds so much credit in the new school, to say nothing that women don't understand, didn't understand anything that they didn't already have in common with women.[26]

Women's intelligence has become a limiting factor in what might be said. Everyone has always known "how they talked in the Cabinet of women at Court" ("comme on devisoit au Cabinet des Dames de Cour," 117), but no one ever thought of using this language as a standard. But, she realizes, for the *poëtes grammairiens,* pleasing these women will lead to invitations to their homes: "But here is the secret.... they can get by the good will of the Ladies, various nice favors like good tables and opulent houses, for which the people who quarrel with us, have persevered." Montaigne would never have stooped so low. He encouraged the reader to hang onto old words, but would not have called words old that everyone uses: "palaces, councils, even kings, and everyone...except for the sweet ladies."[27] Moreover, the so-called old words are only so because these "dames sucrées" refuse to use them—and in fact women never did use most of these words, because they are too vigorous for women:

> For if these words are old because women don't use them today, they were already old seventy years ago: because I can assure you, that I never heard a woman use them, if she didn't desire the honor of intelligence and of the pen: nor did I ever hear women say fifty others as much and more common and legitimate: because their feeble and thin conversation has nothing to do with force, variety, or vigor.[28]

We see a return here to the metaphors about language use—strong and weak, male and female—discussed earlier. The latent sexual associations

Marie de Gournay   287

with different kinds of language are now explicitly applied to the ways in which real men and women talk.

These women seem to have no conception of the natural growth and development of language, refusing the root of a word, for example, while keeping one of its offshoots: "so that we see branches without a trunk, and adjectives or participles without a noun."[29] With a particularly savory parallel, Gournay compares this linguistic use to the idea of producing children without a father: "Well, wouldn't our chambermaids call this, making children without a father, for fear that they might piss in the bed?" ("Quoy donc, nos chambrieres appelleroient-elles point cela: faire des enfans sans pere, de peur qu'ils ne pissassent au lict?") Women's prudery toward etymological roots has something of this prudery about biological roots, and particularly about the role of the male in the generation of language. Gournay's defense of natural language growth shows an earlier Renaissance attitude toward language as part of raw nature, while her suspicion of contemporary Parisian usage is related to her dislike of the urban, indoor, artificial life it reflects, which is essentially female.[30]

During the last section of the "Deffence," Gournay continues to struggle with what it is about women's conversation that she objects to—since normally she takes the position that usage should be taken seriously for its contribution to language change. Aristotle, Cicero, Erasmus, Scaliger—all invented words and built on their predecessors: "all this how far removed from this silly whim, to base one's writings on the conversation of the ladies!" Over and over, as she tries to conclude the "Deffence," Gournay opposes two views of poetry: one, "that of the universal centuries, and most illustrious in doctrine and complacency"; the other, "that one can say, as do these people, that the fashion has changed, in imitation of a dress or a bonnet."[31] One is clearly the humanistic ideal that Gournay inherits from the sixteenth century and, through it, from the great writers of antiquity. The other is a matter of contemporary poetic and linguistic fashion, adopted like the other fashions in an arbitrary and frivolous manner, largely by women.[32]

How are we to interpret Gournay's surprising attacks on women as largely responsible for the crisis of language in her time? It is hard to know, first of all, whether to take these statements seriously or not. Gournay, a "vieille fille" of seventy by the time Les Advis was published, may well have been jealous of the younger women at whose salons such *poëtes grammairiens* as Malherbe were received. Or, she may have wished to distance herself from some of the more superficial women of her time, including feminists, who claimed extravagant abilities with very little education, talent, or accomplishment. Although Gournay was a self-proclaimed feminist, and wrote two feminist tracts ("De l'égalité" and "Grief des Dames"), she seems more concerned to make women similar to men—through education and increased opportunities—than to define any specifically feminine characteristics as superior.

But taking her statements seriously, for the sake of argument, we may be able to see some truth in the theory that women helped to nail the lid on the coffin of humanism, and even, for a moment, to see why they might have done so.

Humanism proposed a very elitist model for intelligence and creativity.[33] Humanists were to be well born, well educated, and, above all, male. Almost without exception, the authors championed by Gournay were members of an elite caste who would certainly have considered women, and probably Gournay herself, to be part of the *vulgaire*. At least some of the hostility, among the women described by Gournay, toward Ronsard and his contemporariesmay have been due to the rising tide of feminism in seventeenth-century France, with its revival of the "querelle des femmes" and heightened awareness of women's point of view in dialogue. These women readers, like many women readers today, may have reacted against what can only be called the male-centered viewpoint of humanist poetry, and the way in which it frequently denies women—even those with whom the poet is supposedly in love—a voice or point of view.

From this perspective, the arguments by seventeenth-century women about language may have covered up for a more profound dissatisfaction with the worldview of humanism. "On ne parle plus ainsi" may refer to more than just changing details of grammar and vocabulary, but rather to a changed view of discourse, to a changed relationship between speaker and listener, writer and reader, toward one of more equality. The importance of "la conversation des Dames" to changing views of poetry may be, in part, that the model of the ode, for example, where the lady, fountain, or forest does not answer back, is no longer adequate to describe a more realistic, social definition of linguistic exchange.

But Gournay herself is totally oblivious to the sexism of her authors, and does not really seem to think of herself, as a writer, as being a woman. For this reason, her attacks on women follow logically some of the borrowed male-centered metaphors for language that we earlier saw developed in her statements about language change.

Contemporary French is weak and lifeless—effeminate—while Latin and the French of the humanists influenced by Latin is strong and vigorous—masculine. Even the *mots/choses* distinction seems to fall into this polarity. Words themselves are weak, prosaic, and ordinary. They are part of the world of women—superficial, like their clothing and cosmetics. The abortion metaphor quoted above shows language as female, as well. But things—ideas—to which words should point are strong, inspired, and heroic. They partake of the divine, which is male.

Attacks on women for their responsibility in the current degeneration of language and literature may themselves therefore function metaphorically. When Gournay speaks of "la conversation des Dames," she may really simply be referring to the worldly, fallen, modern view of language, described as female in the metaphors that she uses. Despite the fact that Gournay's observations may be largely metaphorical, however, they do offer an insight into some of the social changes that accompanied—and perhaps hastened—the demise of humanism. We seem to have a case here of metaphor and social change progressing together: a sort of chicken and egg dilemma.[34]

The two literary quarrels of the seventeenth century—the "Querelle des Anciens et des Modernes" and the "Querelle des Femmes"—are oddly joined in Gournay, who is practically the only "partisan des Anciens" among women, who are generally on the side of the "Modernes." Gournay seems to function as the exception that proves the rule—she recognizes that the lofty humanist ideal of language and literature does not fit the contemporary reality of greater social control of both, by the bourgeoisie as well as by women. When she laments the fact that words are no longer ruled by ideas, but may actually begin to create a separate reality themselves (as Foucault, among others, has suggested),[35] she may also be noting one of the polarities that kept words subordinate to ideas, in poetic theory, in the first place.[36] The association of women with language—*garrulitas*, especially—and the need to keep women's tongues under control may initially have reflected the idea that language itself was wayward, female, needing control by the more rational, orderly, authoritative male mind. Resistance to the emerging view that language in fact creates reality, knowledge, and theory—rather than being created by them—may have come from some of the same deep-seated suspicions we see expressed by Gournay and others in the late Renaissance, toward vernacular language as a powerful but deceptive, wayward, capricious force, which is gaining ground despite attempts by authoritative institutions such as Church and State to repress it. The decline of humanism, and of its language, Latin, may have been hastened by women and by the language that they spoke, the vernacular.[37] But in addition, the conception of language associated with women is one that has become dominant since the seventeenth century—a conception of language based on real, verbal social exchange rather than abstract written statements about language.

Gournay manages to ignore most of the disturbing implications of her rhetoric about "la conversation des Dames" as they might apply to herself. Nonetheless, her book may provide an example of this conversation, and of its increasing power to note and even to dictate language change. Rather than simply observing the process, Gournay, a woman writer, is inescapably part of it.

NOTES

1. Although Gournay's edition of Montaigne's *Essais* (Paris: L'Angelier, 1595) had been in disrepute for centuries, in the past ten years it has reemerged as an authoritative text, in part through the efforts of David Maskell.

2. The full titles of these collected works are: *L'Ombre de la Demoiselle de Gournay; oeuvre composée de meslanges* (Paris: Jean Libert, 1626); and *Les Advis ou les presens de la Demoiselle de Gournay* (Paris: Toussainct Du Bray, 1634, 1641). The essays from these collections that treat literary and linguistic themes have been reprinted in Anne Uildriks, *Les Idées littéraires de Mlle. de Gournay* (Groningen: Kleine, 1962). Unless otherwise indicated, I quote from the Uildriks edition of the "Deffence de la Poësie." Translations are my own.

3. Gournay, 96: "Je sors d'une maison où j'ay veu jetter au vent les venerables cendres de Ronsard et des Poëtes ses contemporains, autant qu'une impudence d'ignorans le peut faire"; "leur grand et general Refrain butte sur leur langage, alleguans: *On ne parle plus ainsi.*" (Emphasis added.) Marjorie Ilsley believes that this house was probably that of Madame des Loges, where Gournay may have met Malherbe and other linguistic theorists of her time (*A Daughter of the Renaissance: Marie le Jars de Gournay, Her Life and Works* [The Hague: Mouton, 1963], 134).

4. Gournay, 96: "elle ne peut marcher qu'à pas d'escrevisse." Richard Katz agrees with Gournay that actually the French language had not changed so much

Marie de Gournay   291

since the sixteenth century as theorists like Malherbe seemed to believe (*Ronsard's French Critics: 1585–1828* [Geneva: Droz, 1966], 50).

5. Gournay, 97: "L'appetit des François si friand au change."

6. Gournay, 97: "Chacun artisan praticque son mestier selon la mesure de son esprit, et nous sommes artisans en nostre langue: c'est à dire, non seulement tenues de la débiter selon que nous l'avons apprise et receuë, mais encore de la mouler, informer et bastir, pour enlasser biens sur biens, et beautés sur beautés."

7. Gournay, 98: "et les langues cherchent autant le progres, qu'elles fuyent ce rebut ou reculement, peste des fruicts qu'elles ont produicts"; "Toutes fois voicy tousjours nostre Refrain triomphant: On ne parle plus ainsi, *la mode est changée.*" (Emphasis added.)

8. Richard Waswo, *Language and Meaning in the Renaissance* (Princeton, N.J.: Princeton University Press, 1987). See especially part 2, chap. 3, "The Challenge from Philosophy." In this chapter Waswo discusses the work of Valla and Vives, and shows how they introduced relativism into what had previously been an absolutist, Platonic view of language.

9. Montaigne, *The Complete Essays of Montaigne,* trans. Donald M. Frame (Stanford: Stanford University Press, 1958), II, 16, 468 A: "Il y a le nom et la chose; le nom, c'est une voix qui remerque et signifie la chose; le nom, ce n'est pas une partie de la chose ny de la substance, c'est une piece estrangere joincte à la chose, et hors d'elle."

10. Gournay, 133: "c'est l'exprimer seulement à moitié, c'est dire l'escorce et non la chose, ou pour mieux parler, c'est la siffler et non pas la dire."

11. Gournay, 133: "La raison est, qu'elle ne se dit que par celuy qui la comprend: et ce doux diseur ou explicateur à leur mode, n'a garde de la comprendre ny partant de la faire comprendre à autruy: son imagination ne donnant qu'une mole et foible atteinte en la superficie des sujets, qui ne se peuvent percer jusques à la mouelle, comme il est requis pour les expremer pleinement, sinon par une atteinte vive et puissante: laquelle le bout de la langue d'un tel homme, aussi timide qu'elle est enervée et flouëtte, n'a garde de leur pouvoir donner, parce qu'elle n'ose entreprendre de percer, de peur de reboucher sa poincte."

12. See Robert Cottrell's discussion of this sort of metaphor in Montaigne, in his *Sexuality/Textuality: A Study of the Fabric of Montaigne's "Essais"* (Columbus: Ohio State University Press, 1981).

13. Gournay, 133: "Quelle merveille, puis qu'un langage est fils de l'esprit, que la pluspart de ses richesses soient abstraictes et profondes à l'imitation de celles de son pere!" See Waswo on the theological aspects of the connections between word and idea, in particular part 3, "Arguments about the Word."

14. Gournay also wrote a treatise on metaphor, "Sur la version des poëtes antiques, ou des metaphores," which ostensibly examines the question of whether it is possible to translate metaphors. But there is also a strong sense, in that essay, that a respect for metaphor was one of the qualities of ancient and

Pléiade poetry that is gradually being lost in the seventeenth century. Metaphors point toward ideas that may be abstract or difficult to grasp—Gournay sees seventeenth-century readers as not willing to make that effort. Ilsley notes the fact that Gournay defends the baroque conception of metaphor, ahead of most of her contemporaries (149).

15. Gournay, 133: "Pour conclure, il faut casser un noyau avec effort, il faut briser un os, et mordre vertement une pomme, non pas les lecher ou morciller doucettement, qui veut extraire l'amande, la mouelle, et la bonne substance qu'ils recellent." The apple metaphor for humanism itself has been discussed by Philippe Desan in his introduction to this collection, with the suggestive notion that "a worm was in the apple" from the beginning. In stating that seventeenth-century readers are no longer willing to bite the apple, Gournay may testify to a decline in the belief that there is a canon or common body of knowledge (the apple of the tree of knowledge?) that readers wish to pluck and eat. The apple metaphor may suggest a decline in consensus about what knowledge is and why it is important.

16. Gournay, 134: "Le parler estant exactement une image de l'esprit (de sorte que selon qu'il est ferme et solide, ou lasche et mol, il faict voir à quel de ces deux divers poincts l'esprit se chauffe)."

17. Gournay, 157: "Me puis-je trop bander sur la revanche de l'antique et legitime Poësie, contre de si furieuses aggressions de la nouvelle, sa parricide fille, qu'elles mettent cette illustre mere en peril de naufrage.... Je serois heureuse et fine, lecteur, si je te pouvois induire d'aymer l'Antiquité; puis qu'estant moy-mesme de cette datte, j'espererois de grapiller parmy le marché quelque parcelle en ta bonne grace."

18. Gournay, 99: "Et je repartiray, que si nous le regardons comme Orateur supreme, telles personnes n'arrivent point en un Estat Monarchique, quand la suffisance de l'esprit et des Lettres, se trouve tousjours devoluë aux autres fonctions des Muses, si ces Deesses daignent honorer de tels Estats de leur faveur."

19. Gournay, 121–22: "Si ne puis-je abstenir icy par exception, de tourner encore les yeux vers les Escrits de l'Ementissime Cardinal Duc de Richelieu, pour voir si leur éloqution est soubmise aux loix de ces nouveaux Docteurs.... Et comment aussi ce Cardinal, pillier de l'Estat, et dont les plus superbes Couronnes ne peuvent pas ouyr le nom sans crainte, si elles sont ennemies de la France; ne seroit-il pas en suitte pillier de la Langue, qui est une partie du mesme Estat, et de la stabilité de laquelle il a tel besoin pour la conservation de ses Escrits."

20. See also Waswo's discussion of cosmetic and clothing metaphors for language, implying that words only "clothe" ideas, rather than creating them. For example, in chapter 4, "The Challenge from Vernaculars," he describes the clothing metaphor used frequently in sixteenth-century language theory (189–90).

21. Gournay, 108: "un perroquet en peut autant dire et taire, et deviendra l'Homère du Siecle à ce prix quand il luy plaira"; and 109: "ils luy eussent donné le coup de pied par le ventre pour la faire avorter."

22. Gournay, 111: "Toutefois il n'y a garçon de quinze ans au College, qui ne leur sçache donner tablature de bien parler et de bien escrire"; 126: "malheureux que nous sommes si nous n'allons à l'habiller de ces Milords et Milordes tous les matins, apprendre en quel langage nous demanderons à disner!"; and 130: "plus volage et flottant que ces plumes qu'ils portent sur la teste."

23. The "Deffence" is dedicated to Madame des Loges, Marie de Blaineau. In the same collection of essays, there are two feminist tracts, "De l'égalité des hommes et des femmes" and "Grief des Dames." These essays have been reprinted in Mario Schiff, *La Fille d'alliance de Montaigne: Marie de Gournay* (Paris: Champion, 1910).

24. In the introduction to *L'Automne de la Renaissance*, Jean Mesnard comments on the connections between the court, Malherbe, and women: "Le véritable usage sur lequel entend se régler Malherbe est celui de la cour, dans la mesure où elle est lieu de haute culture, et sur celui des cercles, le plus souvent féminins, qui en prolongent ou en accusent l'esprit" (*L'Automne de la Renaissance, 1580–1630*, ed. Jean Lafond and André Stegmann [Paris: J. Vrin, 1981], 14).

25. Gournay, 98: "qu'eux mesmes qui les proscrivent sont forcez d'advouer, que le Vulgaire les employe, les Conseils du Roy, les Predicateurs, le Parlement, la Cour mesme, excepté quelque petit nombre d'esprits essorées, feminins sur tout, qu'ils ont recordez à leur mode."

26. Gournay, 115: "J'ay peur que ceux qui furent inventeurs de cette regle de si grand crédit en la nouvelle Escolle, de ne rien dire que les Dames n'entendissent; n'entendoient rien qui ne leur fust commun avec elles."

27. Gournay, 136: "Mais voicy le secret... on peut tirer par la bienveillance des Dames, plusieurs faveurs commodes des bonnes tables et des maisons opulentes, à qui ces personnes qui nous querellent, ont rendu de tout temps plus d'assiduité"; and 139–40: "les Palais, les Conseils, les Roys mesmes, et tout le monde... à la réserve seule des Dames sucrées."

28. Gournay, 142: "Que si ces mots là sont vieux parce qu'elles ne les employent pas à cette heure, ils l'estoient avant 70 ans: car je puis asseurer, que je ne les ouys oncques dire à femme, si elle n'envyoit l'honneur de l'esprit et de la plume: ny ne leur en ouys jamais prononcer 50 autres autant et plus communs et legitimes: à cause que leur foible et mince conversation n'a que faire d'uberté, ny de variété, non plus que de vigueur."

29. Gournay, 143: "affin qu'on vist des branches sans tronc, et des épithètes ou participes sans nom." See Michel Charles's discussion of the use of tree metaphors for language in the seventeenth century, in *L'arbre et la Source* (Paris: Seuil, 1985).

30. Uildriks comments on the fact that women did make up a large portion of the expanded readership for literature during the early seventeenth century. Gournay was not happy with the lowering of intellectual standards that this seemed to bring ("Deffence," 40).

31. Gournay, 147: "tout cela combien eslongé de cette joyeuse humeur, de regler ses Escrits sur la conversation des Dames!"; and 152: "celle des Siecles universels, et plus illustres en doctrine et en suffisance"; "qu'on peust dire, comme font ces personnes, que la mode est changée, à l'imitation de celle d'une robe et d'un bonnet."

32. Carolyn Lougee comments that one of the changes effected through feminism in the early seventeenth century was the denigration of the heroic values that in fact shaped much humanist poetry (*Le Paradis des Femmes: Women, Salons, and Social Stratification in Seventeenth-Century France* [Princeton, N.J.: Princeton University Press, 1976], 31).

33. In his introduction, Jean Mesnard comments, for example, that for the Pléiade humanists, poetry is "un art réservé à une élite, et plus accessible aux humanistes qu'au public de cour" (7).

34. Nancy Miller sums up this relationship when she says, "Feminist criticism has shown that the social construction of sexual difference plays a constitutive role in the production, reception, and history of literature" (*The Poetics of Gender* [New York: Columbia University Press, 1986], xi).

35. In chapter 2 of *Les Mots et les choses* (*The Order of Things*), Foucault describes his sense that by the seventeenth century, words and things are separated from each other, losing the profound "analogy" that linked the two before that. Gournay, like Montaigne, may well be a witness to this shift. A remark of Foucault's that is even more relevant to the present study is his suggestion that spoken language is female, while written language is male (*The Order of Things: An Archeology of the Human Sciences* [New York: Random House, 1970], 39).

36. Richard Waswo has commented that association of sexual processes with mental and linguistic ones lies dormant in most Indo-European languages (178).

37. Father Ong has made this point in a number of his works, for example in *The Presence of the Word: Some Prolegomena for Cultural and Religious History* (New Haven, Conn.: Yale University Press, 1967). In chapter 5, Ong develops the links between "Commerce, Vernaculars, and Education of Women" (241–55): "The link between these seemingly disparate phenomena is their common tendency to eat away at the Latin base for training in verbal expression and in thinking which connected the old dialectico-rhetorical academic tradition directly with the highly oral culture of antiquity" (241).

Descartes and Humanism: The Critique of *Bricolage*

Fernand Hallyn

The subject and scope of this article necessitate a twofold qualifier. Its purpose will be neither to offer analysis based on new texts nor to treat the texts in question in an exhaustive manner within these few pages; this essay simply proposes to shed new light on several crucial passages. Second, Descartes's attitude toward Renaissance humanism should not be viewed as characteristic of the period; the first half of the seventeenth century is well acquainted with many remnants of humanism as well as many forms of "antihumanism,"[1] but it is with Descartes that the will to break with tradition takes its clearest, most decisive form in the history of thought.

Although Descartes clearly affirms his intention to begin anew the thinking process without letting himself be dominated by the cultural memory of humanity, it is not difficult to point out all that he owes or seems to owe to tradition itself. Without dwelling on discussions that had already circulated in the seventeenth century (notably on the antecedents of the *cogito*), and in order to limit ourselves to some of the most important studies, let us remember that Etienne Gilson has undertaken a systematic research project exploring affinities with "medieval humanism";[2] that Henri Gouhier has shown, in the early work, the persistence of traditional metaphysical themes coexisting with topics concerning mathematical physics;[3] and that Giovanni Crapulli has traced the history of the idea of a *mathesis universalis* in the sixteenth century.[4]

It is true, however, that Descartes himself does not in any way deny that one can find "Cartesian ideas" in previous works by other thinkers and other authors. After rejecting all previous conceptions, he reserves the right to "replace them afterwards with better ones, or with the same

296 Humanism in Crisis

ones... squared with the standards of reason."[5] He does not pride himself on the complete originality of each of his ideas: "I do not boast of being the first to discover any of them, but I do claim to have accepted them not because they have, or have not, been expressed by others, but solely because reason has convinced me of them."[6] Perhaps the clearest passage illuminating the relationship between Descartes's writing and its eventual sources can be found in the following passage of Baillet's biography:

> M. Descartes, being the first to admit that what he was saying had already been said by others, excused this charge by likening it to accusing a writer of pillaging the alphabet or the dictionary simply because he had used the letters of the one, and the words of the other. He then added that those who recognize the connection between ideas will soon agree that this man is as innocent of theft as the able orator charged with plagiarizing Calepin and Evandre for having borrowed the words from one and the letters from the other.[7]

The originality to which Descartes lays claim lies not in the particularity of the ideas themselves, but rather in the form that discourse takes, in the new sense of inner cohesion and connection. As we know, the model of this new coherence is found in the deductive logic of mathematics. Everything that enters this realm is called to adhere to the internal structure of reason, and to resist falling prey to the mere imitation of an outside source. No doubt the fourth of the *Regulae* concedes that certain classical thinkers had a presentiment of the discursive method, but they knew it in an imperfect form, or "with a kind of pernicious cunning, later suppressed this mathematics as, notoriously, many inventors are known to have done where their own discoveries were concerned."[8] In no way, then, does the search for actual precursors problematize the relationship to culture in specifically Cartesian terms.

This Cartesian position, however, becomes clearer in the *Discours de la méthode*, where it is illuminated by the oblique light of several comparisons, of which the most famous, and the most inevitable, calls upon the image of a building or of a city.

> Thus we see that buildings undertaken and completed by a single architect are usually more attractive and better planned than those which several have tried to patch up by adapting old walls built for

different purposes. Again, ancient cities which have gradually grown from mere villages into large towns are usually ill-proportioned, compared with those orderly towns which planners lay out as they fancy on level ground. Looking at the buildings of the former individually, you will often find as much art in them, if not more, than in those of the latter; but in view of their arrangement—a tall one here, a small one there—and the way they make the streets crooked and irregular, you would say it is chance, rather than the will of men using reason, that placed them so.[9]

Interchangeable images depicting the history of thought, the building, and the city patched up through the years impose the idea of time without real divisions. Philosophical discourse from antiquity to Descartes consists only of a series of adaptations and extensions. There remains no fundamental distinction between the Middle Ages and the Renaissance,[10] no real innovation by the humanism of the fifteenth and sixteenth centuries. The only true rupture will be the one that Descartes himself seeks to effectuate, and to which Eudoxe, his spokesman in *Recherche de la vérité*, applies the same comparison:

I would compare it [knowledge] to a badly constructed house, whose foundations are not firm. I know of no better way to repair it than to knock it all down, and build a new one in its place. For I do not wish to be one of those jobbing builders who devote themselves solely to refurbishing old buildings.[11]

Accommodation, re-accommodation: these activities of the small-time artisan, which in the first comparison sum up the activity of human thought until Descartes, correspond to the notion of *bricolage*. In addition, to take up the well-known opposition developed by Lévi-Strauss,[12] the discursive break that Descartes seeks to bring to light in the second comparison can be read as the opposition between the work of a *bricoleur* and that of an *ingénieur*. If Lévi-Strauss describes savage or primitive thought as a *bricolage*, the ironies of intertextuality are such that in the letter prefacing the *Passions de l'âme*, Father Picot compares anti-Cartesian thought to that of the savage peoples of America.

[I]t is easy to prove that an undue reverence toward antiquity can be detrimental to the advancement of science, for we witness, in the savage peoples of America, and in several others closer at hand, a standard of living inferior to our own, even though their heritage is as old as our own. Therefore, they are as right as we when they say they are satisfied with the wisdom of their forefathers, and they do not believe anyone could teach them anything better than what has been known, and what has been practiced in antiquity. This point of view is so detrimental that, as long as one clings to it, no new capacities can be gained.[13]

Moreover, primitive thought has often been compared to an infantile mode of thinking, "a timid and stuttering form of science."[14] The comparison of a thought process that dares not cross the threshold of adolescence is a recurring theme in Descartes.[15] We must outgrow our childhood, for we are truly adults, the real ancients of the world:

I do not see why we continue to revere antiquity on the sole grounds that the ancients possess the quality of ancientness. Surely, "ancient" is a name we deserve more than they, because the world is older now than it was in their day, and we have more experience than they.[16]

It is not necessary, in these pages, to judge, to approve, or to condemn the schematic and polemic manner in which Descartes describes the persistence of old modes of thinking, of ancient thought patterns. More pertinent is the analysis of its meaning—or one of its meanings—through examination of the notion of *bricolage*, which illuminates the coherence between the criticism and the images.

Bricolage, before all else, presupposes an innate conservatism, the collection of objects, of elements, even of remnants and of debris. For the *bricoleur*, the pieces of his collection constitute his repertoire of instruments, instruments with which he either repairs and transforms existing objects or constructs new ones. His creed is to always "make do with whatever is at hand," to use the previous ends as present means, to work constantly toward reorganizations of the given repertoire. He "neither extends nor renews it, and limits [himself] to obtaining the group of its transformations."[17] The humanist thinker, writes Descartes in the *Discours*, "makes use of old walls which had been built for other purposes" ("se servir de vieilles murailles qui avaient été bâties à d'autres fins"), instead of forging new and appropriate means when confronted with a specific goal to attain.

The tools at the disposition of the *bricoleur,* like those of the humanist, are constituted by culture and operate by means of signs.[18] Through analysis and new syntheses one might, as is the case with Ficino, "trace from Plato an image as close as possible to Christian truth."[19] With this practice, sign and meaning constantly change status:[20] what was sign for Plato (text) became meaning for Ficino (object of the new philosophical discourse), whereas what was meaning for Plato (his philosophy) becomes for Ficino the sign of a certain apprehension of Christian truth outside of revelation.

Intellectual *bricolage,* especially when applied to the written text, maintains one particularity over manual *bricolage* this being that the re-utilization of the mental object does not necessarily imply the material destruction of this object in its previous form. It remains intact alongside the new objects. One can always read the works of Plato along with Ficino's *Théologie platonicienne.* Old objects then coexist with the new, and the number of elements available to the *bricoleur* continually augments.

For Descartes, the passage through this assemblage of texts and the ensuing task of reciprocal transformation of sign and meaning hardly represent the regal path of knowledge and wisdom. To be sure, there exists a human nature, and each man carries within himself "the seeds of truth,"[21] but these seeds have yet to be methodically cultivated. Furthermore, erudition (the constitution of personal collection) demands an inordinately large investment of time in relation to the value of the acquired knowledge; erudition remains a cluttered workshop where the true and the good coexist with the erroneous and the useless in the greatest disorder:

> But I do not wish to consider what others have known or not known. I am content to observe that even if all the knowledge that can be desired were contained in books, the good things in them would be mingled with so many useless things, and scattered haphazardly through such a pile of massive tomes, that we should need more time for reading them than our present life allows, and more intelligence for picking out the useful material than would be required for discovering it on our own.[22]

Culture ceases to be a value in and of itself; its interest becomes primarily anthropological in nature. If the human spirit proves itself endowed with the seeds of truth, one also finds among these seeds errancy and error. The criticism is that of an *ingénieur* speaking of a *bricoleur*:

> [T]he engineer is always trying to make his way out of and go beyond the constraints imposed by a particular state of civilization while the *bricoleur* by inclination or by necessity always remains within them. This is another way of saying that the engineer works by means of concepts and the *bricoleur* by means of signs. The sets which each employs are at different distances from the poles on the axis of opposition between nature and culture. One way indeed in which signs can be opposed to concepts is that whereas concepts aim to be wholly transparent with respect to reality, signs allow and even require the interposing and incorporation of a certain amount of human culture into reality.[23]

Descartes reproaches this mentality of staying within the limits of a received cultural language. The humanist operates within a terminological universe, which, by virtue of its veneration of classical authors and its superimpositions of successive discourses, clearly possesses a "heavy layer of human culture." For Descartes, humanity is not only "incorporated into reality"; humanity often screens reality completely from view. Instead of being transparent to reality, "almost all of our words have confused meanings";[24] even the "learned," when they conceive of things, "fail to explain them in terms which are quite appropriate."[25] Moreover, if the meaning lacks clarity and distinctness, it is because the signs central to the *bricolage* mindset refer constantly back to other signs, without ever clearly defining their relationship with reality. Thus, when a man is defined as a reasonable animal,

> two other questions arise from this one. First, what is an *animal*? Second, what is *rational*? If, in order to explain what an animal is, he were to reply that it is a "living and sentient being," that a living being is an "animate body," and that a body is a "corporeal substance," you see immediately that the questions, like the branches of a family tree, would rapidly increase and multiply. Quite clearly, the result of

all these admirable questions would be pure verbiage, which would elucidate nothing and leave us in our original state of ignorance.[26]

Of all the tools at man's disposition, the received language is no doubt the most difficult to shed. Descartes knew this, yet without deluding himself with visions of success in the eyes of other men, he nonetheless dreamed of a universal language that, modeled after mathematics, would be of a perfect conceptual transparency:

[I]t [language] could be learnt very quickly. Order is what is needed: all the thoughts which can come into the human mind must be arranged in an order like the natural order of the numbers. In a single day one can learn to name every one of the infinite series of numbers, and thus to write infinitely many different words in an unknown language. The same thing could be done for all the other words necessary to express all the other things which fall within the purview of the human mind.[27]

Intellectual *bricolage,* according to Lévi-Strauss, is intrinsically tied to a science of the concrete. It is precisely this type of science that Descartes challenges when criticizing what constitutes its two principal aspects: the explanation of "the sensible world in sensory terms," and the recognition of both "physical properties and semantic properties."[28]

Descartes reproaches philosophy and the science taught in the schools for having rooted themselves in opinions, which, in most cases, either ring false or even contradict themselves. These opinions are, in turn, signs through which meaning corresponds to the concrete sensory impressions, signs that all too easily suggest a correspondence with things. Doubt should accompany the study of the world of sensory qualities: "because our senses sometimes deceive us, I decided to suppose that nothing was such as they led us to imagine."[29] A science worthy of this name does not content itself with exploring the concrete in which universal truth would already be given; it must include among its methodical inquiries the acid test of the truth of the sensible world: "We need a method if we are to investigate the truth of things."[30] These "things" would be the result of a method first posed in its abstract form, instead of being the concrete realities to which methods adapt themselves.

The *Dioptrique* constitutes a protest against a science of the concrete that studies the world as it appears to the senses. If the telescope is able to augment the power of sight, it also exposes the natural weakness of the sense upon which the concrete science of astronomy has been previously founded. Based on the example of the telescope, one can no longer be content to *bricoler* with the closed universe of instruments that constitute the senses in their natural state. The impulse that made Galileo turn the telescope toward the sky constituted indeed an act of an *ingénieur*, working toward the opening of knowledge rather than simply being satisfied with its reorganization: "though in use for only a short time," these telescopes "have already revealed a greater number of new stars and other objects above the earth than we had seen there before."[31]

Descartes does regret, however, that the telescope was "invented" largely by accident by a *bricoleur*, an artisan who was seeking to construct "mirrors and magnifying glasses" ("des miroirs et des verres brûlants") by combining "different shapes of glass" ("verres de diverses formes"). Descartes himself proposes to undertake the establishment of an optical theory. To him, it is only by way of this theoretical deduction (even if it is made a posteriori) that the telescope can definitively acquire the dignity of a valid scientific instrument. One might even say that for Descartes, the true inventor of the telescope was not the one who first fabricated it, but the one who first transformed it into a concept, rendering transparent its relation to reality.[32]

But this world in which the science of the concrete organizes and exploits the sensory quality in sensory terms is equally endowed with semantic properties. Man never leaves the universe of signs. The world as it appears to the senses is itself the signifier of a transcendental signified. In 1619 and 1620, at a time when many old elements subsist in the mind of young Descartes, the *Cogitationes privatae* admirably sums up this traditional conception of a world of signs:

Just as the imagination employs figures in order to conceive of bodies, so, in order to frame ideas of spiritual things, the intellect makes use of certain bodies which are perceived through the senses, such as wind and light. By this means we may philosophize in a more exalted way, and develop the knowledge to raise our minds to lofty heights.

The things which are perceivable by the senses are helpful in enabling us to conceive of Olympian matters. The wind signifies spirit; movement with the passage of time signifies life; light signifies knowledge; heat signifies love; and instantaneous activity signifies creation.[33]

A barrier separates such fragments from mathematical physics; nature is thought of in terms not of quantitative relationships, but of the qualities and concrete appearances of things that become integrated in a traditional symbolic language. Later, Descartes will refuse this line of reasoning. He will choose to speak the language of "man, purely man," deeming himself incapable of sustaining a theological or mystical discourse.[34] His discourse will remain "humanist," if you will, but only in the sense that Montaigne gives the word when he refers to writings "as being purely human and philosophical, with no admixture of theology."[35]

When speaking of the refusal of semantic properties, the recourse to new instruments is significant. The best example of this is no doubt found in the *Géométrie*. While Kepler still refuses to resort to algebra in his cosmology, and whereas he develops a theory of harmony based entirely on the dignity of figures traced with the ruler and the compass,[36] Descartes *opens* his universe of instruments in the most literal sense of the word, and at the same time deprives the mathematical universe of semantics. On the one hand, the choice between geometric representation and algebraic representation is given uniquely in terms of operativity, or of relational transparence in a given problem; on the other hand, an end is signaled to the reign of the ruler and the compass by the invention of a new instrument, composed of several rulers, that allows one to consider figures such as conic sections as "geometric" (and no longer "mechanical").

The first part of the *Discours de la méthode* can be seen as a Cartesian version of Montaigne's essay on "les trois commerces." After the erudition and the search for knowledge through books, the focus shifts to travel and to the contemporary world, both of which offer experiences that continue to deliver the author from "many errors" ("beaucoup d'erreurs"). Finally the best "commerce," the one upon which Descartes finally attaches the greatest value, is that of self-knowledge: "I resolved one day to undertake studies within myself too." The search for truth demands that the seeker place himself outside of history and society, "like a man who walks alone in the dark."[37]

This solitude does not, however, exclude all ties with humanity. As a whole, the sixth part of the *Discours* constitutes a very complex analysis of communication. If a complete study of it lies beyond the scope of this paper, let us at least cite a well-known passage in which Descartes goes so far as to evoke a new history of humanity spilling over into a utopian future for society:

> For they opened my eyes to the possibility of gaining knowledge which would be very useful in life, and of discovering a practical philosophy which might replace the speculative philosophy taught in the schools. Through this philosophy we could know the power and action of fire, water, air, the stars, the heavens and all the other bodies in our environment, as distinctly as we know the various crafts of our artisans; and we could use this knowledge—as the artisans use theirs—for all the purposes for which it is appropriate, and thus make ourselves, as it were, the lords and masters of nature.[38]

Men could dominate the elements, like "masters and possessors of nature" ("comme maîtres et possesseurs de la nature"). This affirmation resounds like an echo of the frequently heard humanist celebrations of the power of man. Man makes use of earth, water, air, and fire as if he were their master, writes Ficino: "quasi sit omnium dominus."[39] But whereas this mastery is a given for the humanist, it is a future state for Descartes. Furthermore, the text of the *Discours* proposes to supplant "the speculative philosophy that is taught in the Schools" ("philosophie spéculative qu'on enseigne dans les écoles") with a "practical" mode of acting in the world in order to change it. The humanist ideal lay, above all, in the realm of contemplative wonder. Man was to interiorize the world and to reconstitute the perfect reflection of it in his spirit, according to the theme of the intellectual microcosm as it appears notably in the work of Charles de Bovelles.[40] In this view, even the technique of the artisan had a narcissistic implication; Ficino gives a privileged status to work that "does not seek any corporal advantage," but in which reason, imitating natural wonders, finds "proof of its power...closely resembling divine nature."[41]

Other passages in Descartes suggest that he has no intention of proposing that man become a "god on earth" ("dieu sur terre") (not even with the attenuating "quasi" that allows Ficino to avoid blasphemy), but rather that he wants him to develop knowledge and wisdom of "man, purely man"—that is to say, man endowed with limited powers and fully aware of his limitations. Science, for Descartes, has the goal of hunting down and destroying the sense of wonder before the fallacious concreteness of the world (an idea illustrated in *Les Météores* by the example of a man in awe before a rainbow). As for the technique, rather than permit the comparison of human creations to the divine creation, this same divine creation will henceforth be reduced, by an inversion of movement, to a rational explanation of a human product, since we must try to know nature as distinctly as we know the various crafts of our artisans.[42]

André Lelande has correctly acknowledged an aspect of the Baconian ideal of science in the passage we cite.[43] We further add that in the preamble of *Redargutio philosophiarum,* Bacon presents himself, at the beginning of his undertaking, in a solitude as complete as that of Descartes in the *poêle* or in Holland:

—I am preparing a restoration of philosophy, so that it will be neither abstract nor empty, but a philosophy made for bettering the conditions of human life.
—The task is noble; who is helping you?
—Know that I work in complete isolation.[44]

However, when Descartes evokes, in a section following the passage that concerns us, the mastership of man over the world, where "innumerable devices... would facilitate our enjoyment of the fruits of the earth and all the goods we find there,"[45] does he truly believe in the reality of a paradisiacal future? In his letter to Mersenne in which he discusses a universal language, Descartes clearly states his mistrust of all utopian thought of the kind expressed in *The New Atlantis:* "For that, the order of nature would have to change so that the world turned into a terrestrial paradise, and that is too much to suggest outside of fairyland."[46]

How then can one explain the resolutely optimist and lyric sentiment in our passage? No doubt by the fact that the *Discours* belongs, in one of its dimensions, to "fairyland" ("pays des romans"); Descartes offers this text to be read as a fable, and if this genre "awakes the spirit" ("reveille l'esprit"), it does so, he says, by making us "imagine many events as possible when they are not."[47]

In short, science and technology (machines, engines, but also and above all medicine) could create a link with humanity that would be neither contemplative nor speculative, nor essentially utopian, but rather made of solidarity and of mutual aid. In this way Descartes affirms the sense of *humanitas* rejected by Aulus-Gellius in a definition that, based on Varro and Cicero, would dominate the acceptance of the term during the Renaissance:

> Those who created the Latin language, and those who spoke it well, did not give the word *humanitas* the vulgar meaning which is synonymous with the Greek word *philanthropia*, signifying an active complaisance, a tender amiability toward all men. Rather they gave this word a meaning that the Greeks called *paideia*, or what we call education and knowledge of culture. Those who display the most aptitude and the most inclination for this study are those worthy to be called *humanissimi*. For, of all earth's beings, only man is capable of devoting himself to the care and study of this discipline which has been called *humanitas*. Such is the meaning given to this word by the ancients, and by Varro and by Cicero in particular.[48]

Descartes's philosophy is certainly a critique of the Renaissance in the multiple meanings of the word *krisis* (separation, distinction, judgment, contention).

But perhaps it would be useful to recall, along with the Gilson edition of the *Discours*, that the architectural images, by which Descartes so strongly affirms his will to break with tradition, probably refer to certain types of construction (public squares, fortified cities, etc.) whose conceptions are firmly rooted in the architecture of the Renaissance.[49]

Let us also point out that it is in the *Quattrocento* that we find the first large-scale building project conceived in terms of an *ingénieur*, and no longer in those of an *artisan-bricoleur*. We are speaking of Brunelleschi's construction of the Santa Maria dei Fiori: "By applying calculus for the first time in order to solve a technical problem, that of the covering of a space so large as to exclude the possibility of construction on scaffolding, Brunelleschi will have effectively replaced medieval empiricism with a kind of rational method founded upon the geometrization of space, on the assimilation from an architectural space to a Euclidian space."[50] The paradigm of the *ingénieur*, as it is encountered in the seventeenth century, is born with the art of the Renaissance.

Moreover, the significance that Descartes attaches to his work and his place in the history of philosophy seems identical to the self-evaluation that Alberti espouses, two hundred years earlier, concerning his views on pictoral perspective and his place in the history of art. In his

De pictura, Alberti deeply disdains the procedures by which artisans of the day seek to create the illusion of depth by means of a purely empirical diminution of sizes. For them it is simply a matter of *via,* of a technique, without a theoretical *ratio.* Such a practice pays no attention to the specific character of the pictorial representation as a particular kind of space, subordinate to a point of view. "They place their first equidistant line by chance," he writes with contempt. The pictorial representation obtained by these *bricoleurs* is not necessarily ordered in terms of a specific point of view ("certus cuspidis ad bene spectandum locus"), and therefore often contains errors. Alberti sees his advent and its theoretical implications as a new beginning, a rupture from the trial-and-error system.[51] Descartes declares also that from the point of view of true philosophy, "it is far better never to contemplate investigating the truth about any matter than to do so without a method," that is to say, without "rules which are easy to apply," but rather "more favored by fortune" or "casu saepius quam arte."[52]

This parallel with perspective, as well as the fact that Cartesian criticism of the philosophy of the Renaissance follows the very model of art in the Renaissance, does not escape Descartes's contemporaries. Claude Gadroys writes in 1675:

I suppose that philosophers have, in this way, imitated artists who, wishing to draw the same statue, choose different vantage points from which to draw it; some draw it from the front, others from the side, and still others from behind. When we compare the resulting works, there seem to be no similarities; we do not notice a single feature in one drawing that is like that of another drawing, and though they have worked from the same original, we can only see the immense diversity. In the same respect, one can view the world from many vantage points, in order to seize it in all its aspects. Herein lies the reason why so many different opinions co-exist and lead us to believe that philosophers contradict and undermine each other. But in all truth, we have good reason to complain of them. They have hidden from us their point of view, and for some reason they have apparently affected obscurity.... Descartes is the only one to my knowledge who has discovered this truth. Also, just as the beauty of a painting is ascertained only when the viewer perceives it from the artist's vantage point, one shouldn't be surprised that philosophy, once the philosopher's vantage point is defined, seems beautiful, its principles sensible, and its exposition ingenious. We discover right down to the finest detail, and we clearly see the relationship between the elements of which it is comprised.[53]

How better to depreciate a mode of thinking that, by clinging desperately to phenomena, loses itself in the concrete movement of things, than by elevating another thought process that takes itself as the problematic origin as well as the only possible source, in its abstract form, of all representation.

NOTES

This essay was translated by Daniel Bertsche and Philippe Desan.

1. Henri Gouhier, *L'Antihumanisme au XVIIe siècle* (Paris: Vrin, 1987).

2. Etienne Gilson, *Etudes sur le rôle de la pensée médiévale dans la formation du système cartésien*, enl. ed. (Paris: J. Vrin, 1951).

3. Henri Gouhier, *Les Premières pensées de Descartes: contribution à l'histoire de l'anti-Renaissance*, enl. ed. (Paris: J. Vrin, 1979).

4. Giovanni Crapulli, *Mathesis universalis: genesi di un'idea nel XVI secolo* (Rome: Ateneo, 1969).

5. Descartes, *Discourse on the Method*, in *The Philosophical Writings of Descartes*, trans. John Cottingham, Robert Stoothoff, and Dugald Murdoch, 2 vols. (Cambridge: Cambridge University Press, 1985), 1:117: "en remettre par après ou d'autres meilleures, ou bien les mêmes... ajustées au niveau de la raison." All quotations from Descartes are from this edition unless otherwise noted. Note that the very expression by which Descartes lays claim to originality—"squared with the standards of reason" ("ajustées au niveau de la raison")—is modeled after an expression by Naudé ("esquarrer au niveau de la raison," in *Instruction à la France sur la vérité de l'histoire des Frères de la Rose-Croix,* [1623]; observation made by Fausta Garavini, in *La casa dei giochi: Idee e forme nel Seicento francese* (Turin: Einaudi, 1980), 40.

6. Descartes, *Discourse on the Method*, 1:150: "je ne me vante point aussi d'être le premier inventeur d'aucunes, mais bien que je ne les ai jamais reçues ni pour ce qu'elles ne l'avaient point été, mais seulement pour ce que la raison me les a persuadées."

7. André Baillet, *Vie de M. Descartes*, 2 vols. (Paris: Horthemels, 1691), 2:545: "M. Descartes voulant bien accorder que ce qu'il disait avait déjà été dit par d'autres croyait qu'il en était de même que d'un homme qu'on accuserait d'avoir pillé l'Alphabet et le Dictionnaire, parce qu'il n'aurait pas employé de

lettres qui ne fussent dans le premier ni de mots qui ne se trouvassent dans le second. Mais il ajouta que ceux qui reconnaîtraient l'enchaînement de toutes ses pensées qui suivent nécessairement les unes des autres, avoueraient bientôt qu'il serait aussi innocent du vol qu'on lui impute, qu'un habile Orateur que l'on rendrait plagiaire de Calepin et du vieux Evandre, pour avoir emprunté les mots de l'un, et les lettres de l'autre."

8. Descartes, *Rules for the Direction of the Mind*, in *Philosophical Writings*, 1:19: "par une ruse funeste ces auteurs l'ont ensuite eux-mêmes étouffée; car, ainsi que bien des artisans l'ont fait pour leurs inventions, comme chacun sait."

9. Descartes, *Discourse on the Method*, 1:116: "Ainsi voit-on que les bâtiments qu'un seul architecte a entrepris et achevés, ont coutume d'être plus beaux et mieux ordonnés, que ceux que plusieurs ont tâché de raccommoder, en faisant servir de vieilles murailles qui avaient été bâties à d'autre fins. Ainsi ces anciennes cités, qui, n'ayant été au commencement que des bourgades, sont devenues, par succession de temps, de grandes villes, sont ordinairement si mal compassées, au prix de ces places régulières qu'un ingénieur trace dans une plaine, qu'encore que, considérant leurs édifices chacun à part, on y trouve souvent autant ou plus d'art qu'en ceux des autres; toutefois, à voir comme ils sont arrangés, ici un grand, là un petit, et comme ils rendent les rues courbées et inégales, on dirait que c'est plutôt la fortune, que la volonté de quelques hommes usant de raison, qui les a ainsi disposées."

10. Gouhier, *Les Premières pensées*, 143.

11. Descartes, *The Search for Truth by Means of the Natural Light*, in *Philosophical Writings*, 2:407: "je la tiens [la connaissance] pour quelque maison mal bâtie, de qui les fondements ne sont pas assurés. Je ne sais point de meilleur moyen pour y remédier, que de la jeter toute par terre, et d'en bâtir une nouvelle; car je ne veux pas être de ces petits artisans, qui ne s'emploient qu'à raccommoder les vieux ouvrages."

12. Claude Lévi-Strauss, *The Savage Mind*, trans. George Weidenfeld and Nicholson (Chicago: University of Chicago Press, 1966).

13. This letter from Father Picot to Descartes is included in the preface to *The Passions of the Soul*, in Charles Adams and Paul Tannery's edition of *Oeuvres de Descartes* (Paris: Vrin, 1967), 11:309: "il est aisé de prouver que le trop grand respect qu'on porte à l'antiquité est une erreur qui préjudicie extrêmement à l'avantage des sciences. Car on voit que les peuples sauvages de l'Amérique, et aussi plusieurs autres qui habitent des lieux moins éloignés, ont beaucoup moins de commodités pour la vie que nous n'en avons, et toutefois qu'ils sont d'une origine aussi ancienne que la nôtre: en sorte qu'ils ont autant de raison que nous de dire qu'ils se contentent de la sagesse de leurs pères, et qu'ils ne croient point que personne leur puisse rien enseigner de meilleur, que ce qui a été su et pratiqué de toute antiquité parmi eux. Et cette opinion est si préjudiciable que, pendant

qu'on ne la quitte point, il est certain qu'on ne peut acquérir aucune nouvelle capacité." This letter does not appear in Cottingham's translation.

14. Lévi-Strauss, 13: "une forme timide et balbutante de la science."

15. This follows the architectural comparison in the *Discourse*, and also appears in *The Search for Truth*, 2:407.

16. Baillet, 2:531: "Je ne vois pas qu'il faille tant faire valoir l'Antiquité dans ceux qui portent la qualité d'Anciens. C'est un nom que nous méritons mieux qu'eux, parce que le monde est plus ancien maintenent qu'il ne l'était de leur temps, et que nous avons plus d'expérience qu'eux."

17. Lévi-Strauss, 20: "ne l'étend ni le renouvelle et se borne à obtenir le groupe de ses transformations."

18. Lévi-Strauss, 30.

19. Marsile Ficino, *Théologie platonicienne*, ed. and trans. R. Marcel, 2 vols. (Paris: Les Belles Lettres, 1964), 1:36: "tracer de ce Platon une image aussi proche que possible de la vérité chrétienne."

20. Lévi-Strauss, 31; and Gérard Genette, *Figures* (Paris: Seuil, 1966), 148, upon which the following sentence is fashioned.

21. The expression "semences de la vérité" appears in *Cogitationes privatae, Regulae, Discours,* and the French translation of *Principes:* see Geneviève Rodis-Lewis, *L'Oeuvre de Descartes* (Paris: Vrin, 1971), 457–58.

22. Descartes, *The Search for Truth*, 2:401: "Mais je ne veux point examiner ce que les autres ont su ou ignoré; il me suffit de remarquer Que, quand bien même toute la science qui se peut désirer, serait comprise dans les livres, si est-ce que ce qu'ils ont de bon est mêlé parmi tant de choses inutiles, et semé comfusément dans un tas de si gros volumes, qu'il faudrait plus de temps pour les lire, que nous n'en avons pour demeurer en cette vie, et plus d'esprit pour choisir les choses utiles, que pour les inventer de soi-même."

23. Lévi-Strauss, 19–20: "par rapport à ces contraintes résumant un état de civilisation, l'ingénieur cherche toujours à s'ouvrir un passage et à se situer *au delà*, tandis que le bricoleur, de gré ou de force, demeure *en deça*, ce qui est une autre façon de dire que le premier opère au moyen de concepts, le second au moyen de signes. Sur l'axe de l'opposition entre nature et culture, les ensembles dont ils se servent sont perceptiblement décalés. En effet, une des façons au moins dont le signe s'oppose au concept tient à ce que le second se veut intégralement transparent à la réalité, tandis que le premier accepte, et même exige, qu'une certaine épaisseur d'humanité soit incorporée à cette réalité."

24. Descartes, *Descartes's Philosophical Letters*, trans. Anthony Kenny (Oxford: Clarendon Press, 1970), 6: "les mots que nous avons n'ont quasi que des significations obscures."

25. Descartes, *Rules for the Direction of the Mind*, 1:53, rule 13: "les expliquent en termes peu satisfaisants."

26. Descartes, *The Search for Truth*, 2:410: "De cette question... deux

autres naissent: la première, qu'est-ce qu'animal; la seconde, qu'est-ce que raisonnable. Et de plus si pour expliquer ce qu'est un animal, il répondait que c'est un vivant doué de sensibilité, et qu'un vivant est un corps animé, et qu'un corps est une substance corporelle: vous voyez sur le champ que les questions s'augmentent et se multiplient comme les rameaux d'un arbre généologique; et que pour finir il est assez évident que toutes ces belles questions se termineraient en une pure battologie, qui n'éclairerait rien et nous laisserait dans notre ignorance primitive."

27. Descartes, letter to Mersenne, dated November 20, 1629, in *Descartes's Philosophical Letters,* 5–6: "elle pourrait être enseignée en fort peu de temps, et ce par le moyen de l'ordre, c'est-à- dire, établissant un ordre entre toutes les pensées qui peuvent entrer en l'esprit humain, de même qu'il y en a un naturellement établi entre les nombres; et comme on peut apprendre en un jour à nommer tous les nombres jusques à l'infini, et à les écrire en une langue inconnue, qui sont toutefois une infinité de mots différents, qu'on pût faire le même de tous les autres mots nécessaires pour exprimer toutes les autres choses qui tombent en l'esprit des hommes."

28. Lévi-Strauss, 16: "le monde sensible en termes de sensible"; "des propriétés physiques et des propriétés sémantiques."

29. Descartes, *Discourse on the Method,* 1:127: "à cause que nos sens nous trompent quelquefois, je voulus supposer qu'il n'y avait aucune chose qui fût telle qu'ils nous la font imaginer."

30. Descartes, *Rules for the Direction of the Mind,* 1:15, rule 4: "On ne peut pas se passer d'une méthode pour se mettre en quête de la vérité des choses."

31. Descartes, *Optics,* in *Philosophical Writings,* 1:152: "n'étant en usage que depuis peu, [la lunette] nous a déjà découvert de nouveaux astres dans le ciel, et d'autres nouveaux objets dessus la terre, en plus grand nombre que ne sont ceux que nous y avions vus auparavant."

32. For a more detailed analysis of the signification of the telescope, see my article in *Cahier de littérature du XVIIe siècle,* no. 11 (1989).

33. Descartes, "Olympian matters," in *Philosophical Writings,* 1:4–5: "De même que l'imagination se sert de figures pour concevoir les corps, de même l'intelligence, pour figurer les choses spirituelles, se sert de certains corps sensibles, comme le vent, la lumière. D'où il suit que, philosophant de façon plus élevée, nous pouvons conduire l'esprit, par la connaissance, dans les hauteurs.... Les choses sensibles nous permettent de concevoir les olympiques; le vent signifie l'esprit; le mouvement avec la durée signifie la vie; la lumière signifie la connaissance; la chaleur signifie l'amour; l'activité instantanée signifie la création."

34. See Descartes, *Discourse on the Method,* 1:112, 114: "l'homme purement homme." See also Gilson's commentary in his edition of the *Discours de la méthode* (Paris: Vrin, 1976), 94, 134.

35. Montaigne, *The Complete Essays of Montaigne,* trans. Donald Frame (Stanford: Stanford University Press, 1958), I, 56, 234 B: "purement humains et philosophiques, sans mélange de théologie." The letter (B) indicates the 1588 textual strata.

36. See Fernand Hallyn, *The Poetic Structure of the World: Copernicus and Kepler,* trans. D. M. Leslie (New York: Zone Books, 1990), 229–30.

37. Descartes, *Discourse on the Method,* 1:116: "je pris un jour la résolution d'étudier aussi en moi-même"; and 119: "comme un homme qui marche seul dans les ténèbres."

38. Descartes, *Discourse on the Method,* 1:142–143: "Car elles m'ont fait voir qu'il est possible de parvenir à des connaissances qui soient fort utiles pour la vie; et... au lieu de cette philosophie spéculative qu'on enseigne dans les écoles, on en peut trouver une pratique, par laquelle, connaissant la force et les actions du feu, de l'eau, de l'air, des astres, des cieux et de tous les autres corps qui nous environnent, aussi distinctement que nous connaissons les divers métiers de nos artisans, nous les pourrions employer en même façon à tous les usages auxquels ils sont propres, et ainsi nous rendre comme maîtres et possesseurs de la nature."

39. Ficino, *Théologie platonicienne,* 2:224. The use of *quasi* in this text, as well as the use of other attenuating qualifiers by humanists, shows that the mere presence of the word *comme* in the phrase "comme maîtres et possesseurs de la nature" is not sufficient grounds to establish ironic distance for Descartes, as André Glucksmann (*Descartes c'est la France* [Paris: Flammarion, 1987], 224) would like to have it.

40. See Charles de Bovelles, *Le livre du sage,* ed. and trans. P. Mignard (Paris: Vrin, 1982), as well as my study "Le microcosme ou l'incomplétude de la représentation," *Romanica Gandensia* 17 (1980): 183–92.

41. Ficino, *Théologie platonicienne,* 2:224: "n'envisage aucun avantage corporel"; "la preuve de sa puissance... presque semblable à la nature divine."

42. Let us remember that in *Rules for the Direction of the Mind,* the most humble manifestation and the simplest of craftsmen are proposed as models of order and of method for science.

43. André Lalande, "Quelques textes de Bacon et de Descartes," in *Revue de métaphysique et de morale* (1911), 304–5. Also see E. Gilson's comments in *Discours de la méthode* (Paris, 1925), 446. The correspondence between Descartes and Mersennes in 1630 contains several traces of an attentive reading of Bacon.

44. M. Le Doeuff and M. Llasera, *Voyage dans la pensée baroque,* in Francis Bacon, *La Nouvelle Atlantide* (Paris: Payot, 1983), 170.

45. Descartes, *Discourse on the Method,* 1:143: "une infinité d'artifices, qui feraient qu'on jouirait, sans aucune peine, des fruits de la terre et de toutes les commodités qui s'y trouvent."

46. Descartes, letter to Mersenne, dated November 20, 1629, in *Descartes's Philosophical Letters*, 6: "cela suppose de grands changements dans l'ordre des choses, et il faudrait que tout le Monde ne fût qu'un paradis terrestre, ce qui n'est bon à proposer que dans le pays des romans."

47. Descartes, *Discourse on the Method*, 1:114: "imaginer plusieurs événements comme possibles qui ne le sont point."

48. Aulus-Gellius, *Noctes atticae*, 13.16.

49. Descartes, *Discours de la méthode*, ed. E. Gilson, 162.

50. H. Damisch, *Théorie du nuage* (Paris: Seuil, 1972), 235: "En appliquant pour la première fois le calcul à la solution d'un problème technique, celui de la couverture d'un espace si vaste qu'il excluait toute possibilité de construire sur échafaudages, Brunelleschi aura en effet substitué à l'empirisme médiéval une méthode rationnelle, fondé sur la géométrisation de l'espace, sur l'assimilation de l'espace architectural à l'espace euclidien."

51. L. Alberti, *On Painting and on Sculpture*, ed. and trans. C. Grayson (London: Phaidon, 1972), 54–56.

52. Descartes, *Rules for the Direction of the Mind*, 1:16, rule 4: "il est bien meilleur de ne jamais penser à chercher la vérité d'aucune chose, que de le faire sans méthode"; "règles certaines et aisées"; "par une heureuse fortune."

53. Claude Gadroys, *Le système du monde selon les trois hypothèses* (Paris: G. Desprez, 1675), nonpaginated preface: "Je me figure que les Philosophes ont en cela imité les Dessignateurs, qui voulant copier une mesme statuë, la prennent par differens endroits; les uns de front, les autres de profil, et les autres par derriere. Si l'on considère leurs ouvrages, ils n'ont rien de semblable, on ne remarque pas un trait dans l'un comme dans l'autre, et quoy qu'ils ayent travaillé sur le mesme original, on ne voit par tout cependant que de la diversité. Le monde a de mesme plusieurs faces, & on peut le prendre par toutes ces manieres. C'est ce qui a fait naistre tant d'opinions qui paroissent differentes, & ce qui fait mesme penser aujourd'huy que les Philosophes se contrarient et se destruisent les uns les autres. Mais à dire le vray nous avons à nous plaindre d'eux. Ils nous ont caché le point de veuë, d'où ils ont regardé le monde, & par je ne sçay quels motifs ils ont en apparence affecté l'obscurité.... Descartes est le seul que je sçache qui nous l'a découvert sans reserve. Aussi comme on ne commence à voir les beautez d'un tableau, que lors qu'on le regarde de son point de veuë, il ne faut pas s'estonner si la Philosophie paroist belle, ses principes sensibles, & sa manière d'expliquer ingenieuse. On y découvre jusqu'au moindre trait, on voit le rapport qu'ont ensemble toutes les pieces qui la composent."

Contributors

Cathleen M. Bauschatz is Associate Professor of French at the University of Maine. She has published numerous articles on reading and readers in French Renaissance literature. She is currently completing a book on the address of women readers in sixteenth-century France.

Marc E. Blanchard is Professor of French and Comparative Literature and Director of the Critical Theory program at the University of California, Davis. Among his books are: *Sign, Self, Subject: Critical Theory in the Wake of Semiotics* (The Hague–New York, 1980), *In Search of the City* (Saratoga, 1985), and *Trois portraits de Montaigne: essai sur la représentation à la Renaissance* (Paris, 1990). He is now working on postmodern uses of space.

Jean Céard, honorary President of the Société Française des Seiziémistes, is Professor of Renaissance Literature and Culture at the University of Paris-XII. His books include a critical edition of Ambroise Paré's works (Geneva, 1971), *La Nature et les Prodiges* (Paris, 1977), and *Rébus de la Renaissance* (Paris, 1987). He is now completing an edition of Ronsard's complete works.

Bernard Crampé is Visiting Lecturer of French Literature at New York University. A specialist on the history of rhetoric and grammar theory, he is currently completing an edition of Dufour's *Voyage d'Italie* and is preparing a critical edition of Bernard Lamy's *Art de parler*.

Philippe Desan is Associate Professor of French Literature at the University of Chicago. He is the editor of *Montaigne Studies*. His books include *Naissance de la méthode* (Paris, 1987), *Literature and Social Practice* (Chicago, 1989). He has edited works by Le Roy, La Popelinière, the Goncourt brothers, and is currently completing a book titled *Les Commerces de Montaigne: l'émergence du discours économique à la Renaissance*.

Claude-Gilbert Dubois is Professor at the University of Bordeaux-III and Director of the Center for Research on Montaigne and His Time. His books include: *Mythe et Langage au seizième siècle* (Paris, 1970), *La Conception de l'histoire en France au XVIe siècle* (Paris, 1977), *Le Maniérisme* (Paris, 1978), *L'Imagi-*

naire de la Renaissance (Paris, 1985). He is now completing a study on European mannerism, and another on *L'Isle des Hermaphrodites* (1605).

Fernand Hallyn is Professor of French Literature at the University of Ghent (Belgium). His books include: *Forme métaphoriques dans la poésie baroque* (Geneva, 1975), *Méthodes du texte: introduction aux études littéraires* (Gembloux, 1987), and *La Structure poétique du monde: Copernic, Kepler* (Paris, 1987; English trans., New York, 1990).

Timothy Hampton is Assistant Professor of French Literature at the University of California, Berkeley. He is the author of *Writing from History: The Rhetoric of Exemplarity in Renaissance Literature* (Ithaca and London, 1990) and is currently working on a study of literature and politics at the dawn of the French Renaissance.

George Huppert is Professor of History at the University of Illinois at Chicago. His books include *The Idea of Perfect History* (Urbana, 1970), *Public Schools in Renaissance France* (Urbana, 1984), *Les bourgeois gentilshommes* (Chicago, 1977), and *After the Black Death* (Bloomington, 1986). He is currently working on the links between the Renaissance and the Enlightenment.

Frank Lestringant is Professor of French Literature at the University of Lille-III. His books include *Arts et légendes d'espaces* (Paris, 1981), *Le Huguenot et le sauvage* (Paris, 1990), *André Thevet, cosmographe des derniers Valois* (Geneva, 1991). He is now completing a book on *L'Atelier du Cosmographe*.

Timothy J. Reiss is Professor and Chair of Comparative Literature at New York University. His most recent book is *The Uncertainty of Analysis* (Ithaca and London, 1988), and *The Meaning of Literature* is now in press (Ithaca and London, 1991). He is presently researching a book on Descartes, political thought, the Palatine, and the Thirty Years' War.

François Rigolot is Meredith Howland Pyne Professor of French Literature at Princeton University. His publications include *Les Langages de Rabelais* (Geneva, 1972), *Poétique et Onomastique* (Geneva, 1977), *Le Texte de la Renaissance* (Geneva, 1982), Louise Labé's *Œuvres complètes* (Paris, 1986), and *Les Métamorphoses de Montaigne* (Paris, 1989). He is now preparing a new edition of Montaigne's *Travel Journal*.

Zachary S. Schiffman is Associate Professor of History at Northeastern Illinois University in Chicago. He is the author of *On the Threshold of Modernity: Relativism in the French Renaissance* (Baltimore, 1991) and is presently working on a history of "knowledge representation" from antiquity to the present.

James J. Supple is Senior Lecturer in French at the University of St. Andrews in Scotland. He is the author of *Arms versus Letters: The Military and Literary*

Ideals in the "Essais" of Montaigne (Oxford, 1984) and *Racine: "Bérénice"* (London, 1986). He is currently completing an edition of the diplomatic reports of René de Lucinge.

Index of Names

Abbott, Robert, 217
Aeschylus, 272
Agrippa von Nettesheim, Heinrich Cornelius, 183
Alberti, Leo-Battista, 306–7
Aldrovandi, Ulisse, 181, 197, 199
Alfonse, Jean, 159
Ambrosini, B., 197
Andrewes, Lancelot, 217
Aneau, Bathélemy, 267
Apianus, Petrus, 159
Apollonius of Rhodes, 27
Archimedes, 38, 138
Aristotle, 18, 44, 47, 57, 72, 116, 127, 133, 140, 161–64, 169–70, 181–82, 239, 262–63, 287
Arnauld, Antoine, 272
Auerbach, Erich, 245
Aulus-Gellius, 306

Bacon, Francis, 23, 305
Badius, Conrad, 211
Baillet, André, 296
Balzac, Guez de, 9, 266, 269
Baronius, Caesar, 215
Barthes, Roland, 87, 238, 244
Baudouin, François, 70
Beard, Thomas, 217
Becon, Thomas, 211
Beeckman, Isaac, 79
Bellarmine, Robert, 215
Belleforest, François de, 131, 153–55, 158, 170, 188
Bembo, Pietro, 46
Béthune, Maximilien de, 37

Boaistuau, Pierre, 181
Boccaccio, Giovanni, 233
Bodin, Jean, 16–17, 22, 28, 58, 70, 117, 157–58
Boemus, Joannes, 156–57
Boileau, Nicolas, 266, 269
Boissière, Claude de, 134–35
Borges, Jorge Luis, 233
Bouchet, Jean, 36
Bourchenin, P. D., 36
Bouvelles, Charles de, 134–35, 138, 141, 304
Brahe, Tycho, 30
Brantôme, 36, 47
Brightman, Thomas, 217
Brunelleschi, Filippo, 306
Bruni, Leonardo, 70
Bruno, Giordano, 21, 30
Bruyère, Nelly, 134
Bucer, Martin, 217
Budé, Guillaume, 35–36, 39, 41, 86–88
Burckhardt, George, 210

Cabot, Sebastian, 163
Caesar, Julius, 70, 92, 226
Calvin, Jean, 183
Camerarius, Ludwig, 170, 188, 192
Campanella, Tommaso, 23, 30
Camus, Albert, 244
Cardan, Girolamo, 30, 192–93, 198
Carle, Lancelot de, 36
Cassirer, Ernst, 22
Castiglione, 46–47
Cato, 91–94, 102

Index of Names

Chamfort, Nicolas, 225
Champier, Symphorien, 36
Chapelain, Jean, 266
Charles VIII, 11, 13
Charron, Pierre, 5, 70, 77–78, 100
Chartier, Roger, 36
Chateaubriand, François René, 190
Chaunu, Pierre, 244
Cicero, 14, 57, 72, 127–28, 140, 183–84, 189, 226, 260–64, 287
Clichtove, Josse, 44
Cohn, Norman, 219
Colbert, Jean-Baptiste, 17
Coligny, Gaspard de, 160, 167
Colin, Jacques, 36
Commines, Philippe de, 229
Copernicus, 18, 21
Cordier, Mathurin, 58
Corneille, 100–102, 238
Crapulli, Giovanni, 295
Cusa, Nicholas of, 21, 138

Dainville, François de, 36, 171–72
Daneau, Lambert, 212
D'Aubigné, Agrippa, 109, 227, 245
Da Vinci, Leonardo, 168
D'Avity, Pierre, 155, 173–74
De Bry, Theodore, 174
Dekker, Thomas, 211
Descartes, René, 5, 9, 12, 15, 19–20, 23, 65, 70, 79–82, 126, 139, 244, 264, 270, 295–308
Descaurres, Jean, 56
Deschamps, Eustache, 42
Des Masures, Louis, 211
Des Portes, Philippe, 280
Digby, Everard, 134, 142
Digges, Thomas, 21
Dionysius of Halicarnassus, 86
Drouot, Henri, 64
Du Bartas, Guillaume de Salluste, 280
Du Bellay, Joachim, 14–15, 26, 29–30, 111, 227, 267, 269, 280, 283–85
Dubois, Claude-Gilbert, 29
Du Fail, Noël, 237

Dunn, Catherine, 134
Du Perron, Jacques Davy, 108
Du Rosier, Simon, 211
Du Saix, Antoine, 36, 39–42
Du Vair, Guillaume, 70

Eliade, Mircea, 30
Empedocles, 170
Erasmus, 39, 126, 129–30, 160, 260, 287
Eratosthenes, 155
Estienne, Henri, 6, 129–31, 140–43
Estienne, Robert, 137
Euclid, 138
Euripides, 27

Fabri, Pierre, 130
Faret, Nicolas, 45–48
Feugère, Léon, 140
Ficino, Marsilio, 299, 304
Fioravanti, Leonardo, 167
Flaubert, Gustave, 199
Fleurance-Rivault, David de, 37–42, 47
Foisil, Madeleine, 243–44
Foucault, Michel, 281, 289
Fouquelin, Antoine, 133
Foxe, John, 211, 217
Francis I, 74, 85, 87–88
Francis II, 160
Froissart, Jean, 229
Fulke, William, 211

Gadroys, Claude, 307
Galileo, Galilei, 302
Gemma, Cornelius, 193
Gilbert, Balthasar, 271
Gilson, Etienne, 295, 306
Gonzague, Ludovic de, 41
Gouberville, Gilles de, 223, 240–49
Gouhier, Henri, 295
Goulart, Simon, 181
Gournay, Marie de, 9, 279–90
Graves, Robert, 27
Grynaeus, Simon, 153, 157, 174
Guevara, Antonio de, 87

Index of Names   321

Guibelet, Jourdain, 195
Guicciardini, Francesco, 229
Guttierez, Diego, 163

Habermas, Jürgen, 88
Hakluyt, Richard, 154, 172–74
Hallie, Philip, 35
Haydn, Hiram, 2
Henry II, 160, 167, 241
Henry III, 184, 232, 238, 240
Henry IV, 40, 214–15, 237, 240
Herodotus, 160, 167, 172
Hill, Christopher, 217
Horace, 57, 94, 108
Hotman, François, 70–71, 229
Huppert, George, 36
Hurault, Michel, 131, 229
Huss, John, 210–11

Illyricus, Flacius, 211

Jakobson, Roman, 244
Joinville, Jean, 229
Joubert, Laurent, 195
Jouvancy, Joseph de, 272
Juvenal, 57, 108

Kepler, Johannes, 30, 303
Koyré, Alexandre, 20, 22–23

La Bruyère, Jean de, 14, 225, 238
Laffemas, Bathélemy de, 17
La Fontaine, Jean de, 14
Lamy, Bernard, 264, 271
Langer, Ullrich, 109
La Noue, François de, 36, 131
Lapoincte, Bertrand de, 58
La Popelinière, Lancelot du Voisin, 5, 70, 72–73
La Rochefoucault, François de, 14
Lelande, André, 305
Léry, Jean de, 227
Le Roy Ladurie, Emmanuel, 243–44, 249
Le Roy, Loys, 19, 28–30, 131
L'Estoile, Pierre de, 223, 231–40

Le Testu, Guillaume, 160, 164–67, 172
Lévi-Strauss, Claude, 297, 301
Liceti, 196, 198
Livy, 57, 213, 226, 229, 272
Lope de Vega, Felix, 135
Luther, Martin, 114, 183, 186, 213
Lycosthenes, 184

Machiavelli, Niccolo, 16, 28, 224, 229–30
Malebranche, Nicolas, 271
Malherbe, François de, 9, 269, 280, 285, 288
Marco Polo, 164
Marcus Aurelius, 87
Mathé de Laval, Anthoine, 40–44
McLuhan, Marshall, 107
Medici, Catherine de, 16, 142, 235, 241
Meigret, Louis, 137, 140
Melanchthon, Philipp, 183, 211
Ménager, Daniel, 110
Mercator, Gerhardus, 172
Merezhkovsky, Dmitri, 218
Mersenne, Marin, 195, 305
Michelet, Jules, 11, 13, 28
Molière, 9, 26
Monchrestien, Antoine de, 17
Monluc, Blaise de, 223, 225–28, 239–40, 249
Montaigne, Michel de, 4, 5, 9, 12, 15, 16, 20–21, 23, 25, 39, 45, 69, 75–81, 85–102, 107–19, 131, 153–54, 169, 188–89, 196, 215, 223–28, 236, 238–39, 247, 261, 281–82, 286, 303
Moreau, Jean, 63
Moreau, Pierre, 63
Mornay, Philippe de, 216
Münster, Sebastian, 153–56, 158–62, 172–73
Murner, Thomas, 134

Nero, 89
Nietzsche, Friedrich, 218

Ong, Walter, 142
Ovid, 57, 263

Palissy, Bernard, 192
Palsgrave, John, 130
Paré, Ambroise, 22, 181–99
Pascal, Blaise, 14, 225, 238
Pasquier, Etienne, 5, 23, 70, 72–74, 108, 110, 131
Peletier Du Mans, Jacques, 15, 134–37
Pereira, Duarte Pacheco, 168, 214
Périon, Joachim, 140
Persius, 57
Petrarch, Francesco, 11, 15, 87
Plato, 18–20, 44, 72, 96, 139, 162, 299
Plattard, Jean, 107
Pliny, 160, 162, 169, 182
Plutarch, 210, 226
Pluvinel, Antoine de, 36
Polybius, 72
Pomey, François, 272
Pompey, 88
Porteau, Paul, 36
Poseidonius, 155
Postel, Guillaume, 22, 158, 184
Proust, Marcel, 236
Ptolemy, 7, 21, 153–55, 158–61, 165, 169–72
Pythagoras, 138

Quint, David, 110
Quintilian, 116, 127, 262–63

Rabelais, François, 15, 63, 86, 107, 183, 224, 261, 282
Raemond, Florimond de, 210, 214–16
Ramus, Peter, 6, 14–15, 18–19, 125–28, 134–43, 262, 271
Ramusio, Giovanni Battista, 174
Randles, William, 163
Raymond, Marcel, 110
Renan, Ernest, 218
Ribera, Francisco de, 214–15

Richelieu, Cardinal de, 45, 284
Ringmann, Mathias, 134
Riolan, Jean, 193, 196
Robespierre, Maximilien, 65
Ronsard, Pierre de, 5–6, 9, 15, 27–28, 107–19, 227, 245, 266, 269, 279–80, 282–85, 288

Saint Augustine, 171, 182–84, 189, 196, 260
Saint-Hilaire, Geoffroy, 199
Saint Simon, 225, 238
Sallust, 57
Salmon, J. H., 12
Sanders, Nicholas, 211, 215
Sassoferrato, Bartolus of, 71
Saulnier, Verdun-Louis, 12
Scaliger, Julius Caesar, 130, 137–38, 141, 287
Schaefer, David, 17
Schenck, Johann Goerg, 182, 195–96
Sebillet, Thomas, 15, 136–38, 141
Seneca, 14
Seyssel, Claude de, 36, 42
Soarez, Cyprian, 8, 260–73
Socrates, 90, 95, 102
Sophocles, 27, 272
Sorbin, Arnaud, 182–83
Starobinski, Jean, 117
Stendhal, 244
Strabo, 7, 154, 157–58, 161
Sully, 17
Sussanneau, Hubert, 63

Tacitus, 229, 260
Talon, Omer, 127, 133
Terence, 57
Teserant, Claude de, 187
Tetel, Marcel, 17
Thevet, André, 153–56, 159–61, 164–72
Toffanin, Giuseppe, 46
Torre, Alfonso de la, 135
Tory, Geoffroy, 130, 134
Turnèbe, Adrian, 58

Vadianus, Joachimus, 153, 156–57, 160, 172
Valla, Lorenzo, 15, 57, 280
Varro, 306
Vasari, Giorgio, 211
Vergerius, Louis, 156
Vespucci, Amerigo, 164
Viegas, Bras, 214
Vignier, Nicolas, 70, 72–73, 216
Viret, Pierre, 207, 211

Virgil, 57, 97
Vives, Juan Luis, 280
Voltaire, 65, 270

Waswo, Richard, 280–81
Wilson, Thomas, 127
Worde, Wynkyn de, 211
Wycliffe, John, 210

Xenophon, 57, 87
Yates, Frances, 40

www.ingramcontent.com/pod-product-compliance
Lightning Source LLC
Chambersburg PA
CBHW021135230426

43667CB00005B/130